AN IGNATIAN SPIRITUALITY READER

AN IGNATIAN SPIRITUALITY READER

Contemporary Writings on St. Ignatius of Loyola, the Spiritual Exercises, Discernment, and More

VOLUME II

EILEEN BURKE-SULLIVAN • JULIA A. DOWD
MARK MOSSA, SJ • STEPHANIE RUSSELL • LORI STANLEY
EDITORS

LOYOLAPRESS.
A JESUIT MINISTRY

LOYOLA PRESS.
A JESUIT MINISTRY
www.loyolapress.com

Acknowlegments for permission to reprint granted by previous publishers can be found on pages 489–496.

Cover design by Loyola Press
Interior design by Think Design Group
Cover art credit: Philippe Lissac/Getty Images, Jesuits of the Missouri Province

ISBN: 978-0-8294-5621-9
Library of Congress Control Number: 2025942854

Published in Chicago, IL
Printed in Canada
25 26 27 28 29 30 31 32 33 34 MQS 10 9 8 7 6 5 4 3 2 1

The editors dedicate this collection to Father George Traub, SJ,
and to the Chief Mission Officers, past and present,
of the colleges and universities which are sponsored works of the
North American Assistancy of the Society of Jesus.
Among those leaders is the late Eileen Burke-Sullivan,
who served as the first editor of this volume
and in whose loving memory we bring it to fruition.

Contents

IV. Reconciliation

V. Leadership and Mission

VI. Adaptations

VII. Imagination and Creativity

VIII. Ignatian Spirituality and Anti-Racism

IX. Care for Our Common Home

Preface

In 2008, Loyola Press published two collections of essays edited by George Traub, SJ: the first, titled *An Ignatian Spirituality Reader* and the second, *A Jesuit Education Reader*. Both books were well used by Jesuits and lay partners in various programs of the Association of Jesuit Colleges and Universities, the Jesuit Schools Network, and other Ignatian ministries. Father Traub had an extensive history in developing formation programs for lay partners in the mission of Jesuit universities through his work at Xavier University in Cincinnati, Ohio, and these collected works continue to be relevant for introducing lay partners of the Jesuits into the vision and mission of the works of the Society of Jesus.

Sixteen years later, Loyola Press presents the second volume of *An Ignatian Spirituality Reader* (along with another volume of *A Jesuit Education Reader*). The second volume of the *Spirituality Reader* is intended as a companion to the first, providing a sampling of the outpouring of conversations in more recently published blogs, books, essays (both scholarly and pastoral), presentations, homilies, and lectures. This second volume of textual materials published in the last dozen years has been collected and edited by a team of scholars and practitioners who have worked with colleagues, friends, and supporters of Jesuit works to enable our lay partners to deepen their appreciation of the values and attitudes that animate the Christian tradition, and—in dialogue with other religions—ground their experience in St. Ignatius's *Spiritual Exercises*.

While this second volume is longer than the original and the selected works more diverse in style and purpose, we remain greatly appreciative of Father Traub's work and we wish to honor his efforts. Recognizing the rapid expansion of subject areas that are now influenced by Ignatian reflection, we have put forth nine chapters, each of which includes three or more texts. We want to stress that in no way have we tapped all of the excellent content that has been created in these subject areas. Like Father Traub's first *Ignatian Spirituality Reader*, this book shares portions of a few excellent Ignatian conversations and ecclesial and Jesuit commentary that we hope will serve as resources and conversation starters in a range of Ignatian pastoral, educational, and scholarly settings.

In Part II of this collection, we have included the papal address at the 36th General Congregation of the Society of Jesus in 2016, in which Pope Francis counsels the Jesuits that an essential outcome of Ignatian discernment is development and change. This transition from one historical moment to another is the work of the Holy Spirit, moving always toward the benefit of those whom we serve and with whom we stand in solidarity. We embrace this charge from Pope Francis to recognize growth and change as graces of Ignatian discernment, and we invite the reader to approach the selections in this volume through this lens.

Some selections demonstrate scholarly probing of the developing understanding of Ignatian spirituality; others explore the praxis of Ignatian spirituality in ways that were not even imagined fifty years ago, much less in the sixteenth century. Nonetheless, these areas of growth can be well understood today under the umbrella of the ordinary practice of the wisdom and grace that the Ignatian vision and tradition discloses.

The editors of this collection are deeply grateful to the graces and gifts that Ignatian spirituality has provided in our diverse circumstances. We have been blessed to be Jesuit and partners in this work of expanding the formation of our colleagues. We fully expect that our more knowledgeable colleagues will ask why this article or that blog post, or the remarkable chapter of this-or-that book, has not been included, and we can only say there is always further reading and listening to do. For those who wonder why these particular texts were chosen, we say that they seemed to us to add to the conversations that are going forward this year, and address the characteristic topics we selected at this point in time. We hope perhaps others will offer volume three to this series in another few years.

We wish to gratefully acknowledge the support of Diana Vara and Caitlyn Rei in the final editing stages, and Gary Jansen and Maura Poston of Loyola Press.

We invite all of us to the development of understanding which the Holy Father commended to the Society of Jesus at their most recent General Congregation, and we further join our prayers with the Society of Jesus that all may grow to their full measure as human persons.

Eileen Burke-Sullivan
Julia A. Dowd
Mark Mossa, SJ
Stephanie Russell
Lori Stanley

I. Foundations, History, and Current Context

Part I Introduction

We found ourselves assembling this collection in the context of two key Jesuit initiatives in the last decade. The first is the Society of Jesus's Universal Apostolic Preferences (UAPs), articulated and implemented in 2019, after two years of consultation with Jesuits and their colleagues in ministry around the world. According to these preferences, the Jesuits have committed to giving special attention to four key missions until at least 2029: Showing the Way to God, Walking with the Excluded, Journeying with Youth, and Caring for Our Common Home. As the inclusion of an excerpt from Fr. General Arturo Sosa's book *Walking with Ignatius* will show, the focus of this volume is more on the first, stated in the form of a mandate, to "show the way to God through the Spiritual Exercises and discernment." This first preference demonstrates something of which the Jesuits and their colleagues in ministry are keenly aware: that at the heart of Ignatian spirituality is what is often referred to as simply "the ministry of the Exercises." This is the foundation for all Jesuit ministries and thus something that requires continual attention as we seek to remind ourselves and come to understand both the origins of the Exercises themselves as well as the spiritual insights that helped form them and which emerge from them.

Undoubtedly the Ignatian Year, which was celebrated from 2021–2022 and marked the anniversary of the moment that changed the course of Saint Ignatius's life, a life-threatening injury suffered when his leg was shattered by a cannonball at a battle in Pamplona in 1521, was meant as a concrete manifestation of that first preference. Jesuit ministries around the world invited people to share their own "cannonball moments," finding a meeting place in the conversion experience of this sixteenth-century soldier with their own life-changing experiences of pain, transformation, and conversion in their twentieth and twenty-first century lives. This was a reminder to us all, as Jean Luc Enyegue explores in the included essay, both of a sameness in human experience over the centuries when it comes to finding our way to God, but also the ways in which such experiences must be understood according to the particular time, place, and circumstances in which we find ourselves. We can only imagine what it would have been like to be a soldier on a sixteenth-century battlefield. Similarly, when composing the *Spiritual Exercises*, Saint Ignatius could hardly have anticipated how different an experience of conversion might be for a woman in the twenty-first century.

Coincident with these two Jesuit initiatives, this section assembles a variety of essays and book chapters published in the last two decades which further plumb the depths of the origins of Ignatian spirituality and continue to examine the possibilities for the practical application of Ignatian principles in the midst of the diverse experiences of our lives today.

Ignatius's cannonball moment was just the beginning of a conversion story that spanned years—indeed, a lifetime—and provided the opportunity for prayer, reading, learning, spiritual conversation, and friendships that would shape the text which would come to be known as *The Spiritual Exercises*. The first piece of this section, by Eileen Burke-Sullivan, is taken from her introduction to the book *The Ignatian Tradition*, which she co-authored with Kevin F. Burke, SJ. Here she explores "The Biographical Roots of the Ignatian Tradition," focusing on the ways in which Ignatius's life and experience offer insight both into whom he would become and what would become of the spirituality and way of life inspired by his experience. In doing so, she anticipates and echoes a central insight of many contemporary Ignatian scholars that what we understand to be Ignatian spirituality cannot be accounted for simply by the text of *The Spiritual Exercises*, or even by the experience of the retreat for which it is a guide, but that it must also be seen in light of the lived experience of the first Jesuits, which could hardly be encapsulated by that one text. Similarly, as many of the contributions to this volume illustrate, our contemporary experience of Ignatian spirituality relies on the collective wisdom and adaptations of generations of Jesuits, and, increasingly so in recent generations, of their colleagues in study and ministry.

In a complementary spirit, Mark Mossa builds upon insights taken from his book *Saint Ignatius Loyola: The Spiritual Writings*, to highlight an often-overlooked source of Ignatian wisdom: the collected letters of the saint who was not only the emerging leader of a dynamic religious community but also one of the most prolific letter writers of his time. The letters provide practical wisdom for everyday experiences and struggles that the more focused experience of the Spiritual Exercises and the foundation of the Jesuit order do not. They also allow us to see how Ignatius engages the experience of the wide variety of people in a multitude of circumstances, to whom he wrote.

This is not to say that no attention has been given to Ignatius's letters. Some sixty years ago, Hugo Rahner published *St. Ignatius Loyola: Letters to Women*, which explored how Ignatius may have applied his spiritual principles to the lives of the women of his day. This provides an interesting bridge to two other essays included in this volume. The first is a reflection by Margo Heydt and Sarah Melcher inspired by their experience of an Ignatian pilgrimage to Spain and Rome. "Mary, the Hidden Catalyst" is the account of how these two self-professed "Protestant feminist pilgrim professors" were taken by the role that Mary clearly played in Ignatius's conversion experience as they themselves moved through his pilgrim journey. This inspired them to further research the role that women played in the life of Ignatius, and the ways in which his relationships with women, and with Mary, offer an alternative perspective for our understanding of the Exercises in particular, and Ignatian spirituality as a whole. Later, in chapter six, this feminist perspective is further explored in an innovative way in an essay by Elizabeth Liebert, "The Spiritual Exercises and Gender," appearing here, in English, for the first time.

Finally, we include the Society of Jesus's announcement and outlining of the Universal Apostolic Preferences, as well as an excerpt from chapter six of Jesuit Father General Arturo Sosa's 2021 book, *Walking with Ignatius*, titled, "Showing the Way to God." This more expansive question-and-answer interview demonstrates how the first of the UAPs does not simply involve leading people in the Spiritual Exercises or articulating the riches of Ignatian spirituality, but rather witnessing how Ignatian spirituality can infiltrate our daily life. The conversation includes questions and answers specifically focused on Jesuit mission, the Exercises, and how these inform our understanding of the Church and our lives of faith. As the title of his book suggests, all of this has to do with endeavoring to understand what it means to walk with Ignatius, both in his day and our own. Each of the pieces in this section offers its own perspective on this basic question.

Mark Mossa, SJ

The Biographical Roots of the Ignatian Tradition

Eileen Burke-Sullivan

Ad majorem Dei gloriam, a favorite phrase of Ignatius, emerged from the heart of medieval ideals of honor and glory that shaped his early ambition, but had then been purified in the fires of mystical love. Literally translated "to the greater glory of God," the phrase provides a summary statement that, like hypertext in the world of computers, springs open when pressed, to reveal a dense description of attitudes and behaviors. This manner of living the Christ life provides one of the great historical spiritualities found within the Christian tradition. In relationship to the major historical spiritualities of the monastic and the conventual traditions, the Ignatian pattern is the youngest. As such it draws on these earlier methods for living the Christian life but remains distinct from all of them because of its various emphases.

Ignatius Loyola was a man of his own time, but, like Martin Luther with whom he shares the 16th-century religious stage, seems to stand above that era. Born in the Basque country of northern Spain in 1491, within months of the completion of the Reconquista by Isabella and Ferdinand, and the discovery of the Americas, Ignatius entered history at a moment of extraordinary change in European culture. It was the dawn of Spain's golden age of wealth and power. Initiated by Isabella's material and social support of Christopher

Excerpt from *The Ignatian Tradition: Spirituality in History*, with Kevin F. Burke, SJ, & Eileen Burke-Sullivan (Liturgical Press, 2009).

Columbus's exploration voyage, this period of extraordinary wealth and power was fueled by the discovery of gold, silver, lands, crops, and slave labor of the peoples of the Americas.

From the larger world of European culture, the Renaissance inaugurated dramatic intellectual growth, as well as strong biblical and spiritual reform in the Spanish Catholic Church.

Renaissance thinking set the stage for the Protestant Reformation, which in turn led to the end of Christendom as a united political reality. The printing press, invented only forty years before Ignatius's birth, had already contributed to a revolution of language, literacy, and learning throughout Europe, even while he was a child. In this period of epochal change in Western culture the fundamental theistic worldview of the medieval period gave way to the dawn of an anthropocentric premodernity. Newly formed nations sent ambitious younger sons to unmapped continents where they claimed land and resources in the name of their monarchs, achieving both wealth and power.

In the midst of these momentous cultural quakes, Ignatius discovered a similar tectonic movement within his own heart and mind. He was drawn by circumstance and grace from a life of self-glorification to a clear-eyed realism oriented to God's glory. His experience of God's gracious intervention in his personal human struggles, which he learned to carefully observe and methodize, provided the matrix of insights and practices that defined his own spiritual journey and became the foundation for the way of Christian life that is named for him.

Ignatius's Early Life

Ignatius of Loyola was born into a Basque family of clan chiefs and baptized Íñigo, a common name in the Basque language of Euskadi. One of the youngest children in a family of eight boys and three girls, he lost his mother as a small child and his father when he was fifteen. The wife of an older brother cared for him after his mother's death; that same brother inherited the estate and title of Loyola when their father died.

Because of the medieval law of primogeniture and as a younger son in a large noble family, Íñigo had few choices about the direction of his life. He could enlist in the king's army, join in the exploration and conquest in the Americas, enter the service of the church as clergy, or serve one of the lords of the Spanish or imperial court. He had only a minimal education, but he learned to read and write in Spanish. Apparently he also received tonsure—the first step toward the clerical state—at the age of thirteen. But after he turned fifteen an undisclosed reversal of fortune sent him to the court of his mother's cousin, Juan Velazquez de Cuellar, the royal treasurer of King Ferdinand and Queen Isabella.

While at court, Íñigo acquired the style and flourish of a young courtier and began signing his name according to the Latin, Ignatius.[1] He also became enamored of the popular romantic literature of the day: stories of heroic battles, glorious knightly competitions, and the conquest of the hearts of wealthy and beautiful women. He described this period of his life in a single sentence: "Up to the age of twenty-six he was a man given to the vanities of the world; and what he enjoyed most was warlike sport, with a great and foolish desire to win fame" (*Autobiography*, 68).

---

1. Baldassare Castiglione describes the kind of person Ignatius was expected to become by his appointment to the court of de Cueller: "So in jousts and tournaments, in riding, and handling every kind of weapon, as well as in the festivities, games and musical performances, in short, in all the activities appropriate to a well-born gentleman, everyone at his court strove to behave in such a way as to be judged worthy of the Duke's noble company" (Baldassare Castiglione, *The Book of the Courtier*, trans. George Bull [London: Penguin Books, 1967], 42).

A French cannonball fired at the small, fortified city of Pamplona where he served among the defenders suddenly turned Ignatius's life upside down. From all historical evidence Ignatius had committed himself to a hopeless cause, for the French completely outnumbered the Spanish. His sense of chivalrous honor, however, required him to serve king and country to the end. The cannonball seriously damaged his knee, but the French treated him compassionately. They moved him back to Loyola Castle where family physicians using the primitive surgery of the day did what they could for him. He nearly died after septicemia set in.

As he began to recover Ignatius realized the extent of his injury: a bone protruded near his knee leaving one leg significantly shorter than the other. Unwilling to have either his looks marred or his mobility impaired, Ignatius required the local doctors to saw off the segment that jutted from his knee and reset the bones. Again he endured serious infection and again he barely survived. Aided by tortuous physical therapies that straightened and lengthened the leg, however, he did recover.

During this period of enforced immobility, Ignatius requested books to while away the time and take his mind off the pain. His pious sister-in-law had only two: a popular *Life of Christ* by Ludolph of Saxony (which included significant portions of both the Old and New Testaments) and *Golden Legends*, a collection of saints' lives told in a chivalrous style that captured his imagination and enthusiasm. For over six months Ignatius read, reread, considered, and fantasized about these books. He even copied large segments of both into personal notebooks.

Conversion and the First Steps in Discernment

The Lutheran Reformation caused Catholic authorities in Spain to frown upon vernacular translations of the Bible. Because of this and because he knew no Latin, Ignatius had never read or studied Scripture. Ludolph's *Life of Christ*, however, represented a theological and popular exposition of the doctrines of creation, incarnation, and paschal mystery. It also contained a conflation of the gospel narratives surrounding Jesus's birth, public ministry, and death. Since Ignatius was born and raised in a Catholic family in that most Catholic of countries, the biblical stories provided him with no new data. But having time to read and consider their implications enabled him to experience the truth of the Christian message in an entirely new way. During these months, he ceased to be merely culturally religious and became profoundly faithful.

The *Autobiography* witnesses that from the days of his long physical recovery at Loyola Castle, Ignatius learned to pay careful attention to his affective response to the reading and the fantasies that he wove under the influence of both books. In his imaginary life he entertained himself by daydreams that at one time featured him pursuing and winning a very attractive woman's favor through chivalrous deeds, and at other times described him as a poor and humble servant winning souls for God in the manner of St. Francis or St. Dominic. Both kinds of dreams gave him pleasure in the imagining, but the different states of mind and heart that resulted after spending hours weaving the various fantasies astonished him. When he dreamed of winning human praise and adulation, he later felt bored and tired, but when he imagined that he accomplished deeds for God he later felt energized and alive. He told de Camara that initially he didn't take much note of this, but then a time came when "his eyes were opened a little and he began to marvel at the difference and to reflect upon it" (*Autobiography*, 71).

This first stage of discernment—observing his own thoughts and feelings—led him to begin to address God less through structured formula and instead to practice what he later named "a colloquy." This prayer is an intimate conversation, face-to-face, "in the way one friend speaks to another, or a servant to one in authority—now begging a favor, now accusing oneself of some misdeed, now telling one's concerns and asking counsel about them" (SE 54).[2] This very intimate, conversational prayer opened his mind and heart to discover the great love that God had for him and the personal interest God took in his choices and in his way of life. This experience of being radically loved and carefully guided compelled Ignatius to leave the comfortable and politically powerful life of a courtier and to seek God's desire for his future. He began a relationship with God that, in these beginning stages, he likened to study with a good teacher who carefully guides his student.

Generally recovered in health, though permanently crippled, Ignatius set out walking on a new path—a path toward living in a way more fully responsive to God's desires for him. Years later, Ignatius would call himself the pilgrim—the one on the journey toward God—on the way of companioning Jesus. He determined to visit Jerusalem, but he stopped on the way and dwelt for almost a year in a cave near the town of Manresa, Spain, down a steep hill from the Benedictine monastery of Montserrat.

The Months at Manresa

In this setting, Ignatius spent hours in prayer accompanied by rigorous physical penances that occasionally left him near death from the extreme privation of food, sleep, and shelter. His impulse was at least in response to the medieval influence undertaking an overwhelming challenge to prove his worth and his devotion. Later he judged that such efforts may not necessarily have been guided by God but could well have been responses to a more arrogant spirit of pride where he wanted to "outdo" the giants of medieval spirituality, Francis and

2. *The Spiritual Exercises of Saint Ignatius*, ed. and trans. George E. Ganss (St. Louis, MO: Institute of Jesuit Sources, 1992). Throughout this book citations to the text of the Spiritual Exercises will be identified in the classical method that employs paragraph numbers, i.e., SE 54. One can thus find the reference in any translation or version of the book. Such citations will be located within the text rather than in endnotes. It should be noted that throughout this book we distinguish the written text of *The Spiritual Exercises* from the act of doing the Spiritual Exercises (or directing another who is doing them) by placing the former in italics.

Dominic. During these periods of severe self-deprivation, he often suffered intense bouts of scrupulosity and an obsessive guilt about his past that seemed to reject the power of God's mercy to forgive him. He even spiraled toward suicide at least once during this period. He later actively discouraged his followers from imitating this extreme penitential behavior and suggested that they carefully discern the reasons for wanting to. It became clear to him that the matter of doing penance had to be an individual response of love, not an effort to achieve God's love or attention. There should be no uniform expectation of certain ascetical acts required of all because each person is called to demonstrate love uniquely.

Once he discovered that his impulse toward severe penances and the scrupulosity that afflicted him were not from God, he set the penitential behavior aside, the scruples subsided, and he began to live a somewhat more ordered life. At this point he was granted a series of mystical graces, which he later described in his autobiographical account. These graces altered his understanding of his human nature, of God, and of God's desire for Ignatius's responsive love and service. He understood better his own dissolute history, and received God's absolving mercy. He experienced himself as freed, by God's grace, to seek and discover that which is truly of God. Conversely, he understood in a new way how self-destructive was his former attraction to sin.

Ignatius uses the classical phrase "the discernment of spirits" to name the process of distinguishing between "movements" toward God's desires and "movements" toward his own sinful self-will. While the phrase was not new (numerous discussions about the necessity and practice of discernment appear in the New Testament and throughout the tradition), Ignatius made a striking contribution to this tradition: a psychologically sound and spiritually astute methodology for individual discernment of spirits and discernment of God's will.

The ability to sort among the various attractions in one's life and to discover a concrete expression of God's desires within one's talents and history is based on a graced freedom from compulsions, addictions, or inordinate attachments of all kinds. Ignatius's mystical experience taught him that such freedom is ultimately based on an interior knowledge that God is both the source of all creation and the summit of all our genuine desires. He was convinced that each human person is created for a relationship with God and that all things and relationships given to each person are given to assist in the journey back toward God. Indeed, the purpose of human existence is to respond in freedom to the God of love. This knowledge serves as the foundation of a Christian spiritual life. Without a firm grounding in this first "principle and foundation" one cannot fruitfully pursue the spiritual journey (SE 23).

Rooted in Ignatius's experiences in Manresa, the *Spiritual Exercises* move from this foundation to a series of meditations on the nature of sin and God's redeeming grace. Beginning with sin itself in macrocosmic terms, Ignatius narrowed the focus to meditations on the patterns of sin and weakness in each human life. He recognized that unless one experiences repentance, sin ultimately leads to eternal alienation from God and God's goodness. Therefore, it is sheer grace to recognize that one has participated in disrupting God's ordered plan of love, and to experience feelings of sorrow for collaborating in such destruction. Seemingly, for many Christians, that recognition alone enables them to live reasonable Christian lives thereafter. But some, including Ignatius himself, experience the call to do greater things in the service of Christ and the reign of God.

He invited such persons to move, even as he did, into a second phase of spiritual maturity. In this phase he was drawn to contemplate the life events of the mission, sufferings, and death of Jesus, and of the glory of the Lord's Resurrection. His prayer involved imagining himself present within the events recounted in the biblical texts he had so carefully copied from Ludolph's *Life of Christ*. His contemplation of the mysteries of Christ formed a doorway through which he entered experientially into the Lord's human life. Given a series of extraordinary graces, or "consolations," he encountered the mystery of Jesus's human and divine reality, the gift of Christ's presence in the Eucharist, and the role of Mary in the Church. The climax of Ignatius's experiences at Manresa occurred on the banks of the Cardoner River near the town. He received a graced insight so profound that he understood the created order, the mysteries of faith, and his relationship to God with such clarity that he later said that if he added up every grace he ever received from God through his entire life it would not equal the clarity and completeness of those few moments. In the course of these eleven months of purification and enlightenment, his deepest desire shifted. Instead of a life of solitude and penance, he now sought a life filled with the apostolic purpose of "helping souls" the way he had been helped.

Years of Study and Ordination

Leaving Manresa with this conviction of call and his desire to respond, Ignatius first fulfilled an earlier commitment to go on pilgrimage to Jerusalem. Once there he was tempted to stay and try to convert Muslims, but the Franciscans in charge sent him back to Europe in order to keep a precarious peace with the Muslim authorities. This pilgrimage was particularly important because it helped Ignatius gain a memory of the physical place of Jesus's life in the world. For the rest of his life he would be able to imagine Jesus on earth more poignantly because he had a capacity to "compose the place" of an encounter in his memory and imagination. The use of these mental faculties was important to Ignatius. They are the personal doorways through which God's Spirit works on the consciousness and affections of the individual disciple.

Returning to Spain, he discovered other men and women who were hungry for a deeper spiritual life. He guided them through a series of prayer exercises based on his notes. This ministry brought him face-to-face with the Spanish Inquisition and forced him to experience imprisonment for brief periods as he awaited trials. He was tried and found innocent.

Nevertheless, the religious authorities ordered him to limit, and in some cases cease, his work. He soon realized that, given the structures of the medieval Spanish Church, he could not fulfill his mission from God unless he became a vowed religious or an ordained priest. Uncertain about finding the right religious community, he opted to prepare for the priesthood. In his mid-thirties he enrolled in Latin, studying with preadolescent boys.

A year later, with the goal of ordination to the priesthood firmly in mind, he studied philosophy and theology at the Spanish universities in Alcalá, Barcelona, and Salamanca. In each of these cities he engaged in spiritual conversations and gave his Spiritual Exercises to men and women, clergy and laity, always inviting others to discover the interior freedom he had come to know. The inquisitors of each city, however, continued to harass him. Finally, he left Spain and matriculated at the University of Paris to complete his religious training. At every stage of his formation into the priesthood he begged for his daily bread and for enough resources to pursue his studies as well to help others pay their tuition. He gave spiritual counsel and guided various people in the Spiritual Exercises. During the Paris years, he took extended trips to Flanders and even to England to beg from wealthy patrons there. Many of those he directed became his greatest benefactors, while others introduced him to ecclesial authorities capable of providing protection for his studies and his work.

The Founding of the Society of Jesus

Ignatius studied at the University of Paris for seven years. During that time, he met the men who eventually joined him in his way of companioning Christ. Among them he discovered yet another crucial dimension of his "way": the treasure of spiritual companionship with others in Christ. He became a master at the art of spiritual conversation. He liked to say that he attempted always to enter through another's door in order to draw that person out through his door. Thus, Ignatius invited his friends to discover the distinctive way God acted directly on and within their own lives.

When he had nearly finished his studies at Paris, he and six companions professed vows together on the Feast of the Assumption in 1534, both the traditional vows of poverty and chastity and then a third vow to either make their way to Jerusalem on a mission to preach the gospel among the Muslims—if that would be possible within a year or two—or to go to Rome and place themselves at the direct service of the pope.

These *compañeros*, a company of friends committed to service of God, did not yet see themselves as a religious community. For this reason, they did not profess a vow of obedience to one of their own companions. But when an unusual combination of war, famine, and terrible weather made their mission to Jerusalem impossible, they journeyed to Rome to fulfill their alternative vow. On the way, two further events shaped the final form of this "way of Ignatius." The first was a remarkable vision of God the Father and Jesus carrying his Cross that came to Ignatius while he was praying at a wayside shrine at La Storta. In the context of the vision, the Father turned to Jesus and asked him to take Ignatius as companion and servant. God then told Ignatius that God would guide and support him and his companions in Rome. Quite reasonably, the companions took this profound experience of their leader as a sign of God's blessing on the group, on their choice of the name Society of Jesus, and on their commitment to apostolic service to the whole Church. For Ignatius it was a confirmation of the companionship and their common call to help souls through preaching, spiritual conversation, and giving the Spiritual Exercises.

The second singular occurrence was an activity that the companions undertook among themselves in relationship with God and each other. Over the course of the next three months, while engaged apostolically in ministries of teaching, preaching, and consoling the sick, they met together in a process of focused deliberation to discern whether to bind themselves to one another and effectively become a new religious community. They also took up a related but more problematic question as to whether to make a vow of obedience to one of their number. This so-called Deliberation of 1539 became a classic model of corporate decision-making. The men committed themselves to hours of prayer, extensive fasting, and other penances. They pondered the situation and needs of the world. They spent long hours sharing with one another their deepest desires, fears, spiritual consolations, and desolations. In the end they determined, with great joy and peace, that God was calling them to form a religious community. Likewise, in addition to their previous vows of poverty, chastity, and service to the Holy Father, they agreed to take a vow of obedience to one of their companions. This deliberation gave birth to the Society of Jesus.

Almost immediately after this decision, some members of the group took up residence in Rome while others assumed missions to other parts of Europe. New opportunities to proclaim the gospel soon followed in the recently discovered worlds of the Americas and Asia. Pope Paul III formally approved their petition to found a new order in 1540. Ignatius, but for his own vote, was elected the first general. He remained in Rome for the last sixteen years of his life, overseeing the initial growth of the new order, composing the Formula of the Institute and, with the help of his secretary, Juan de Polanco, eventually writing the *Constitutions of the Society of Jesus*.

Letters to the Twenty-First Century: The Incomparable Value of Ignatius's Letters for Understanding the Practicality of Ignatian Spirituality Then and Now

Mark Mossa, SJ

"The same divine Spirit could move me to this course for one set of reasons, and move others to the opposite for different ones, with the outcome being what the Emperor indicated."[1] Quite unexpectedly, and in an entirely different context, my eyes set upon these words, written in the sixteenth century, during the tumult of September 2001. The article they were quoted in had nothing to do with the crisis I was then facing, but they leaped from the page as an answer to the inner disquiet I was feeling. I was barely four years into my life as a Jesuit, living and studying in New York City and, like other Jesuits I lived with—some only two years and others but a handful of weeks removed from our first vows—I was struggling with how to respond to the horrors that had unfolded on September 11, but a short train ride away. As I saw the varied reactions and resolutions of my brothers to both the event and our country's response to it, I wondered why we could have responses that were morally at odds with each other. Hadn't I joined a company of men who would not differ as to what

Adapted from *Saint Ignatius Loyola: The Spiritual Writings, Selections Annotated and Explained* (Skylight Communications, 2012). All citations in this article, whether in the text or in a comment are taken from Martin E. Palmer, John W. Padberg, & John L. McCarthy, eds., *Ignatius of Loyola: Letters and Instructions* (St. Louis: Institute of Jesuit Sources, 2006).

1. Letter to Francis Borgia, June 5, 1552, p. 377.

was a just or unjust response to violence and terror? I was naive perhaps, but genuinely concerned about the implications of this for my chosen vocation. Maybe I had made the wrong choice.

Maybe this wasn't the Society of Jesus I thought I had bound myself to. If other Jesuits with ease could hold what seemed contradictory views to my own, views that I thought were God's views, how could we all call ourselves Jesuits?

The words of that letter might not meet others with the same force that they were impressed upon me that day, but Saint Ignatius's words taken not from *The Spiritual Exercises*, not from his famous *Autobiography*, but from one of his letters, offered a spiritual insight that continues to guide me powerfully. At the time the letter was written, the question was whether the also inexperienced young Jesuit, Francis Borgia, to whom the letter was addressed, should be made a cardinal, as the emperor had recommended and the pope seemed inclined to approve. Ignatius, as a devoted servant of the Church, found himself conflicted because of his strong conviction that Jesuits should not be bishops (and probably some reluctance related to the fact that the motivation had largely to do with the prominence of Francis's family). Yet, despite his strong initial resistance, he tells Borgia, before reaching the above conclusion, "However, being unsure of God's will because of the many reasons that occurred to me on both sides, I ordered all the priests in the community to say mass and those not priests to offer their prayers for three days that I might be guided wholly to God's greater glory."[2] Ignatius emerged from those three days even more convinced that it was God's will and thus his obligation that he must "do all I could with the Pope and the cardinals to oppose it . . ."[3] But, as the above qualification suggests, he emerged equally convinced, and at peace with, the possibility that the Holy Spirit might for different reasons guide the Church to what would be essentially the opposite course of action. As Ignatius's words touched my heart nearly five hundred years later, and in a quite different circumstance, I realized that this same conviction was the answer to my current crisis: that the apparently contradictory views

2. Letter to Francis Borgia, June 5, 1552, p. 376.
3. Letter to Francis Borgia, June 5, 1552, p. 377.

of me and my brothers, even if I felt certain that another was wrong, might actually be inspired by that same Spirit who guided each of our lives. We could hold opposing views, even regarding matters of such great import, and still be good and faithful Christians, and Jesuits. For others, these same words might have passed unnoticed, but in that moment they were the answer to my questions and prayers, and Ignatius's spiritual insight continues to guide me to this day when I find myself tempted to demonize someone with whom I disagree.

Saint Ignatius is thought to be the most prolific letter writer of his time, at least among the most prominent figures of his day, and so it is surprising that his letters are still not more widely known and their spiritual insights not more often promoted. Several years ago, when invited to organize into a book a collection of key excerpts from Ignatius's spiritual writings, I convinced the publishers that if they wanted to make an important and unique contribution to the understanding of Ignatian spirituality the book ought to include not only excerpts from Ignatius's *Spiritual Exercises* and *Autobiography*, but also his letters.

As I poured through hundreds of Ignatius's letters, I was struck by the variety of addressees and the multitude of contexts in which he offered advice about practical and spiritual matters or, in the context of letters written to individual Jesuits, Jesuit provinces, or the Society of Jesus as a whole, not just advice, but orders. Regardless of the addressees and the circumstance, I found often that the spiritual insight and practical wisdom dispensed could be applied more broadly to one's everyday experience, even in our own time. For example, Ignatius's 1547 letter to the Fathers and Jesuit Scholastics at Coimbra offers words of inspiration that certainly touched the hearts of those to whom they were addressed, but which can also speak to anyone then or now reflecting on what it means to follow Christ:

> To sum up my meaning in a few words: If you thought carefully about how deeply you are bound to defend the honor of Jesus Christ and the salvation of your neighbor, you would see how much you are obliged to dispose yourselves for every toil and labor to make yourself apt instruments for God's grace for this purpose, particularly nowadays, when there are so few real laborers, so few persons who seek "not the things

> that are their own but the things that are Jesus Christ's" [Philippians 2:21]; you need to strive all the harder to make up for what others fail to do, since God is giving you such a special grace in this vocation and resolve.[4]

Perhaps this has been the case throughout history, but certainly many of us today see the challenge of our God-given vocations in relation to the fact that it can often seem that there are "so few real laborers" that we are obliged to take our responsibilities as disciples all the more seriously.

Saint Ignatius was well aware of the challenges that would accompany accepting so prominent a figure as Francis Borgia into the Society of Jesus, so much so that he kept the process of Borgia's incorporation into the Society largely a secret as it was happening. Because of Borgia's status, we already see how it eventually led to an effort to make Borgia a cardinal. However, it was both Borgia's status and his personal and spiritual dispositions that made Borgia one of Ignatius's more frequent correspondents. One can imagine that this caused Ignatius a certain amount of grief, but it also led to letters offering both simple and profound insights into how we ought to conduct ourselves in our spiritual lives.

Early in the history of the Jesuits, we can see how some, even among the members of the Society itself, sought to use both Borgia's prominence and his sometimes overly pious disposition to their advantage. Less than a decade into the beginnings of the Society of Jesus, two early Jesuits who worked in Gandia, Andres de Oviedo and Francisco Onfroy, were suggesting some reform in the Society with regard to individual Jesuits' time spent in prayer. They each had arrived at the conviction that engaging in lengthy hours of prayer each day was essential to the spiritual life. When it came to light that Borgia might be inclined to their view, they sought to enlist him to their cause. This prompted letters from Ignatius to Borgia in which Ignatius explains various reasons he believed their view to be in error in general, and not just in regard to Jesuit life. He explains to Borgia, offering seven different points to make his case (it will suffice to offer

---

4. Letter to the Fathers and Scholastics at Coimbra, May 7, 1547, p. 170.

two here): "To say that a meditation of one to two hours is no prayer and that more hours are required is bad doctrine and opposed to the opinion and practice of the saints . . . Second, this can be seen from the prayer Christ himself taught us: he called it prayer even though it is short and does not take more than one or two hours to pray; one should not deny that this is prayer."[5] As there are few of us who think that we give sufficient time to prayer, I personally find these insights consoling and often share them with others.

Lest we think that Ignatius's correspondence was restricted to noble persons and Jesuits, one will find that among his correspondents were all manner of persons. We find numerous letters to Teresa Rejadell, a Benedictine nun in Barcelona who wrote to Ignatius on numerous occasions seeking spiritual advice. Again, it seems that Ignatius is advising not overdoing it when it comes to prayer but, in this instance, he relates it to care for one's health and well-being: "The second is something that happens to many people given to prayer or contemplation: because they exercise their minds much, they cannot sleep afterwards because they keep thinking about matters they have contemplated and pictured. Hence, the enemy tries hard to preserve good thoughts, so that the body will suffer from the loss of sleep."[6] What was true of prayer in Ignatius's day is true today of the pictures that can linger in our minds from excessive time spent at the computer or on the internet before bed. Studies have shown that such habits can have a detrimental effect on our sleep. Again, Ignatius seems somewhat ahead of his time! He also shares, in similar words in his *Autobiography*, the kind of obstacles that he himself faced in his own journey to his life's vocation:

> [T]he enemy's general practice with persons who have a desire and have begun to serve our Lord is to bring up obstacles and impediments. This is the first weapon with which he attempts to wound them; namely, "How are you going to live your whole life amid such penance, with no enjoyment from friends, relatives, or possessions, leading such a lonely

5. Letter to Francis Borgia, July 1549, p. 281.
6. Letter to Teresa Rejadell, September 11, 1536, p. 23.

life, and never having any ease? There are other less perilous ways you can save your soul." He suggests that we will have to live a longer life amid all these hardships than any human ever lived.[7]

He offers similar insights in his correspondence with Isabel Roser, a lay woman who was one of the Society of Jesus' greatest benefactors and most ardent supporters (Ignatius even allowed her to make private vows tying her to the order):

> You mention how many acts of spitefulness, intrigue and untruthfulness have besieged you on every side. This does not surprise me in the least, even if it were much worse. For at the moment you decide, will and strive with all your strength for the glory, honor and service of God our Lord, at that moment you join battle and raise your standard against the world, and prepare yourself to cast away lofty and embrace lowly things, resolving to treat equally the high or the low, honor or dishonor, wealth or poverty, love or hatred, welcome or rejection—in short, the world's glory or all its abuse.[8]

Ask anyone who has pledged themselves to following God in some radical way, whether as a religious or priest, married or single lay person, and they will likely tell you of similar experiences. Indeed, the ways in which the "battle" that one joins are described might ring familiar, as they are not unlike the words of traditional marriage vows we might have heard or spoken ourselves.

Even while the bulk of Ignatius's letters are addressed to Jesuits, this does not mean that they are irrelevant to the lives of non-Jesuits or those who don't work for the Church. Indeed, it is remarkable how at times Ignatius offers advice that speaks to the concerns of the everyday people of his time and of our time as well. Who doesn't complain these days about the challenges of busyness? Addressing Fulvio Androzzi, who distinguished himself as one of the earliest Jesuit spiritual writers, Ignatius offers practical advice:

7. Letter to Teresa Rejadell, June 18, 1536, p. 19.
8. Letter to Isabel Roser, November 10, 1532, p. 9.

> When you are very busy, you need to make a choice and devote your efforts to the more important occupations, that is, those in which there is a greater service to God, greater spiritual advantage for the neighbor, more universal or perfect good, etc. If there are people from the area who could take your place in some matter, it would be good to share some of the labor with them so as to be free for more important matters.[9]

In other words, focus on what is most important to God, and have the good sense to ask for help. In this spirit, Ignatius was also quite serious about challenging those who neglected their own health in the service of God or others, as he once did. Two zealous Jesuits whom he took to task for such behavior were Gaspar Berze, who succeeded Francis Xavier as superior of the mission in India, and Francis Borgia, who would eventually succeed Ignatius as the third Superior General of the Jesuits. To Berze, he writes, "There are two dangers in treating yourself so harshly. The first is that, barring a miracle, Your Reverence will not be able to last very long in the holy ministries you undertake . . . The second danger is that, being so hard on yourself, you could easily become too hard on those under you . . ."[10] Ignatius went even further with Borgia to ensure he took care of himself, assigning another Jesuit to take charge of his treatment of his own body, noting, "We understand that you do not treat yourself—your body, I mean—with the same charity you show toward others. You eat badly, overwork, and do not let others assist you."[11] This is a scenario familiar to many today and, in the absence of a doting religious superior, one might still see to it to choose someone to whom they can be accountable for caring for oneself as one would others.

Ignatius also offers some perspective and advice regarding a struggle that can vex many: being confounded by one's own expectations of what the spiritual life should be like, what form prayers should take, what emotions they ought to feel, in order that they might go about doing the work of the Lord in the "right way." As prescriptive

9. Letter to Fulvio Androzzi, July 18, 1556, p. 694.
10. Letter to Gaspar Berze, February 24, 1554, p. 473.
11. Letter to Francis Borgia, June 13, 1555, p. 574–75.

as some of the meditations and contemplations that Ignatius outlines in the Spiritual Exercises can be, they always come with the recognition that the particulars of the experience may very well be different for different people, and for good reason, not because they are doing something "wrong." Nicholas Floris was a Jesuit who was very successful in his ministry but was troubled by the experience of spiritual dryness in his prayer and, most especially, the fact that he did not experience the "gift of tears" in his compassion for others. This would be especially troubling for one who knows that in the Third Week of the *Spiritual Exercises* tears are among the primary graces that Ignatius suggests one pray for. Having struggled to experience this myself, I know the frustration that accompanies the apparent failure not to "achieve" this gift. But Ignatius reassures Nicholas, making clear that such expectations can be unreasonable and that such gifts are not meant for everyone, or are indicators of blessings or success. Ignatius writes:

> While some people have tears because their nature is such that the affections in the higher part of their souls easily overflow into the lower, or because God our Lord, seeing that it would be good for them, grants them to melt into tears, this still does not mean that they have a greater charity or accomplish more than other persons who are without tears but have no less strong affections.[12]

Then, rather sharply, he continues:

> Moreover, I would tell Your Reverence something of which I am convinced: There are persons to whom I would not give the gift of tears even if it were in my power to do so, because it does not help their charity and damages their heads and bodies, and consequently hinders any practice of charity. So, Your Reverence ought not to be distressed over the lack of external tears; keep your will strong and good and show it in your actions, and that will suffice.[13]

12. Letter to Nicholas Floris (Goudanus), November 22, 1553, p. 449.
13. Letter to Nicholas Floris (Goudanus), November 22, 1553, p. 449–50.

For those of us for whom the gift of tears is infrequent, Ignatius's words are indeed consoling, as is the reminder that sometimes we get in our own way by thinking that one feeling, one experience of prayer, or one particular approach is essential to the success of our ministry, the effectiveness of our compassion, or our relationship with God.

Ignatius also addresses what in my experience is one of the most common things that people complain about in their efforts to pray and to serve God: distraction. This can take various forms. Many of us, like the Jesuit Manoel Godinho, treasurer of the Jesuit college at Coimbra, find ourselves frustrated by the apparent disconnect between our day-to-day work and our spiritual lives. Godinho was convinced enough that his work as treasurer was so disconnected from his spiritual life that he sought Ignatius's permission to be relieved of his duties. Ignatius, instead, invited him to see things from another perspective:

> Although responsibility for temporal business may appear and be somewhat distracting, I have no doubt that your holy intention and your directing everything you do to God's glory makes it spiritual and highly pleasing to his infinite goodness. For when distractions are accepted for his greater service and in conformity with his divine will . . . they can be not only equivalent to the union and recollection of constant contemplation, but even more acceptable to him, since they proceed from a more vehement and stronger charity.[14]

Ignatius writes to Borgia, again in the context of the entreaties of Oviedo and Onfroy for more lengthy and intensive prayer in Jesuit life, of the certainty of distraction, especially if one attempts to do too much in prayer, or otherwise. He offers his opinion that "even very devout servants of God complain about wanderings and instability of the mind . . . It is true that sometimes, even many times, numerous

14. Letter to Manoel Godinho, January 31, 1552, p. 367.

servants of God have a great and vivid awareness, quite certain and stable, of his eternal truths; but for them to remain permanently in this state is impossible to believe."[15]

This, I hope, will suffice to convince those who seek a greater insight into and awareness of Ignatian spirituality that the letters of Ignatius are indispensable. Only there can we receive the kind of practical insight, which to our great surprise and joy, speaks not only to the concerns of those to whom they are addressed, but speaks powerfully to many challenges we encounter today, both as we strive to serve and be in relationship with God, and to find God in the many distractions of daily life.

15. Letter to Francis Borgia, July 1549, p. 278–79.

Mary, the Hidden Catalyst: Reflections from an Ignatian Pilgrimage to Spain and Rome

Margo J. Heydt and Sarah J. Melcher

In the summer of 2006, we undertook a ten-day Ignatian pilgrimage with several Jesuit university colleagues. Our intention was to write from a feminist perspective about our experiences learning about the history of a religious order of men. We set out to discover how women fit into the history of the early Jesuits to which we would be exposed, thinking that the focus would arise from the holes in the story—the places where women should have been found but were missing. What we encountered on the pilgrimage, however, differed in several ways from what we expected. This chapter develops one of our discoveries: the influence of Mary, the mother of Jesus, on the transformation of Ignatius of Loyola from a Spanish soldier of nobility to the spiritual founder of the Jesuits.

These reflections on our journey, combined with our research, demonstrate the impact that such an exploratory trip can have on two Protestant feminist pilgrim professors. The trip led us to a new understanding of the role that women played in the life of Ignatius of Loyola and so to a better grasp of the individual himself and the order that he founded. Two standard texts had been suggested to all on the pilgrimage: *The First Jesuits,* by John W. O'Malley, SJ, and *Saint*

From *Jesuit and Feminist Education: Intersections in Teaching and Learning for the Twenty-first Century*, edited by Jocelyn M. Borczyka and Elizabeth A. Petrino (Fordham University Press, 2012). Note that the original publication includes images not reprinted here.

Ignatius of Loyola: Personal Writings, translated by Joseph A. Munitiz and Philip Endean.[1] The historical information we learned from tour guides and artifacts throughout the pilgrimage revealed the role of Mary to be considerably more significant to Ignatius throughout his life and in the founding of the Society of Jesus than had been portrayed in the books we read. The visual representations of Mary and of the life of Ignatius that we saw on the pilgrimage left a great impression, making the recommended readings come alive. The extent of Mary's impact was confirmed by the research we began upon our return. Through the lens of the pilgrimage, we invite the reader to journey along with us and see images of Mary, who so strongly influenced St. Ignatius.

The Pilgrimage and Imagery in Art

The pilgrimage retraced the steps of the early Jesuits, with stops at important Ignatian sites in Spain and Rome. It spanned the lifetime of Ignatius of Loyola, from his birth (1491) at the Loyola family castle to his death at age sixty-five (1556) in his simple apartment next to the Gesù, the church of the Society of Jesus in Rome. Along the pilgrimage path, we were delighted to find that representations of women were considerably more abundant in European religious settings than (in our experiences) in the United States. This was particularly true of the art we observed at the religious sites we visited in Spain. Not only were these representations more numerous, but most were also qualitatively different. We became fascinated by differences between the images of Mary we observed in Spain and Rome and those more commonly described images of Mary by those we queried from the United States during and after the pilgrimage.

1. John W. O'Malley, *The First Jesuits* (Cambridge, Mass.: Harvard University Press, 1993); Joseph A. Munitiz and Philip Endean, trans., *Saint Ignatius of Loyola: Personal Writings* (London: Penguin, 1996).

Before you continue reading, we invite you to pause for a moment and close your eyes to see what image of Mary comes to mind. In informal questioning of others, we found that the image that comes to mind for many is that of a solemn, light-skinned bust with downcast eyes, surrounded by folds of flowing blue and white fabric. Some envision a simple, gold halo floating above her head. If the image is full-bodied, it is usually a full-length version of that bust. Often she is seated and holding a barely visible infant well-wrapped in more blue and white fabric.

There is no visible hair, no eye contact, and no hint of activity in the depiction of either Mary or the baby Jesus.

The representations in Spain and Rome were quite diverse from this more conventional image. The eyes of the woman depicted in the sculpture or painting appeared to be looking at the viewer or at other figures in the artwork itself. The figure's hair was often visible. In addition, the representation was more likely to be full-bodied or standing. Mary's arms or hands were often raised or engaged in some kind of activity rather than folded or used only to hold the baby. The images of Mary that included Jesus showed him making eye contact and represented him at various stages of childhood instead of as a perpetually sleeping infant with closed eyes. A wide range of colors was present in Mary and Jesus's skin tones and the fabrics they wore.

Crowns of many styles worn by both Mary and Jesus tended to be large and ornate. In some images, there was both a crown and a halo. Most significantly, these empowering representations tended to portray a woman-as-agent very much engaged with and affecting those around her. This was especially true of the statue of Mary in the Basilica of St. Mary Major in Rome, where Mary appears to be blessing her audience while holding a squirming Jesus as a toddler.

The extent of Mary's influence on Ignatius of Loyola became increasingly evident to us throughout the pilgrimage. From the very first stop at the hospital where Ignatius was treated for his war wounds, we were intrigued to hear of his vision of Mary while he was hospitalized and to see the displays telling the story. At the Loyola family castle, a diorama (a collection of figurines arranged in twenty-six vignettes) illustrated the major events of Ignatius's life. Almost immediately, we were struck by how prominently

Ignatius's devotional relationship to Mary was portrayed throughout the vignettes. Later, however, what stood out to us was the minimal emphasis given in most Jesuit history accounts to this relationship. The vignettes and the accompanying narrative demonstrated how images of the Madonna inspired Ignatius's initial conversion experience. Along his lengthy spiritual path, the continued appearance of such images was instrumental in confirming Ignatius's decisions. The diorama clearly showed that Ignatius became devoted to Mary, imploring her throughout his lifetime to help him be more like her son, Jesus.

To our knowledge, neither the diorama nor the accompanying text is a product of critical historical research. Since we found them at the Loyola family castle, they could represent authentic family history or be significantly embellished, or both. They are, however, building blocks in a hagiography of Ignatius of Loyola. The diorama focused our interest on the influence of Mary on Ignatius and sparked our pursuit of further evidence of this, as well as our joint reflections, which prompted us to begin researching the relationships among Ignatius, the Jesuits, Mary, and other women. In this chapter, we share both our reflections and some of our research thus far.

Mary and Ignatius

Supporting the story told by the diorama at Loyola Castle, numerous sites along the pilgrimage path emphasized the spiritual connections that Ignatius had with Mary and how pivotal these were in his turning away from his previous lifestyle and in this founding of the Society of Jesus. We learned of a number of significant Marian visions, occurrences of spiritual inspiration sparked by a painting or statue of Mary, and other kinds of Marian connections in Ignatius's life:

- Ignatius's father and nurse taught him about Mary when Ignatius was a child, setting a foundation that made him receptive to Marian influence later.[2]
- He is profoundly affected by a painting of Mary hanging in the family castle.
- Ignatius's first vigil of conversion, during which he pledges to live his life as Jesus lived his, takes place before an image of Mary in Aránzazu.
- Ignatius seriously considers murdering a Muslim who questions Mary's virginity in order to defend her honor.
- After a three-day vigil, Ignatius lays down his sword in front of the Black Madonna at Montserrat to take up the life of a religious.
- Ignatius feels the strong influence of Mary at Manresa while meditating and writing the Spiritual Exercises in the cave.
- Ignatius has a vision of Mary in the hospital of the Magdalena at Azpeitia.
- He takes vows with some companions in front of the Mary statue at St. Paul's Outside-the-Walls Basilica in Rome.
- A painting of Mary and Jesus hangs in a prominent location in his simple apartment in Rome.
- The first church ever held by the Jesuits, and the site of the future Gesù in Rome, is called Santa Maria della Strada, or Our Lady of the Way.

It is possible that the early circumstances of Iñigo de Loyola's life explain his openness to the influence of Mary, the mother of Jesus. According to Azpeitian witnesses at Ignatius's canonization process (1595), Ignatius was one of thirteen children of Beltran Yanez de Loyola. His mother, Marina Sanchez de Licona, died soon after his birth. The boy was raised and taught religious devotion in the home of Maria de Garin, his nurse and the wife of a local blacksmith.[3]

---

2. Louis A. Bonacci, "The Marian Presence in the Life and Works of Saint Ignatius Loyola: From Private Revelation to Spiritual Exercises–The Cloth of Loyola's Allegiance" (doctoral thesis, International Marian Research Institute, University of Dayton, 2002), 16–17.
3. W. W. Meissner, *Ignatius* of *Loyola*: *The Psychology of a Saint* (New Haven, Conn.: Yale University Press, 1992), 8–9.

According to W. W. Meissner, "the combination of the loss of his mother and exile from the castle of Loyola must have had great psychic impact on the infant who was to become the great saint and founder of the Society of Jesus."[4] Meissner observes that the early loss of a parent can result "in attachment to idealized substitute figures or devotion to idealized causes."[5]

As James W. Reites explains it, Mary's more prominent role in Ignatius's life began with the wedding gift of a painting of Mary from Queen Isabella the Catholic to Ignatius's sister-in-law Magdalena, who had been a lady-in-waiting to the queen.[6] Young Ignatius contemplated this painting, which played a role in his conversion.[7] According to the diorama text, Ignatius first considered following a spiritual path after reading about the lives of saints in books that Magdalena brought him during his convalescence from his war wounds.[8] Despite Ignatius's request for some of the tales of chivalry that he loved, Magdalena brought him a *Life of Christ* and *The Golden Legend*.[9] He formed an idea of living out his life in the "land of Jesus," afflicting upon himself penances more severe than those endured by the saints. Ignatius felt that this plan was confirmed by a vision he had one night of the Madonna with the infant Jesus in her arms, a vision that filled him with immense joy: "Being awake one night, he saw clearly a likeness of Our Lady with the Holy Child Jesus, at the sight of which, for an appreciable time, he received a very extraordinary consolation."[10]

The Loyola Castle diorama text and Ignatius's *Reminiscences* relate how Ignatius's devotion to Mary continued. After leaving Loyola Castle to make his way to Jerusalem and the land of Jesus, Ignatius stopped first at Aránzazu, a Marian sanctuary in the village of Oñate. There Ignatius hoped to gain strength for his journey to Jerusalem through a vigil before a statue of Mary.[11] The diorama text describes

4. Meissner, 11.
5. Meissner, 10.
6. James W. Reites, "Ignatius and Ministry with Women," The *Way*, Supplement 74 (Summer 1992): 7–19.
7. This painting's influence on Ignatius is discussed in Hugo Rahner, ed., *Saint Ignatius Loyola: Letters to Women*, trans. Kathleen Pond and S. A. H. Weetman (New York: Herder & Herder, 1960), 116.
8. See also Munitiz and Endean, *Saint Ignatius* of *Loyola*, 14–16 and O'Malley, *The First Jesuits*, 24.
9. O'Malley, *The First Jesuits*, 24.
10. Munitiz and Endean, *Saint Ignatius of Loyola*, 16.
11. Munitiz and Endean, *Saint Ignatius of Loyola*, 18.

this as Ignatius's premier vigil of conversion, during which he pledged before an image of Mary to live his life like Jesus. In a letter written much later (1554), after the sanctuary at Aránzazu was damaged by fire, Ignatius describes how much his experience in the chapel there had meant to him:

> Indeed, the fire was a great pity and misfortune, especially for those of us who are acquainted with the devotion which flourished there and the great service rendered to God our Lord. Whatever measures are necessary for the restoration of the monastery should be undertaken with much devotion. I may say I have a particular and personal reason for desiring it. When God our Lord granted me the grace to make some change in my life, I remember having received some benefit for my soul while watching one night in that church.[12]

On the road to his next stop in Montserrat, Ignatius seriously disagreed with a Muslim who questioned the virginity of Mary. After the encounter, Ignatius apparently experienced an intense internal battle, feeling that he had not done his duty toward Mary.[13] In reconsidering the disagreement, Ignatius felt that he should have defended Mary's honor more devotedly and contemplated catching up with the man to kill him. In the end, however, he headed in another direction, one literally determined by the mule on which he was riding, and he left the Muslim alone.

According to the well-known and broadly circulated medieval (pre-1850) poem "Ordene de Chevalerie," a chivalrous man must make himself available to a woman in need, honor her, and perform whatever mighty deeds may be necessary.[14] Ramon Lull of Majorca, author of *Libre del Ordre de Cavayleria*, indicates that a knight had the obligation to "maintain and defend the holy Catholic faith, by which God the father sent his son into the world to take human flesh ain

12. William J. Young, trans., *Letters of St. Ignatius of Loyola* (Chicago: Loyola Press, 1959), 349–50.
13. Munitiz and Endean, *Saint Ignatius* of *Loyola,* 19.
14. The requirement to treat women with chivalry is part of the "four commandments." See Keith Busby, ed., *Raoul* de *Hodenc: Le Roman des Eles / The Anonymous Ordene* de *Chevalerie* (Amsterdam: John Benjamins, 1983), 112–13 (lines 263–303). See also Maurice Keen, *Chivalry* (New Haven, Conn.: Yale University Press, 1984), 6–8.

[sic] the glorious virgin our lady Saint Mary."[15] Ignatius's background prepared him for religious devotion, as the classic orders of chivalry recommended daily attendance at Mass. Lull closely follows the earlier "Ordene de Chevalerie" in declaring that the "office of a knight is to maintain and defend women, widows and orphans, men diseased; and those who are neither powerful nor strong."[16] Perhaps even more pertinent is the requirement outlined in Geoffroi de Charny's *Libre de Chevalerie*: "Hence all good men-at-arms are rightly bound to protect and defend the honor of all ladies against all those who would threaten it by word or deed."[17] Ignatius's background as a noble prepared him to defend and honor Mary in the encounter with the Muslim and probably played a role in the later events that occurred on his journey.[18]

Both O'Malley and the diorama offer the better-known story of Ignatius's conversion experiences at the Benedictine monastery of Montserrat, where he undertook a vigil before the famous Black Madonna statue in the basilica. The full-bodied statue is of a dark-skinned Mary and Jesus. Mary sits straight and tall, with Jesus as a little boy sitting in her lap. They are wearing heavy gold crowns and gold robes and sit regally on a massive throne, looking straight at the viewer. Both the tour guides and our research revealed several possible explanations for the darkness of the skin other than that this was the artist's intention. But as far as we have been able to determine, there is no consensus as to whether the skin color seen today is the original. The colors of their apparel are all golds, browns, and black. At another location in the same basilica was a ceramic tile relief of the Black Madonna that bears little resemblance to the statue in terms of colors. This representation shows Mary and Jesus wearing crowns and about the same age as they appear in the statue, depicted in a similarly straightforward and regal pose. In this tile representation,

15. Brian R. Price, ed., *Ramon Lull's Book of Knighthood and Chivalry*, trans. William Caxton (Union City, Calif.: Chivalry Bookshelf, 2004), 25.

16. Price, 35.

17. Geoffroi de Charny, *A Knight's Own Book of Chivalry*, trans. Elspeth Kennedy (Philadelphia: University of Pennsylvania Press, 2005), 53.

18. Though Ignatius read romances rather than treatises on chivalry, the latter genre gives a better overview of the requirements and the culture of chivalry. In addition, the treatises on chivalry were influenced both by the romances and by ecclesiastical opinion. See Keen, *Chivalry*, 6.

however, both Mary and Jesus are portrayed in incredibly full and colorful attire. The Black Madonna statue that Ignatius honored as well as the ceramic tile representation in the same basilica emphasized the authority and power radiating from a queen mother through colors and her attire, facial expressions, and pose.

In spite of the fact that Ignatius's legs were not fully recovered from his battle wounds when he was in Montserrat, he was determined to perform a traditional chivalrous act toward the Black Madonna statue of Mary. As a noble in the age of chivalry, he was conscious of his obligation to maintain religious devotion and to honor women with all his might. Ignatius maintained his vigil of arms for Mary, standing for the entire night despite his war wounds. He then made the commitment to become a man of peace, laying his sword and dagger down in surrender before the Black Madonna.[19]

Continuing on his way to Jerusalem from Montserrat, Ignatius next journeyed to Manresa, where he wrote the *Spiritual Exercises* during lengthy meditations in a cave. The *Spiritual Exercises* became the foundation piece of the Society of Jesus. The cave of Ignatius's meditations was later enclosed by a marble wall and is now a small chapel replete with a wide variety of grand works of art. Although several pieces of art, including the one within the altar of the Manresa cave itself, show Ignatius looking up at Mary while he writes the *Spiritual Exercises* in the cave, to date we have not found supporting textual documentation of that vision of Mary.

Mary is, however, frequently cast as intercessor in the *Spiritual Exercises*. For instance, the Third Exercise suggests a series of colloquies, the first addressed to "Our Lady." The colloquy asks for her to intercede with Jesus Christ:

> This is to be made to Our Lady, so that she will obtain for me grace from her Son and Lord for three things, (i) that I may feel an interior knowledge of my sins and an abhorrence for them, (ii) that I may feel a sense of the disorder in my actions, so that abhorring it I may amend

19. Munitiz and Endean, *Saint Ignatius of Loyola*, 20. See also O'Malley, *The First Jesuits*, 24–25.

> my life and put order into it, (iii) I ask for knowledge of the world so that out of abhorrence for it I may put away from myself worldly and aimless things. Then a Hail Mary.[20]

Similarly, in the meditation on the Two Standards, Ignatius recommends another colloquy that also asks for Mary to intercede with Jesus so that the reader may obtain physical and spiritual poverty, receive insults and reproaches, and have the ability to accept these without sin.[21] Mary is mentioned as well in the "First Day: First Contemplation on the Incarnation," where Ignatius exhorts his reader to reflect upon Gabriel's appearance to Mary in the Annunciation story.[22]

The Loyola Castle diorama text closes by stressing again the role of Mary in Ignatius's life. Reflecting on what it means to be a Jesuit, the narrative suggests that Jesuits should emulate Ignatius, who prayed to Mary without ceasing to place him at the side of Jesus, her son.

Investigating this devotion in the life of Ignatius, we discovered numerous instances of Ignatius entreating Mary to intercede with God or Jesus to enhance his relationship with the Deity. Particularly notable in this regard is *The Spiritual Diary*, in which Ignatius asks Mary to intercede on his behalf with God. Throughout *The Spiritual Diary* Ignatius perceives Mary as being very receptive to him. In his meditations, he sees her as highly willing and ready to intercede with God.[23] So central was Mary in this role of intercessor in the *Diary* that Ignatius recalls his meditation during the Mass of Our Lady in the Temple, saying, "I could not but feel or see her, as though she were part, or rather portal, of the great grace that I could feel in my spirit."[24]

In some of Ignatius's letters, his devotion to Mary is evident when he indicates his intention to pray to the Mother on behalf of the addressee.[25] On a number of occasions in his *Autobiography*, Ignatius speaks of Marian visions or of his devotion to and communication with the Madonna. In the epilogue to the *Autobiography*, Gonçalves da

---

20. Munitiz and Endean, *Saint Ignatius of Loyola*, 297–98.
21. Munitiz and Endean, *Saint Ignatius of Loyola*, 311–12.
22. Munitiz and Endean, *Saint Ignatius of Loyola*, 305–6.
23. Munitiz and Endean, *Saint Ignatius of Loyola*, 74, 77, 78, 81.
24. Munitiz and Endean, *Saint Ignatius of Loyola*, 78.
25. For example, see Young, *Letters*, 11.

Cámara relates how Ignatius envisioned Mary or received confirmation from her throughout the forty days during which he meditated upon the Constitutions.[26]

Jesuit Women Who Wished to Follow Ignatius

The pilgrimage, the background readings for the pilgrimage, and the text accompanying the diorama at Loyola Castle, as well as the diorama itself, opened up to us an important aspect of Ignatius's spiritual life and sparked our interest in researching the Marian connection. Our research indicates that Mary was a very influential figure throughout Ignatius's spiritual journey. Our discoveries about this, along with the varied representations of Mary that we encountered, fueled an interest not just in Mary but in the role of women in general in the life of Ignatius and the early Jesuits. During the pilgrimage, we heard stories about Ignatius and women—from tour guides and other pilgrims. From the confluence of all this, we began to focus on some areas of special interest to us beyond Ignatius's devotion to Mary, including the secret ordination of one woman, Princess Juana of Austria, into the Society of Jesus very early in its history.[27] In addition, we discovered information about an early Jesuit-affiliated order under Ignatius himself composed of a handful of women who were engaged in ministries to prostitutes. Unfortunately, as a result of some difficulties arising from interactions with the women who wanted to join the Jesuits, Ignatius approached the pope, who granted a decree in 1547 "freeing" the Jesuits from the spiritual direction of women; that decree has been in effect for almost five hundred years.[28]

---

26. Munitiz and Endean, *Saint Ignatius of Loyola,* 64.
27. For more information about this ordination and the circumstances surrounding it, see John W. Padberg, "Secret, Perilous Project," *Company* 17 (1999): 28–29, and Joan Roccasalvo, "Ignatian Women Past and Future," *Review for Religious* 62 (2003): 38–62.
28. Rahner, *Saint Ignatius Loyola*, 290.

Ignatius's devotion to Mary and her extraordinary influence upon his life were unknown to us—two Jesuit university faculty members and Protestant feminist researchers, one of us a biblical scholar, the other a clinician and social worker—prior to the pilgrimage. To the biblical scholar, this was a source of great "consolation," to use Ignatian terminology. To the clinician and social worker, the consistently empowering portrayals of Mary were of greater interest. As two feminist professors teaching at a Jesuit institution for nearly ten years, we pondered how it is that this aspect of Ignatius's spiritual development seems to have received much less attention than other aspects of the founding of his order, such as his relationships with other early Jesuits. The secret agency of Mary as a hidden catalyst in the formation of the Society of Jesus through her influence on Ignatius was an exciting as well as puzzling discovery.

While it was personally gratifying to make the discoveries recounted here, as professors, we believe that the implications of these discoveries for Ignatian education serve as an example of how uncovering lesser-known "herstory" through the experiential learning of a pilgrimage sparked new insights into both "history" and "herstory." As feminists and educators have discovered through the decades, experiential learning can be a crucial means of delivering a holistic education in which the learner gains understanding in both cognitive and affective ways. Although the focus here is on the diverse, complex images of Mary in Spain and Rome and especially on the influence of Mary in the devotional life of St. Ignatius of Loyola, there are other important aspects of the influence of women on the early Jesuits in general.[29] The implications of this discovery for us are developing in unexpected ways that contribute to new understandings of how Jesuits and feminists can work together toward greater inclusion of women at every level, including in relating the "history" of the Society of Jesus.

29. Research uncovering the influence of women on the early Jesuits continues. For example, see Lisa Fullam, "Juana, SJ: The Past (and Future?) Status of Women in the Society of Jesus," *Studies in the Spirituality of Jesuits*, November 1999.

Missing "Herstory" and Decree 14

Both our reflections and research emphasize the need for greater recognition of the historical role of women in the formation of the Society of Jesus. Some of our findings thus far regarding evidence of "herstory" in documented "history" follow. In his popular 1993 volume, *The First Jesuits*, O'Malley briefly mentions the vigil of Ignatius in front of the Black Madonna but includes nothing about the role of Mary in the conversion of Ignatius prior to that event. There is some description of Princess Juana of Austria as well as mention of the unsuccessful two-year venture when Ignatius "accepted a few 'devout women' to live in obedience to him."[30] In his more recent work published in 2007, *The Jesuits II: Cultures, Sciences, and the Arts, 1540–1773,* O'Malley includes a chapter by Elizabeth Rhodes titled "Join the Jesuits, See the World: Early Modern Women in Spain and the Society of Jesus." In the 1998 second edition of *Jesuit Saints and Martyrs: Short Biographies of the Saints, Blessed, Venerables, and Servants of God of the Society of Jesus*, Joseph N. Tylenda, SJ, does not mention Princess Juana of Austria or the other women who tried to become Jesuits. He does, however, briefly discuss the influence of Mary on both Ignatius and the Society in four sections of the book and states: "At all important junctures in the life of St. Ignatius, our Lady had an important role to play."[31]

In the hundred-plus-page glossy coffee table book *"Ours": Jesuit Portraits*, published in 2006, M. C. Durkin provides a fascinating illustrated review of the Jesuits who have contributed to Jesuit history through the centuries.[32] Chapter 1 highlights the beginning of the Society, with a focus on Ignatius of Loyola, Peter Faber, and Francis Xavier. It includes a photo of the famous fresco of Mary and Jesus called *Madonna della Strada (Our Lady of the Way)*, which was moved from the original church into the Jesuits' Church of the Gesù. Princess Juana of Austria is not included in the list of thirty-two significant Jesuits throughout the centuries. Even more recently than Durkin's volume,

30. O'Malley, *The First Jesuits*, 75.
31. Joseph N. Tylenda, *Jesuit Saints and Martyrs: Short Biographies of the Saints, Blessed, Venerables, and Servants of God of the Society of Jesus* (Chicago: Loyola Press, 1998), 110.
32. M. C. Durkin, *"Ours": Jesuit Portraits* (Strasbourg: Editions du Signe, 2006).

Amalee Meehan picks up the theme in her 2008 article "Partners in Ministry: The Role of Women in Jesuit Education." She examines the missing "herstory" in light of the cultural context of the times. Meehan concludes: "Jesuits, in their 'way of proceeding,' need to recognize that women are a rich and still largely untapped resource. Recalling the origins of the Society of Jesus, when Ignatius invited women to enter into the spirituality of the Exercises, will help us conserve the past while creating the future."[33]

Throughout the pilgrimage, the early stories we heard about women and the Society of Jesus offered historical lessons that can aid in the quest for greater solidarity among the Society, Jesuit institutions, and the many women like us who contribute to the Jesuit mission on a daily basis. We offer our reflection and research to stress the value of continuing to incorporate such experiential learning in the future in Jesuit institutional contexts, especially toward the end of making these contexts more inclusive. After nearly five hundred years of silence, the groundbreaking nature of Decree 14, "Jesuits and the Situation of Women in the Church and Civil Society," must be emphasized. Emanating from the 34th General Congregation of the Society of Jesus in 1995, this amazing call for "solidarity" with women officially recognizes Jesuit complicity with the Church and society in gender discrimination against women. Our research indicates, however, that when individual Jesuits take that brave step to truly align with women in solidarity, trouble tends to brew for them and the women themselves or the history of their roles is again omitted.

More specifically, Decree 14 calls for Jesuits "to listen carefully and courageously to the experience of women."[34] As Susan A. Ross points out, Decree 14 has indicated that solidarity with women is integral to the Jesuit mission. If that is so, states Ross, "Making such solidarity a reality will require a profound conversion, a conversion in which knowledge of women's lives and experiences is central."[35] In the context of Jesuit institutions, she also stresses how crucial

33. Meehan, "Partners in Ministry," 24.

34. Mary Garvin, "Dusting off a Document," *Conversations* 29 (Spring 2006): 38.

35. Susan A. Ross, "The Jesuits and Women: Reflections on the 34th General Congregation's Statement on Women in Church and Civil Society," *Conversations* 16 (Fall 1999): 21–22.

it is for Jesuits and others to establish and nurture ongoing relationships with women: "Real listening is not possible apart from trusting relationships."[36] This is where experiential learning can become crucial to Jesuit education in the future by providing occasions and opportunities to "listen carefully and courageously to the experience of women" and establish healthy and lasting relationships with women.

This pilgrimage stands as a case in point. The pilgrimage introduced us not only to the significance of Mary in the life of Ignatius but also to other female figures who were influential among the early Jesuits and who may have had an impact on the very shape of the Society. If university administrations, faculty, staff, and students are given similar experiential learning opportunities to explore the influence of Mary and other women on the early Jesuits, they will be better able to analyze those historical interactions. Of course, it is in the reflection aspect of experiential learning where the greatest integration can take place. Participants are then more likely to draw out implications for today's relationships between Jesuits and women if they are thoroughly informed about the past. The influence of Mary on the early Jesuits was significant to their experience and thus it is significant for those involved in Jesuit education today.

Conclusion

In closing, we leave you with two final artistic images from our pilgrimage. For us, these images epitomize the role of Mary in the founding of the Society of Jesus. The first image, of which we do not have a photograph, is a grand painting within the Gesù in Rome, and one of the most powerful portrayals of Mary with several of the early Jesuits. The title of the painting is *Regina Societas Gesù*, or, *The Queen of the Society of Jesus*. With Mary as the central figure, fondly gazing down upon many of the early Jesuits along with some of the followers of each, it recalls to us Ignatius's frequent references in *The Spiritual*

36. Ross, 24.

Diary to Mary at being receptive to him and, by inference, to his many followers as well. In our view, it resonates with the description of the diorama regarding what it means to be a Jesuit, suggesting that Jesuits should emulate Ignatius in his unceasing prayers to and relationship with Mary.

And finally, in the Loyola family castle was one of the most powerful Ignatius-Mary images of all: a life-sized statue of Ignatius cradling a full-bodied Mary attired in flowing blue and white. Although reducing Mary to the size of a doll may seem to minimize the significance of her role, the look of adoration on the face of Ignatius overrides that possibility, displaying his total absorption in the sense of "I will carry you with me everywhere." This is what he did.

Throughout the pilgrimage to Spain and Rome, experientially engaging with such diverse but lesser-known representations of Mary as agent and uncovering her significant role as a hidden catalyst to Ignatius's spiritual journey encouraged us to initiate research regarding the role of "herstory" in Jesuit "history." As well, the pilgrimage was spiritually empowering to us as women, as feminists, and as professors at a Jesuit institution of higher education. These unexpected outcomes move us to include a theological comment about the implications of experiential learning of this kind for Jesuit education. As Roger Haight, SJ, argues, the turn to the human subject and experience by the highly influential theologian Karl Rahner marked a "monumental achievement" in Catholic theology.[37] Haight derives a lesson from this: "The house of Christian meaning lies in the experience of the Christian subject."[38] Feminist theologians argue that Christian theology will not be balanced until the experiences taken into consideration are themselves gender balanced.

Experiential learning, such as the pilgrimage we were privileged to embrace, can help create that balance in individual theological reflection as well as institutional practice. Women will be more likely to occupy a position of equality with men when women's "herstory" is seen as worthy of treatment and as integral to the

37. Roger Haight, "Lessons from an Extraordinary Era: Catholic Theology since Vatican II," *America*, March 17, 2008, 11–16.
38. Haight, 11–16.

narrative as men's "history." In addition to encouraging engagement in similar avenues of experiential learning, these reflections are shared in the hopes of stirring others to make similar discoveries, to dust off Decree 14, and to continue taking brave steps toward the kind of solidarity envisioned therein. We suggest that substantial and consistent support from Jesuit leaders and educational institutions is needed to restore the centrality of the role of Mary to its original prominence within the Society's historical documents. This in turn would begin to move the Society toward greater solidarity with women, in keeping with the stated intent of Decree 14. Along with the Jesuit emphasis on the whole person, the history of the Jesuits also needs to be made whole.

What the Conversion of St. Ignatius Can Teach Us 500 Years Later

Jean Luc Enyegue, SJ

In 1597, on the same day that she went completely blind, a woman from Mallorca named Noguere was touched by the relics of Saint Ignatius. She reported that a scent of roses filled her with a sweet consolation. The acute pain in her eyes suddenly subsided. She began to see things faintly, and the next day she saw perfectly. This healing was one of the supporting miracles for the canonization of St. Ignatius Loyola.

This year, beginning on May 20 and continuing until July 31, 2022, the Society of Jesus worldwide, and the entire Ignatian family, celebrate St. Ignatius's spiritual journey from the 500th anniversary of his conversion in 1521 to his canonization in 1622. In the context of this Ignatian Year, Noguere's story helps explain conversion as a process of recovering from blindness to better sight.

On May 20, 1521, in a battle at the Spanish town of Pamplona, a cannonball broke one leg of Iñigo López de Loyola and wounded the other. With the incident, Iñigo had reached the bottom of what had been a rather shattered existence marred by loss and insatiable ambition. The man wounded in Pamplona was a twenty-six-year-old orphan who lost his parents at an early age. One of his brothers died in war. Another ventured to the Americas and never returned home. By the time of the battle of Pamplona, his new master and stepfather,

Originally published in *America* magazine in May 2021.

Juan Velásquez de Cuéllar, the chief treasurer of the Crown, who had introduced Iñigo to court decorum and diplomacy, had lost his privileged position.

Ignatius's conversion took place during his long recovery from his injuries, as he read about the lives of the saints, like Francis and Dominic. Ignatius's dreams transferred from heroic feats on the battlefield to heroically serving Christ. The bull of canonization on March 12, 1622, reported that Ignatius was called from worldly honors and earthly military service to a holy life that led to the founding of the Jesuit order and, ultimately, the consolation of souls worldwide.

While the general theme of this jubilee year is conversion, the underlying invitation related to this conversion is to "see, everything has become new!" (2 Corinthians 5:17). To see "perfectly," like Noguere, or to see everything new, like St. Paul, is to first acknowledge some form of blindness. Then, when touched by Ignatius's relics—which is to say, once inspired by his experience and spiritual tradition—we will be able to let God console us, and so embrace our present and future with renewed hope and faith.

Our world faces new challenges. COVID-19 alone has shattered our normal ways of life. We need faith to be able to see anew. The 34th General Congregation of the Society of Jesus in 1995 declared that "without faith, without the eye of love, the human world seems too evil for God to be good, for a good God to exist. But faith recognizes that God is acting, through Christ's love and the power of the Holy Spirit, to destroy the structures of sin which afflict the bodies and hearts of his children."[1]

The congregation was significant in part because it took place at a moment of self-examination for the Society. It was a moment in which, as Jesuits, as the congregation wrote, "we faced our limitations and weaknesses, our lights and shadows, our sinfulness." Yet amid the brokenness of the world, the Jesuits "also found much that was wise and good." They were able to see everything new and recommitted themselves to "follow this Christ, the Crucified and Risen Lord, in pilgrimage and labor."[2]

1. General Congregation 34, Decree 2, 11.
2. General Congregation 34, Decree 1, 3.

The conversion of Ignatius was not completed instantly, following his fall in Pamplona. This incident, however, set a new course for his life. It turned his life upside down and forced him into self-examination. Out of this spiritual awakening, Ignatius had a burning desire for holiness and a zeal to do great things for God, which ultimately led him to a lengthy process of self-surrender.

The appeal of this conversion today is that, when confronted with a hopeless situation, Ignatius created greater intimacy with God. As he renewed his relationship with God, he was able to refocus his unsettled existence. Ignatius put God at the center of his life. He could look at the world not with fear but with hope and the desire to set it on fire with the love of Christ.

This Ignatian Year is not limited to Ignatius's conversion but culminates with his canonization. His cause was bolstered by miracles attributed to his intercession, like Noguere's recovery of sight through the use of relics. Though the language of relics and miracles itself might seem at odds with the extreme rationalism of our world, all of us are tasked to make these "relics" and miracles meaningful for our own time. As heirs of the Ignatian tradition, we are the guardians of Ignatius's spiritual "relics." We remain indebted to the rich Ignatian tradition, which, though rooted in medieval Christianity, boldly embraced the modern world. The opportunities offered by the world of Ignatius's time shaped the Society of Jesus, which in turn helped transform the Church and the way it reached out to the world.

Miracles are still a part of our spiritual practice. When faced with a tragedy, an incurable disease, the loss of a job, a beloved friend or sibling, we may pray to God in the secrecy of our hearts to intervene. The true miracle might not be the immediate realization of our wishes or prayers for various needs. It is, instead, the consolation that grows out of the deepening of faith in God. The miracle is to believe that for those, like Ignatius, who believe in God and trust in God's care and providence, there is no accident, no tragedy or failure that they cannot overcome. The bottom that Ignatius hit in 1521 became a stepping stone for greater adventures, self-realization, and success. The Church considered Ignatius's journey from 1521 to 1622 exemplary for others.

In Africa and its growing Church, there are ample reasons for hope, but also for despair. Celebrating a jubilee reinforces our hope that things can change for the better. The sick can be healed. Peace can be restored. The joy of the gospel can blossom. The kings of Spain, France, and Bavaria were able to put aside their bloody rivalries to push for the canonization of St. Ignatius. Like them, all Christians can help build a peaceful global community and create new networks of solidarity and friendship for the greater glory of God and the service of the poorest among us. To see all things new is to renew our commitment to Ignatius's original vision of spiritual depth, love, and service of the Church and society.

Universal Apostolic Preferences of the Society of Jesus, 2019–2029

Arturo Sosa, SJ

Dear Friends in the Lord:

The Universal Apostolic Preferences, which I promulgate with this letter, are the fruit of an election. A choice has been made among several possibilities, all of them good. Our desire has been to find the best way to collaborate in the Lord's mission, the best way to serve the Church at this time, the best contribution we can make with what we are and have, seeking to do what is for the greater divine service and the more universal good.

At the end of the sixteen months that the process lasted at the various levels of the Society, I presented to the Holy Father four universal apostolic preferences:

1. To show the way to God through the Spiritual Exercises and discernment;
2. To walk with the poor, the outcasts of the world, those whose dignity has been violated, in a mission of reconciliation and justice;
3. To accompany young people in the creation of a hope-filled future;
4. To collaborate in the care of our Common Home.

In his confirmation letter of 6 February 2019, Pope Francis observed that "the process that the Society followed to arrive at universal apostolic preferences was (...) a real discernment." He affirmed that the proposed preferences "are in agreement with the current priorities of the Church as expressed through the ordinary Magisterium of the pope, the synods, and the episcopal conferences, especially since *Evangelii gaudium*."

The Holy Father insisted that "the first preference is crucial because it presupposes as a basic condition the Jesuit's relationship with the Lord in a personal and communal life of prayer and discernment." And he added: "Without this prayerful attitude the other preferences will not bear fruit."

I. Universal Apostolic Preferences 2019–2029

Thanks to the Universal Apostolic Preferences formulated by Peter-Hans Kolvenbach, which have guided us for more than fifteen years, several processes have been initiated which must be continued. These include a qualified presence in Africa and China, the responsibility of the whole Society for the interprovincial works in Rome entrusted to us by the popes, the consistency of our intellectual apostolate, and our service to refugees and migrants. During the next ten years, the following preferences will guide us in incarnating the mission of reconciliation and justice in all the apostolic services to which we, along with others, have been sent.

1. To Show the Way to God through the Spiritual Exercises and Discernment

We sense that secular society today profoundly challenges the Church in its task of proclaiming the Gospel. As believers we feel an urgent need to overcome both new secularisms and the nostalgia for cultural expressions of the past. We resolve to collaborate with the Church in experiencing secular society as a sign of the times that affords us the opportunity to renew our presence in the heart of human history. A mature secularized society opens up spaces for the complex dimensions of human freedom, especially religious freedom. In a mature secular society, the conditions exist for the emergence of circumstances conducive to personal religious processes, independent of social or ethnic pressure, that allow people to ask profound questions and to choose freely to follow Jesus, to belong to an ecclesial community, and to adopt a Christian lifestyle in social, economic, cultural, and political spheres.

The Spiritual Exercises of Saint Ignatius of Loyola are a privileged instrument for making the life and action of the Lord Jesus present in diverse social contexts of today's world. Therefore, we resolve to gain a deeper experience of the Spiritual Exercises so that they lead us to a personal and communal encounter with Christ that transforms us.[1]

At the same time, we resolve to offer the Spiritual Exercises in as many ways as possible, providing many people, especially the young, the opportunity to make use of them to begin or to advance in following Christ. Experiencing the Spiritual Exercises and the spirituality derived from them is our preferred way of showing the pathway to God through commitment to the redemptive mission of Jesus Christ in history.

We also resolve to promote discernment as a regular habit for those who choose to follow Christ. The Society of Jesus is committed to practicing and spreading spiritual discernment, both personal and communal, as the ordinary way of making decisions guided by the Holy Spirit in our lives, our apostolic works, and our ecclesial communities. This is a choice to seek and find the will of God, always, letting ourselves be guided by the Holy Spirit. Through our discernment in common with the apostolic preferences, we have experienced a renewal in our way of proceeding. Therefore, we resolve to make regular use of spiritual conversation and discernment in our implementation of the preferences at all levels of the life-mission of the Society.[2]

We want to share with others the most fundamental discovery of our lives, namely, that discernment and the Spiritual Exercises of Saint Ignatius show the way to God. We need to follow the call to

1. Cf. GC 36, d. 1,18.
2. Cf. Pope Francis, *Gaudete et Exsultate*, 167 and 169.

deepen our knowledge and experience of Ignatian spirituality, and we want to do so out of a living faith that is incarnate and consistent, a faith nourished by familiarity with God that is the fruit of a life of prayer, a faith that enters into dialogue with other religions and with all cultures. Our faith is manifested in works of justice and reconciliation because it comes from the crucified and risen One who leads us to the crucified of this world so that we might be bearers of hope in the new life that the Lord gives us. Ours is a faith lived in community that becomes a testimony to hope.

2. To Walk with the Poor, the Outcasts of the World, Those Whose Dignity Has Been Violated, in a Mission of Reconciliation and Justice

Sent as companions in a mission of reconciliation and justice, we resolve to walk with individuals and communities that are vulnerable, excluded, marginalized, and humanly impoverished. We commit ourselves to walk with the victims of abuse of power, abuse of conscience, and sexual abuse; with the outcasts of this world; with all those whom the biblical tradition knows as the poor of the earth, to whose cry the Lord responds with his liberating incarnation.

The necessary condition for becoming companions "on the way" in the style of Jesus is, out of closeness with the poor, "to announce his Gospel of hope to the many poor who inhabit our world today."[3] To come closer to the poor means going out to the human peripheries and to the margins of society, adopting a style of life and work appropriate to the situation so that our accompaniment will be credible. To achieve this goal, we resolve, at all levels of the Society, to discern who are the most vulnerable and excluded persons in our midst and to find ways to walk closely beside them.[4]

The path we seek to follow with the poor is one that promotes social justice and the change of economic, political, and social structures that generate injustice; this path is a necessary dimension of the reconciliation of individuals, peoples, and their cultures with one

3. GC 35, d. 2,13.
4. Cf. GC 36, d. 1,15.

another, with nature, and with God. Care for indigenous peoples, their cultures, and their basic rights occupies a special place in our commitment to reconciliation and justice in all their dimensions.

We confirm our commitment to care for migrants, displaced persons, refugees, and victims of wars and human trafficking. We also resolve to defend the culture and the dignified existence of indigenous peoples. Consequently, we will continue to help create conditions of hospitality, to accompany all these people in their process of integration into society, and to promote the defense of their rights.

We want to contribute to strengthening political democracy by imparting good civic formation, especially among those at the base of the social pyramid. By promoting social organizations committed to seeking the Common Good, we want to help counteract the pernicious consequences of the diverse forms of neo-liberalism, fundamentalism, and populism.

We commit ourselves to help eliminate abuses inside and outside the Church, seeking to ensure that victims are heard and properly helped, that justice is done, and that harm is healed. This commitment includes the adoption of clear policies for the prevention of abuse, the ongoing formation of those who are committed to mission, and serious efforts to identify the social origins of abuse. In this way, we effectively promote a culture that safeguards all vulnerable persons, especially minors.

We join many other people and institutions in promoting a culture of hospitality[5] and of protecting the rights of children and others made vulnerable by changing social structures.[6]

Accompanying the impoverished requires us to improve our studies, our analysis, and our reflection in order to understand in depth the economic, political, and social processes that generate such great injustice; we must also contribute to the elaboration of alternative models. We commit ourselves to promoting a process of globalization that recognizes multiplicity of cultures as a human treasure, protects cultural diversity, and promotes intercultural exchange.

---

5. Cf. GC 36, d. 1,16.
6. Cf. GC 36, Matters entrusted to Father General.

We accompany the poor, inspired by our faith in God the Father of mercy who invites us to embrace reconciliation as the foundation of a new humanity.

3. To Accompany the Young in the Creation of a Hope-filled Future
The 2018 Synod recognized young people and their situation as a crucial place from which the Church seeks to perceive and discern the movement of the Holy Spirit through this moment of human history. The poor and the young are a complementary and interwoven *locus theologicus*. Young people, most of whom are poor, face enormous challenges in our world today, including reduced job opportunities, economic instability, increased political violence, multiple forms of discrimination, progressive degradation of the environment, and other ills, all of which make it difficult for them to find meaning in their lives and to draw closer to God. Youth is the stage of human life when individuals make the fundamental decisions by which they insert themselves into society, seek to give meaning to their existence, and realize their dreams. By accompanying the young in this process, teaching them discernment and sharing with them the Good News of Jesus Christ, we can show them the way to God that passes through solidarity with human beings and the construction of a more just world.

Young people continue opening up to the future with the hope of building a life of dignity in a reconciled world that is in harmony with the environment. It is the young who, from their perspective, can help us to understand better the epochal change that we are living and its hope-filled newness. Today, young people are the principal protagonists of an anthropological transformation that is coming to be through the digital culture of our time, opening humanity to a new historical epoch. We are living through a period of change from which will emerge a new humanity and a new way of structuring human life in its personal and social dimensions. Young people are the bearers of this new form of human life that can find, in the experience of encounter with the Lord Jesus, light for the path toward justice, reconciliation, and peace.

The apostolic works of the Society of Jesus can make an important contribution to creating and maintaining spaces that are open to young people in society and the Church. Our works seek to be spaces open to youthful creativity, spaces that both foster an encounter with the God of life revealed by Jesus and deepen the Christian faith of the young. Such spaces should help young people discern the path by which they can achieve happiness by contributing to the well-being of all humankind.

Young people experience the tension between the drive toward cultural homogeneity and the emergence of an intercultural human society that respects and is enriched by diversity. The logic of the market economy leads to homogeneity, but young people aspire instead to diversity that corresponds to the exercise of true freedom and opens up creative spaces that contribute to the emergence of a humane, intercultural society. With that as a base, they can commit themselves to building a culture of safeguarding that guarantees a healthy environment for children and young people, creating conditions that allow all to develop their full potential as human beings.

To accompany young people demands of us authenticity of life, spiritual depth, and openness to sharing the life-mission that gives meaning to who we are and what we do. Having these, we can learn, along with the young, to find God in all things, and through our ministries and apostolates we can help them live this stage of their lives more profoundly. Accompanying young people puts us on the path of personal, communitarian, and institutional conversion.

4. To Collaborate in the Care of Our Common Home

In the encyclical *Laudato Si'*, Pope Francis reminds us that all human beings share responsibility for care of creation, considered to be many peoples' "mother earth." "This sister now cries out to us because of the harm we have inflicted on her by our irresponsible use and abuse of the goods with which God has endowed her. . . . This is why the earth herself, burdened and laid waste, is among the most abandoned and maltreated of our poor; she 'groans in travail' (Romans 8:22)."[7]

---

7. *Laudato Si'*, 2.

The damage done to the earth is also damage done to the most vulnerable, such as indigenous peoples, peasants forced to emigrate, and the inhabitants of urban peripheries. The environmental destruction being caused by the dominant economic system is inflicting intergenerational damage: not only does it affect those now living on earth, particularly the very young, but it also conditions and jeopardizes the life of future generations.

We resolve, considering who we are and the means that we have, to collaborate with others in the construction of alternative models of life that are based on respect for creation and on a sustainable development capable of producing goods that, when justly distributed, ensure a decent life for all human beings on our planet. The preservation over time of the conditions of life on our planet is a human responsibility of immense ethical and spiritual importance. Our collaboration should include both participating in efforts to analyze problems in depth and promoting reflection and discernment that will guide us in making decisions that help to heal the wounds already inflicted on the delicate ecological balance. We are especially concerned about areas that are so crucial for maintaining the natural equilibrium that makes life possible, such as the Amazon region; the river basins of the Congo, India, and Indonesia; and the great extensions of open sea. Caring for nature in this way is a form of genuinely worshipping the creative work of God. Bold decisions are required to avoid further damage and to bring about lifestyle changes that are necessary so that the goods of creation are used for the benefit of all. We want to be actively present in this process.

Laudato Si' reminds us that "disinterested concern for others, and the rejection of every form of self-centeredness and self-absorption, are essential if we truly wish to care for our brothers and sisters and for the natural environment. These attitudes also attune us to the moral imperative of assessing the impact of our every action and personal decision on the world around us."[8] It is logical to conclude that what Christians "need is an 'ecological conversion,' whereby the

8. *Laudato Si'*, 208.

effects of their encounter with Jesus Christ become evident in their relationship with the world around them. Living our vocation to be protectors of God's handiwork is essential to a life of virtue."[9]

It is necessary, therefore, to step out of oneself and lovingly care for everything that is good for others. A model of human life reconciled with creation will not be possible if we are not able to break out of individualism and inaction.

Conversion for us, Jesuits and our companions in mission, begins by changing the habits of life promoted by an economic and cultural system based on the consumption of an irrational production of goods. The words of Pope Francis encourage us in this direction: "There is a nobility in the duty to care for creation through little daily actions, and it is wonderful how education can bring about real changes in lifestyle."[10]

II. Guided by the Spirit

The process we have gone through has its source in the winds of ecclesial renewal inspired by the Spirit in the Second Vatican Ecumenical Council. That same Spirit, present and active today in the Church, has been at work also in General Congregations 31 to 36, leading the Society through a demanding process of spiritual and apostolic renewal. Inspired by the image of our first companions in Venice (1537), as they pondered where the Spirit was leading them (Cf. *Autobiography*, 93–95), the 36th General Congregation sent us forth as companions on a mission of reconciliation and justice.[11]

Inspired by the words of Pope Francis, GC 36 felt the need to return with greater confidence to our origins and to the practice of discernment in common. In sharing our experience during these months, we have come to realize the grace involved in the very process of discernment in common, lived at all levels of the body of

9. *Laudato Si'*, 217.

10. *Laudato Si'*, 211.

11. "This reconciliation is always a work of justice. . . . The Cross of Christ and our sharing in it are also at the center of God's work of reconciliation. . ." GC 36, d. 1, 21.

the Society. For many, it has meant a rediscovery of some dimensions of Ignatian spirituality: it has helped us to renew the practice of spiritual conversation in order to seek together the way of Jesus; and it has been an exercise of discernment in common as a way of finding God's will in our life-mission. We have experienced the grace of feeling ourselves to be one united body and of growing in indifference and availability so as to become a discerning community with open horizons.[12] With these apostolic preferences we commit to continue forward on the path that we have begun, taking up this fundamental dimension of our life and mission.

We have lived through a process that has produced, step by step, a consensus that we believe is guided by the Holy Spirit. We began with many doubts and concerns, not knowing the path well and struggling to overcome skepticism. Like the first companions, we, too, come from diverse origins and cultures, and we have different ways of seeing and understanding things.

But we have found a unity of desire, a common passion to serve Jesus as he carries his Cross to all the ends of the earth. Slowly we learned to believe and to trust. We could say that the Lord took us by the hand, like a schoolteacher, just as he led Ignatius in Manresa (Cf. *Autobiography*, 27). The contributions from the communities, apostolic works, regions, provinces, and from Jesuits in formation provided a vital starting point.

The contributions of the six Conferences of Major Superiors were in surprising agreement. Like the first disciples, we rowed out into the deep and found ourselves in the midst of the storm, but we were amazed to experience how the Lord came to us. It is he, the incarnate, crucified, and risen Lord, who shows us his wounds and invites us to join with him in the quest for justice. He impels us toward new frontiers, accompanying those whom society has discarded, announcing the Good News to one and all, so that they might be transformed by the love of our God. Our hardened hearts are also changing day by day, becoming filled with mercy and compassion.

12. Cf. GC 36, d. 1, 7–16.

This process has taught us that Universal Apostolic Preferences are a means for continuing to be guided by the Spirit. Moreover, the preferences are an instrument for deepening the style of life-mission indicated by GC 36 when it invites us to spiritual and apostolic renewal, incorporating discernment, collaboration with others, and networking into our daily lives.

We are deeply convinced that the preferences will help the apostolic body of the Society if they maintain a clear unity between life and mission, if we understand them as orientations that go beyond "doing something" and enable us to achieve our transformation as persons, as religious communities, and as apostolic works and institutions in which we collaborate with others. Consequently, while each preference points to some important aspect of our apostolate, it also invites us to renew our own lives so that our work will be credible and effective.

The preferences seek to embody concretely the mission received as the Lord's response to the cry of a wounded world; the cry of the most vulnerable, who have been displaced and marginalized; the empty rhetoric that divides and dismantles our cultures; the growing chasm between rich and poor; the cry of the young in search of hope and meaning; the cry of the earth and its peoples, who have been degraded to the point of having their very existence put at risk. The preferences seek to respond to a world in which entire generations have never heard about Jesus and his Gospel.

Our Church has been wounded by the sin of its members and all the suffering this has brought. Our Church is sailing in the midst of strong winds. In the Society we have become painfully and humbly aware of our own vulnerabilities and our sin. We feel shame and confusion when we stand before the Lord, asking him to forgive us, to heal us, and to show us his merciful love. Only as sinners forgiven and loved can we continue forward. We can bring his compassion to others only if we ourselves, individually and as a body, have experienced that compassion.

Indeed, it is our own experience of being loved and saved that gives our desire for mission its depth and energy. It is precisely in the challenges of our wounded world and our own wounds that we hear the gentle but insistent call of the Lord.

The Universal Apostolic Preferences seek to deepen these processes of personal, communal, and institutional conversion. They are orientations for improving both the apostolic work of the whole body of the Society and the ways in which we accomplish our ministries, in which the preferences are expressed. At the same time, they seek to help Jesuits and our companions in mission to make their apostolic lives a pathway to God. We want to invite all people to follow the path opened up by Jesus of Nazareth, a path on which we ourselves are walking, following in his footsteps, encouraged by his Spirit.

They are not our preferences. We have followed the Holy Spirit, who has guided and inspired us. We receive them confirmed by the pope, trusting, like Ignatius and the first companions, that he is the one who has the best vision of the needs of the world and of the Church. The Universal Apostolic Preferences will help us to overcome every form of self-centeredness and corporatism, so that we may become authentic collaborators in the Lord's mission, which we share with so many people inside and outside the Church. The preferences are an opportunity for us to feel that we are the least Society in collaboration with others.

III. The Necessary Personal, Communal, and Institutional Conversion

The Contemplation to Attain Love begins with a point that seems to be common sense but which must be continually kept in mind: "Love ought to manifest itself more by deeds than by words" (SE 230–237).[13] The process of discerning the Universal Apostolic Preferences filled the participants with a profound sense of gratitude for the abundant graces received. At the same time, we experienced a strong call to personal, communal, and institutional conversion.

Receiving the preferences means that we initiate their implementation immediately by changing any styles of life or work that hinder the renewal of the persons, communities, and works committed to

13. Cf. 1 Jn 3, 8.

mission. We are inspired by the response of the first apostles, who promptly abandoned their nets and their lives as fishermen in order to set out on the path of discipleship following Jesus.[14] After the promulgation of the preferences, all the apostolic units of the Society will be provided with resources to help in planning their effective implementation.[15] A necessary dimension of our conversion is taking responsibility for seeking and properly managing the economic and financial resources needed to support the apostolic initiatives inspired by the universal apostolic preferences.[16]

The call is to share the life and mission of Jesus Christ. At the heart of this call is the love of the one and triune God who is not paralyzed in the face of the world's situation but who sends Jesus to take on our humanity and give his life in order to open the gates to divine life and love for all human beings. In dying, Jesus expresses the supreme love that vanquishes death. To accept that call is to give one's life for love expressed in deeds of reconciliation and justice; it means being transformed into authentic followers of Jesus and active members of the Church and the Society that serves the mission in collaboration with so many other persons. Conversion empowers us to take part in the mission: conversion to faith in the Good News that the Reign of God is at hand, and conversion to a living faith that expresses itself in works that make possible the fulfillment of God's promise in human history.

Keeping vividly in mind the experience of our first companions in Venice, GC 36 invites us to return to our roots. We reaffirm "what they . . . found to be life-giving: sharing their lives together as friends in the Lord; living very close to the lives of the poor; and preaching the Gospel with joy."[17] Making our communities spaces for communal discernment where a life of prayer is encouraged, the Eucharist is shared and spiritual conversation is practiced which enables us to share the gift of discernment as a way of letting ourselves

14. Cf. Mark 1, 14–20.
15. For example, see https://jesuits.global/uap.
16. "General Congregation 36 affirms that, keeping in mind our commitment to poverty, various financial strategies, opportunities, and implications must be considered in apostolic planning and decision-making at all levels of Society governance. The treasurer and other skilled and knowledgeable persons should assist in these processes" (d. 2,18).
17. GC 36 d. 1, 4.

be guided by the Spirit in apostolic works and in all ministries. Living simply, close to the poor, awakens the creativity we need to do more with less, and it gives greater credibility to our apostolic work offered freely to others.[18]

At the same time, responding to the call of the Universal Apostolic Preferences necessitates that we strive more than ever for the intellectual depth that our foundational charism and tradition demand; such depth must always be accompanied by an attendant spiritual depth. The Society is committed to the intellectual apostolate because intellectual depth should characterize all forms of the apostolate of the Society of Jesus. We want to continue serving the Church through the intellectual apostolate, expressing our faith with intellectual consistency.

Consequently, all members of this apostolic body are called to continue their formation throughout their lives. Intellectual depth demands habits of thought, and so we must not neglect ongoing formation. If we fail in this regard, the Society's contribution to the mission of the Church will not respond to the demands of the Ignatian *magis*.

The apostolic renewal of the Society of Jesus that will flow from the implementation of the Universal Apostolic Preferences has as a condition the deepening of collaboration among Jesuits and our companions in mission and among the ministries and apostolic units, other bodies in the Church, and all the persons and institutions that contribute to the inseparable realities of reconciliation among human beings, with creation, and with God. "That mission is deepened and ministry is extended by collaboration among all with whom we work," states GC 36, confirming the orientations of GC 34 and GC 35.[19]

The experience we have had during the communal discernment of the preferences confirms the perception of GC 36: "Noting remarkable progress in collaboration across the Society, obstacles remain. . . . Inclusive discernment and ongoing planning and evaluation of our efforts to go beyond the obstacles is required in order

18. Cf. GC 36, d. 1, 11–16.
19. GC 36, d. 2, 6. Cf. GC35, d. 6, 30; GC 34, dd. 13 and 14.

to mainstream the participation of mission partners further in various levels of the Society's apostolic activities and governance."[20] Complete incorporation of the dimension of collaboration into our life-mission is an essential condition, one without which our desire to render greater service to the Lord's mission will run the risk of not being realized in our works and our way of life.

With these Universal Apostolic Preferences, we resolve to concentrate and concretize our vital apostolic energies during the next ten years, 2019–2029. We accept them as a mission of the Church through Pope Francis, who has approved them by confirming the communal discernment that was undertaken by the apostolic body. It corresponds to us, as a body obedient to the Holy Spirit, to plan with diligence the implementation of the preferences in every dimension of our life-mission. The preferences seek to unleash a process of apostolic revitalization and creativity that makes us better servants of reconciliation and justice.

Let us undertake this process, designing it and assessing it in accord with persons, times, and places in the light of the Church's orientations and the Spirit's guidance.

May Our Lady, the Mother of the Society of Jesus, obtain for us from her Son the grace of integrity of life so that, preaching what allows us to know the Lord and doing what we preach, we may be witnesses to the love of God poured out upon humanity, and impelled by the Holy Spirit, we may effectively collaborate for the reconciliation of all things in Christ.

Arturo Sosa, SJ Superior General
Rome, 19 February 2019
(Original: Spanish)

20. GC 36, d. 2,7.

Showing the Way to God

Arturo Sosa, SJ

"And what if God spoke to you? What would he tell you?" With those two questions, the new Universal Apostolic Preferences (UAPs) of the Society of Jesus were introduced. The first one aims to show the path to God via the Spiritual Exercises and discernment. Why does this UAP come first?

It is a fundamental premise of the spiritual life of Christians that God maintains a continual dialogue with human beings and with history. Without that, nothing else would make sense. The Bible is a selection of examples of the very long story of God's communication with mankind in different contexts. If we define God through the word *love*, then the deepest form of communication is what love means. Those who love go beyond verbal communication and give of themselves fully. But for two-way communication to take place, a few basic conditions are required: God speaks to those who want to begin a dialogue with him. It is his desire to speak to us, and those words in the video introducing the Universal Apostolic Preferences are an invitation to listen. If you allow God to speak to you, you realize that he has something important to tell you.

God is the Word, as the prologue to the Gospel of John tells us. This can also be expressed through other words: Let God love you because he is the one who attracts you. The prophet Jeremiah said that

From *Walking with Ignatius* (Dublin, Ireland: Messenger Publications, 2021).

[Editors' Note: The chapters in *Walking with Ignatius* are presented in a question-and-answer format, with the questions posed by Dario Manor and answered by Jesuit Superior General Arturo Sosa.]

the Lord seduced him . . . and that he allowed himself to be seduced. This communication has a dimension beyond listening. It relates to feelings and affectivity. That is why the UAPs are essential for us. If we are not open to God speaking to us, there is no way forward. We find the meaning of life in the love of God, which turns into love for our neighbor. When God speaks to us, it is to tell us to love, to draw close to our neighbor, and to initiate a relational dynamic of loving and giving. When we enter a process of listening to the Lord, we discover the truth of that saying of Teresa of Avila that might seem utterly crazy: "Only God is enough."

The first UAP begins with the phrase "showing the way to God." How does the Society interpret this "showing" in our societies today?

Showing means making something available to people, which is quite different from imposing it upon them. It involves respecting the freedom of each person to choose or reject the path shown. This is nothing new: This has always been the way that the Lord has made his presence known since the beginning. In the Bible, we see that God communicates with human beings by revealing himself rather than imposing his presence on them. The Lord becomes present, he offers himself to us, but each individual is then free to accept or reject him. With Jesus, this becomes something even more radical. The Gospels give us a panorama of every conceivable way that God reveals himself to us through Christ. We chose the word *showing* in the UAPs because it suggests freedom, both that of other people to choose this path and also our own to teach freely what we are offering.

What is the greatest strength of the Spiritual Exercises and spiritual discernment?

They are a pedagogy in how to communicate with God from the deepest part of ourselves: our affections. They lead us into a dynamic of affective communication with the Lord. They take us by the hand to listen to him and enter the loving dialogue he offers. The starting point of the Spiritual Exercises is as much that God wishes to communicate with us as that each person is free to communicate with him. Only by starting from a place of freedom can we enter a relationship with him. The Exercises also offer a pedagogy in spiritual discernment by revealing how, over time, God moves within each of us. On his retreat, Ignatius reflected on how the Lord communicates by stirring our affections; Ignatius's reflection led to the development of a pedagogy to grasp and understand this way of communicating. That is what the Spiritual Exercises are. Their name is not a random choice. We exercise to be in shape. In this case, we are doing exercises in the Spirit so we can train in the process of accompaniment that helps us discern. Although some people say it is enough to do the Spiritual Exercises once in a lifetime, the tradition of the Society teaches us that it is worthwhile doing them every year and to keep up the practice of doing them regularly. Discernment requires a spiritual workout if we are to make decisions in freedom.

There is a danger, however, that the Spiritual Exercises might be hawked as a commercial product that is for sale. This can happen if the experience of God is stripped out and they become an end in themselves, or if it is thought that people can "save themselves" through doing them, or become someone of "spiritual stature." What the Spiritual Exercises really do is help you meet the true God and remain active in the service of others.

Why do so many people (Jesuits, other religious, lay people, clergy) do the Spiritual Exercises without it leading to a real change in their lives? What is the secret to the Exercises really changing people?

If the Exercises are just a one-off incident in your life rather than the beginning of an ongoing process, they will not lead to a real change. You might have a moving experience, but the Exercises will not take you any further than that if they do not reinforce or nourish a process of developing a spiritual lifestyle. In our last General Congregation, we addressed the question of why the Spiritual Exercises do not always spark the change that they should, even in Jesuits. I believe this situation reveals the fragility of our own spiritual lives.

We do not make enough use of the Daily Examen. This is a key tool in Ignatian spirituality. Ignatius's Examen begins with a grateful recognition of God's presence in our lives so that we can then explore our response to this. If you learn how to continually apply that attitude of the Examen to everything you do, then you probably will change. That is what Ignatius recommends. But this form of discernment in the spiritual life works only if you have begun an ongoing spiritual process, and the Exercises, prayer, or the Eucharist are not one-off instances in your life. If there is a process, then it is possible to grow into a way of life modeled on Jesus.

It was the reading of religious books during his convalescence after being wounded in Pamplona that changed Ignatius and led to his conversion. Do you believe that literature still has the same power to move us today, or are we now more influenced by other media such as videos?

Many things can help, although I'm of a generation for whom there is no substitute for reading. While there's no doubt that videos, films, or pictures have the power to move us, what is unique to reading is its power to completely grip you and get inside your head, which is what happened to Ignatius. Literature is essential in the Christian life, to the extent that the reading of the Word is central to our liturgical celebrations. And, although we often read the Bible, the experience is different every time. I've been fortunate enough to read widely since I was a small child. My parents hardly allowed us to watch television, and we were always greatly encouraged to read. If I went out into the street without a book under my arm to turn to in idle moments, I felt like something was missing.

Where do we most frequently find the spark that triggers conversion?

That spark can happen when you discover another person and who they truly are beneath the surface. That's conversion: when you abandon your assumptions or prejudices and see the person before you as they truly are. That discovery of difference enriches you and shows you something you didn't know before then, with both its good and bad points. That's when you discover suffering, joy, and also occasional emptiness.

In my case, the journeys I made as a young man throughout Venezuela and my experiences in the novitiate, when for a time I worked alongside rural workers, and in a factory, were immensely significant. My eyes were opened to ways of living unfamiliar to me. I recall one particular experience in the countryside. A man had died, and during his funeral, his wife embarked on a very beautiful dialogue with the deceased. It was her way of saying goodbye to someone she had loved deeply. Witnessing that triggered a conversion process. The Jesuit universities in Latin America have Ignatian leadership programs that encourage their students to discover other social realities. A number of different factors can trigger conversion in us, including discovering who other people truly are, reading, or sharing our life with others.

Is it possible to talk about conversion and a path towards God in societies that regard being free of religion as something positive?

Part of the process of secularization is about being set free from religion, understood here as a social convention or a way of imposing a vocabulary or identity that allows little space for individual freedom and faith. Christianity is not simply a religion: it is a religious faith because it leads to a personal relationship with God. If society helps set you free from a religion that feels like a straitjacket, it can actually help you grow in faith. However, to have this openness to faith, it is important to be aware of the role the sacred plays in society. The Gospel shows us that Jesus was very "antireligious" in the sense described above. He placed the human person above the law and had no time for empty and exclusive ritualism, and because of that, he was condemned to death. For Jesus, the heart of religion was the living God, the God of life and the communion of love among persons, with him, and towards the environment. He destroyed an image of God mixed up with power structures and oppression. Setting that kind of religion free was a step towards a genuine faith in God.

What would you say to those who believe in God and consider themselves Catholic but reject the Church?

First of all, I would listen to what they have to say, to understand how they arrived at that conclusion. That idea of holding onto God but parting ways with the Church probably comes from a personal experience that would be worth exploring. Based on that conversation, I'd share what it means to me to have an intimate relationship with Jesus and to belong to the Church.

Faith in Christ leads you to reach out to others to share your faith with them and cannot be separated from belonging to the community, which is the Church. That does not mean you cannot be critical of the Church. Indeed, the saints themselves were, and they suggested ways to improve her. The person who steps away from the Church is completely right to reject whatever has scandalized them. But what needs looking at is how they might move on from this experience in order to try and improve the Church, in order to ensure that their personal faith in God is complemented by belonging to a community based around the Eucharist.

How do you explain the success of New Age beliefs, alternative spiritualities, and sects?
People's thirst for faith is slaked in many different ways. It is another consequence of secularization because these phenomena do not emerge in societies where there is one dominant religion. I am no expert on this area, but some of these beliefs are very individualistic and do not demand any commitment at all to your neighbor. Christianity, in contrast, when it is authentically lived out, brings you into communion with others, and into contact with things you don't like. It makes you open to other people's pain and problems.

Some intellectuals are suggesting that, thanks to technological development, mankind could become immortal. Is it possible for this reality to coexist alongside the concept of God that has prevailed up until now?
Any form of immortality which, hypothetically, might be possible thanks to technological advances, would certainly be different from the eternal life spoken of by the Christian faith. Immortality means prolonging this life but does not consider a perspective beyond human life. The length of our lives is changing, as we have seen in the past few decades as life expectancy in some countries has shot up from thirty or forty years old to more than seventy, with consequent problems. What age might we live to with the immortality offered by technology? I'd love to regain the energy I had at the age of twenty, but not the doubts nor the ignorance I also had then.

What is so interesting about the Christian faith is not that it offers us immortality but that it invites us to share in the life of God. It implies life in its fullness: We have our origin in God, and we end in him. In his book about Jesus, Benedict XVI is very enlightening on this point when he explains that the Resurrection is a step towards full participation in the life of God and that is why death is necessary. It is Easter, and without Easter this experience cannot be had. One dies to this life to reach the next. But in a way, we are also dying through the transformations we go through over the course of our lives. In his letters, St. John says we have passed from death to life, and that, as we adopt the way of life shown by Jesus, we enter into a new life. Death means going towards more love and having a greater share of the life of God. That is why we speak of Easter and not of immortality. This is about a gift, not the fruit of our scientific endeavors.

The lack of serenity and reflection in the contemporary world is obvious. Does this scenario offer the Church an opportunity to help people slow down and reflect on the important things in life?
The spiritual life as such cannot exist if it allows no room for peace. That is something we religious also experience: We are determined to do so many things that at times we do not leave enough room to go deeper in our relationship with God. Times of peace and prayer are necessary for us to examine the life we are leading and enjoy a joyful interiority. If not, we can end up doing too many things and not living. Little by little, this strips our life of meaning. Many vocational crises in the religious life are connected to this.

The Spiritual Exercises, which we talked about earlier, teach you to retain a certain discipline in order to preserve time for prayer. However, this is a problem for everyone. In the life of a couple, there needs to be time dedicated to their mutual affection, beyond the responsibilities. The same thing happens with professionals. I recall a great friend, a social activist, who became the head of a trade union but realized at that point he had lost control of his daily schedule and no longer had the time to do what he set out to do when he had chosen that direction in life.

Unamuno wrote in *El sentimiento trágico de la vida* (*Tragic Sense of Life*): "Act so that in your own judgment and in the judgment of others you may merit eternity, act so that you may become irreplaceable, act so that you may not merit death. Or perhaps thus: Act as if you were to die tomorrow, but to die in order to survive and be eternalized."[1] Should death give meaning to life?

Anyone involved in pastoral care in parishes is well aware that, day-to-day, the subject of death never goes away. People come to churches during funerals and Masses of the Dead, and you can end up in tune with what they are going through. I once knew a Jesuit who said that he preached only during funerals because everyone present hung on his words, far more so than during a normal Mass. When someone comes to a burial or funeral, they do so out of affection for the person they are saying goodbye to. During the First Week of the *Spiritual Exercises*, St. Ignatius recommends that you imagine the moment of your death and think about how you would have liked to have lived. That helps you examine your life and change your present. The presence of that limitation which is death enables us to live with meaning and integrity. That phrase of Unamuno's is an invitation to conversion, to change our lives.

What role can popular religiosity play in spirituality, e.g., pilgrimages?
Popular religiosity is a richly symbolic form of spiritual life, whether expressed on the level of individuals or of groups. It makes a powerful use of images. The great challenge popular religiosity entails is how to ensure that people actually experience what the activity they are involved in represents, as opposed to this just being about doing something together in a group. For example, some people who join a *cofradía* (penitential lay brotherhoods common to Spain and Latin America who process in public during Holy Week carrying sculptures representing the Passion of Christ) lose touch with the deep meaning of what is actually being represented. Popular religiosity enables people to connect very quickly to an experience of God, as I

1. *Tragic Sense of Life*, M. de Unamuno. Trans. by J. Crawford Flitch. e-artnow, April 24th, 2020.

experienced in base communities in Latin America, and I know this happens in the religious experience of the poor in other continents. When these forms of popular religiosity exist, the atmosphere of liturgical celebrations is much richer and deeper. That is the challenge: ensuring that expressions of popular religiosity based on deep experiences of faith do not turn into empty rituals. Contexts need to be established that allow people to express their experience of the divine. This pope, during his time as an auxiliary bishop of the Archdiocese of Buenos Aires, and later as the archbishop, was in close contact with the faith of the working classes. He has broad experience of this kind of pastoral care.

II. Contemporary Interpretations

Part II Introduction

Interpreting Ignatian spirituality has been an ongoing process for those who are called to follow the gospel through this lens, from the early corporate discernment of Ignatius and his first companions to the present day. In the early days of the renewal of the Society and its spirituality after Vatican II, scholars, spiritual guides, teachers, as well as companions in other religious orders and the lay members of Christian Life Community have sought to discover and implement the experience of Saint Ignatius in relationship to the Trinity by practicing his Spiritual Exercises and the discernment demanded by them. The publication of the fruits of this work in *The Spiritual Exercises*, letters, journal excerpts, the "Formula of the Institute" (two versions), and the *Constitutions* have made up a body of published literature which, in turn, established methods and practices that require this process of interpretation to take place in multiple cultures and languages across the five-hundred-plus years of time and the distance of the whole world. Additional publications in the *Monumenta* volumes by the co-founding fathers of the Society of Jesus have added remarkable insight into the practices of this spirituality.

No one should be surprised, then, that practitioners of Ignatian spirituality would seek to interpret the founding experience in the human development of the present time. Part II and subsequent Parts of this second volume of *The Ignatian Spirituality Reader* point to lives committed to making Ignatian spirituality real in our time and in the U.S. American culture(s).

Part II begins with the allocution (address) given by Pope Francis to the delegates of General Congregation 36 of the Society of Jesus. The tasks of General Congregations are to elect a new Superior General if necessary and to interpret Ignatian spirituality in ways that allow the Jesuits to serve the Church and the world in timely and meaningful ways for new eras or cultures. The current popes have been important voices at General Congregations through the years, and often the papal allocution is about the Society's essential works of service to faith. The striking difference of this allocution is that since Pope Francis is a Jesuit, the papal voice is both from the Church and within the Society itself. His insights offer all Jesuits, and their lay and religious partners in the works of the Society, wisdom regarding interpretation.

The second essay in Part II is from the voice of an academic theologian (Matthew Ashley) who is speaking of Pope Francis as a theologically valuable voice of interpretation of Ignatian spirituality in our time given his role as leader of the Catholic Church.

Part II continues with five shorter chapters, blogs, and essays that offer practical insight into specific ways of interpreting the most necessary characteristics of Ignatian spirituality for the present decade, which the Jesuits and their partners have determined in the discernment of the four Universal Apostolic Preferences (UAPs). Care for those on the margins of culture (Julia Dowd), social media's impact on human development (Eric Clayton), human growth in the face of social conflicts (Alex Hale), cognitive development and spiritual growth (Thanh-Thao [Sue] Do), and the care of the identity of the poor through medical care often imagined for the rich (Ryan Mak) are critical concerns of this century. But they raise practical questions that we can respond to well by implementing a sixteenth-century interpretation of a first-century call to the full humanness of holiness.

Each problem/solution demonstrates how Ignatian spirituality is alive in this historical moment because of measured and appropriate interpretation.

Eileen Burke-Sullivan

Address to the 36th General Congregation of the Society of Jesus

Pope Francis

Monday, October 24, 2016

My dear Brothers and Friends in the Lord,

While I was praying about what to say to you today, a fond memory came to me of the last words blessed Paul VI said to us at the end of our 32nd General Congregation: "This is the way, this is the way, brothers and sons. Forward, in Nomine Domini! Let us walk together free, obedient, united in the love of Christ, for the greater glory of God."[1]

Saint John Paul II and Pope Benedict XVI also encouraged us "to walk in a manner worthy of the vocation to which we are called"[2] (cf. Ephesians 4:1) and "in the ecclesial and social context that marks the beginning of this millennium . . . to continue on the path of this mission in full fidelity to your original charism. As my Predecessors have said to you on various occasions, the Church needs you, relies on you, and continues to turn to you with trust, particularly to reach those physical and spiritual places that others do not reach or have difficulty in reaching."[3]

From the General Curia of the Society of Jesus.

1. Address to the 32nd General Congregation of the Society of Jesus, 3 December 1974.
2. Homily, Mass at the opening of the 33rd General Congregation of the Society of Jesus, 2 September 1983.
3. Address to the participants of the 35th General Congregation of the Society of Jesus, 21 February 2008.

To walk together—free and obedient—moving toward the margins of society where no one else reaches, "under the gaze of Jesus and looking to the horizon which is the ever greater glory of God, who ceaselessly surprises us."[4] As Saint Ignatius reminds us, a Jesuit is called "to think and to live in any part of the world where there is a greater need of service to God and assistance for souls" (Constitutions [304]). The fact is that "the Society must feel at home anyplace in the world," as Nadal used to say.[5] Saint Ignatius wrote to Francis Borgia about the criticism against the Jesuits that they were too "angelic" (Oviedo and Onfroy), for some people were saying that the Society was insufficiently trained and needed more instruction in the spirit. The spirit that guides them, Ignatius wrote, "ignores the state of things in the Society because these things are always in fieri, except for what is absolutely necessary."[6] I rather like Ignatius's way of seeing everything—except for what is absolutely essential—as constantly developing (in fieri), because it frees the Society from all kinds of paralysis and vain ambition.

What is necessary and essential is the Formula of the Institute, which we should keep constantly before our eyes after gazing at the Lord: "The nature of this Institute which is his pathway to God." This is the way it was for the first members of the Society, just as they foresaw it would be "for those who will follow us along the path." In this way, whether it be poverty or obedience or the dispensation from certain obligations such as praying in choir: All these things are neither needs nor privileges but rather aids given to the Society so that its members may be available "to travel along the way of Christ Our Lord" (Constitutions [582]), so that, thanks to their vow of obedience to the pope, they may receive "more certain direction from the Holy Spirit" ("Formula of the Institute," 3). The Formula contains Ignatius's insight, and its essence is what accounts for the

---

4. Cf. Francis, Homily, Liturgical Memorial of the Most Holy Name of Jesus, Church of the Gesù, 3 January 2014.
5. Nadal V, 364–365.
6. Letter 51, to Francis Borgia, July 1549, 17 n. 9. Cf. M. A. Fiorito and A. Swinnen, La Fórmula del Instituto de la Compañía de Jesús (introducción y versión castellana), Stromata, July–December 1977, n. 3/4, 259–260.

Constitution's insistence on always keeping in mind the priority of "places, times, and persons" and the fact that all the rules are intended to help us in concrete situations.

For Ignatius, the journey is not an aimless wandering; rather, it translates into something qualitative: It is a "gain" or progress, a moving forward, a doing something for others. This is how it is expressed in the two Formulas of the Institute approved by Popes Paul III (1540) and Julius III (1550), centering on the Society's solicitude for the faith—its defense and propagation—and on the lives and instruction of the people. Here Ignatius and his first companions use the word *aprovechamiento* or "benefit" (ad profectum, cf. Philippians 1:12, 25) to describe the practical criterion of discernment in Ignatian spirituality.[7]

Aprovechamiento is not individualistic but communal. "The purpose of this Society is not directed merely at the salvation and perfection of the souls of its members by divine grace, but rather by the same grace to work assiduously for the salvation and perfection of the souls of our neighbors" (SE 1 and 2). And if Ignatius's heart was inclined in one direction or the other, it was toward helping his neighbors, so much to the point that he would get angry whenever he was told that someone wanted to spend time with the Society "in order to save his soul. Ignatius did not want people who were good for their own sake if they did not want to place themselves at the service of their neighbors.[8]

Aprovechamiento pervades everything. Ignatius's Formula expresses an inherent tension: "Not only . . . but . . ." This mentality of holding tensions together—one's own salvation and perfection with the salvation and perfection of others—beginning with the higher order of grace, is a distinctive characteristic of the Society. The harmonizing of this and all tensions (contemplation and action, faith and justice, charisma and institutions, community and mission . . .) is not contained in abstract formulas but rather obtained over the course

7. "Ad profectum animarum in vita et doctrina Christiana" in *Monumenta Ignatiana*, *Constitutiones* T. I (MHSI), Rome, 1934, 26 and 376; cf. Constitutions of the Society of Jesus, annotated by General Congregation 34, and the Complementary Norms, Rome, ADP, 1995, 32–33.

8. Aicardo I, point 10, p. 41.

of time through that which Fabro calls "our way of proceeding."[9] By walking and "moving forward" in following the Lord, the Society is harmonizing the tensions of the different groups of people who make it up and the missions it embraces and undertakes.

Aprovechamiento is not elitist. In the Formula, Ignatius goes on to describe the means of a more universal aprovechamiento specific to priesthood. But first let us note that works of mercy are taken for granted in the Formula. It says: "Without these being an obstacle" to mercy! The works of mercy—the cure of the sick in the hospital, alms and their distribution, the teaching of the young, bearing hardships patiently—these were the vital milieus in which Ignatius and his first companions moved and existed. These were their daily bread. They took great pains to prevent anything from getting in the way of these!

In the end, this kind of aprovechamiento is "what is best for us." It is a *magis*, that plus that leads Ignatius to undertake initiatives, to follow them through, and to evaluate their real impact on people's lives in matters of faith, justice, mercy, and charity. The *magis* is the fire, the fervor of action that rouses us from slumber. Our saints have always been an incarnation of this. It was said of Saint Albert Hurtado that he was "a sharp dart stuck in the sleeping flesh of the Church." This counters the temptation that Paul VI labeled *spiritus vertiginis* and what De Lubac called "worldly spirituality." A temptation that is not primarily moral but spiritual as it distracts us from what is essential: namely, to be aprovechamiento, to leave an imprint or a mark in history, especially in the lives of the smallest.

"The Society is zealous," Nadal affirmed.[10] In order to reignite the mission's fervor for "benefiting" people in their concrete lives and through teaching, I would like to ground my reflections in three points which, from the moment the Society established itself in the missions it undertook, have especially enhanced our way of proceeding. These three points are joy, the Cross, and the Church—our Mother—and they have the purpose of taking a step forward, taking away the impediments that the enemy of human nature places in front of us when, in the service of God, we rise from good to better.

9. Cf. MF. 50, 69, 111, 114, etc.
10. Cf. Nadal V, 310.

1. Ask Persistently for Consolation

We can always improve in praying persistently for consolation. The Apostolic Exhortations *Evangelii Gaudium* and *Amoris Laetitia*, along with the Encyclical *Laudato Si'*, were meant to highlight the importance of joy. In the Exercises, Ignatius asks his companions to contemplate "the task of consolation" as something specific to the resurrected Christ (SE 224). It is the specific task of the Society to console the Christian faithful and to help them in their discernment so that the enemy of human nature does not distract us from joy: the joy of evangelizing, the joy of the family, the joy of the Church, the joy of creation . . . Let us never be robbed of that joy, neither through discouragement when faced with the great measure of evil in the world and misunderstandings among those who intend to do good, nor let it be replaced with vain joys that are easily bought and sold in any shop.

This "service of joy and spiritual consolation" is rooted in prayer. It consists in encouraging ourselves and others "to ask persistently for God's consolation." Ignatius expresses this in a negative formulation in the sixth rule of the First Week when he affirms: "It is very helpful intensely to change ourselves against the same desolation" by persisting in prayer (SE 319). It is helpful because in desolation we realize how weak we are without grace and consolation (cf. SE 324). To practice and teach this prayer of asking and begging for consolation is our main service of joy. If one does not consider himself worthy (something that happens often in practice), he should at least persist in asking for this consolation out of a love for the message, since joy is constitutive of the Gospel, and he should ask it also out of a love for others, his family, and the world. One cannot deliver good news with a sullen face. Joy is not a decorative "addition" but a clear indicator of grace: It indicates that love is active, operative, present. Therefore, searching for it should not be confused with searching for some "special effect" easily produced today for the mere purpose of consumption, but, rather, it should be sought in its essential trait of "permanence": Ignatius opens his eyes and awakes to this discernment of spirits by discovering the difference between the joys that endure and the joys that pass away (*Autobiography*, 8). Time becomes the element that offers him the key to recognizing the action of the Spirit.

In the Exercises, progress in the spiritual life is made through consolation: It is a moving from good to better (cf. SE 315) as well as "every increase of hope, faith, and charity" (SE 316). This service of joy was what led Ignatius's first companions to establish rather than disband the Society to which they offered themselves and shared spontaneously, and whose distinctive characteristic was the joy it gave them of praying together, being sent as missionaries together, and reuniting in imitation of the life that the Lord and his apostles led. This joy of an explicit proclamation of the Gospel—by means of the preaching of the faith and the practice of justice and mercy—is what drives the Society out to the margins of society. The Jesuit is a servant of the joy of the Gospel, be it when he is working "in the workshop" of giving retreats—even if to one person, helping him or her to encounter that "interior place whence comes the strength of the Spirit that guides, frees, and renews"[11]—or when he is working in a structured way by organizing works of formation, mercy, and reflection, all of which are an institutional outgrowth of that point of "inflection" in which we allow our will to be overcome and the Holy Spirit comes into action. M. De Certeau said it well: The Exercises are "the apostolic method par excellence" insofar as they make possible "a return to the heart, to the principle of docility to the Spirit, who awakens and encourages whoever undertakes the exercises to personal fidelity to God."[12]

11. Pierre Favre, *Mémorial* (Paris: Desclée, 1959); cf. "Introduction" by M. De Certeau, 74.
12. de Certeau and Favre, 76.

2. Allow Ourselves to be Moved by the Lord on the Cross

We can always improve somewhat in allowing ourselves to be moved by our crucified Lord, both in person and as present in the sufferings of so many of our brothers and sisters—indeed, the majority of the human race! Just as Fr. Arrupe said, wherever there is pain, the Society is there. The Jubilee of Mercy is a privileged time to reflect on the "services" of mercy. I use the plural because mercy is not an abstraction but a lifestyle consisting in concrete gestures rather than mere words: reaching out and touching others and institutionalizing the works of mercy. For those of us who perform the Exercises, this grace by means of which Jesus commands us to become like the Father (cf. Luke 6:36) begins with a conversation of mercy that is an extension of our conversation with the crucified Lord because of our sins. The entire Second Exercise is a conversation full of sentiments of shame, confusion, sorrow, and tears of gratitude by seeing precisely who I am—by making myself small—and who God is—by magnifying him—he who "preserved my life until now" (SE 61); and by seeing who Jesus is, hanging on the Cross for me. The way in which Ignatius lives and formulates his experience of mercy is of great personal and apostolic benefit and requires an acute and elevated sense of discernment. Our spiritual father said to Saint Francis Borgia: "As for me, I persuade myself both before and after that I am nothing but an obstacle; and from this I derive great spiritual contentment and joy in our Lord insofar as I cannot take credit for anything that appears good."[13] Ignatius therefore lives completely on God's mercy even in the littlest things. He felt that the greater the obstacle in life, the greater the goodness with which the Lord treated him: "The Lord's mercy was so great and the tenderness and sweetness of His grace so abundant within him, that the more he wished to be castigated in this way, the greater was God's goodness toward him and the more generously He showered him with the treasures of His infinite generosity. Laonde said he believed there was no other man in the world

13. Ignatius of Loyola, Letter 26 to Francis Borgia, c. 1545.

in whom these two things came together more strikingly: failing God so much on the one hand, and receiving so many graces from Him on the other."[14]

Ignatius, in formulating his experience of mercy in these comparative terms—the more he felt he was doing wrong in the Lord's eyes, the more the Lord showered him with his grace—liberated the dynamic strength of mercy that we so often dilute with abstract formulae and legalistic conditions. The Lord, who looks upon us with mercy and chooses us, sends us forth with the same powerful mercy to the poor, the sinners, the abandoned, the crucified, and anyone who suffers from injustice and violence in today's world. Only when we experience this healing force in our own lives and in our own wounds—as individuals and as a body (i.e., the community)—will we be able to lose our fear of allowing ourselves to be moved by the immense suffering of our brothers and sisters so as to go out and walk patiently with our people, learning from them the best way to help and serve them (cf. *General Constitutions*, 32d, 4, n. 50).

3. Do Good with a Good Spirit by "Feeling with the Church"

We can also take a step forward in doing good with a good spirit: "Feeling with the Church," as Saint Ignatius says. It is also a distinctive service of the Society to facilitate the discernment of how we do things. Fabro formulated it by asking the grace that "all the good that can be realized, thought, and organized, has to be done with a good spirit, not a bad spirit."[15] This grace of discerning is not limited to thinking, doing, and organizing well, but rather of doing these things with a good spirit: This is what roots us in the Church in which the Spirit works and distributes his various gifts for the common good.

14. P. Ribadeneira, *The Life of Saint Ignatius of Loyola* (Rome, La Civiltà Cattolica, 1863), 336.
15. Pierre Favre, *Mémorial*, cit. n. 51.

Fabro used to say that in many cases those who wanted to reform the Church were well intentioned, but God did not wish to correct the Church using their methods.

It is distinctive of the Society to do things by "feeling with the Church." To do this joyfully and without disturbing the peace, considering the sins we perceive within ourselves and the structures we have created, entails carrying the cross and experiencing poverty and humiliation, the locus in which Ignatius encourages us to choose between patiently enduring them and desiring them.[16] Whenever the contradiction was more pronounced, Ignatius gave the example of reflecting before speaking or acting in order to work in a good spirit. The rules of "feeling with the Church" are not to be read as precise instructions on controversial points (some of them arise spontaneously), but rather as examples where Ignatius extended the invitation to "act against" the anti-ecclesial spirit of his time, inclining always and decisively on the side of our Mother, the Church; not to justify a controversial point, but rather to open up space in which the Spirit could work in his own time.

The service of good-spiritedness and discernment makes us men of the Church—ecclesial men, not clerical men—men "for others," having nothing that isolates us but placing everything we have in common and at the service of others.

We walk neither by ourselves nor for our own comfort; we walk with "a heart that does not rest, that does not close in on itself but beats to the rhythm of a journey undertaken together with all the people faithful to God."[17] Let us walk by making ourselves all things to all people by seeking out someone to help.

This shedding of ourselves makes it possible for the Society to always have the face, the way of speaking, and the way of being of all peoples, all cultures, by inserting ourselves into all of them, into the specific heart of each people, to build up the Church with each of them, by inculturating the Gospel and evangelizing every culture.

---

16. Cf. Directorio Autógrafo, 23.
17. Francis, Homily, "Liturgical Memorial of the Most Holy Name of Jesus," Church of the Gesù, 3 January 2014.

Let us ask Our Lady of the Way, speaking as a son with his mother or as a servant with his mistress, to intercede for us in the presence of the "Father of mercies and the God of all consolation" (2 Corinthians 1:3), that he may place us once again together in the presence of his Son, Jesus, who takes up the Cross of the world and asks us to take it up with him. Let us entrust him with our "way of proceeding," that it may be ecclesial, inculturated, poor, ministerial, and free of worldly ambition. Let us ask our Mother to guide and accompany each Jesuit to that portion of the faithful People of God to which he is sent, on the ways of consolation, compassion, and discernment.

Pope Francis as Interpreter of Ignatius's Spiritual Exercises

Matthew Ashley

In September of 2015, Pope Francis recorded a message for a meeting of the International Congress of Theology, held in Buenos Aires on the occasion of the 100th anniversary of the founding of the theology faculty at the Catholic University of Argentina. In his address, he communicated his understanding of theology, beginning with a reflection on the relationship between what I call "academic theology" and "pastoral theology."

> Not infrequently an opposition is generated between theology and pastoral thinking and action, as if they were two opposing, separated realities that didn't have anything to do with one another. Not infrequently we identify the doctrinal mindset with being conservative and retrograde, and, conversely, we think about the pastoral mindset from the perspective of adaptation, reduction, accommodation. As if they had nothing to do with one another. What gets generated in this way is a false opposition between the so-called "pastorally minded" and the "academics," between those on the side of the people and those on the side of doctrine. What gets generated is a false opposition between theology and thinking pastorally, between believing reflection and believing life. And then life has no room for reflection and reflection

Originally appeared in *Spiritus* 17, no. 2 (Fall 2017): 165–180.

> finds no room in life. The great fathers of the Church, Irenaeus, Augustine, Basil, Ambrose, just to name a few, were great theologians because they were great pastors.[1]

Francis states that one of the main contributions of Vatican II was overcoming this opposition, and, because of this, one of the principal tasks of theology is "the arduous work of distinguishing the message of Life from its forms of transmission, from its cultural elements that have a time encoded within." He continues, "not to do this exercise in discernment leads in one way or another to a betrayal of the message." He concludes, "This meeting of doctrine and the pastoral mindset is not optional; it is constitutive of a theology that aims to be ecclesial."[2]

While this understanding of theology can be taken as a brief for the centrality of pastoral or practical theology to the work of academic theology, I follow two hints for arguing that it can also be understood as pressing the centrality of the discourse of spirituality. First, "believing life" (*vida creyente*) strikes me as an apt synonym for spirituality, which is often described as "lived faith." Both namings intend to point to the way that life is actually lived out in the ambient of belief. Francis's point here, I believe, is that vida creyente, "believing life," has its own integrity and structures that should be taken more seriously by theology. Homologously, as recent scholarship has stressed, Christian spiritualty, or "lived faith," incorporates in its own way the conceptual parameters, the doctrines that belong to Christian faith at one particular moment in history, which academic theology, for its part, labors to understand and interrelate more conceptually and abstractly. Second, Francis names this work of integrating the doctrinal element of Christian faith (*lo doctrinal*) and

1. Francis, Video Message of His Holiness Pope Francis to Participants in an International Theological Congress Held at the Pontifical Catholic University of Argentina (Buenos Aires, September 1–3, 2015), accessed November 11, 2016, https://www.vatican.va/content/francesco/en/messages/pont-messages/2015/documents/papa-francesco_20150903_videomessaggio-teologia-buenos-aires.html. I have modified the translation slightly based on the Spanish original: https://www.vatican.va/content/francesco/es/messages/pont-messages/2015/documents/papa-francesco_20150903_videomessaggio-teologia-buenos-aires.html. As Cardinal Archbishop of Buenos Aires, Francis made the same point in an address to the Pontifical Commission for Latin America in February 2009: Francis, "The Importance of Academic Formation," in *Only Love Can Save Us: Letters, Homilies, and Talks of Cardinal Jorge Bergoglio* (Huntington, Ind.: Our Sunday Visitor Publishing Division, 2013), 139–149, especially 143–45.
2. Francis, Video Message.

the pastoral element (*lo pastoral*) as a work of discernment, a term of art from Christian spirituality in general, and from his own spiritual tradition, founded by Ignatius of Loyola in particular. He elsewhere names discernment as the element of Ignatian spirituality that is most important for his exercise of the Petrine ministry, and describes it in strikingly similar terms to those he used when addressing the theologians gathered in Buenos Aires.[3] For him, discernment exemplifies the attitude of John XXIII, the architect of the Second Vatican Council, and takes place "in the presence of the Lord, looking at the signs, listening to the things that happen, the feeling of the people, especially the poor."[4]

We may add to these hints the fact that Francis has made it clear on more than one occasion that his Jesuit formation and his experience as a Jesuit, including as provincial of the Jesuits of Argentina in the 1970s, have decisively shaped his thought and papal practices, much more so than particular theological figures or schools. Unlike his two predecessors, the Argentinian pope was never an academic, and does not turn readily and spontaneously to the parlance of academic philosophy or theology. His difference in style is amply evident from the encyclicals and apostolic exhortations that have emerged during the first four years of his pontificate. Striking too is his frequent deployment of the language and traditions of Christian spirituality as shown in *Laudato Si'*. Both this encyclical and the apostolic exhortation, *Amoris Laetitia*, conclude with lengthy sections devoted to spirituality.[5] He explains this feature, novel for this genre of magisterial statement, in these terms:

---

3. Antonio Spadaro, SJ, "A Big Heart Open to God: A Conversation with Pope Francis." (New York: Harper One, 2013), 12–14. Here and elsewhere, Francis associates discernment with a motto coined a century after Ignatius to encapsulate his spirituality: "Non coerceri maximo, contineri tamen a minimo, divinum est." He says the motto "offers parameters to assume a correct position for discernment, in order to hear the things of God from God's 'point of view.' According to St. Ignatius great principles must be embodied in the circumstances of place, time, and people" (13). Discernment is precisely the arduous and time-consuming task of deciding how great and timeless principles (or doctrines, or theological assertions) can be detected and applied in particular contexts. For further reflection on this issue, see Peter Schineller, SJ, "Pope Francis–Deeply Ignatian and Deeply Jesuit" (Toronto: Salt and Light Media Foundation, 2017), accessed March 17, 2017, https://slmedia.org/blog/pope-francis-deeply-ignatian-and-deeply-jesuit.
4. Francis, "A Big Heart Open to God," 14.
5. *Laudato Si'*, §§216–245; Amoris Laetitia, §§313–325.

> More than in ideas or concepts as such, I am interested in how such a spirituality can motivate us to a more passionate concern for the protection of our world. A commitment this lofty cannot be sustained by doctrine alone, without a spirituality capable of inspiring us, without an "interior impulse which encourages, motivates, nourishes and gives meaning to our individual and communal activity."[6]

While Francis of Assisi has pride of place in *Laudato Si'*, it seems abundantly clear that the spirituality that has been most formative of the pope's thought and practice is that of Ignatius.[7] With this in mind, I explore here the hypothesis that Christian spirituality (including Ignatian spirituality in particular) is a constitutive element and source of theology for Pope Francis, rather than an ancillary "frosting" on the doctrinal cake or a merely subjective application of universal, self-sufficient principles worked out elsewhere. That is, not only is Francis an interpreter of the Spiritual Exercises, as the title of this essay suggests, but the Exercises interpret him, as it were. The spirituality laid out in such detail in Ignatius's masterwork provides a hermeneutical lens for deepening our understanding of Francis's theological assertions.

As a test case for this hypothesis, I take up the theme of mercy and its relationship to justice, a theme with a long and complex career in the history of theology.[8] I draw from *The Name of God is Mercy*, a book that includes the bull, *Misericordiae Vultus*, which proclaimed the year of mercy, as well as an interview with Francis on his thoughts and hopes about this jubilee year.[9] I argue that his working out of the relationship between mercy and justice is best illuminated against the backdrop of his understanding of Ignatian spirituality. Outlining the pope's

---

6. *Laudato Si'*, §216. The quotation he gives is from his first apostolic exhortation, *Evangelii Gaudium*, §261.

7. I use "Ignatian spirituality" as a shorthand for the spirituality which, as recent scholarship has emphasized, was not created and shaped only by the nobleman-turned-ascetic from Loyola, even though he was the pathbreaker, but also by others among the first Jesuits, including the original companions and subsequent members of the Society of Jesus. Figures such as Peter Faber, Diego Lainez, and Jeronimo Nadal, each made important contributions. Indeed, Francis himself names Peter Faber as one of his models. *A Big Heart Open to God*, 19–21.

8. For a review of this complex history, see Walter Kasper, *Mercy: The Essence of the Gospel and the Key to Christian Life*, trans. William Madges (New York: Paulist Press, 2014), 52–55, 75–129.

9. Francis, *The Name of God is Mercy: A Conversation with Andrea Tornielli*, trans. Oonagh Stransky (New York: Random House, 2016).

understanding of Ignatian spirituality in a comprehensive way exceeds the limits of this essay. As it seems to me, a plausible shortcut is to use a preached retreat, "in the manner of St. Ignatius of Loyola," that he gave to Spanish bishops in 2006, for which we have the text of his talks.[10]

My argument proceeds in three stages. First, I argue that Francis's overt statements on the relationship between justice and mercy are theologically underdetermined and thus open to a variety of interpretations. Second, I argue that the most satisfying way of resolving this polysemy is to read these statements using the pattern established by the relationships of the first and the Second Week of the Spiritual Exercises, and the graces that they open up to those making the Exercises. These are, from the First Week, an experience of one's weakness and sinfulness together with a deep sense of being forgiven; and from the Second Week, an experience of being called to a deeper intimacy with Christ and to following him. Together, these graces inform the choices we make in life and enable us to experience union with God in and through these choices. For Francis, this is how people fulfill the demands of justice. Francis's innovation as a reader of the Exercises is to place these "moments" of the Christian spiritual itinerary in the tightest possible relationship. This close interweaving on the level of the Christian's spiritual itinerary provides the proper backdrop for interpreting the set of claims he makes about justice and mercy, which are not otherwise easily systematized. Third, as a contrastive case, I conclude with a brief comparison with John Paul II's approach to this issue in his encyclical, *Dives in Misericordia*.

Mercy and Justice: The Problematic

Probing the relationship between mercy and justice brings us quickly to the heart of the mystery of God's grace and entangles us in perennial questions that arise when one plumbs that mystery: the relationship between God's mercy and God's justice, between God's merciful

10. Francis, *In Him Alone is Our Hope: Spiritual Exercises Given to His Brother Bishops in the Manner of St. Ignatius of Loyola* (New York: Magnificat, 2013).

action and the response of human free will, as well as the relationship between the response of faith and the response of works of justice. In the bull *Misericordiae Vultus*, Francis is spare in his comments on the relationship between justice and mercy. He starts by saying that they are "two dimensions of a single reality that unfolds progressively until it culminates in love."[11] He then distinguishes between justice as a principle in civil society and justice as the principle governing "that which is rightly due to each individual." Reading the Hebrew Bible with the latter definition in mind, he argues that justice is understood as "full observance of the Law and the behavior of every good Israelite in conformity with God's commandments."[12] Yet, lest this become a legalistic rigorism, Francis is quite clear when he adds, "We need to recall that in Sacred Scripture, justice is conceived essentially as the faithful abandonment of oneself to God's will."[13] I will return to this point since I think it provides the key to unlocking his approach by giving a bridge to the spirituality of Ignatius's Spiritual Exercises.

Looking at the New Testament, Francis argues that "faced with a vision of justice as the mere observance of the law that judges people simply by dividing them into two groups—the just and sinners—Jesus is bent on revealing the great gift of mercy that searches out sinners and offers them pardon and salvation."[14] The "rule of life" for Jesus' disciples, then, "must place mercy at the centre."[15] Francis frequently uses this kind of language: Mercy is not only the defining feature of an action or a disposition to act, but an orienting center or a "rule of life." It is a key to the "logic" of God's gratuitous and overabundant love.

11. Francis, *Misericordiae Vultus: Bull of Indiction of the Extraordinary Jubilee of Mercy*, §20 (Vatican City, April 11, 2015), https://www.vatican.va/content/francesco/en/bulls/documents/papa-francesco_bolla_20150411_misericordiae-vultus.html. I cite from this text printed as an appendix to *The Name of God is Mercy*, 105–151; here, 138.

12. *Misericordiae Vultus*, §20, in *The Name of God is Mercy*, 138.

13. *The Name of God is Mercy*, 138. Francis's remarks concerning legalism here should not be directed at a caricatured Old Testament Judaism. But rather, in the context of his remarks, he is clearly addressing contemporary Catholicism in particular.

14. *The Name of God is Mercy*, 139.

15. *The Name of God is Mercy*, 140.

Mercy, then, is "not opposed to justice, but represents God's way of reaching out to the sinner, offering him a new chance to look at himself, convert, and believe."[16] It does not devalue justice or render it superfluous. "On the contrary: anyone who makes a mistake must pay the price. However, this is just the beginning of conversion, not its end, because one begins to feel the tenderness and mercy of God."[17] Mercy is also a marker of God's transcendence: "If God limited himself to only justice, he would cease to be God, and would instead be like human beings who ask merely that the law be respected." God is not like human beings, because God acts with mercy; yet, this mercy does not deny justice. In and through mercy, "God envelops [justice] and surpasses it, with an even greater event in which we experience love as the foundation of true justice."[18] The pope sums up in this way: "When there is mercy, justice is more just, and it fulfills its true essence."[19]

This cryptic set of statements is difficult to systematize, although the biblical background against which it is drawn, both from the Old and New Testaments, is clear. What does it mean for justice to be enveloped and surpassed? How precisely is justice "more just" where there is mercy? If justice and mercy are two parts of a single, unfolding reality, then what are the stages of that unfolding, and how are the two parts related as this single reality unfolds? Two hints in *The Name of God Is Mercy* lead me to turn to the Spiritual Exercises to provide a framework in which to place and interpret these statements.

First, when asked about the meaning and place of mercy in his own personal history, Francis refers to Gaston Fessard's classic early theological commentary on the Exercises, *La Dialectique des Exercices Spirituels de Saint Ignace de Loyola*.[20] He is interested in Fessard's account of the dialectic interplay of shame, mercy, and hope that

16. *Misericordiae Vultus*, §21, in *The Name of God is Mercy*, 141.
17. *The Name of God is Mercy*, 143.
18. *The Name of God is Mercy*, 143.
19. *The Name of God is Mercy*, 80.
20. *The Name of God is Mercy*, 10. cf. Gaston Fessard, La dialectique des Exercices Spirituels de Saint Ignace de Loyola (Paris: Aubier, 1956). For an English introduction to this text, see Edouard Pousset, *Life in Faith and Freedom: An Essay Presenting Gaston Fessards' Analysis of the Dialectic of the Spiritual Exercises of St. Ignatius* (St. Louis: Institute of Jesuit Sources, 1980).

Ignatius expects to occur when placing oneself before the Cross of Christ. This associates the experience of mercy with the so-called First Week in the Spiritual Exercises.

The second clue, to which I already alluded, is Francis's claim "that in Sacred Scripture, justice is conceived essentially as the *faithful abandonment of oneself to God's will*."[21] This statement expresses the second of two purposes that Ignatius names for the Spiritual Exercises: "the name of spiritual exercises [is] given to any means of preparing and disposing our soul to rid itself of all its disordered affections and then, after removal, of seeking and finding God's will in the ordering of our life for the salvation of our soul."[22] This suggests that for Francis, the full achievement of "justice" goes beyond conformity to a particular codification of God's will, and also includes "faithful abandonment" to that will. What is faithful abandonment, and how is it achieved? It is the fruit and goal of the spiritual life as a whole, and the Spiritual Exercises propose a set of practices to move progressively closer to it. Moreover, to the extent that the grace of experiencing mercy is central to the first stage or "week" of the Exercises, and to the extent that Ignatius insisted that, if one did not find and embrace that grace, then she or he should not continue on, we already have a rendering in this spiritual classic of the theological claim that mercy is fundamental to justice. Or, as Francis states, "Where there is mercy, justice is more just and fulfills its essence."[23] Hence, we have an initial framing of the relationship between mercy and justice.

Francis's Reading of the Spiritual Exercises as Interpretive Lens

Next, I follow these clues and explore this correlation suggested in the pope's remarks on mercy and justice, drawing from the text of the retreat given to the bishops of Spain. Before doing so, a few brief

21. Francis, *The Name of God is Mercy*, 10; emphasis added here.

22. George E. Ganss, SJ, *The Spiritual Exercises of Saint Ignatius: A Translation and Commentary* (St. Louis: The Institute of Jesuit Sources, 1992), §1, 21.

23. Francis, *The Name of God is Mercy*, 80.

words on the structure of Ignatius's exercises are perhaps in order.[24] Ignatius structures the retreat into four stages, which he names "weeks." They are distinguished by the materials for prayer proper to each but, more fundamentally, by the type of grace Ignatius has the retreatant seek during each week. During the First Week, one contemplates the death-dealing presence of sin in the world, one's own complicity in that sin, and its ultimate outcome: death and hell. The grace one prays for is shame and confusion over how many times one has deserved damnation because of her or his sins, and intense sorrow and tears for those sins.

However, the First Week is not just about self-accusation, shame and confusion, or self-loathing; for Ignatius, it involves equally the experience that, my sins notwithstanding, God is still faithful to me. Ignatius expects that I will utter "an exclamation of wonder" that I am still held in existence and given the gifts of creation; the created world continues to sustain my life; and the angels and saints still intercede for me (SE 60 and 44).[25] In other words, my sinfulness is met by God's mercy reaching out to me and sustaining me in existence—indeed, precisely, in my sinfulness. In a colloquy, or intimate conversation, Ignatius has me "extoll the mercy of God our Lord, pouring out my thoughts to Him, and giving thanks to Him that up to this very moment he has granted me life. I will resolve with His grace to amend for the future" (SE 61 and 44). Encountering both the depth and power of sin and also the deeper and more efficacious

24. For context and interpretations of Ignatius's masterwork, see the notes to Ganss's translation cited above. For a sampling of other works on this Christian spirituality classic, see David L. Fleming, SJ, *Like the Lightning: The Dynamics of the Ignatian Exercises* (St. Louis: Institute of Jesuit Sources, 2004); William Barry, *Finding God in All Things: A Companion to the Spiritual Exercises of St. Ignatius* (Notre Dame, IN: Ave Maria Press, 2009); Anthony DeMello, *Seek God Everywhere: Reflections on the Ignatian Exercises*, eds. Gerald O'Collins, SJ, Daniel Kendall, SJ, and Jeffrey LaBelle, SJ (New York: Image/Doubleday, 2010); and Katherine Dyckman, Mary Garvin, and Elizabeth Liebert, *The Spiritual Exercises Reclaimed: Uncovering Liberating Possibilities for Women* (New York: Paulist Press, 2001). Francis also refers to another commentary on the exercises by the late Cardinal Archbishop of Milan, Carlo Maria Martini, *Letting God Free Us: Meditations on Ignatian Spiritual Exercises*, foreword by George Maloney, SJ, trans. Richard Arnandez (New Rochelle, NY: New City Press, 1993).

25. In a telling echo of our theme, I should wonder that the angels, "although they are the swords of God's justice . . . have borne with me, protected me, and prayed for me?"

mercy of God, will elicit, Ignatius believes, a powerful and energizing disposition of gratitude and hope essential to an authentic choice, or election, of how to live my life.

It is only on the basis of the profound and personal appropriation of this realization, this grace, that Ignatius advises one to proceed to the Second Week, made up of a series of imaginative exercises that frame the process of discernment of the choice that will enable me more fully to seek and find God's will in ordering my life. Some exercises of that week are meant to continue the work of detecting and confronting the continuing presence of sin in my life, "inordinate attachments," in order to achieve a state of indifference in which my affective responses to the world are supple enough to be reoriented by a choice for a particular good that gradually emerges in the process of discernment of God's will for my life. Other exercises place me imaginatively with Jesus, walking with him from nativity and hidden life through the conclusion of his public ministry as portrayed in the Gospels. Generally, one asks for the grace of "an intimate knowledge of our Lord, who has become human for me, so that I may love him more and follow him more closely" (SE 104). Finally, in the Third Week one meditates on the Passion and Death of the Lord, noting how "the divinity hides itself" (SE 196) and asking for the grace of "sorrow, compassion and shame because the Lord is going to his suffering because of my sin" (SE 193) and "sorrow with Christ in sorrow, anguish with Christ in anguish, tears and deep grief because of the great affliction that Christ endures for me" (SE 203). The Fourth Week takes up the Resurrection, in which one prays for the grace "to be glad and rejoice intensely because of the great joy and the glory of Christ our Lord" (SE 221).[26]

Francis's presentation of the Spiritual Exercises follows Ignatius's advice that the exercises be accommodated to the needs and capacities of the one making them (SE 18). He spends the greatest part of his

26. Anthony DeMello notes that the graces of each week mark a gradual decentering of the one making the Exercises. The focus turns more and more from my sinfulness, my shame and confusion, my choice, to identification with Christ's suffering and then joy. The first-person pronoun gradually withdraws from the graces to be desired, which DeMello explains as the Spiritual Exercises' way of modeling and effecting the Pauline assertion that "it is no longer I who live, but it is Christ who lives in me" (Galatians 2:20). See Anthony DeMello, SJ, *Seek God Everywhere*, 141–143.

time on the exercises of the Second Week.[27] With the materials of that week, he spends little time with the contemplations on episodes from Jesus' life, devoting most of his attention to the week's less scripturally grounded exercises: the Contemplation on the Call of the King; the Meditation on the Two Standards, the Meditation on Three Classes of Person, and the reflection on Three Ways of Being Humble. Furthermore, his presentation is in the style of a "preached retreat" rather than the individually directed retreat that was originally envisioned by Ignatius, and which was only widely recovered and practiced in the last century. In the preached retreat, the different parts of the Exercises are the subject of lengthy talks, which the retreatants then take away for their private reflections.[28] In his talks, Francis evinces a clear awareness of the challenges, perils, and pitfalls that face a bishop (unsurprisingly, as he too faced similar issues for more than fifteen years prior to writing his talks). He also shows an awareness of the dispiriting prospect that a rapidly secularizing Spanish society and culture presented its hierarchy. Many themes for which the future pope would come to be known show up here: the dangers of corruption, clericalism, and spiritual worldliness; the need to pray for and cultivate a combative hope in the face of challenges facing the Church; and the importance of discernment. And, central to our theme, mercy appears frequently and prominently.[29]

That Francis associates the First Week with the experience of mercy is clear from the very outset of the retreat, as he chooses to frame the entire retreat with a reference to the Magnificat, "his mercy is from age to age": "As with Mary [he tells them,] our acts of thanksgiving, adoration and praise found our memory in the mercy of God that sustains us. With hope that is firmly rooted in him, we are

27. After a brief introduction, a chapter is devoted to the Principle and Foundation (fourteen pages), two chapters to the First Week (twenty pages), and six chapters to the Second Week (fifty-six pages). One chapter treats Death and Resurrection (Third and Fourth Weeks totaling twelve pages), and a final chapter covers the famous Contemplation to Attain Love which concludes the Fourth Week and the Exercises (sixteen pages). About forty percent of the text is devoted to the Second Week.

28. This practice began or was foreseen during Ignatius's own lifetime and became more the rule as time went on. See Joseph de Guibert, *The Jesuits: Their Spiritual Doctrine and Practice* (St. Louis: Institute of Jesuit Sources, 1994), 301–304; John O'Malley, SJ, *The First Jesuits* (Cambridge, Mass.: Harvard University Press, 1993), 127–133.

29. It figures prominently in the opening lines of his talks: Francis, *In Him Alone is Our Hope*, 9; and also 29, 33, 88, 116 (quoting James 3:17), 122, 124.

thus prepared to fight the good fight of the faith and of love, on behalf of all those entrusted to our care."[30] The itinerary of the Spiritual Exercises, as the pope interprets and presents it here, is a remembering of God's mercy (First Week) giving rise to a hope that will enable the bishops to make the difficult pastoral discernments required of them to fulfill their calling and vocation (Second Week). The activist character of his approach is indicated by the kind of hope that he has in mind, which he marks as the outcome of the retreat: "The grace of a combative hope."[31] The influence of Fessard's articulation of the dialectic of mercy, shame, and hope is also clearly evident.

There are many interesting features of the way that Francis interprets and presents the complex weave of Ignatius's Spiritual Exercises following this itinerary. For our purposes, I want to call attention to the way that he very tightly connects the First Week of the Exercises with the second. That is, instead of seeing the First Week as a stage through which we pass and then leave behind in order to advance to the Second, he presents them as dialectically interrelated. This, as I will suggest, patterns how he understands the relationship between mercy (First Week) and justice (Second Week). They are not separate stages but are internal to one another, each entailing the other.

The intercalation of the two weeks is most prominent in the chapter in which he treats the First Week contemplations on sin. He proposes what he calls a "paradoxical pattern" emerging from the Gospels:

> As we read the Gospels, a paradoxical pattern emerges: the Lord is more inclined to warn, correct, and reprimand those who are closest to him—his disciples and Peter in particular—than those who are distant. The Lord acts in this way to make it clear that ministry is a pure grace. . . . In this context of the Lord's gratuitous choice and his absolute fidelity, to be reprimanded by him means that one is receiving a sign of God's immense mercy.[32]

30. *In Him Alone is Our Hope*, 9. He also chooses this because of a document that the Spanish bishops penned. The quote from Luke 1:50 is in a passage from a document approved by the Spanish Bishops Conference in November 1999: La fidelidad de Dios dura siempre. Mirada de fe al siglo XX.

31. *In Him Alone is Our Hope*, 10.

32. *In Him Alone is Our Hope*, 29.

To illustrate this paradox, he uses what he calls "the first confession of Simon Peter" in the story of the miraculous catch of fish (Luke 5:1–11 New Revised Standard Version Catholic Edition). The context, Francis notes, is evangelization. The well-known story of the Lord teaching the crowds from Peter's boat is presented. Having completed his teaching, Jesus has the disciples put out into deep water and, their night of fruitless toil notwithstanding, has them throw their nets over one more time, only to have their nets filled to the bursting point. His commentary on what follows is worth quoting in full:

> At the sight of this prodigy, Simon Peter confesses himself a sinner. And in this very act, the Lord converts him into a Fisher of men. Conversion and mission are thus intimately united in the heart of Simon Peter. The Lord accepts his "'Go away from me, Lord, for I am a sinful man'" (Luke 5:8), but he reorients it with his "'Do not be afraid; from now on you will be catching people'" (Luke 5:10).
>
> From that moment on, Simon Peter never separates these two dimensions of his life: he will always confess that he is a sinful man and a fisher of men. His sins will not prevent him from accomplishing the mission he has received (and he will never become an isolated sinner enclosed within his own sinfulness). His mission will not allow him to hide his sin, concealed behind a pharisaical mask.[33]

This is for Francis the fruit of a genuine, graced experience of the First Week: "The Lord is the ever greater One: when he calls us to conversion, far from diminishing us, he is giving us stature in his Kingdom. From the hand of the Lord who corrects us also comes his abundant mercy."[34] This is, I think, Francis's way of taking into account the "Colloquy before the Cross" of the First Week, in which, fresh from the experience of God's faithful love and mercy even in the face of one's sin, one places oneself before the cross and asks, "What have I done for Christ?"; "What am I doing for Christ?"; "What will I do for Christ?" The experience of mercy is not just the experience of being pardoned but the experience of being "given stature in the

33. *In Him Alone is Our Hope*, 30.
34. *In Him Alone is Our Hope*, 48–49.

Kingdom of God," being given the dignity of being not just the object of God's saving mercy and love, but also its subject, making it a reality for oneself and for others. Thus, for the pope, experience of mercy without an experience of being given a mission is incomplete. On this reading of the Spiritual Exercises, the movement to the Second Week—with the Call of the King, in which one imagines oneself along the model of a generous knight called into battle by a just king, and the Two Standards, in which one contemplates the "logic" of Christ in contrast to the "logic" of Satan, the enemy of our human nature—is not something totally new but simply an elaboration of a dynamic already unleashed in and by the First Week meditations on sin, mercy, and the call to conversion. They are bridges that allow that dynamic to flow into the precise articulation of how I will respond to God's mercy, which is the subject for discernment and choice during the Second Week.

There are other ways in which Francis's presentation of the Exercises keep the First and Second Weeks tightly connected. For example, chapter 4, "The Spirit of the World or the 'Anti-Kingdom,'" looks ahead to the Meditation on the Two Standards in Week Two, yet the chapter also keeps the focus on sin and turns to the "Colloquy before the Cross" of the First Week.[35] When he begins his discussion of the Meditation on the Call of the King proper to the Second Week, he keeps the focus (rightly enough) on the way this meditation "frames the contemplations on the life of Jesus within the context of a great vocation," which refers back to his presentation of "the first call of Peter" in the reflections he drew from the First Week.[36]

Let us consider this close interrelating of the First and Second Weeks and the mutually implicatory experiences of mercy and of mission, to unpack and interpret Francis's statements about mercy and justice. He has said, "Justice and mercy are two dimensions of a single reality that unfolds progressively until it culminates in love."[37] The Spiritual Exercises map such an unfolding process, which begins with the transformative experience of mercy in the First Week,

35. *In Him Alone is Our Hope*, 51.

36. Francis, *Misericordiae Vultus*, §20.

37. *Misericordiae Vultus*, 124.

passes through the conforming of oneself with the will of God in the discernment and choice of life in the Second Week, and culminates in the Contemplation to Attain Love at the end of the Exercises, which is an active love of the "contemplative in action." Satisfying the demands of justice is the ever-renewed work of conforming one's life with God's will for oneself and for the world. This certainly requires attention to specific norms. Francis expounds, "The Church remembers the mercies of God and therefore tries to be faithful to the Law. The Ten Commandments are the juridical aspect that provides a human framework for God's mercy."[38] A graced response, as Ignatius envisions it in the Spiritual Exercises, and which Francis takes up in his retreat talks, also elicits and nourishes a discernment that is not only about applying those norms in and to the particularities of one's own situation, but of revising and extending them in response to an "ever greater God." This "ever greater God's" call to act justly is heard more clearly and more radically (in the Second Week) the deeper our experience is of the depths of God's mercy in coming to terms more radically with the power of sin in the world and in our own lives (in the First Week). The process is not one driven by guilt or by demonizing oneself or others but by the logic of gratitude and hope (as the Contemplation to Attain Love makes clear).[39] It is also a commitment to justice that never gives up on others because it comes from the experience of mercy in which I realize that God has not given up on me. In short, as laid out by the dynamism of the Spiritual Exercises, "When there is mercy, justice is more just, and it fulfils its true essence."[40]

Finally, if we use this map for thinking about mercy and justice, we avoid the problem that mercy becomes a patronizing act of condescension on the part of someone in power over the weak and powerless, which often ends up simply confirming the powerless

---

38. Francis begins his reflection on this famous contemplation: "When Saint Ignatius asks us to renew our memory of 'the blessings of creation and redemption, and the special favors I have received' (SE 234) he wants us to go much further than merely giving thanks for all that we have received. He wants to teach us to have more love" (119).

39. *Misericordiae Vultus*, 80.

40. Although Francis does not draw attention to this, what is remarkable in the story of Peter's "first call" is that Jesus does not deny Peter's confession of sinfulness in Luke 5:8; but neither does he respond with explicit words of forgiveness. The act of forgiving is implicit to the call to follow him.

in that state and viewing mercy as a kind of divine noblesse oblige. The action of mercy, as Francis describes it by tying the First and Second Week closely together, is not just the forgiveness of a debt that the debtor cannot otherwise repay, but also, and indissolubly, an invitation to participate in God's own agency in the world.[41] Mercy's pardon is found precisely in a call to agency that confers a unique dignity on the one pardoned by calling her or him to join in the process of bringing others into this unfolding process. I think that this is an important framing of what the pope means by mercy when he states that "Jesus Christ is the face of the Father's mercy. These words might well sum up the mystery of the Christian faith."[42]

Mercy and Justice in *Dives in Misericordia*

To highlight the difference made by the background of Ignatian spirituality for Francis's understanding of mercy and justice, I venture a brief comparison to another powerful expression of the centrality of mercy, this time from the Magisterium of Pope John Paul II. In his 1980 encyclical, *Dives in Misericordia*, John Paul also emphasizes that "in Christ and through Christ God also becomes especially visible in His mercy."[43] Francis's predecessor agrees as well that "true mercy is, so to speak, the most profound source of justice."[44] Yet, John Paul's mode of argumentation is quite different from Francis's. There was, in fact, a profound spiritual life that nourished the pope's interest in mercy. John Paul canonized the Polish nun, Faustina Kowalska, an Apostle of Divine Mercy, and in her memory declared the Sunday after Easter "Divine Mercy Sunday." However, her life and reflections do not appear in *Dives in Misericordia*.[45] Besides noting this difference

---

41. *Misericordiae Vultus*, §1.

42. *Dives in Misericordia*, §2: https://www.vatican.va/content/john-paul-ii/en/encyclicals/documents/hf_jp-ii_enc_30111980_dives-in-misericordia.html.

43. Francis, *Dives in Misericordia*, §14.

44. Francis does mention her in his bull: *Misericordiae Vultus*, §24. On the impact of Faustina on John Paul II, see George Weigel, *Witness to Hope: The Biography of Pope John Paul II* (New York: HarperCollins, 2001), 158, 187, 386–87.

45. *Dives in Misericordia*, §7.

from Francis, who readily cites saints and spiritual authors, the principal point I would make here is that locating the differences between the two on the relationship of mercy and justice requires us to pay attention to the role that Ignatian spirituality plays for Francis. In his explanation of the relationship between justice and mercy, John Paul is guided by 2 Corinthians 5:21, "For our sake he made him to be sin who knew no sin, so that in him we might become the righteousness of God," from which he elaborates very densely presented atonement soteriology: "In the Passion and Death of Christ—in the fact that the Father did not spare His own Son, but 'for our sake made him sin'—absolute justice is expressed, for Christ undergoes the Passion and Cross because of the sins of humanity."[46] For Francis, on the other hand, I have argued that he sets the relationship in terms of the dialectic of shame, mercy, and combative hope as the driving force of being a follower of Christ. His is a discipleship soteriology. One is saved in and by becoming a disciple, one's sinfulness and frailty notwithstanding.

This is not the place for a full-fledged comparison of these two soteriologies and the understandings of mercy and justice that arise from them. The approaches diverge but are not, at least in their main features, opposed. My point in sketching the contrast, however briefly, is that it can be done securely only by allowing the Spiritual Exercises to provide an interpretive grid for locating their differences when it comes to Francis's articulation of the theme. For example, attention to the cross is not absent from his approach, evidenced by the crucial place that the First Week "Colloquy before the Cross" has in his understanding of the experience of mercy. That being said, it is very clear that Francis does not deploy the mystery of the Cross to construct an atonement soteriology to figure the relationship between justice and mercy, as does John Paul.[47] It is also true that, while Francis is far clearer on the insistence that the grace of mercy has an

46. Francis alludes to the cross in saying that "God's justice is his mercy given to everyone as a grace that flows from the Death and Resurrection of Jesus. The Cross of Christ is God's judgment on all of us and on the whole world, because through it he offers us the certitude of love and new life" (*Misericordiae Vultus*, §21). He does not elaborate these points into an atonement soteriology.

47. On the latter, see *Dives in Misericordia*, §6: "Nevertheless, the causes of this emotion [of the father at the end of the parable] are to be sought at a deeper level. Notice, the father is aware that a fundamental good has been saved: the good of his son's humanity . . . Going on, one can therefore say that the love for the son, the love that springs from the very essence of fatherhood, in a way obliges the father to be concerned about his son's dignity."

inherent and dignifying call to discipleship, John Paul insists in his own way (by means of an interpretation of the parable of the prodigal son) that integral to mercy is a restoration of dignity to the one who is the object of mercy.[48] Francis's approach shows a far greater attention to the synoptic Gospels in comparison to John Paul's approach, which relies on Paul, at least for working out the relationship of mercy and justice. This is just what one would expect given the centrality of the Gospels to the Spiritual Exercises. Moreover, Francis aligns himself more closely to those who argue that theological claims drawn from reflection on the Cross and Resurrection have to be far more closely integrated with those drawn from attention to the life and ministry of Jesus prior to his death than they often have been in atonement soteriologies. Lastly, knowledge born of discipleship is crucial for the current pope. He has what Johann Baptist Metz has called a "discipleship Christology"—that is, one that stresses that knowledge of who Christ is has to arise from the experience of following him.

One could continue in this vein by noting that both John Paul and Francis understand attention to, and a living appropriation of, mercy to be vital if the Church is to fulfill the promise of the Second Vatican Council.[49] The differences in emphases on how they attend to mercy and propose the logic of how it is authentically appropriated could shed light on their different styles in leading the Church. Perhaps I have provided enough evidence that such a comparison is significant and, that for it to succeed on the side of Francis, one must attend to his relationship to Ignatian spirituality.

---

48. "The contemporary Church is profoundly conscious that only on the basis of the mercy of God will she be able to carry out the tasks that derive from the teaching of the Second Vatican Council, and, in the first place, the ecumenical task which aims at uniting all those who confess Christ," *Dives in Misericordia*, §13. In *Misericordiae Vultus*, Francis highlights the fact that he opened "the year of mercy" on the 50th anniversary of the closing of the Second Vatican Council, adding, "The Church feels a great need to keep this event alive." He then quotes the words of John XXIII in opening the council: "Now the Bride of Christ wishes to use the medicine of mercy rather than taking up the arms of severity" (*Misericordiae Vultus*, §4).

49. It would be ridiculous to deny that John Paul had a deep and deeply motivating spirituality, and it may well be the case that a more fully adequate account of John Paul's understanding of mercy would equally require identifying and surfacing resources in Christian spirituality integral to his own practice of theology. Minimally, though, it seems clear that he keeps the discourses of academic theology and spirituality more distinct than Francis, and this difference in style is significant when it comes to content, as I have just argued.

Conclusion

I have argued that understanding what Francis means by mercy and how he frames the relationship between mercy and justice, requires attention to his experience and interpretation of Ignatius of Loyola's Spiritual Exercises. I believe this puts him in the company of other Jesuits such as Karl Rahner and Ignacio Ellacuría, who used the Exercises to reconfigure theology in order to confront contemporary problems. This is not to claim that this is the only source of Francis's integration of *lo doctrinal* and *lo pastoral*. Nor is Ignatian spirituality the only approach in which to frame a theological response to the question of how to relate justice and mercy. Julian of Norwich's *Showings* also comes to mind as a powerful constellation of insights that move on a parallel track, and the pope's own attraction to the spirituality of Francis of Assisi in order to extend the reach of this theology beyond the merely human to include the rest of the natural world is testament to his own ecumenicity, if I might put it that way, when it comes to the beautiful array of spiritualities in the Christian tradition. I still contend that the creativity, depth, and Christian force of Francis's "theology of mercy" come from an embrace of the mystery of God's merciful response to our world's situation that is configured by his own experience and appropriation of the spirituality of Ignatius of Loyola in particular. Our own attempts to take up, extend, and correct where needed, his thought, need to take this into account. A further intriguing question is whether it might be possible to read his act of declaring a jubilee of mercy for the Catholic Church (along with the many powerful symbolic gestures by which he has incarnated the dynamic of mercy-justice) to be something like an attempt to actualize the dynamic of the Spiritual Exercises not just on the individual level but corporately, for the whole Church. This is a topic worthy of further study for which this reflection could provide valuable insights.

In Our Bones: The Spiritual Exercises and Call to Justice in Jesuit Education

Julia A. Dowd

For more than forty years, Jesuit universities have been sharing the Spiritual Exercises with staff, faculty, and students as a tool for leadership development and mission formation. Over this same period, Jesuit institutions have made a concerted effort to rigorously engage a mission of faith doing justice. As the Society of Jesus reaffirms its commitment to discernment and sharing the Spiritual Exercises in its newly ratified Universal Apostolic Preferences (UAPs), now is an opportune time to consider what we have learned over these past several decades of sharing the Exercises with college and university faculty and administration. Has the process of sharing the Exercises with colleagues had an effect on our institutions? Have the Exercises enabled our universities to be focused and bold in living out our Jesuit mission of reconciliation, justice, and inclusion?

If you are reading this article, then you likely share with me a deep desire to build robust programs and conversations promoting our Jesuit Catholic mission, identity, and heritage at our colleges and universities. This desire is heightened in these increasingly challenging times financially, politically, and existentially.[1] The COVID-19 pandemic has disrupted our university communities and nearly every aspect of human life as we know it in ways most did not imagine just

From *Conversations on Jesuit Higher Education* 58 (Fall 2020).

1. See "Reading Ignatius in Dystopia," by Michael C. McCarthy, SJ, *America*, October 1, 2018, vo. 219, no. 7, 20–24.

months ago. Our communities have erupted yet again in grief and anger over state-sanctioned violence against black and brown people, with desperate calls for racial justice. Leadership at all Jesuit institutions will be required to think in radical new ways over the next several years about what it means to be a Jesuit university, how we will participate in the social and economic recovery of our communities, and how to learn, heal, and teach with a renewed commitment to facing and abolishing racism and white supremacy.

The Universal Apostolic Preferences offer a path forward by training our eye on four priorities, the first of which, "showing the way to God through the Spiritual Exercises and discernment," is the focus of this article and current issue of *Conversations*. In response to the call from Superior General of the Society of Jesus Fr. Arturo Sosa, SJ, Jesuit provincials within the United States are asking Jesuit universities to consider ways of sharing the Spiritual Exercises with colleagues. Jesuits West provincial Scott Santarosa, SJ, asked higher education leaders to take discernment "into our bones" and "take the Exercises seriously"[2] as a tool for leadership development and decision-making in the years ahead, even suggesting that Jesuit directors of works do the Exercises with their professional teams.

There is a long precedent for this. The Spiritual Exercises have always been at the root of the Jesuit apostolic mission. Ignatius's own prayer life, his spiritual conversion, and his ongoing reflection on God's activity in his life as described in the Exercises inspired and guided the foundation and early growth of the Society of Jesus. Ignatius's reflection on his direct experiences in prayer and with the Exercises guided his personal and corporate decisions as founder of the Jesuits. Reflection on the Exercises, including faith-sharing with women, enabled Ignatius to occasionally think outside the box, beyond the social and ecclesial restrictions of his time.

In recent decades, the practice of using the Exercises to guide institutional mission has continued, a notable example being Ignacio Ellacuría's leadership of Central American Jesuits in response to the

2. From "A Family Reunion with 'Jesuit Muscle,' by Tracey Primrose, *Jesuits West Magazine*, Fall 2019, https://www.jesuitportland.org/uploaded/Principal_Blog/Pages_from_JW_Fall2019_pp12-16.pdf.

Salvadoran political and economic turmoil of the 1980s.[3] Ellacuría recognized the Exercises as a means to reflect theologically on the current historical reality, which allowed him, as rector of the University of Central America in San Salvador, to radically reconsider the role and purpose of the Jesuit university, arriving at the conclusion that the university should be a social project actively engaged in social transformation for the liberation of the poor—a decision that had prophetic consequences.

Today the Exercises remain a means through which reflection and imaginative thinking can take place to discern our mission in our current contexts and illuminate future directions. Philip Endean describes the Exercises as "a way of handling realities as yet unforeseen."[4] The Exercises have never been intended as a prescriptive or dogmatic approach to Ignatian spirituality or Jesuit identity. Quite the contrary. There is an inherent flexibility, a dynamic and responsive process that ultimately trusts the activity of God in human history as well as in the life of the institution itself. Ignatius and later Jesuit superiors set a precedent of using prayer, discernment, and reflection on the Exercises as a way of guiding not only the broad vision of the Society but also its operational, fiscal, personnel, and strategic functions. Reflection on the Exercises was a way of instilling a sense of shared mission and purpose among Jesuits and colleagues across vast distances. We have a historical and Ignatian rationale to turn to the Exercises as a resource for helping us understand our mission and our social context today.

Yet it may be easier said than done. There are obstacles to our consciously sharing faith and spiritual experiences in professional settings. First of all, it is generally considered unprofessional to do so. Secondly, we are multi-religious, multi-faith communities in which not everyone shares the same language, experience, or sacred texts, a topic that Erin Cline addresses in this issue and her recent book, *A World on Fire*. Thirdly, Jesuit institutions and the Catholic Church

3. See Matthew J. Ashley, "Ignacio Ellacuría and the Spiritual Exercises of Ignatius Loyola," *Theological Studies* 61 (2000): 16–39. See also Matthew J. Ashley, Kevin F. Burke, SJ, and Rodolfo Cardenal, SJ, *A Grammar of Justice: The Legacy of Ignacio Ellacuría* (Maryknoll: Orbis, 2014).

4. Philip Endean, "The Spiritual Exercises," in *The Cambridge Companion to the Jesuits*, ed. Thomas Worcester (Cambridge, UK: Cambridge University Press, 2008), 64.

have not always stood on the right side of history when it came to the social and racial conflicts we face today; thus, returning to our roots will be fraught with tensions requiring great humility and willingness to face our collective failings. Despite the challenges, there are some very good reasons to at least give it a try—in addition to the specific request of provincials.

Two years ago, as part of a research project, I surveyed and interviewed female-identified faculty and staff from seventeen Jesuit universities across the United States who had completed the Exercises. I asked them to reflect on their experience of the Exercises and to consider whether anything they encountered might relate to the mission of their Jesuit institution. My interest was in whether women's experiences might fill in critical lacunae in the vision and mission of Jesuit higher education, lacunae that prevent us from achieving our fullest potential as Jesuit apostolates, particularly in the areas of justice and inclusion. And if we learned something new from women's experiences with the Exercises, what else could we learn from other voices, especially from other marginalized voices, on our campuses?

Over the course of a year, I collected stories, words, and images that shed new light on our language around Jesuit and Ignatian mission. One example came when two women independently shared with me that, as a result of doing the Exercises, they recognized their university as the "beloved community." This is not a phrase we commonly use in Jesuit education, but it is one that connects us powerfully to a rich history of faith in action for civil rights and social justice. The beloved community is not the status quo whereby everyone simply gets along. The beloved community is a new reality whereby the hierarchies and systems that oppress have been dismantled, so that all can flourish and prosper. What a beautiful image brought forth through reflection on the Exercises.

Individually, the Exercises have an effect on individuals by illuminating personal biases and sinfulness, as well as pointing to individual gifts of courage and freedom. Collectively, the Exercises have an effect on an institution by improving teaching and community relationships and by prompting responses to social problems that stem from the collective wisdom of the entire community rather than from only the cultural and academic mainstream.

Likewise, the Exercises can be a tool for deepening our commitment to anti-racism work. University of San Francisco law professor Rhonda Magee, in her book *The Inner Work of Racial Justice*,[5] suggests that daily meditation and mindfulness work "will help you develop the capacity to stay with the challenges of racism as it arises in the world and strengthen your ability to work against it." There are concrete practices within our Ignatian spiritual tradition, such as the Daily Examen, that build one's inner capacity for mindfulness, courage, and freedom.

Mission officers might consider inviting individuals who have completed the Exercises to meet and reflect on their experiences. This brings more people, more voices, into the work of interpreting our sacred texts, traditions, and future directions. Shawn Copeland describes the centrality of genuine conversation in Jesuit education. "Jesuit education," she writes, "draws inspiration from Ignatius's penchant for and insistence on conversation. Conversation requires hospitality, openness, testing, revision, and discovery. Genuine conversation may lead as well to the disruption of conventional opinion, to encounter an 'other' who may change us radically. Genuine conversation lays the ground for solidarity and justice."[6] Through conversation we have an opportunity to gather the graces of the many retreats, spiritual direction sessions, prayer groups, and 19th annotation programs we have held over many years so that they may inform our communal, public, and official discourse on mission. I learned that the Spiritual Exercises and reflection on the Exercises can lead us to:

- Thinking outside the box.
- Examining unexamined implicit biases.
- Working through creative tensions.
- Discovering new paths forward beyond our current imaginations and perceived possibilities.
- Breaking through social and ecclesial tensions—often by giving individuals a stronger sense of their own voice and freedom.

---

5. Rhonda Magee, *The Inner Work of Racial Justice: Healing Ourselves and Transforming Our Communities Through Mindfulness* (New York: TarcherPerigee, 2019), 37.
6. M. Shawn Copeland, "Race, Class and Gender in Jesuit and Feminist Education," in *Jesuit and Feminist Education: Intersections in Teaching and Learning for the Twenty-first Century*, edited by Jocelyn M. Borczyka and Elizabeth A. Petrino (New York: Fordham University Press, 2012), 130.

- Engaging depth of thought and imagination.
- Sharing stories and discovering a particular narrative as an institution.
- Recognizing collective experiences of Cross and Resurrection, for ourselves personally and for our communities.

Christopher Pramuk writes, "For Jesuits and laypersons alike, the spark that sets our common vision aflame is freedom itself, personal and communal, sustained by grace, centered in the heart, and the desire to join our freedom with others in a story larger than ourselves."[7] This engagement with suffering, this authentic empathy with the excluded, the poor, the suffering of the world is what in my view gives Jesuit education its teeth; this is what keeps us distinct. The Exercises, and shared reflection on the Exercises, provide one way in which we begin to recognize the suffering of the world not as a *they* but an *us*, which is at the heart of the Universal Apostolic Preferences.

Over these weeks I have seen that our practice of "showing the way to God through discernment with the Exercises" was our hard-wired response in the midst of unprecedented crises. It is in our bones. Amid the coronavirus pandemic and the killing of George Floyd and others, Jesuit-educated students and institutional leaders have shown up in creative and unprecedented ways to express support, solidarity, and love to one another and to build community across distances. In the midst of panic and fear, our students, faculty, and staff turned to our spiritual foundations, sought comfort and guidance from Ignatian prayer and texts, led Examens on YouTube and prayer services on Zoom, stood up for the most vulnerable in our communities, and presented creative innovations to maintaining community with our students, faculty, staff, and alumni spread far and wide. It makes me prouder than ever to be engaged in this work and more convinced than ever of the value of Jesuit education. In these uncertain times, I find consolation and hope in our future.

---

7. Christopher Pramuk, "The Emergency of a Lay Esprit de Corps: Inspirations, Tensions, Horizons," *Jesuit Higher Education* 8 (2): 21–36, 2019, 21.

Something I Never Thought About: Jesuits as Plastic Surgeons?

Ryan Mak, SJ

Throughout my four years as an undergraduate pre-med student, and my seven years as a Jesuit walking the path to become a physician, I never considered a career in plastic surgery. Like most, I have been influenced by media portrayals (i.e., the TV show *Nip/Tuck*) in thinking that plastics (as it is referred to in the medical field) primarily consisted of wealthy and privileged individuals spending a large amount of money to look "beautiful."

It was new territory this past December during my third year of medical school surgery rotation when I found myself spending one month as part of the Plastic and Reconstructive Surgery team. As someone planning to go into work as a surgeon, I was blown away by the incredible advances in medicine, and, in particular, what we as humans can do in the operating room to fix injuries and appease disease. I worked long hours, usually from 5:00 a.m. to 7:00 p.m., seeing patients in the hospital and spending hours upon hours in the operating room (OR). I love the hands-on work in the OR, and, debunking my stereotypes of plastic surgery, I discovered that ninety-five percent of our cases were non-cosmetic, meaning there was a medical necessity for the surgery.

I assisted with bilateral facial lacerations in a fifty-five-year-old Polish immigrant who had his head caught in machinery at work. I witnessed the removal of a cancerous mass and reconstruction of a

From *The Jesuit Post*, March 23, 2021.

seventy-year-old man's ear. We even performed an eyebrow lift on an eighty-year-old Catholic priest who had to push up his eye every time he read a book due to complications from a prior skin cancer surgery.

However, one surgery I discovered was our team's "bread and butter"—the one we did most commonly: breast reconstructions. When I entered the Jesuits and expressed interest in going to medical school, my thoughts centered around a desire to use my academic abilities in the health sciences and serve God's people. However, performing breast reconstructions was not exactly how I pictured it playing out. Once again, our God is one of surprises, gracing us in ways we least expect.

The plastics team often worked with the surgical-oncology team to treat women with breast cancer. First, a woman would have a significant portion of her breast removed (mastectomy) and then have silicone implants placed with surrounding tissue and blood vessels to reconfigure the breast. These are significant procedures, usually taking up to five hours, and often our surgical team did multiple breast mastectomy and reconstruction surgeries each day.

One day I saw one of our returning breast-cancer patients in the outpatient clinic. The attending physician closed the door. She asked a few questions to see how the patient was doing, and then began to unwrap the forty-year-old woman's dressings from around her chest. As I stood there watching, the patient looked at me and said, "I'm sorry, it must be terrible for you [a guy] to have to see this ugly chest."

I was stunned but responded quickly, "Oh my gosh, no, of course not. There's nothing to be sorry about."

The attending chimed in too: "Don't be ridiculous, you are beautiful." But as I stood there watching the rest of the patient visit, it hit me: *Here was a relatively young woman whose life was not only completely altered by a cancer diagnosis, but also a significant part of her physical identity as a woman was taken away.*

Her voice dominated my prayer that evening. I felt a hint of the shame that filled her voice when she spoke to me with doubts about her own beauty and physical appearance. I prayed that she not only be physically healed from cancer and the surgical scars on her chest, but also that she experience a deeper healing—one of inner peace and love. It struck me then: A plastic surgeon can be a powerful mediator of God's healing. The plastic surgeon has the ability to repair the superficial wounds while also having the opportunity to attend to a patient's deeper emotional and spiritual needs that come from our embodied human experience.

At the beginning of the Spiritual Exercises, Ignatius invites us to pray about our principle and foundation as people living on this earth. All things were created to glorify God and serve souls. There is no aspect of life that is exempt from God's grace. There is no human endeavor that cannot be used for Christian service and for the greater glory of God.

While I may personally struggle with accepting how much society and media influence a definition of beauty and attractiveness, this experience also helped me realize just how deep a physical wound can cut. I am grateful for this reminder that God's people are everywhere and that the moments in which we mutually connect with God have no limit.

Although I am not planning to pursue a career in plastic surgery (my heart is in orthopedic surgery), perhaps one day there will be a Jesuit plastic surgeon repairing skin and soft-tissue cuts, rebuilding ears and noses after major accidents, and even performing breast reconstructions all while reminding a patient what I believe God would want to say: "Don't be ridiculous, you are beautiful."

Catholics Need to Learn How to Deal with Disagreements. St. Peter Faber Can Help.

Alex Hale, SJ

There is evidence that American Catholics are just as influenced, if not more so, by partisan politics than their Catholic faith on a number of hot-button issues.

According to Pew Research, 56 percent of Catholics are in favor of legal abortion in most cases and 53 percent of Catholics are in favor of the death penalty. This is despite years of emphasis by Church leaders on the sanctity of life from conception until natural death. This dynamic has influenced not only people's positions on given issues but also the way they treat folks on the opposing side.

In January 2021, Fr. Casey Cole, OFM, released a video titled "Fight Abortion. Don't Lose Your Soul Doing So." In the video, Fr. Cole adheres to Church teaching, acknowledging that abortion is wrong and must be opposed. He argues, however, that following Jesus is above any political or social issue.

He called out some on the political left who he believes "care more about immigration than the church. Care more about preserving the environment than their enemies, care more about justice in this time, in this place, than they do in trusting God's eternal justice." He also criticizes those on the right who have replaced Jesus with the issue of abortion as the defining mark of the Catholic faith.

From *The Jesuit Post*, March, 2021.

His message is simple, prophetic, and blatantly Christian: Jesus Christ is the most important thing in our lives. Everything else comes after our love for him and his love for us. Yet, Fr. Casey was attacked so much for his video that he had to release another video to respond to the hate mail and death wishes.

The critics of Fr. Cole appear not to have given him the benefit of the doubt but reacted to the video without actually watching it (Fr. Cole says that 40 percent of viewers didn't make it past the first minute of the video). The vitriol commenced, but minds were not changed. The nasty comments by those attacking and, as Fr. Casey has pointed out, those defending him did not contribute to a meaningful discussion where people's views were changed or challenged in any legitimate ways.

If these reactions are so strong over content that isn't even against Church teaching, then it would appear that there is no hope for the work of changing hearts and minds. How can we possibly evangelize non-Catholics if we spend so much time shouting at each other on social media?

We can find a model in St. Peter Faber, one of the founders of the Jesuits and, according to St. Ignatius, the best person to guide people through the Spiritual Exercises. Faber spent a good deal of his ministry in places that were heavily Protestant. He quietly worked and converted thousands back to the faith. He was not known for his arguments or for his brilliant takedowns of Protestant theology. Yet, he was still able to convert massive numbers of people.

How did he do it? The answer is simple: He loved those he talked with.

Faber realized that people fell away from the faith not necessarily because of good arguments (though those play a role for sure). Rather, he wrote, "They are led astray not so much by the teaching and seeming good of the Lutherans as by the wickedness of those very ones who should be examples of zeal."[1]

Why would someone want to stay or become Catholic when they saw the hypocrisy of priests living in opulence during Faber's time? Why would someone want to become Catholic when Catholics are

1. W. Bangert, SJ, *To the Other Towns* (Newman Press, 1959).

publicly messaging each other that they are "jealous of the angel that will get to throw their opponent into hell?" This display of hatred is a major reason people run away from the faith. Faber understood that the core of our faith is the love of Jesus.

Faber understood that the anger against the Church and God came from a place of pain. There is a story of Faber meeting a priest who had become a Protestant. The priest began yelling at Faber about what was wrong with the Church's position on married priests. Faber let the man rage before acknowledging him and then moving into a deeper spiritual conversation. After a while, the man was so moved by the fact that Faber did not return his anger with anger that he opened up about having a mistress. The man found himself in tears. He promised to repent of this sin and come back to the Church. Here is another lesson we can learn from Faber: Once an individual is able to address God how they have made mistakes without the fear of being hated, their relationship with God begins to heal. The same can be extended to those who feel hurt either by the Church or by their perception that God has abandoned them. Once there is an outpouring of love in response, hearts become soft, and people desire to follow God more closely.

The Church is meant to be a unifying presence in the world. We are meant to encounter as many people as we can and to love as many people as possible. It is possible for us to have differences of opinion in how the Church and our society function, but let's remind ourselves that following Jesus is the most important thing.

How Ignatian Spirituality Enhanced My Cognitive Behavioral Therapy

Thanh-Thao (Sue) Do

In 2015, I became depressed during my transition to a new university after three years of attending my local community college. As a disabled Vietnamese student whose parents escaped Vietnam to seek better opportunities in the United States, I was raised in a faithful home where my educational pursuits were the expected way for me to contribute to the family.

Living away from my home was a new experience for me. I missed my parents' home cooking, my local parish, my choir friends. Most of all, I missed the familiarity of the local eateries in San José, where I have lived since I immigrated to the United States.

I have dealt with language barriers, adjusting to a new country and making new friends. But the primary challenge of moving to my new school came from my cerebral palsy, which requires me to use a wheelchair at times. At home, I moved easily around town and had assistance from my friends and family. The streets of my new cities of Oakland and Berkeley were filled with unfamiliar faces and crowded with cars.

Don't show your emotions. Be strong, I told myself.

One day, as I was crossing the street to get to my class, a red car zipped by so fast I was seconds away from getting hit. Later, as I made my way back to my apartment, I found myself battling a wave of exhaustion. I fumbled for my iPhone and dialed my dad. Three rings

From *America*, July 30, 2021.

later, his tired voice answered my call. "Hello?" I forced myself not to cry. *Don't show your emotions. Be strong,* I told myself. "I want to go home, Dad. I'm tired."

Home is where the heart is, right? But where is God? After giving myself a moment to pause, I asked my dad to call the paramedics for me.

A few minutes later, the paramedics arrived and took me to the ER. Like a scene out of *Grey's Anatomy*, several doctors asked me endless questions. I mumbled my answers, mostly in a dazed state of mind. They diagnosed me with a panic attack and then transferred me to another hospital when I started exhibiting symptoms of suicidal ideation. In that moment of stress, I was emotionally blind and could not see the purpose of living.

After coming out of this ordeal, I ended up deciding to leave Berkeley and move back home to San José. I remember wheeling myself with my dad into an advisor's office and picking up a pen to scribble my signatures on the medical leave documents. The moment of truth came as I sat with the acceptance that I needed to practice better self-care and compassion before taking on new endeavors. It's okay not to be okay. God doesn't judge you.

This moment of truth also led me to two tools that helped me practice self-care and compassion: therapy and Ignatian spirituality. Over time I realized I could deepen my own spirituality and self-acceptance with the practices of a 16th-century saint combined with the techniques of modern psychology. *It's okay not to be okay. God doesn't judge you.*

When I met my therapist, she spoke to me briefly in Vietnamese. I was shocked because she did not look Vietnamese. I mustered up the courage to ask her about her background, and I found out she was half-Vietnamese. She had lost both of her parents as a child and learned Vietnamese in her upbringing by her grandmother. *Ah, God, this is what you were preparing me for.* Her speaking in my mother tongue felt like a warm hug.

I opened up to her about the difficulties of school, but mostly about how I always seemed to feel anxious about my expectations as the eldest daughter in a Vietnamese Catholic family. I grew up attending

Mass and following my dad to his weekly Saturday catechism classes. These were followed by Vietnamese language immersion classes. I felt the need to be a great example for my siblings.

Ah, God, this is what you were preparing me for.

Gently, my therapist asked me what I wanted most in life. I grew quiet, and after a few minutes of silence, I responded, "I want to be peaceful in my heart and mind." She asked me what peace meant to me. The question made me reflect on how I dealt with my trials previously. As a child I was taught the Hail Mary and the Our Father as part of our nightly family rituals of prayer and petitions for safety and protection. Like any other young child, I was guilty of dozing off halfway through long homilies. *Am I a good Catholic?*

I sat in my therapist's well-lit office every two weeks, processing my need for self-care along with my role as an immigrant daughter in a religious family. My therapist made eye contact with me, at times nodding and validating my feelings. When I finished my conversation with her, she reminded me of the grounding techniques of using my five senses to focus on being present and feeling gratitude.

My year-long break from school allowed me to rest and take walks on the grounds of Our Lady of Peace Church in Santa Clara. As I walked slowly up to the big statue of the Virgin Mary, I bent down with my eyes closed while the cool wind blew around me. A wave of calmness washed over me as I felt tears dripping from the corners of my eyes. Silently, I asked her for guidance about which school to transfer to.

After applying again and with careful discernment, I transferred to Santa Clara University, where I met many Jesuit mentors and friends from Christian Life Community groups. Fr. Manh, the CLC director, guided us each week with conversations and themes of Ignatian spirituality for different stages of our lives. Most of all, these weekly meetings gave me new friends to accompany me through my joys and sorrows.

In the five steps of the Examen prayer of St. Ignatius, I found the "reviewing of my day" to be a crucial part of my resilience and recovery. Facing my struggles and talking to God about them through journaling is similar to confronting my distorted thoughts through cognitive behavioral therapy techniques. Positive affirmations are similar to the awareness of one's needs and asking for graces in Ignatian spirituality.

Ignatian spirituality and the Examen prayer joined the rosary and petitionary prayers as parts of my own path to God. I discovered that I can experience God's love in all things. I developed a new habit of finding God in the little moments throughout my days. On breaks from classes, I would ride in my wheelchair while the cool wind blew in my face. Every day, I would grab my phone out of my pocket and snap as many pictures of the sun and clouds as I could.

As the sun emitted its light, I felt God's presence through the warmth. The white clouds fascinated me as they shifted shapes. I marveled at the gift of nature, of God's creation.

Reviewing my day and observing moments led to new appreciation of the stillness amid the chaos and constant distractions from my never-ending busyness. In these realizations, I found God to be a friend rather than the judgy father figure I had imagined as a child. He carried me with the grace of patience rather than the usual impatience that contributed to my anxiety.

Each breath I inhaled and exhaled became the movement inside me. The movement of the spirit calmed me down in the stillness of the day. The prayers became a mantra that I focused on. The distractions became more like pebbles than rocks, much easier to overcome.

It occurred to me: St. Ignatius must have created the Examen as a form of spiritual cognitive behavioral therapy.

When I spoke with my therapist, she did not deny my struggles; rather, she listened and comforted me. She acknowledged that my struggles were valid and gave me the tools to change my distorted thoughts. In those sessions, I sometimes broke down in tears—a very natural part of my recovery process—but those tears have surprisingly helped me find God by allowing me to release my anxiety. Letting go is an ongoing process that I constantly strive to practice.

These acknowledgements from my therapist are similar to how I utilize the Examen to help me recognize God working in my daily life. While my therapist sat down physically to help me process my feelings, I have also learned to recognize God by becoming aware of the happenings of my days. God is present the whole time, and I had not realized it until I experienced the gift of slowing down. He is in control.

Mental health is seldom talked about in my home due to the cultural barriers between me and my parents' generations. However, I have learned that every living human being has a yearning to be understood at the deepest levels of ourselves. We are all broken in some ways, and no one is perfect. I have found that God loves me despite my brokenness. He is patiently waiting for me to come to him.

Through the gift of encouragement from my psychotherapist and the Examen prayer, I have embraced my healing journey as one that, like the Jesuit motto, *Ad Majorem Dei Gloriam*, glorifies God by finding him in all things and seeing him in the good, the bad, and the little moments that make me aware of how I can improve myself each and every day. He walks with me no matter what I am going through, and I am grateful for that.

Story Standards

Eric Clayton

There's a line from Peter Jackson's 2001 film adaptation of J. R. R. Tolkien's *The Lord of the Rings: The Fellowship of the Ring* that's always stuck with me: "But they were, all of them, deceived, for another Ring was made."[1] Brief as this line is—and easily missed, as it's part of a longer prologue sequence—this sentence captures the stakes of the entire trilogy. Because the people of Middle Earth were deceived, because they didn't know the whole story, pain and suffering resulted.

On screen, we watch as rings of power are made and distributed to all the key players of Middle Earth: the Elves, the Dwarves, and the Race of Men. These rings represent influence, clout, prestige, and they bestow great power. We are led to believe they've been appropriately distributed. For whatever reason, these rings seem to reflect an agreed-upon order of things, how Middle Earth is organized and governed, how the inhabitants of Middle Earth make sense of their lives.

But they were, all of them, deceived, for another Ring was made.

This deception is quite literal in *The Lord of the Rings*. Sauron made another ring, told no one about it, and amassed unimaginable amounts of power and influence as a result. The rest of Middle Earth went about their days assuming they understood how the various rings of

From *Cannonball Moments* (Chicago: Loyola Press, 2022).

1. Spoken by Galadriel in the prologue of the film.

power would influence their lives and livelihoods, but they were wrong. They didn't have all the information. They didn't know that the scales were tipped against them and had been from the start.

And thus, our heroic Hobbits appear on the scene to destroy the One Ring and make things right.

Stories help us see truth: in ourselves, our communities, and our world. But stories can also be used to conceal truths, intentionally and unintentionally. Stories can be used to maintain a status quo that's based on a lie. If we think we know about all the rings, then we tell stories that reflect that knowledge. But if we know there's *another* ring and that we're all potentially in danger as a result, then our stories should point that out.

Much in the same way that we may not realize the privileges we enjoy and how they affect the stories we tell about ourselves and others without doing some deep, personal reflection . . . we may also fail to see the structural, cultural, and systemic injustices that make up the world around us. And if we fail to see those problems, we are doomed to repeat—even praise—them in our stories.

This chapter aims to provide a framework through which we can assess how larger, systemic issues are impacting our stories, and it offers a way to tell stories that act against these harmful systems. To do so, we'll reflect on the Two Standards, a pivotal meditation from Ignatius's Spiritual Exercises. Again, as we attempt to answer the question *Whose am I?* in our storytelling, we're invited deeper into the realities experienced by people different from ourselves.

Here's another example, taken from our own time and place: social media. I've taught courses in social media to undergraduate students, and I always begin the semester with an easy icebreaker: Tell me your name, what you study, and why you're in this class.

"I took this class because I want to be a YouTube star."

I remember doing a double take at the young man who had spoken. "Oh, really?" I replied, eyebrows raised. "Say more."

"Yeah. I've been working on my channel, building up my subscribers. You can make a lot of money on YouTube." He was a tall kid, loud, confident. He earned himself a few glares from around the room and perhaps a few admirers.

I nodded. "You can," I said, wondering if anything in my syllabus would help this aspiring YouTuber rake in his hoped-for millions.

For the majority of my students, the role social media can and should play in their professional and personal lives is assumed; it's taken for granted. The question isn't *if* they'll use it; it's *how.* How might I employ this tool for my personal gain? After all, no one takes a filmmaking course and questions the use of a camera. And yet what I try to get my students to grapple with over the fifteen or so weeks we're together is that social media isn't just a tool; it's an ecosystem. It's a cultural force. You don't just make use of social media in the same way you might make use of a camera. The camera can't use you back.

I remember one young woman from a different semester. She was quiet, sat near the back. And her answer on that first day had something to do with her Instagram account. She wanted to become an influencer, someone others looked to for advice, tips, and life hacks, and she saw Instagram as her ticket into that world. She had already amassed a number of followers, and her account looked clean, well-curated, and overall, professional.

This semester happened to kick off right after the Dolly Parton Meme Challenge went viral. Dolly Parton had created a square graphic, split into four parts. Each quadrant held a different image of Dolly. Underneath each image was written the name of a different social media platform: LinkedIn, Facebook, Tinder, or Instagram. Each picture of Dolly was distinct: some risqué, some professional, some fun and casual. They more or less matched the visual experience a user would expect to find on the social media platform listed beneath the image. The Internet loved it, and countless users—famous and not so famous—spent the next few weeks making their own.

This became our topic on that first day of class. I asked my students to talk me through how they'd approach the Dolly Parton challenge.

Attending that class were aspiring influencers and brand managers and students who were already interning in the world of social media. These weren't amateurs.

"Facebook is where most of my family is," one said. "So I'd post a photo of me with my friends doing something I wouldn't worry about others seeing."

"Yeah," another student weighed in. "This is where I'd post stuff I'd want my mom to see." Everyone laughed, agreeing.

"Now, Instagram," the first student continued, "that's where my friends are. That picture would be me being cute, doing something cool. Like at a party or something. And Tinder—well, that photo would probably be—"

That's when I held up my hand. "Don't tell me anything I don't want to know," I said.

We went around discussing images, what was appropriate and what wasn't, depending on the platform in question. "So, do you have different identities on these different platforms?" I asked.

"Well, yeah," several students replied.

"Does that trouble you?"

"No," that first student chimed in. "That's just what you have to do. You have to act a little differently depending on what platform you're on."

"But who's the real you?" I pressed. "Where does the real you come into play?"

That was when the students averted their eyes, scratched their heads—thoughtfully, I guess—and hoped I wouldn't call on them. It was a good enough place as any to wrap up the first class.

Weeks later, I was grading the first assignment. It was a reflection paper, and students were tasked with thinking about their own relationship to social media. Did anything about it give them pause? What might they hope to work on? Were they happy with how they related to and through their social media channels? They were supposed to connect their thinking to something we'd discussed thus far in class.

The quiet girl who sat in the back and hoped to be an Instagram influencer wrote about the Dolly Parton Meme Challenge and our subsequent class discussion. Despite that well-curated Instagram feed—all those pretty pictures—she confessed to not really knowing who she was, who she was trying to represent on Instagram. She didn't know how to express her true self. She was under such pressure to share only pretty pictures, images that would convey the kind of life she was creating. It was all a fiction, though. The images on her feed didn't represent who she really was, and she didn't know how to process the feelings she had about the highly selective—and increasingly dishonest—process of becoming the influencer she thought she should be. She felt like she was losing sight of who she actually was and who she was becoming.

She committed herself to trying harder to be more honest with herself as the semester continued. But I don't know if she succeeded. Because the very nature of social media—the ecosystem so many of us are forced to play in—is powered by clicks and likes and comments, and if you fall out of favor, which can happen quickly and decisively, it can be all but impossible to claw your way back.

And so, if your identity, your income, and your relationships all depend on that kind of constant affirmation, constant recalibration to the changing whims and algorithms of the system, you can understand how a person might get lost. But you can also see how this system works just beyond our realm of understanding: Who changes those algorithms and why? What impact does it really have, and who does that impact serve?

This kind of systemic dependency is not limited to social media. Think of your own life. Think of the various systems of which you are a part: a belief system, an economic system, an education system, a media ecosystem. Are there assumptions that go unchallenged? Do you feel pushed to do things, to make decisions based on how the system works? Is that good for you, your family, your community?

Our stories are tied up in these systems. That's not inherently a bad thing. But, as in the case of my students, sometimes we lose ourselves in these systems; we forget who we *actually* are and what makes us unique.

One thing I never talk about in my communications classes is the downward mobility of Christ. There are several reasons for that, one being that I don't teach in the theology department of a Jesuit school, and another being that, well, it's kind of a bummer.

This downward mobility, reflected in the Gospel, speaks to how Jesus set his priorities. He's unconcerned with possessions or wealth; he doesn't even have a permanent home. He constantly pushes aside any honors or praise, often telling those recipients of his miracles to quiet down, hush up, say not a word of whatever healing powers have been revealed. And, of course, the great paradox of the Crucifixion: Jesus, the Son of God, exerts no power or influence over his captors but simply allows himself to be led to his death, exposing the cruel violence embedded in the structures of his society and embracing nonviolence, a tactic so often used by those who have no power, no force to call upon to save the day.

Poverty, rejection, and humility: These preferences mark the way of Christ. St. Ignatius, in *The Spiritual Exercises*, even goes so far as to encourage us to pray for these things in our own lives, if God so wills it. Why? Not simply for some masochistic endeavor. Rather, if we are constantly prioritizing this downward trajectory, this antithetical path to all that the world so often calls us to, then we find ourselves more able to see through the fog, hear through all the noise, and pinpoint exactly where we are being tempted to go astray.

I wish I could talk about these things in my courses more frequently, because I think in many ways this downward path is the answer to what that quiet, would-be Instagram influencer was looking for: a radical rejection of the narrative that beckoned her forward, dangling likes and shares and retweets as though they were salvation itself.

Failing to recognize the role these systems play in our lives without our even realizing it means we can never truly become who we are called to be. Rather than heal, we haphazardly place Band-Aids.

I think, for example, of the young Black man living in fear of the criminal justice system in the United States, a fear that, as a white man, I simply do not share. The system looks differently at me than it does at him because of the centuries of prejudices and biases that have become so ingrained in our way of thinking that it takes work even to see them. The neighborhood I live in, the security net I rely on, the network of friends and colleagues I enjoy, and the way society sees me—all these things contribute to a system where I am seen very differently from my Black counterpart.

And yet, how do I extricate myself from this system? Is it even possible?

Our stories must grapple with these larger forces. We ask why things happen to us and our neighbors. And we point to that why . . . as a way to understand what values—good, bad, and ugly—are being promoted in our society. As we find our way through our own stories, through the stories we share with and about others, we must point out these unseen forces and the impact they have. Is our society living up to the values it professes to hold dear? As we practice prophetic listening—as we hear the hurt experienced by others—we may find that we are pointing not just to the hurt, but through it to the systems in our society that continue to poke at the wound.

St. Ignatius gives us a powerful reflective tool as we attempt to navigate these problematic systems, and it's built upon the downward mobility of Christ. At the end of the Second Week of his Spiritual Exercises, the retreatant is asked to meditate on what's called the Two Standards.

Imagine a great battle between the forces of good and evil, of Christ and the enemy. Imagine these two opposing forces represented by standards—flags, of a sort—upon the field of battle. You know which side you represent based upon which standard you stand beneath.

The Standard of Christ is represented by those three virtues of downward mobility: poverty, rejection, and humility. Harsh words, but definitive ways in which to map the trajectory of our lives. Do we pursue only our own benefit, whether through ever-increasing wealth, status, praise, power, or privilege? Or do we set those things aside in favor of others and their needs? Do we allow those more self-centered things to get in our way, to guide our lives, to serve as the North Star of all our decision-making? Or do we put Christ's mission of peace, justice, and reconciliation first and foremost?

The enemy's standard is the opposite of Christ's standard. It is represented by riches, honor, and pride. The one who stands beneath this standard seeks out wealth above all else, is obsessed with his or her reputation and status, and is always mindful of ways to gain power and influence over others.

We might simplify the difference in the Two Standards as this: Am I seeking my own benefit, or am I seeking that of others?

When it comes to storytelling, these questions are much the same. Do I tell stories to draw attention only to myself, my own work, my own accomplishments, or do I use my platform to shine a light on others, their needs, and their gifts? Do I manipulate and make use of others' voices, or do I allow them to speak for themselves? Do my stories challenge the status quo, or do I go along to get along, to maintain my comfortable position, income, and follower count?

In *The Fellowship of the Ring*, we experience the moment the wizard Gandalf has his worst fears confirmed: The ring in Frodo's possession *is* the One Ring, that great source of evil and suffering. I imagine Gandalf did some soul-searching in that moment. Here he'd known—or at least, suspected—that Bilbo, Frodo's uncle, had long had a ring of power in his possession. And Gandalf had done nothing about it. Here he was now, witnessing the slow, painful destruction of Middle Earth, and he'd had it within his power to stop it all along.

And now that the truth has been discovered, when Frodo tries to give Gandalf the ring, he refuses. He fears that he would succumb to the ring's power. He fears he would bring even more harm to Middle Earth. What he can do, though, is accompany Frodo on the path to the ring's destruction.

Perhaps that interpretation of Tolkien's work is incomplete, but in reflecting on Gandalf's character, I wonder if we can't see something of ourselves. We look out at the world, and we know things aren't quite right. Certainly not as God intended. We see racial injustice and the destruction of the environment. We see war and disease and hunger. We see corruption and the accumulation of unfettered power and wealth.

And yet, for so many of us, we get along just fine. Things could be better, sure, but things are good enough in our immediate circles. The larger systems haven't hurt us, not directly, not too much, at least. We turn a blind eye, as Gandalf did, to the rings in our midst.

If the outbreak and global spread of COVID-19 has taught us anything, it's that we're much more interconnected than we ever realized. And while our stories start in the deeply personal—who we are, what we believe to be important—they necessarily expand to include others, set against the backdrop of God's whole creation. If everything and everyone are connected, then how can we not point out those dangerous rings when we find them? How can we not, in our stories, highlight the fractures in the larger systems, the harm they will inevitably do?

The image I have in my mind is that of an otter covered in oil. Think of it: When you see a picture of an otter in oil, do you say, "I hope that otter gets cleaned up" and walk away? No, you're more curious than that. We ask how he got dirty—why is he covered in oil? Was there an oil spill? Are there other otters out there covered in oil? Have we found them? What about the other animals? What about that part of the ocean? How do we prevent this from happening again—and why did it happen in the first place? This otter's story is not a singular event; we find him in a larger context. And we want to know all the factors in play.

It's the same with us, with our stories, and with the people we meet. The Two Standards help us know if we're on the right track.

If we set aside our desire for wealth, we may not concern ourselves with telling sensational stories that get a lot of clicks, a lot of likes, and a lot of commentary. Instead, we're free to tell those stories that need to be told: true stories. We aren't beholden to the preferences and priorities of those holding the purse strings. We uplift the voices at the heart of the story, unafraid if some may find those voices too challenging.

If we set aside our desire for honors, we free ourselves from the affirmation of the masses. We aren't beholden to the changing whims of our followers but can speak truth to power, and we can call people to be their best selves through our stories rather than settle for the lowest common denominator.

And if we set aside our pride, we won't be forced to create a fictional version of ourselves. The stories we share can be truthful, accurate representations of the joys and challenges of real life. We don't need to filter out images that are unflattering. We don't need to constantly check our phones to see if anyone has said something new about our work. And when we inevitably make a mistake, we can admit to our failure and move on. We can tell a new story.

Ultimately, this kind of storytelling is healing for all of us.

An Exercise in Ignatian Storytelling

Opening Prayer

I desire the grace to clearly see systems and structures that perpetuate harmful narratives and to identify how I might contribute counter-cultural stories.

Prayer Text

Filled with the Holy Spirit, Jesus returned from the Jordan and was led by the Spirit into the desert for forty days, to be tempted by the devil. He ate nothing during those days, and when they were over he was hungry. The devil said to him, "If you are the Son of God, command this stone to become a loaf of bread." Jesus answered him, "It is written, 'One does not live by bread alone.'" Then he took him up and showed him all the kingdoms of the world in a single instant. The devil said to him, "To you I will give their glory and all this authority; for it has been given over to me, and I give it to anyone I please. If you, then, will worship me, it will all be yours." Jesus said to him in reply, "It is written, 'Worship the Lord your God, and serve only him.'" Then he led him to Jerusalem, made him stand on the parapet of the temple, and said to him, "If you are the Son of God, throw yourself down from here, for it is written, 'He will command his angels concerning you, to protect you,' and 'On their hands they will bear you up, so that you will not dash your foot against a stone.'" Jesus said to him in reply, "It is said, 'Do not put the Lord your God to the test.'" When the devil had finished every test, he departed from him until an opportune time'" (Luke 4:1–13).

Reflection Exercise

- I put myself in the story. When the evil spirit comes to me, what am I tempted with? What riches? What source of power? What tug at my own ego?
- I think of the many systems of which I am a part: cultural, religious, economic, racial, etc. Are there aspects of these systems that pull me toward wealth, honors, and pride? Are there aspects that pull me toward poverty, rejection, and humility? How do I respond?
- As I consider my response to the previous question, I begin to recognize the larger narratives at play, the stories I've been told and that I tell myself, that I hear others tell to condone certain behaviors. What stories might I tell in response?

Conversation

I hear God whisper those words—*poverty, rejection,* and *humility*—in my heart. I share how they make me feel. I share, too, my struggle to make sense of Christ's standard in a world that hardly seems cut and dried, a world filled with nuance. How do I move forward? How do I avoid paralysis?

Journal

Write the words *poverty*, *rejection*, and *humility* on a piece of paper. Under each, note moments in your life—in your story—that exemplify the given word. How might these moments help others pursue Christ's downward path?

III. Freedom and Discernment

Part III Introduction

In his "Crash Course on Ignatian Discernment," included in this section, Mark Thibodeaux points out that discerning God's will in an Ignatian manner involves contending with a variety of movements and spirits within us. While Saint Ignatius often meant for these principles outlined in this brief introduction to be applied to larger, more consequential decisions, Thibodeaux reveals how paying attention to the process of making smaller decisions, and seeking insight from trusted companions, can help us to know whether we are in a good position to make important decisions, or whether more time and a better disposition is needed. Indeed, there is a presumption in Ignatius's approach to the spiritual life that, although certain approaches and principles regarding prayer, discernment, and decision-making will in most cases prove most effective, sometimes one's circumstances, or the movement of the Holy Spirit, will eventually lead one in another—and perhaps unforeseen—direction. This is apparent in the fact that the Spiritual Exercises do not just propose one way, but many, through which authentic discernment can come about.

The essays that follow in Part III bear that out. Gemma Simmonds reminds us that, though our tendency in speaking of Ignatian discernment might be to focus on "big" decisions, within such decisions always lies a series of smaller choices that have the potential to reiterate, refine, or reshape the initial decision, and that the everyday decisions can lead to both positive and negative turns. One might describe this as the "discernment of spirits" on a smaller scale. She calls it "becoming who we are."

Becoming who we are is rarely done in isolation and is indeed a lifetime project. Increasingly, practitioners and researchers of Ignatian spirituality seek to explore how principles of Ignatian discernment can be used by groups seeking a way forward in missional or institutional contexts, and in different life vocations or stages of life. Issued shortly after his election at General Congregation 36, Jesuit Superior General Arturo Sosa outlines the ways in which the principles of communal discernment applied by the Society of Jesus most prominently at an event like a congregation can and should be used more broadly by both Jesuit communities and apostolates to fulfill their missions more effectively. Of course, these principles could be employed in a variety of collaborative contexts, extending beyond the Jesuit world. We see often enough how rash decision-making by institutions affiliated with the Church cause unnecessary hurt and anger that might have been avoided with more time spent in prayer and attention to the movements of the Spirit. Hung Pham offers additional insight into these roots of communal discernment by reflecting on how he experienced basic principles from the Spiritual Exercises at work in General Congregation 36.

Turning to a different kind of communal discernment, Eileen Burke-Sullivan explores how Ignatian principles might be incorporated into decision-making within the context of marriage. Barbara Lee, in a chapter from her book of the same name, "God Isn't Finished with Me Yet," explores how discernment continues even toward the end of one's life, not only with regard to the many anxieties of those years but also in reflecting upon and discerning the future of one's "spiritual legacy."

Mark Mossa, SJ

A Crash Course in Ignatian Discernment of Spirits

Mark Thibodeaux, SJ

In this section, I present a "travel pack" of information on Ignatian discernment. I cover just the basics.

Ignatian Discernment: What Is It?

Practically every minute of our waking day, we are making decisions: most of them really small, and some of them far-reaching. We know that even the small decisions add up to define who we are and what we are doing with our lives. The problem is that we tend not to take the time and trouble to discern our paths. Instead, we let circumstance and our unconscious emotions (especially our fears and desires) decide for us. All of us are guilty of DUI, so to speak—we are driving under the influence of movements within us of which we are hardly even aware.

This is the genius of St. Ignatius: He knew that God can be found in all things, but he also knew that we cannot find God in every decision unless we consciously seek God out. Thus, Ignatius challenges us to explore the movements within us that are leading us to lean one way or another. I know that I'm drawn to option B, but why?

Excerpt from *Ignatian Discernment of Spirits for Spiritual Direction and Pastoral Care: Going Deeper* (Chicago: Loyola Press, 2020).

What movement inside of me draws me that way? If I don't take the time to ponder that question, I may well choose option B for all the wrong reasons.

Inside all of us is a movement away from God and God's plan. There is also a movement toward God and God's plan. Ignatius calls the inner pull away from God "the evil spirit," whereas he calls the inner pull toward God "the good spirit." Our task in discernment, then, is to determine whether it is the evil spirit or the good spirit that is drawing us toward one option and away from another.

How Do We Identify the Various States of Being?

When we are in a mood of listening to the evil spirit—when we are "driving under the influence" of the evil spirit—Ignatius says that we're in desolation. Today, when we say, "I'm in bad space right now," we often mean that the evil spirit has gotten hold of us and we're struggling not to follow it. When we are in a mood of listening to the good spirit—Ignatius calls this consolation—we say, "I'm in good space." Sometimes when we are in desolation, we are well aware of it, but other times we're convinced that we're in good space—that we're doing the right thing—when in fact we are moving away from faith, hope, and love. In these situations, the evil spirit has played a double trick on us: It has drawn us away from God's plan for us, and it has also convinced us that we are on the right path. This state of self-deception is what Ignatius calls false consolation.

And so, we ask ourselves, "Which spirit is moving me? What is my spiritual state of being—my spiritual 'mood'? Am I in consolation? Desolation? Or false consolation? How can I tell?" Obviously, it is not always easy to know what state of being we are in at any given moment. There is no foolproof way of knowing, but we can look out for a few signs that might indicate the state of being in which we find ourselves.

Detecting Consolation

Among the telltale signs of consolation, two stand out as most important:

- **Being "in sync" with God and God's action in the world.** Do you have a strong sense of the presence of God in your life at this moment? Do you have a sense of God's will for you, and does it come fairly naturally for you to do God's will? Do you feel as though God and you are in a groove together? Does it feel like God and you are dance partners and no one is stepping on toes? Do the wise people in your life who know you well also believe that you're tapping into God's will and following God's lead at this moment? (This last question helps prevent false consolation.)
- **Having great desires for faith, hope, and love.** Do you sense in your heart a strong desire to do the most loving thing possible in this situation? Do you have genuine care for the people you live and work with, including the difficult people? Are you hopeful and faithful? Are you optimistic? Do you have a sense that God is going to help you sort everything out and that it'll turn out fine in the long run? Do the wise people who know you well also believe you are acting out of sincere faith, hope, and love? (Again, this last question helps prevent false consolation.)

Here are other characteristics of a person in consolation:

- **Experiencing peace and tranquility.** In consolation, you may well be experiencing turmoil, anxiety, or stress on the *surface*, but even in the midst of the emotional challenges of your life, there is a *deep down* tranquility—a sense that God is present and that all will be well. Consider the famous words of Psalm 23: *Even though I walk through the valley of the shadow of death, I will fear no evil, for you are with me; your rod and your staff comfort me.*

Note that the psalmist is on a terrible journey . . . valley (bad!) . . . shadow (worse!) . . . death (worst of all!). On the surface, it is an emotionally trying time. But deeper down, the psalmist is comforted knowing that God is near. “I fear no evil for you are with me.” The psalmist, despite being in a valley, is in consolation.

- **Being transparent with [your spiritual director] and with trusted loved ones.** In consolation, you are naturally more inclined to be open about your behaviors and your inner life. Even if you’re a bit embarrassed about some things in your life, your peace and tranquility give you the courage to say what you need to say to those whom you trust. And your desires for faith, hope, and love lead you to pursue spiritual growth, even at the expense of embarrassing yourself.

Detecting Desolation

Ignatius tells us that desolation is simply the opposite of consolation.[1] Therefore, the telltale signs of desolation are the opposite of those described above.

- **Being “out of sync” with God and God’s actions in the world.** You are in desolation when you don’t have a strong sense of God’s presence in your life. It isn’t necessarily a crisis in faith—you aren’t necessarily doubting the existence of God. But you just can’t seem to feel God’s presence. It feels as though God is distant. Wise people in your life are telling you that you seem “out of sorts” or that “you are not yourself lately.”

1. Fourth Rule of the First Week.

- **Having a lack of desire for faith, hope, and love.** You feel unmotivated to do the right thing. Maybe you're still more or less behaving like a good Christian, but interiorly it feels as though you're just "going through the motions." You feel spiritually lethargic, depleted, apathetic.
- **Experiencing disquiet, fear, and inner disturbance.** When you are in consolation, you may well be feeling emotionally challenged—in a valley of the shadow of death—but deeper down, you are at peace. In desolation, you feel a deep-down disquiet, regardless of how things are going in your exterior life. You feel deeply anxious, upset, alone, or threatened. Or maybe you just feel surly, crabby, or cranky.
- **Lacking transparency.** When in desolation, you are guarded, unforthcoming, closed—even with those you love and trust. You are less willing to open your heart to your director or to your loved ones. You find yourself dodging questions and avoiding vulnerable conversations.

Detecting False Consolation

The trickiest state of being to recognize is, of course, false consolation. It's tricky because on the surface it looks and feels like consolation. Your actions and inclinations seem loving and hopeful. You feel like you are in sync with God. So how would you discover "serpent's tail"?—as St. Ignatius once called it.[2] These are a few telltale signs (pardon the pun):

- **A very subtle rebelliousness.** You are a tiny bit cheeky with the people around you. You are not quite as open to constructive criticism or to exploring the possibility that

2. See Sixth Rule of the Second Week. In Fleming, "Draw Me into Your Friendship," *Institute of Jesuit Sources*, 1996, 262.

you are being misled at the moment. You might start to act in subtly rebellious ways—a rebelliousness that you yourself do not pick up on.

- **Secrecy, or at least a lack of transparency.** You are not as forthcoming with your account of all that's going on in your life—your emotions, reasonings, and behaviors. You might even avoid coming to see your director or consulting your spouse. This, as opposed to a person in consolation, who might say, "I really want to keep this to myself, but I probably should tell you everything. So here goes . . ." or "I feel strongly that I am doing the right thing, but I want to know what you think about it."
- **A reversal of past good decisions.** For the most part, subsequent good decisions will be a progression from past good decisions. God will not capriciously lead you from one direction to another. God leads you on a discernible trajectory. Sometimes false consolation can be determined by the unusual reversal of course that you seem to be making.
- **A false urgency.** A person in false consolation often feels compelled to act dramatically and quickly despite the fact that the wise and loving people in your life believe there is no rush and that it would be better to spend more time discerning before acting. You lack Ignatian indifference—the spiritual freedom—either to act on this immediately or to hold off for a while, as opposed to a person in true consolation, who might say, "I feel intensely drawn to this right now, but I don't need to rush. I can pray and deliberate a while more if need be." As already stated, the person in false consolation who does not receive affirmative reactions from trusted advisers and loved ones might then start to act in subtly rebellious ways.

Once We Have Identified the State of Being, What Should We Do Next?

When you are in *consolation*, you have "the good spirit as your counselor," so you can trust your spiritual instincts. Because you are in sync with God, you can move in the direction you feel inclined. If you feel it best to wait and discern some more, you can trust that instinct, too.

Desolation, however, is trickier. Ignatius says that a person in desolation has the evil spirit as his counselor. So you can't trust your gut. You're going to have to use your instruments to fly the plane rather than rely on your own perceptions. Here are five things you should do:

- **Name the desolation** and articulate its characteristics. Half the battle is won when you have correctly diagnosed the problem.
- **Avoid making important decisions or sweeping judgments** about yourself, other people, or about your present situation.
- **Lean more heavily on your support network.** Visit your "elders" more frequently. Consult your spouse or good friend. Seek out professional help through books, counselors, and the like.
- **Be firm with the evil spirit.** Don't allow yourself to engage in unhealthy or sinful behaviors. Don't "check out" of life-affirming activities. Force yourself to think and act out of hope and optimism, even if you don't feel very hopeful or optimistic. Do not let your prayer routines slip. If anything, increase them a little bit in order to spiritually fortify yourself (but only a little bit, otherwise you might experience burnout, which will only exacerbate the problem).
- **But be gentle on yourself.** Meanwhile, don't think harshly of yourself and don't beat yourself up for mistakes or for feeling low. Treat yourself to some wholesome and enjoyable activities like going for a hike, listening to good music, or watching an uplifting movie.

As already stated, *false consolation* is the trickiest state of all. If you're truly in false consolation, you won't know it, so you won't follow my or anyone else's advice! I'll say only this: If you have loved ones who are wise and reliable, why don't you trust them when they are warning you that you might be deceiving yourself? Do you really think that you're above self-deception? Why not consider the possibility that you've taken a wrong turn and haven't noticed? Take a sober and honest look at yourself, pondering the telltale characteristics of false consolation that are stated above. Play the devil's advocate by building a case against your supposed consolation. Might your loved ones be right? If you begin to suspect that you have been in false consolation, then treat it as the desolation that it is. Follow the five instructions above.

Discernment: Becoming Who We Are

Gemma Simmonds, CJ

Pope Francis often talks of "discernment." It is not only the engine of decision-making in the synodal process throughout the Church, which begins next month—it is vital to living and choosing well in our everyday lives.

From the moment we wake up to the moment when we fall asleep, we are making choices, some of them trivial and incidental, others involving the building up or deconstructing of good or bad habits that may have a significant impact on the rest of our lives. How we choose to live our daily lives, even in the small details, can play a major role in how we either grow into the fullest version of who God created us to be, or dwindle and diminish into a shell of that person.

Few people get out of bed in the morning and idly decide to get married, start up a company, commit a murder, or cheat on their partner. Both positive and negative decisions are usually the cumulative build up over time of smaller choices that might appear insignificant in themselves. We make our major life decisions in linear time, on a particular date, but we also go on constantly reiterating and refining or reshaping these decisions as we grow and change. We make decisions and then spend time growing into them. Many of us make life promises without any real notion of what the living out of those promises might entail. Only time and experience teach us what we have taken on. We live in a permanent state of becoming, so that the more we live, the more we become the person we are in the process of turning into.

Originally appeared in *The Tablet*, September 25, 2021.

In the book of Deuteronomy, Moses presents the people with a stark choice: Will they choose to live in relationship with God (life and prosperity) or will they go their own way (death and adversity)? He urges them to "choose life" (Deuteronomy 30:15–20). Believing in God does not give us a safe package deal on how to live a trouble-free existence, but faith gives us the assurance that the Holy Spirit is at work within us and, by nature, we have the capacity to make choices that are in tune with the mind of God.

One word for getting things into better focus is *discernment*. It is a way to practice making choices in small things so that listening for the voice of the Spirit becomes a habit of awareness and reflectiveness, which will serve us well when it comes to the bigger choices and the general orientation of our lives. The COVID-19 pandemic has pulled many people's lives apart in ways that were experienced as shattering and destructive. But while this has had lasting and devastating consequences, it has also provided some opportunities for rebalancing lives that had become oppressive in subtle ways.

How do we develop a capacity for discernment? Making well-discerned choices generally requires a regular habit of serious prayer and reflection; it also requires the ordinary human elements of adequate information: weighing reasons for and against a particular option, and confirmation over time. A discerning person needs to be equipped with self-knowledge, self-acceptance, the ability to integrate dreams and desires with the reality of the lived context, and the validation that comes from sharing these thought processes with wise and trusted friends and companions.

In discernment, our desires matter. An image of God that tells us we are not allowed to have desires of our own will not help us make good decisions, any more than will our using God to legitimize whatever our plans may be. Finding out what we truly want and being willing to engage with those desires can be a challenge, especially if we are not used to connecting with our desires. Equally, we may find ourselves being invited to let go of certain dreams and desires if they have become rigid and compulsive.

In the garden of Gethsemane, we see Jesus afraid, not wanting to die. He admits this to himself and his Father but places himself trustfully into the Father's hands. Paradoxically, this handing over of his own will leads to the freedom and authority that he displays through his entire trial and Crucifixion. If our desires matter, then our questions also matter; whether they be practical/informational questions, without which we cannot make a well-grounded choice, or our own inner questions, denoting a level of uncertainty or misgiving. A key part of discernment is to know what lies at the heart of our questions. Are there fears and anxieties there, an inability to let go and walk forward in trust? The fact that we are uncertain does not always carry negative implications. It may be that, in our heart of hearts, we don't want to make a choice that has been wished on us by others or by circumstances. If we have not been used to having our own desires taken seriously, we may need to find courage to admit to ourselves that we have preferences. If we have always been used to being the decision-maker, we may need to become more sensitive to the unspoken hopes, fears, or objections of others.

Having adequate information and reliable self-knowledge are crucial aspects of making trustworthy decisions. But sometimes we have to make a leap of faith based not on rational thought so much as intuition. In this sense, we need to learn to take our instincts and intuitions seriously. If we have had a "sort of feeling" over a long period or recognize a pattern of orientation that persists toward a particular choice, it is worth exploring this as the guiding light of God's Spirit. It may also be worth taking our dreams seriously in this context as they reveal from our unconscious mind hidden desires or fears that can be essential data in our decision-making. We may also need to pay attention to unadmitted negative feelings. Reason and imagination are not opposites: They are different faculties of the mind that enable us to get in touch with responses to God's grace; both are affective and the fruit of careful consideration.

Our body must also be taken seriously in a process of discernment. All sense experience is data for discernment, and most of it comes to us first through our bodies, which can be a source of

God's Revelation. Even our language tells us something important about the wisdom carried by our bodies. When we talk about being "unable to swallow" something, "feeling choked up" about something, or something "being a pain" or "giving us a headache," we may be speaking figuratively but also revealing a point of tension within the physical self that reveals unresolved conflicts and anxieties to which the conscious mind is not yet attuned. All of this needs to be taken into account if we are to make reliable choices.

However hard we try to discern according to the promptings of the Holy Spirit, time and experience may prove that we were mistaken in our judgment in a given instance. It may simply be that circumstances are beyond our control and we cannot make "the right choice"; we can only make the least bad choice. Sometimes we gain greater wisdom from our failures and mistakes than from our successes. This, in its own way, is a form of discernment, when we learn to put our trust in God, whatever the outcome.

Confirmation of a choice made can be found in the Scriptures and in the doctrine and moral teaching of the Church. It can also be found in the wisdom and experience of the faith community or that of family, colleagues, and friends. It takes courage and inner freedom to face the answer, but we can ask ourselves what the most frequent criticism is when we receive it.

Other factors can be obstacles to good discernment. Poor physical or emotional health might suggest that we need sufficient rest and relaxation or recovery time to enable us to pray and reflect seriously. The aftermath of a major loss or bereavement, or the breakdown of a significant relationship, is not a good context for making choices and decisions that require inner freedom. It is important that we take our emotions seriously before engaging in discernment. We may have formed attachments or compulsions that prevent us from exercising freedom of mind and will. This is also important when it comes to having rigid attitudes, whether they be patterns of religious thinking or prejudices to which we cling. We may have become disconnected from feelings and memories that make us feel uncomfortable, or we may have got out of practice in using our imagination. This will make the charting of our affective responses difficult, as will being dominated by fears and anxieties or social and cultural factors that make it hard for us to think broadly.

The development of a discerning heart happens over a long period of time. Some people enter retreat or a time of discernment with the express purpose of coming to a momentous decision. Sometimes it turns out that they are not so much coming to a decision as coming to accept and acknowledge a decision already made, though that news has not yet reached their brain. It is often best not to focus on the decision itself but to "park" it in a corner, where it can be acknowledged and treated with respect but not made the sole focus of attention. When the time is right, the choice often emerges organically, without having to become the focus of a specific or separate process. It's as if the decision creeps up on us and makes its presence felt without us having noticed that we are making it.

To Allow the Creator to Deal Immediately with the Creature

Hung T. Pham, SJ

To assist the retreatant in maximizing the space of personal encounter with the divine, the author of *The Spiritual Exercises* recommends two points. First, for a greater disposition of oneself to receive graces and gifts from the divine, Ignatius insists that "an exercitant will achieve more progress the more he or she withdraws from all friends and acquaintances" so as to "live in the greatest possible solitude . . . alone and secluded" (SE 20).[1] Second, Ignatius encourages retreatants to enter the Exercises "with great spirit and generosity toward their Creator and Lord" (SE 5 and 22). Both points aim "to allow the Creator to deal immediately with the creature and the creature with its Creator and Lord" (SE 15 and 26). Note, too, that the first point is focused on the external, the second on the internal. The first is about withdrawing, the second pertains to engaging.

The experience of attending General Congregation 36—which included being present in the aula—engaging in processes of discernment and decision, and benefiting from the insights of so many learned and holy men—taught me how such a privileged space of divine encounter had been incorporated into our highest form of governance. The experience of a general congregation can represent a concrete model for how to extend a similar space in our Jesuit apostolates and communities. It requires courage and generosity.

From *Studies in the Spirituality of Jesuits*, September 1, 2017.

1. *The Spiritual Exercises of Saint Ignatius*, trans. and ed. George E. Ganss (Chicago: Loyola Press, 1992).

When I entered the aula for the first time, I was sobered by the spartan ambiance and minimal decor. I saw no portraits or statues of Ignatius or the First Companions. In the middle of the room, there was only Jesus on the Cross. There were, however, four painted panels by the Slovenian Jesuit Marko Ivan Rupnik. Now, typically, Rupnik's mosaics depict biblical figures in bright colors. But these four canvases were relatively minimalistic. There were no detailed figures, only a few, simple brush strokes descending on an opaque background. Each panel also contained a phrase from scripture or from Jesuit spirituality, but depicted so abstractly that they were difficult to read unless one looked closely.

But then I understood that the purpose of these canvases was to provide a mysterious space of encounter. One banner read, "for in this tent, we groan, longing to be further clothed with our heavenly habitation" (Corinthians 5:2). The other banners seemed to hint at how the participants of the congregation might engage each other, and the directions in which that engagement might focus. One read, *En todo amar y server* ("In everything, to love and to serve"). Another contained a verse from the first letter of John (4:8), reminding participants of the foundation of Christian faith: "Whoever is without love does not know God, for God is love." The fourth panel seemed to remind the congregation of the one principle and foundational direction: *a su divina majestad* ("to his divine majesty").

The process of electing a new superior general well exemplifies how a congregation allows the Creator to deal immediately with creature. Even after having deliberated among ourselves for four days, and even after having sought to be informed by those who are capable of supplying good information—the period known as the *murmuratio*—members were expected to attend the Mass of the Holy Spirit and to receive communion on the day of election.[2] I was furthermore surprised to hear that we should make no decision until

2. Constitutions [697].

we had entered the aula and been locked into the place of the election, and again, that we should withhold our decision, and cast our votes, only after having observed one hour of silent prayer.[3]

Pope Francis's address to the congregation was another occasion of leaving space for the Creator. In an off-script remark, he noted that "initiating processes is different from occupying spaces. The Society initiates processes and leaves spaces. This is important. Other religious occupy spaces, the monasteries. The Society initiates processes." Here, I believe that the pope was locating the unique charism of the Society within the long history of Christian religious life. In the beginning, the desert fathers and mothers encountered the divine in barren wasteland. Later, monasteries provided a communal locale for monks to encounter God. Still later, mendicants extended the place of encounter to include cities and universities.

But Ignatius was convinced that an encounter between the divine and the individual takes place in the heart of every individual. For Jesuits, the encounter makes one free to be sent anywhere in the world to labor in the vineyard of the Lord. For that reason, Jerome Nadal told Jesuits that "the world is our home."

Since Jesuits are not supposed to limit themselves to any one space—that space being either physical or emotional—we encounter God anywhere and everywhere, in ever-changing landscapes under the guidance of the Holy Spirit. Thus, Pope Francis continued his remarks, that the "rules of thinking with the church are not to be read as precise instructions . . . [they should not be used] to justify a controversial point, but rather to open up space in which the Spirit could work in his time."

The members of General Congregation 36 explicitly confirmed that God took the initiative in allowing us to encounter him directly and immediately. Decree 1, "Companions in a Mission of Reconciliation and Justice," was inspired by the First Companions' failure to find passage to Jerusalem. Having recognized their powerlessness, they committed themselves once again to be men of prayer, seeking divine guidance as to where they should go. In a similar way,

3. *The Constitutions and Complementary Norms of the Society of Jesus*, ed. John W. Padberg, SJ (St. Louis: Institute of Jesuit Sources, 1996), 337–38.

the decrees of the GC 36 engage the space created for Jesuits by God, who has called us to share in the divine service. In return, we might imagine the creation of new spaces with and for others. Like construction workers who labor in the background to repair and improve city streets and highways, the 36th General Congregation likewise provides the Society a vital infrastructure of Ignatian discernment: the means to allow space for the Creator to deal immediately with the creature.

Maintaining the Tension: Freedom, Commitment, and Discernment

Eileen Burke-Sullivan

In the last century, Karl Rahner wrote:

> One thing remains certain: God can and will come directly to the [person] whom he has created; the [human], his creature, will know him truly when this happens; he will be aware of the sovereign power of God's freedom in his life, a freedom which cannot be computed—philosophically, theologically, nor existentially, nor dictated by human intelligence from appropriate arguments. This very simple and yet in reality stupendous conviction . . . seems to me to be the core of what you today usually term my spirituality.[1]

Pedro Arrupe, General of the Society of Jesus in the last third of the 20th century further asserted:

> Communion among us reflects the divine *koinonia*, for God wanted to bind us to himself in love, for a mission given to us, under obedience, not only as individuals but as sharers together in an apostolic conspiration proceeding from him. The union that exists among us follows a

An earlier version of this essay was published in *The Way*. October, 2004. Vol 43, #4.

1. Karl Rahner, *Ignatius of Loyola. Historical introduction* by Paul Imhof. Trans. Rosaleen Ockenden (London: Collins, 1979), p. 13. Originally published in German as *Ignatius von Loyola* (Frieburg im Breisgau: Verlag Herder, 1978). Rahner places himself in the mind and mouth of St. Ignatius by attempting to interpret Ignatius's key insights in the context of modern concerns and post-Vatican II faith sensibilities.

> divine pattern. The unification that the spirit brings about in a community proceeds from that very unity which operates in the heart of the Trinity.[2]

These texts from Rahner's and Arrupe's writings on the spirituality of St. Ignatius offer entry points into the heart of the dialectic that arises between the distinct human experiences of freedom and commitment. At first blush, in a postmodern cultural context, the terms *freedom* and *commitment* seem to describe opposing existential realities. Two brief narratives might illuminate that cultural sensibility. Earlier this year, in a theology course with college freshmen, a lengthy discussion on the nature and experience of freedom took place in my class. In the midst of the discussion it became clear that the young people, who were for the most part living without close adult supervision or directive guidance for the first time, felt some uneasiness about the demands of choices that were being placed upon them, but they were also strongly resistant to the notion of those choices being limited in any way. They recognized that long-term commitments were frightening and held the power of happiness or misery. They were also quite aware that one or another choice led them to further choices while simultaneously closing off some of the possibilities they now had. They wanted some help—even someone to "tell" them what to do about these multiple and often interwoven strands of choice—but they resisted giving up any of their perceived power of determination. The evident outcome of this confusion in their own thoughts and feelings caused a kind of paralysis for them. In effect, the very banquet of choices undermined their capacity to choose and thereby realize their freedom. When I suggested that one way to work through these multiple decisions was to determine to whom or to what they felt they owed a level of primary commitment—God, country, family, moral values, etc.—many of them reacted as if stung. Many of them felt that the very idea of a prior commitment framing—limiting—their choices caused a denial of their freedom to

2. Pedro Arrupe, SJ, "The Trinitarian Inspiration of the Ignatian Charism" [1980], 98f.: *Legacy* 133.

choose. Furthermore, a number of them stated that they could think of nothing and no one that they were so committed to as to be willing to suffer for, much less give their lives for.

They were willing to concede that freedom, once instantiated in a contingent being, a mortal creature, is no longer absolute. They actually felt the very contingency of their genetic make-up, social setting, and economic resources among an array of other limiting factors. But they were clearly afraid of establishing other permanent limits on their seemingly limitless choices.

Working with slightly older students in another setting brought the foundation of this somewhat generalized fear into clearer focus. I was invited to participate in a weekend program for sophomore women who were looking for some help toward decision-making, specifically around their declarations of a major course of study. When asked to assist, I was also instructed to consider the reality of a whole host of decisions that university students are being forced to make and offer some guidance toward a method of decision-making. In the small group discussions with the women, what emerged from their comments was a deep and abiding fear of making important decisions badly—with possible lifetime consequences. They had observed this reality in others and in some cases were victims of poor choices by their own parents. Even with this experiential background among them, it was evident that their decision-making skills were negligible, and it was even more evident that reflection on possible contexts for good decision-making was lacking.

Western secular culture has provided an extraordinary array of possibilities for young men and women, especially young men and women with access to material wealth and education. What secular culture alone cannot or seemingly will not offer is a context of life-giving commitment(s) that makes the task of competent decision-making reasonable and possible.

What becomes evident in the dilemma of the young people I am working with today is that giving up a certain level of freedom through commitment to key life-giving relationship(s) is the ground or context of realizing freedom; and realized freedom opens up and leads to the possibility of further authentic commitments. It is this character of dialectic between these seemingly opposing movements that must be understood if any real decision-making process can be undertaken. In this sense I am not speaking of a Hegelian dialectic whereby the opposites are subsumed into a synthesis but rather a sustained polar tension that at one time or the other seems to pull a person first one way and then another. It is the maintenance of the tension that protects the reality of each pole. In this case, freedom without the seeming curtailment of commitment is an abstraction rather than a reality; and commitment without freely chosen assent from among possibilities is a lie—it is not commitment but enforcement or slavery.

It is obvious from the writings of Ignatius that, after important conversion experiences, his spiritual awareness became firmly grounded in a commitment to the Trinitarian God. His pursuit of freedom then emerged and flourished in the context of that commitment. Contemporary studies on the Spiritual Exercises nearly uniformly agree that the purpose of the preparatory meditations on the Principle and Foundation is to ground an exercitant in a conscious commitment to God before undertaking the process.[3] If a loving commitment to God is not secured by a preparatory graced experience of God's prior love, then the Exercises of the First Week may very well not provide the internal ground for the appropriate graces of self-knowledge as loved—saved and repentant—sinner, leaving the exercitant less free than before. Similarly, without these graces it would be impossible to enter upon the decision-making process accomplished within the context of a committed personal relationship to the human/divine Jesus that is the locus for graces of the Second Week.

Following the wisdom of the Exercises, when one's responsive and fundamental commitment to God and to God's purposes is deepened, one also experiences the deepening of the interior freedom to pursue the intention of God—which is the exercitant's greatest joy and peace. It is only through the love exchanged in the committed

---

3. Virtually all commentators since the 1960s stress the importance of an expressed love and reverence that flows from a received grace of God's overwhelming mercy, as the appropriate diagnostic for one's readiness to engage the Spiritual Exercises, at least in their entirety. There is historical evidence that Ignatius was unwilling to lead Peter Faber into the Exercises for some time because this grace was not manifest in his experience.

relationship with God that knowledge of God's merciful intention can be experientially ascertained. This remains true not only in the context of the Spiritual Exercises formally undertaken, but also in the whole life of the person who pursues this spiritual wisdom as a way of growth into genuine personal fulfillment.

What appears less obvious about Ignatius's wisdom, but can be deduced from his own development, is that his spiritual experience of freedom is also grounded in his commitment (in faith and service) to the Church and subsequently in his commitment (in fidelity and companionship) to the Society of Jesus. Simply put, the more committed he becomes to specific human relationships in relationship to God, the greater his ultimate freedom to make choices toward a lifetime of joy and peace.

It is evident in his story that some level of commitment to the institutional Church antedated his real commitment to God. The *Autobiography* attests that from his youth Ignatius had deep and abiding loyalty to persons and institutions beyond himself, for whom (or which) he seemed even willing to die. But it is also evident that his commitment to the Church was realized in the form of social, familial, and cultural loyalties, bound to some degree in patterns of sin and self-aggrandizement rather than an informed, personal commitment to the mystery of the Church. Whatever the mix of motivations, however, Ignatius's commitment to the Catholic faith was deep enough and true enough to provide the horizon and the categories that made his availability to God's grace possible after the Battle of Pamplona.

Once Ignatius turned his life over to God, in a real way, his commitment to the Church, as God's instrument, became the context for realizing his freedom. Once other students at Paris began to recognize that their own best futures lay in companionship with him in his enterprise of God's glory through service of the Church, his personal freedom became interwoven with theirs. In one way his freedom seemed to be more limited, but in another way, it opened to a whole new horizon of choices, heretofore not possible for him as one person alone.

It seems possible to assert at this point that discernment—that is, the practice of discovering the best choice for oneself among an array of choices—is the negotiation of a graceful path between freedom and commitment. Based on Ignatius's insights, discernment is the discovery of one's greatest hope for happiness and peace within one's "providential life setting" that is the matrix of human possibilities, human commitments, and other contingencies of ordinary life given by God in the first instance.[4] This greatest hope for happiness and peace is grounded in the discovery of God's desire for each person and the liberating power of God's Spirit to overcome the forces of evil that operate within the human experience to blind, deafen, and defeat one's capacity to choose through multiple forms of fear.

Thus far, I have not suggested anything new or startling about commitment, freedom, or decision-making from an Ignatian spiritual context, but the data, arranged in this category of dialectic between freedom and commitment, leads to one possible conclusion that may be somewhat less unanimously agreed upon, which is the real point I want to make in this short essay: In contemporary Western circumstances, most genuine discernment, even so-called personal discernment, needs to take place within realized committed relationships rather than individual contexts or settings. In nearly all instances this would necessitate communal rather than private discernment processes. One could go so far as to say that theologically it may be necessary if we take the revived consciousness of the communal character of Trinitarian life, and of the Church, seriously.[5]

I couch this assertion in tentative terms because it seems to fly in the face of the practice of discernment by many disciples of Ignatius's method. Even if Ignatius himself, however, seemed to come to know God in a rather privatized setting of the cave at Manresa—and here one could question just how much his interaction with people during those months gave a real context for his prayer and discernment that is not precisely recorded—is it not probable that the post-Enlightenment, twenty-first century Western culture demands

4. I owe this language and some of these insights to a long-time friend and colleague, Fr. Thomas Swift, SJ, formerly of the Missouri Province and now deceased.

5. There is an extensive bibliography of theological writing being done at present on the retrieval of the analogy of communion as a way of penetrating the mystery of the Trinity. See, for example, Catherine LaCugna's text *God For Us* (New York/London: HarperCollins, 1991) as one among many. Since Vatican II nearly all ecclesiologists have focused on the communio-character of the Church—even if that term does not mean exactly the same thing in all of the studies. See for example Dennis Doyle's *Communion Ecclesiology: Visions and Versions* (New York: Orbis Books, 2000).

an adjusted context? For one thing, contemporary Western culture expects a certain parity between men and women, among employers and employees, and even between parents and children that was not the case in the sixteenth century. While Francis Borgia may have been able to discern his future—and also determine that of his ten children—without consultation with family or friends, the same did not seem to be true for Isabel Roser or the other women who sought to follow Ignatius.[6]

Not only are sociological role differences a case in point, but, perhaps more importantly, the personalist orientation of contemporary moral theology from the Magisterium requires some serious reflection on the ethical appropriateness of attempting to make a genuine discernment of God's desire outside of some deliberation and co-discernment with those whose lives will be deeply affected by the outcome. It seems obvious that vowed religious in communities claiming Ignatian spirituality as their source would undertake all significant discernments communally rather than privately.

Since I do not have more than consultative experience with vowed religious, however, the examples I would prefer to consider would be the communal discernment of couples and possibly children in a marriage, or members of lay faith communities such as CLC or Ignatian Associates, ministry work groups such as school faculties, administrative teams, etc. As long as a group or institution professes an Ignatian spiritual base and is built on some level of personal commitment of the participants to the life and work, then genuine effort needs to be put toward enacting decision-making through discernment that allows key actors some voice in the process.

For the purpose of briefly exploring the implications of this reflection, it might be helpful to consider two disparate examples of different levels of commitment.

6. One of the best resources for some data about this cultural disparity among those who Ignatius directed in the Exercises is *The Spiritual Exercises Reclaimed: Uncovering Liberating Possibilities for Women*, by Katherine Dyckman, Mary Garvin and Elizabeth Liebert (New York: Paulist Press, 2003).

Sustaining the Dialectic of Freedom and Commitment within Marriage[7]

Doug and Martha met as young professionals after college. Doug had spent a year in the novitiate of a religious community, determined that he did not have a priestly or religious vocation, and had gone back to school for an advanced degree in his field of study. Martha was employed as a Catholic campus minister at the large state university where Doug enrolled. In early summer, shortly after she met Doug but before they began dating, Martha decided to fulfill a long-time dream and make a thirty-day Ignatian retreat at a Jesuit retreat center only about an hour from the campus. Martha had been thinking seriously about applying to enter a women's missionary religious community or about joining the Peace Corps, Jesuit Volunteers, or some other lay missionary-type project, but the ministry team leader, Fr. Ted, recognizing her gifts with the young adults they served, encouraged her to think of her work at the campus as another form of real service of the poor.

Martha's retreat was a wonderful experience for her. During the retreat itself she had asked Fr. Ted and several other members of the campus ministry team to join her at the retreat center for a few days of prayer for themselves, and to help her by offering some deliberative input with her and her director about her gifts and skills. In the end, she felt strongly that God desired her service and took her into his companionship, but that the specifics were still "cloudy." She was strongly convinced that God would illuminate her situation and remove any barriers she was raising to a fuller and more generous service.

Within a few weeks after her return to campus and the start of the fall term, Martha organized some small communities of students for prayer together and service at a local homeless shelter. Doug heard about the groups at Sunday Mass and decided to participate in order to sustain his own spiritual energy, which he did not want to lose.

7. Names and all specific details of this couple's life have been changed, but the case is a real one.

Over the months, the couple found that they had much in common, especially a deep faith in God and a desire to be of service to God's Kingdom. In the spring, Doug asked Martha to consider marrying him, and she suggested that they enter prayer together to determine if this was God's invitation. Their mutual attraction, which had been growing slowly, was rapidly and deeply connected after they began to pray together about a possible future, and by May the couple announced to their respective families that they planned to marry within the year.

So far, so good, one might say. So, did they live happily ever after? Not in any fairytale sense. The couple determined that together they were called to lay ministry and to support each other in ministry. Doug finished his degree work and Martha returned to school for a Master of Divinity degree so that she could minister more competently in parish leadership. Through the years both have had to re-discern the location of their service several times. They also decided at the time of their marriage that theirs would always be a hospitable home where guests would be welcome when convenient and inconvenient. With the arrival of children into the family this had to be adjusted, but the basic commitment remained stable. Above all they have consistently submitted important personal and familial decisions to a process of prayerful discernment. Furthermore, they have taught their children to value a commitment to God and to pay attention to God's desire in their own thoughts and affections. By the time each of the children reached middle school, he or she was invited to participate in making family decisions as long as they were willing to pray deeply about such decisions and to be honest about their concerns and feelings.

This couple has known heartache and wonderful joy. They have had to fight to save the intensity and beauty of their love for one another as children joined the family and required their full complement of parental attention and private time. They have struggled with the contemporary secular culture and its relegation of their values to the social ash heap. They have sought to remain faithful to the vision of the Second Vatican Council in their ministry, remaining deeply faithful to the Catholic Tradition while becoming more ecumenical in outlook. Their parochial participation has had many ups and downs, but they have actively participated in small faith communities and stayed close to the sacramental practice of the Church. Through Ignatian discernment they have been able to weave their fundamental commitments to God and to one another in Christ, to their children as God's gift and call, and to their ministry of service into a tapestry of remarkable grace for themselves and the other lives they touch. The demands of growing freedom have not been lessened by their commitments, but have rather been expanded and shaped within the blessed boundaries of those commitments.

Is it a simple thing for married couples to practice discernment following the wisdom of Ignatian spirituality? I can personally attest that it is not, but it is possible and necessary, if either one or both partners believe that God has a desire for them and for their marriage, and if the partners want to walk in a quality of freedom that is expressed in the *Contemplatio*. How can two, who have sacramentally become one flesh, be called by a loving God in ways that do not take into account the needs, hopes, dreams, and desires of each other? The transparency toward one another required for an authentic mutual discernment of God's desire can only serve to enrich and enliven the union as well. Is it ever certain or perfect? Not on this side of eternity.

How does it come about in a marriage? I think it begins in conversation between the partners about what is really important to them. It begins often with the necessity of a decision that will affect both their lives. Both partners have to be willing to pray and to talk about their fears. The conversation must also extend to non-defensive disclosure of the needs each one feels, as well as the risks each one is willing to take. Then serious discussion of options, again submitted to prayer and reflection, are essential. When a decision is made, that too must be submitted to prayer and to conversation about the hopes and fears of each. Such processes may be lengthy at first, but as couples strengthen their communication and their willingness to listen to each other, they will discover a deeper love for one another that makes the process less threatening. It does not come about overnight if it is not the habit of the married partners. Perhaps beginning with mutual conversation with a spiritual director that both partners are comfortable with is a safe way to try to engage this process.

Obviously, communal discernment in a marriage is not possible if there is not a viable and healthy human relationship and a reasonable level of Christian faith in both partners. Easiness with prayer and conversation about prayer will also help a couple undertake this practice of discerned decision-making.

Sustaining the dialectic through small community commitment

My own experience of participation in Christian Life Communities in the United States is of some three decades' duration. During that time I have seen a range of spiritual maturity in groups, from those that were barely more than social gatherings for good friends to groups that were so committed to one another that they supported each other financially, supported members through long and painful dying processes, cared for one another's children, held members in life who were suicidally depressed, and celebrated every sacramental and ritual event a family could have from baptism, marriage, orders, to anointing of the sick and burial of the dead. In the most genuinely life-giving of these groups the practice of spiritual direction, discernment of significant life choices, and various forms of accountability for one's growth in faith have been the "business" of the communal life.

In my earliest years of CLC, shortly after its reform from the pre-Conciliar Marian Congregations (in the U.S. the Sodality of Our Lady), the groups in the United States seemed somewhat skittish about the notion of commitment and many were vague—at best—about the meaning and experience of Ignatian Spirituality. This was reflected in membership that rose and fell, participation that was on-again, off-again, members who participated in prayer but were not interested in service (or vice versa), and members interested in participating in local communities but not drawn to the larger commitment of communities to one another nationally or internationally. As the communities became serious about making the Spiritual Exercises, a notable change could be observed. First there was a growing appreciation for and application of principles of personal discernment of God's call to each one, and gradually an awakening to the fact that God's call is never for private growth and happiness only but for the sake of, and in the context of, the community of one's genuine commitments.

Christian Life Communities in the United States have yet to begin to reach their potential as agents for evangelizing culture, but that is changing as some groups take their Ignatian vocation more seriously. Where there are efforts toward real discerned decisions among members, there is greater evidence of commitment to community life. Correlatively those communities where bonds of mutual care appear stronger are the most likely communities to be able and willing to offer greater response to the needs of the poor, and greater freedom to speak out in the service of justice.

Is communal discernment in Christian Life Communities easy? One could not say so at any level of community life. Are the varying efforts made to corporately discern "authentic"? If we can only use as a criterion for judging the "Deliberation of the First Fathers," perhaps some would and many would not be that rigorous.[8] The work of discovering God's desire within the world and for the world, in a context of hundreds of possible choices, remains the vocation of Christian Life Community members, however, and so the work of growing in discernment skills remains important to our formation process at all levels of participation.

8. For a detailed description of this famous communal discernment see "The Deliberation That Started the Jesuits," by Jules J. Toner, SJ, *Studies in the Spirituality of Jesuits*, Vol. 6, no. 4, June, 1974.

Sustaining the Dialectic between Freedom and Commitment

I began this essay with two brief narratives of the dilemma of educated young adults in the contemporary U.S. culture. From a Christian faith perspective, the response to that dilemma is grounded in a commitment to the Triune God. That commitment is realized in key relationships with whom God invites us to realize his love. It is in the context of these commitments that discernment among a startling array of possibilities can be accomplished toward the goal of joy and peace in God. That process is a careful negotiation between commitments and options. It seems self-evident that entering into dialogue with the various persons to whom we are committed is an essential part of the process of real discernment of God's desire for each one of us. We cannot afford to pretend to be isolated individuals before God when we are not, and one wonders how we can authentically hear God's deepest desire for ourselves apart from the voices of those committed relationships.

God Isn't Finished with Me Yet

Barbara Lee

Inevitably the time comes when we see that the road ahead of us is much shorter than the one we have already traveled. We can give in to sadness, or we can savor the abundant graces all around us, even now.

Another Stage of the Journey

The idea of "journey" as a metaphor for human life is at least as old as Dante. His *Divine Comedy* begins:

> *Midway on our life's journey, I found myself*
> *In dark woods, the right road lost.*

Like Dante, many writers and thinkers have focused on middle age as a time of crisis, change, and self-discovery. There is a vast popular literature on midlife crisis as well as articles and publications directed to psychologists and other professionals. Even Cicero's classic *De Senectute* (*On Old Age*), written in the century before Christ, has recently been published in a modern translation subtitled *Ancient Wisdom for the Second Half of Life*. The Australian theologian Gerald O'Collins popularized the term *second journey* to describe these experiences. He cites the stories of Ignatius, St. Teresa of Calcutta,

Excerpt from *God Isn't Finished with Me Yet: Discovering the Spiritual Graces of Later Life* (Chicago: Loyola Press, 2018).

Dietrich Bonhoeffer, and the disciples on the road to Emmaus, among others, as examples of sudden changes of direction in midlife that led to profound spiritual growth.[1]

If we use the metaphor of journey, there is no reason to divide it into only two parts.

Shakespeare, of course, described seven ages of man, although he found little to aspire to in any of them. O'Collins refers in passing to the possibility of "one last journey" at the end of life.

Whatever the divisions, the boundaries are often indistinct. On the spiritual journey, there are many detours and wrong turns, and we sometimes seem to be caught in an endless roundabout. Those of us who have left middle age behind but are not in Shakespeare's "second childishness and mere oblivion" are in another stage of the journey. I invite you to consider its potential for grace by looking at where we have come from and where we are going.[2]

Looking Back

No matter how old we are or how we have lived, we all have some "unfinished business." There are disappointments that still hurt: the couple who couldn't have children; the manager who was downsized from a satisfying job. There are missed opportunities that we recognize only with the wisdom of maturity, "the road not taken," in Robert Frost's phrase. There are old hurts and resentments that still burn.

---

1. Dante, *The Inferno of Dante: A New Verse Translation*, trans. Robert Pinsky (New York: Farrar, Straus and Giroux, 1994), lines 1–3; Cicero, *How to Grow Old: Ancient Wisdom for the Second Half of Life*, trans. Philip Freeman (Princeton, NJ: Princeton University Press, 2016); Gerald O'Collins, *The Second Journey: Spiritual Awareness and the Mid-Life Crisis* (Mahwah, NJ: Paulist Press, 1978), 38–40 (Ignatius); 46 (Mother Teresa); 40–42 (Dietrich Bonhoeffer); 81 (disciples). His "third journey" encompasses "aging and the last years before death," which he sees as consisting of "beauty and simplicity," in part because of the "comforting advantage" of the company of "millions of fellow travelers," 12–14.
2. William Shakespeare, *As You Like It*, act II, scene 7, lines 139–166. In middle age, he sees one "in fair round belly, with good capon lin'd . . . full of wise saws" who next "shifts into the lean and slippered pantaloon with spectacles on nose and pouch at side," lines 154–156.

We cannot change the past, but we can mine it for spiritual wisdom. As a way into the graces to which our memory may lead, I suggest a variation on the Examen, covering not one day but a longer period. A retreat is an optimal setting for this exercise, but it can be done whenever you have an uninterrupted period of quiet.

Ask the Holy Spirit for guidance in choosing a period of time to focus on. You may want to start from the last major transition in your life or go further back. The period can be long or short—whatever seems right to you. I usually try to do this on New Year's Day, looking back over the preceding year.

Next, focus on feelings and memories. Each person's life story will present different questions, but some examples are as follows:

- Of all that happened in that period, for what am I most grateful?
- Have I expressed my gratitude to the people involved? To God? Can I do that now? *Often, the people who have been instruments of grace for us are no longer with us, but we can hold them in our hearts as we thank God for them.*
- What are the most powerful emotions that surface as I look back?
- What gave rise to joy, anger, disappointment?
- Did these emotions spring from an action, an event, or an attitude of mind or heart that prevailed at that time?
- Which ones led me to God, and which ones led me away?
- Can the memory of these feelings lead me to God in the present?
- Are there emotional doors that were closed in the past that I can open now?
- How can the wisdom of the present illumine my understanding of the past?

The answers to these questions will often lead naturally to the next:

- For what do I need forgiveness?
- Is there someone, living or dead, whose forgiveness I need to ask?
- Is there someone I need to forgive for past hurts, trivial or serious?
- Can I forgive myself for missed opportunities or mistakes or the persistence of negative feelings?
- Has God forgiven me?
- Have I asked God's forgiveness?

Finally, ask God for the grace to look forward in hope.

Looking Ahead

At some point in the aging process, we confront financial planning, estate planning, health-care proxies, and other matters that look to the end of life and beyond. It can be difficult to deal with these things; some people postpone taking action precisely because doing so involves thinking about death. Ignatius's rules for decision-making and discernment . . . can be helpful here. Following are some suggestions to pray about:

- A health-care proxy and a living will can relieve the anguish of a loved one who might be called upon to make difficult decisions.
- People who have no close relatives also need someone to make decisions for them if they cannot. Is there a friend who knows and shares your values about end-of-life care? If he or she is willing to be named as your health-care proxy, you are more likely to receive care in accordance with your own values and wishes than if the decisions are left to doctors and nurses.

- Pre-planning of funerals and burial arrangements saves money and reduces stress on survivors who would otherwise have to make these decisions on short notice, with little time for research.
- Thoughtful estate planning can reduce the possibility of quarrels or animosity among children or grandchildren, especially in large or blended families or where some children or grandchildren have special needs.
- Even people with few assets should have a will, especially if they have no immediate family. A friend of mine, a psychologist who worked with developmentally disabled adults, used up most of her savings during a long illness. She steadfastly refused to make a will on the grounds that "I don't have an estate." When she died, the few thousand dollars in her bank account went by default to the State of New York. It wasn't much money, but it could have been put to better use helping the people to whom she had devoted her entire career.

But what about our spiritual legacy? Have our loved ones, our friends, and those whose lives we may have touched without realizing it experienced grace because of us? My immigrant grandparents died when I was in my late teens. I often think of questions I wish I had asked them. Children and teenagers growing up today have an unparalleled facility with audio and video technologies that can lend themselves to oral history projects. Tell them your stories.

Can you share your spiritual journey? For some people, the feelings they share with Jesus are too intimate to be shared with anyone else. For others, there may be some insights that are so powerful they cry out to be shared. It isn't necessary to preach to your friends and family about what you have learned. But don't overlook opportunities to share your story.

Living in the Present

As we age, especially in the later years, it can be all too easy to focus on the past and to think of the future in terms of planning for death. But we are alive in the present, and no matter how long or short our life span, we live our spiritual life in the present. Prayer, always a constant in a God-centered life, can become ever richer with the experience of years.

Ministry of Prayer. Whether or not we are engaged in active ministry, some of us may have the time and space to develop a more contemplative attitude. Thomas Clarke, SJ, has argued for a ministry of intercessory prayer:

> If intercession, then, is the name of the game, I believe that the group best fitted to lead it is the world's elders. We qualify for that role not through our wisdom or even through our prophetic gifts, if we have them, but through our special brand of poverty. In generational terms, it is we who are the *anawim*—the poor—through whom God works wonders. However reduced in physical, mental, emotional powers, and whether we are still "active" or "retired," we can model for all that intercessory offering of "prayers, works, joys and sufferings" through which the world is graced.[3]

Fr. Clarke is not advocating a passive attitude of prayer as a substitute for an active life. Rather, he is inviting those impoverished in the ways particular to old age to claim their place in the communion of saints, as active instruments of grace for all the people in their lives and many they will never know. In the words of the popular hymn, "The Lord hears the cry of the poor."

Praying through the Pain. Anyone who has ever tried to read the Bible or use a popular prayer app while recovering from surgery or undergoing chemotherapy can describe how difficult it is to pray in these circumstances. The words swim on the page; the meanings

---

3. Thomas E. Clarke, SJ, "Elderhood for the World," *America* (July 29, 2000), 9.

don't register; the mind wanders; the pain blots out all other thoughts; when the pain subsides, drowsiness takes over; some passages trigger worries and anxieties; the joyful ones seem irrelevant.

At first glance, Ignatius seems an unlikely guide to prayer in such circumstances. As a soldier, he prided himself on not showing any sign of pain and, for a period after his conversion, he was drawn to extreme penances.[4] Where his wisdom speaks to the aging, and particularly the suffering aging, is in the overriding objective of modeling ourselves after Jesus.

To know, love, and follow Jesus means experiencing pain as Jesus experienced it. In reading the Passion narratives and about the post-Resurrection appearances of Jesus, applying the principles of imaginative prayer or *lectio divina* may show us how to let go of our fears and lead us to a new experience of hope. Or, as Jesus told the disciples at the Last Supper, "And you know the way to the place where I am going" (John 14:4).

Death as Part of Life

The early Christians had a much deeper appreciation of the continuity of earthly life and life eternal. For St. Paul, the disciples who had died after seeing the risen Jesus had merely "fallen asleep" (1 Corinthians 15:6). For his and the immediately succeeding generations, martyrdom was an imminent threat. St. Perpetua, imprisoned in Carthage around AD 202, wrote of a dream of heaven in which a deacon of her community called out to her, "Perpetua, come, we are waiting for you."[5] Those who faced martyrdom, or who knew the stories of those who had experienced it, identified with the death and

4. Not showing any sign of pain: *Autobiography*, 2; extreme penances: 14–17.

5. Perpetua's vision: Herbert Musurillo, trans., *The Acts of the Christian Martyrs* (New York: Oxford University Press, 1972), 117. The text of "The Martyrdom of Saints Perpetua and Felicitas" is one of the earliest primary sources about the lives of the martyrs. Perpetua is believed to have kept a diary while imprisoned, and her story was continued by an unknown editor after her death. The narrator described how Perpetua and her companions "marched from the prison to the amphitheatre joyfully as though they were going to heaven, with calm faces, trembling, if at all, with joy rather than fear" and viewing martyrdom as "a second baptism." The full text is available online at a number of sites, e.g., https://www.scribd.com/document/249295097/Musurillo-Acts-of-the-Christian-Martyrs.

Resurrection of Jesus as the meaning of the Christian life. For them, the Resurrection was not merely a proof of Jesus' divinity or a fact to celebrate at Easter; it was a promise of eternal life that was as real as the Christian's life on earth.

In modern times, we have lost that sense of the continuity of earthly and eternal life. The martyrs' stories—so long ago in such a different world—have no immediacy for us. Where cancer and terrorism are more immediate threats than dying for the faith, there is little feeling of connection with the martyrs. Even those listed in the Roman Canon (now Eucharistic Prayer I) are rarely invoked, since at least in the United States the shorter forms of the Eucharistic Prayer are much more common. In a secular society where belief in the afterlife is a minority view, we keep our thoughts to ourselves.

Although Ignatius prescribes a meditation on hell for the First Week and includes among the criteria for decision-making the advice that we imagine ourselves "at the point of death" (SE 186) or "on judgment day" (SE 187), he has little explicit advice on how one should look on death (for a meditation on hell, see SE 67–82). This is not surprising, since his expectation was that the Exercises would most often be made by young people making decisions about their state of life (SE 169, 171–172). For those of us who are long past such milestones, it is significant that a person making the full Exercises spends the entire second half of the experience meditating on the Passion and Resurrection of Jesus. While anyone, at any stage of life, can experience abundant grace meditating on the Passion and Resurrection of our Lord, these mysteries can be particularly consoling to those who are aware that the time remaining on their spiritual journey is diminishing.

[I have meditated] on the women at the foot of the cross, deep in sorrow because they did not know about the Resurrection. We don't know when or how our own stories will end, but we do know how the story of Jesus ended. Instead of looking backward toward what has been lost or given up, we can ask for the grace to look forward with hope to life eternal, remembering the promise of Jesus: "I will see you again, and your hearts will rejoice, and no one will take your joy from you" (John 16:22).

Ignatian Prayer: Suscipe

At the end of the Spiritual Exercises, Ignatius prescribes the following prayer, usually called the *suscipe*, from the first word in the Latin version:

> *Take, Lord, and receive all my liberty, my memory, my understanding, and all my will—all that I have and possess. You, Lord, have given all that to me. I now give it back to you, O Lord. All of it is yours. Dispose of it according to your will. Give me your love and your grace, for that is enough for me.* (Suscipe prayer: SE 234)

This kind of surrender is vastly different from giving up material goods. I have often wondered whether the middle-aged Ignatius had any inkling of the reaction this prayer might evoke in someone whose liberty was circumscribed by declining health, whose short-term memory was fading, and who was worrying about the loss of understanding and will in the event of dementia. I venture to suggest that people in their seventies and eighties might have a fuller grasp of the magnitude of this prayer than a young person choosing a state in life.

Can a person confined to a nursing home after a stroke or an accident freely and sincerely ask God to "take . . . my liberty"? What about surrendering my understanding? It is no surprise that some people find this prayer difficult or impossible. But even for those of us who have difficulty with consenting to the diminishment that comes with age, the words of the Suscipe are a reminder that everything is God's gift: every breath we take, every beat of our hearts, every memory we cherish, every thought that fills our minds. God may not be asking us to give up any of these gifts, just yet. But as we grow older, we should be able to be more grateful for all the graces God has showered upon us and never cease to thank and praise God every day of our lives. When we are asked to surrender, the grace will be there.

On Discernment in Common

Arturo Sosa, SJ

Dear Brothers in the Lord,
This past 10th of July, I addressed a letter (2017/08) to the whole Society, inviting all Jesuits to reflect on the intimate relationship between our lives and the mission to which we are called and sent. The letter was an invitation to discover, embrace, and live out in depth the message of the 36th General Congregation. In continuity with that reflection, I would now like to share with you some considerations about discernment in common, which is a prerequisite for implementing the decisions of the General Congregation, in keeping with the characteristics of the spirituality which animate our religious and apostolic body.

Called to Discern

Two great challenges proposed to us by the 36th General Congregation are 1) discerning the consequences of formulating the Society's mission as a contribution to reconciliation and 2) choosing Universal Apostolic Preferences at this particular moment in history for the world and the Society. These challenges demand that we, and our partners in mission, improve our ability to discern in common. There are other areas in which we are invited to grow in our capacity for

Arturo Sosa, SJ, Superior General, Rome, 27 September 2017, on the Anniversary of the Bull *Regimini militantis* of Pope Paul III (1540).

communal discernment, among others, constituting ourselves as an intercultural body, deepening our dialogue with other cultures and religions, and promoting a culture of protection for children, young people, and vulnerable persons.

The 36th General Congregation confirmed that discernment in common is inherent to the way of proceeding of the Society of Jesus. The image of the first companions in Venice (1537) highlights the capacity they acquired of deliberating in common, led by the light of the Holy Spirit, even though they were such a culturally diverse group.[1] Nevertheless, they all had an active spiritual life, characterized by their having fallen in love with Christ in the Spiritual Exercises, by their service to the poor, and by their availability to be sent by the Church to any place where the need was greater.

Today, the Society of Jesus, in collaboration with others in the Church's mission of reconciling all in Christ, is also faced with the challenge of discerning in common, at all important decisions. At the same time, the Society must encourage the participation of the whole apostolic body, which is called to elect the best possible ways to contribute to the proclamation of the Good News and the transformation of the world, in this epoch of swift and profound changes.

Pope Francis, for his part, has repeatedly insisted on the importance of spiritual discernment for the Church as a whole, and he has especially asked the Society of Jesus to contribute to the diffusion of discernment in all aspects of ecclesial life. From this perspective, we feel that having regular recourse to spiritual discernment as the means for seeking and finding the will of God in every dimension of our life-mission will bring about a revitalization of our life-mission and also an increase in our capacity to serve the Church in these present times.

1. We read in the *Deliberatio Primorum Patrum*: "The time was approaching for us to be scattered and parted from one another. We were eagerly anticipating this time so that we could the sooner achieve our appointed goal on which we had set our minds and hearts. We therefore resolved to get together for a good long time before our dispersal and to discuss our vocation and covenanted way of life. Some of us were French, others Spanish, Savoyards, or Portuguese. After meeting for many sessions, there was a cleavage of sentiments and opinions about our situation. While we all had one mind and heart in seeking God's gracious and perfect will according to the scope of our vocation."

Discernment in Common and Apostolic Planning

Discernment in common takes place both in our communities and in our apostolic works, with the active participation of our partners in mission. It makes sense that the particular group which discerns in common should vary with the decision that is to be made. In the life of the Society many decisions require that more than one group contribute to the discernment in common so that a final decision may be reached that is in consonance with the will of God that is earnestly sought. Discernment in common can be fruitfully practiced in the Consults of the Province, in board meetings of institutions with a Jesuit identity, and in all instances of apostolic governance.

Discernment in common is the prior condition for *apostolic planning* at all levels of the Society's organizational structure. Thus, discernment in common and apostolic planning work in tandem to ensure that decisions are made in the light of the experience of God, and that these decisions are put into practice in such a way that they realize the will of God with evangelical effectiveness.

The positive tension between discernment in common and apostolic planning requires, according to the Ignatian vision, a spiritual Examen of what we have experienced, so that we continually grow in fidelity to the will of God. Therefore, a systematic evaluation of our apostolates is not sufficient. We must supplement that systematic evaluation with the spiritual perspective of the Examen, a practice by which Ignatius invites us to recognize the action of God in history, to be grateful for his gifts, to beg pardon for our failure to measure up, and to ask for the grace to be ever better collaborators in God's work in the world. Thus, apostolic planning born of discernment in common becomes an instrument of our apostolic effectiveness, and we avoid the dangers of a trendy type of planning that makes use of only the techniques of corporate development.

The Practice of Discernment in Common

The conviction that God is acting in history and is constantly communicating with human beings is the assumption on which our efforts to discern in common are based. For this reason, we should seek out those conditions which allow us to hear the Holy Spirit and be guided by him in our life-mission. The personal and group disposition to receive and follow the Spirit who communicates with us prevents a false type of discernment in common, which seeks only to clothe in correct Ignatian language decisions that were already made based on the criteria of one's own group.[2]

There have been many valuable experiences of discernment in common both in our tradition and in the present life of the Society. Gathering together the *best practices* of discernment in common, as well as providing a pertinent bibliography that is made available to all who participate in our mission, would be a most helpful means of strengthening the common. I encourage apostolic works, provinces, regions, and conferences of major superiors to undertake this task promptly and resolutely, and I urge them to design formation processes for discernment in common that are accessible to all those persons with whom we share our mission, as well as with all those members of the Church who feel called to grow in this dimension of Christian life.

Properties of Discernment in Common

Desiring to foster the growth of this dimension of our life, but without claiming to replace other good aids to and excellent studies on the topic, I wish to describe the principal properties of discernment in common. These properties are present in different degrees, depending on the circumstances in which the discernment is done. The following enumeration is not intended to propose stages or steps in a process, but rather, simply to describe the main features of discernment in common. Sometimes we will find that all these properties

2. Jeremiah 42 and 43 recount a clear example of false discernment in common.

are present, while at other times they will not be present in the same form. Discernment in common follows traditional Ignatian criteria, taking into account *the persons, the times, and the places.*[3] Thus, good discernment in common requires the following:

1. **Choosing the matter well.** Not every decision requires discernment in common. The aim of discernment in common is *seeking and finding the will of God* in important matters, in which it is not completely clear what is to be done or how it is to be done, what is best or how to do it in the best way possible. It is therefore crucial that we know how to choose the matter or the matters that require an *election* through discernment in common. At the same time, full information, of good quality and accessible to all, about the matter to be treated is needed. Good discernment depends on having a precise knowledge about the matter to be decided and about the result that is to be expected from such a complex and demanding process. In this way we avoid banalizing "discernment," using the word as a way to justify either major or minor decisions.
2. **Knowing who should take part in the discernment and why.** It is necessary to establish clearly *which persons* will participate in the process of discernment, *why* they participate, and *under what conditions* they do so. The matter about which the *election* is to be made will determine who is invited to participate in the process. This means that each participant should know precisely and should freely accept both the reasons for which he/she forms part of the group that is discerning and the conditions under which he/she does so. Depending on the group, the matter being discerned, and other conditions in which the process takes place, it may be convenient and prudent to invite other persons to accompany the process or to provide expertise in the matters being treated.

3. See for example: *Constitutions of the Society of Jesus* [64, 238, 343].

3. **Interior freedom**, or Ignatian *indifference*, is a condition without which it is not possible to make a good election. Those who take part in the discernment should cultivate interior freedom; that is, they should be detached from their own interests and be free to assume whatever is the greater good in the light of the Gospel. Indifference is the fruit of an authentic spiritual life in which life and mission are inseparable, as the 36th General Congregation has made clear. It is possible and necessary also for those who share in our mission but not in our Christian faith to acquire that interior freedom which enables them to divest themselves of self-love, self-will, and self-interests (SE 189).[4] This interior freedom is the human possibility to grow as persons in gratuitous relationship with others, seeking the greater good of all, even when such a pursuit involves, as a consequence, personal renunciation and sacrifice.
4. **Union of minds and hearts.** Discernment in common requires the existence of what Ignatius Loyola calls the *union of hearts and minds* in the group that is discerning, because the purpose of the process is to make an *election* freely according to the will of God. This union of hearts and minds is born of the shared sense of purpose possessed by all who form part of the group since what is at stake in the discernment directly affects all and each one. Thus, good mutual knowledge of each other is needed, a mutual knowledge that gives birth to trust in each other and motivates the active participation of each one.
5. **Knowledge about how to discern.** In the Exercises Ignatius presents three different times for making good, sound decisions (SE 175–188). In the *first time*, there is no doubt about what the will of God is (SE 175). In the *second time*, discernment in common may be done, by taking account of spiritual movements and their confirmation

4. There are many cases where persons who do not share our Christian faith collaborate in works of the Society or join with us in providing services to persons in need. Finding respectful and genuine ways to make them participants in the process of discernment in common is a challenge to our creativity and our freedom as sons and daughters of God.

(SE 176, 183, and 188), or it may also be done by reasoning and deciding according to what is described in the *third time* (SE 177 and 178).

For a group of persons who have experience in the discernment of spirits, discernment in common can take the form of a process in which they perceive and weigh the *movements* which the spirits provoke in the group that is seeking the will of God. The capacity of the group to discern the spirits in this way is thus a condition for its being able to make use of the second time of election. The discernment of spirits makes it possible for the group to become aware of the direction that its life would take if it were to follow one or another movement of spirit, in order to follow the movements of the good spirit. In Ignatian language, the movements that are most relevant for discernment are called *consolation and desolation* (SE 313–327).[5] "For just as in consolation it is more the good spirit who guides and counsels us, so in desolation it is the bad spirit, and by following his counsels we can never find the right way" (SE 318).

The spiritual *movements* are not states of soul. They are palpable effects of the spirits that are trying to move a person's will in one direction or another. Thus, *consolation* and *desolation* are not synonyms for being happy or sad, for feeling good or bad, for being contented or discontented, for agreeing or disagreeing with someone else's idea or position. The scene of Jesus praying in the Garden of Olives before the Passion can help us to distinguish the movements from our states of soul (Matthew 26:36–46). The movements appeal to our freedom to choose. Although feeling sadness and anguish (vv. 37–38), Jesus *elected* to follow the will of the Father.[6] The movements of the good Spirit bring about

5. See the *Rules to Aid Us toward Perceiving and Understanding the Various Motions* and *Rules for the Same Purpose, with a More Probing Discernment of Spirits* (SE 328–336).

6. Sacred Scripture offers many examples of the difference between following the Spirit and the state of soul of persons. The vocations and the lives of the prophets are clear examples. The decision of Joseph to accept Mary, already with child, as his spouse illustrates for us this difference between being led by the Spirit and the states of soul during the journey (Matthew 1:18–24).

a growth in faith, hope, and charity (SE 316). Profound interior peace is the sign of being in consonance with the Holy Spirit as a fruit of discernment. That interior peace, which may be felt even in situations of great suffering, is the sign of having *found* the will of God. Such confirmation of being in consonance with the Spirit is perceived in the *joy* of the Gospel—experienced interiorly in each person and sensed by the group that discerns in common—or in the *consolation* that Pope Francis urged us to ask for insistently during his visit to the 36th General Congregation.

On occasion, depending on the conditions experienced by those who make up the group that is discerning, it may be advisable to make use of reasoning or deliberating the advantages (pros) and the disadvantages (cons) of making a certain election against the horizon of the greater and better service of the glory of God. In this case the condition for a good discernment is the group's ability to use its understanding lucidly to perceive what the greater good is according to the values of the Kingdom and to offer the decision made to the Lord for confirmation (SE 183).

6. **Prayer in common** is another requirement for good discernment. The group that proposes to discern in common should find ways and spaces for personal and communal prayer, in accord with its particular characteristics. Personal prayer and communal prayer maintain a healthy tension between heaven and earth as we seek the *magis* that derives from our relationship with God and his Word (SE 101–105). Such prayer helps us to keep in mind that *as a body* we are servants of the *missio Dei*. The Eucharist is the privileged mode of prayer in common. Thus it may have special significance and a central role in the processes of discernment in common. A community or a group that is able to celebrate the Eucharist as a source of life in the Spirit increases its ability to perceive the action of the Spirit in history and to experience how the Lord fulfills his promise to be with us all days until the end of history (Matthew 28:20).

7. **Spiritual conversation** characterizes discernment in common. The 36th General Congregation strongly recommended that we improve our capacity to converse spiritually.[7] Discernment in common should include periods of time dedicated to sharing the fruit of prayer or personal reflection. The sharing is an opportunity to present to others, with simplicity and without making speeches, what one has perceived as movements of the Spirit or as the fruit of one's personal reflection on the point in question. On the other hand, our disposition to "listen to the other person" respectfully, without contradicting the spiritual movements that the other person has felt interiorly, can produce a spiritual echo or new spiritual movements in the person listening, giving rise to a fresh way of perceiving things. The custom of spiritual conversation, the habit of listening attentively to others and knowing how to communicate one's own experience and ideas simply and clearly contribute to good discernment in common when the matter under consideration requires it. Sharing in a spiritual conversation is different from a business discussion in which the aim is to make the most reasonable decision according to administrative logic. It is also different from a parliamentary exercise in which consideration is given to the majority, minority, alliances, etc., in function of individual or group interests, making use of oratorical ability and other parliamentary "techniques." Such forums have in common with discernment the need to offer good information about matters to be decided and the capacity to argue rationally. Discernment needs these elements but is not limited to them. Discernment ultimately has to do with spiritual movements, or if there is no clarity about these,

---

7. "An essential tool that can animate apostolic communal discernment is spiritual conversation. Spiritual conversation involves an exchange marked by active and receptive listening and a desire to speak of that which touches us most deeply. It tries to take account of spiritual movements, individual and communal, with the objective of choosing the path of consolation that fortifies our faith, hope and love. Spiritual conversation creates an atmosphere of trust and welcome for ourselves and others. We ought not to deprive ourselves of such conversation in the community and in all other occasions for decision-making in the Society" (GC 36, d. 1,12).

with that which can reasonably generate greater love and service for the glory of God, seeking also the confirmation which comes from on high.

8. **The systematic practice of the Examen** during the process of discernment in common allows us to pass from *seeking* to *finding* the will of God. The Examen helps us to perceive the true nature of spiritual movements and to confirm that we are on the right path. The personal Examen of each participant needs to be combined with the Examen of what is happening in the group as a whole. Learning to examine the movements of the group allows us to take the pulse of the process or to confirm it, so that we can know whether we should continue onward, and how, guided by the Spirit. The constant monitoring of the movements of the group reflected in the Examen is an instrument which helps us maintain a memory of the process. Just as we learn to perceive our interior movements, discernment in common requires that we develop the ability to perceive and interpret spiritual movements of the group which is listening to the Spirit in order to find the will of God.
9. **Establishing how the final decision is to be made** should be clearly and precisely settled from the very beginning of the process of discernment. Those who take part in the discernment should know and accept from the start the manner by which a final decision is to be made. For example, we understand clearly that a General Congregation of the Society of Jesus makes its decisions by a majority of votes, except when the Formula prescribes otherwise. Similarly, it is known that, in the discernment of a religious community of Jesuits, the final decision rests with the local superior, and the decisions of a province or a region are the responsibility of the major superior. The apostolic works and institutions are governed by their own statutes and norms, which determine how decisions that affect the whole are made and who makes them.

Placing All Our Confidence in God

Discernment is a rich heritage of the Spiritual Exercises, one that is especially useful at moments of making the elections that our life and mission require. Discernment and good elections demand that we free ourselves from our disordered attachments and affections so that we can place ourselves completely in the hands of the Lord. Promoting discernment in common was an intuition of the 36th General Congregation in its search for ways of improving our common life through deeper personal prayer and a richer sharing of our faith and our lives.

The allocution of Pope Francis to the members of General Congregation 36 ends with this prayer: *"We beg Our Mother to direct and accompany every Jesuit, along with that part of the faithful people of God to whom he has been sent, along these paths of consolation, of compassion, and discernment."*[8] Let us make this prayer our own, requesting this grace for each one who is called to share this mission of serving reconciliation and the justice of the Gospel, as well as for our communities and the works and institutions through which we carry out our apostolate.

Let us therefore ask for the grace of personal and institutional conversion, and that the contemplation of Jesus in the Gospels helps us learn, from his loving and faithful relationship with the Father, how to perceive where the Spirit leads, and how to elect to live according to the will of God.

---

8. *Allocution of the Holy Father to the 36th General Congregation*, 24 October 2016.

IV. Reconciliation

Part IV Introduction

From the earliest days of the Society of Jesus, practicing various kinds of reconciling work has been a vital aspect of the charism (spiritual gift and ministerial requirement) of the Jesuits and the works they are sent to do. In the brief Papal Bull, *Exposit Debitum*, finally promulgated by Pope Julius III in 1550 in response to the revised "Formula of the Institute," written by Ignatius and the other founding fathers of the Society in 1540, the Church asserts:

> Whoever desires to serve as a soldier of God beneath the banner of the cross in our Society, which we desire to be designated by the name of Jesus, and to serve the Lord alone and the Church, His spouse, under the Roman pontiff, the vicar of Christ on earth, should, after a solemn vow of perpetual chastity, poverty, and obedience, keep what follows in mind.
>
> He is a member of a Society founded chiefly for this purpose: to strive especially for the defense and propagation of the faith and for the progress of souls in Christian life and doctrine, by means of public preaching, lectures, and any other ministration whatsoever of the Word of God, and further by means of the Spiritual Exercises, the education of children and unlettered persons, and the spiritual consolation of Christ's faithful through hearing confessions and administering the other sacraments.
>
> Moreover, he should show himself ready to reconcile the estranged, compassionately assist and serve those in prisons or hospitals, and indeed to perform any other works of charity, according to what will seem expedient for the glory of God and the common good.

For some members of the Jesuits, this primarily was a reconciliation of a sinner with God in the Sacrament of Reconciliation; for others, including Ignatius himself, however, this involved the labor of mediating conflicts and reconciling spouses in marriage, communities with the Church or civil government, and whole nations with one another. Jesuits today find themselves needing to reconcile all of these broken relationships, current and historical, and even those between the human race and the earth, our common home (see Pope Francis's encyclical letter *Laudato Si'*). In some cases, this reconciliation needs to take place between the Jesuits as a social institution and those they have structurally wounded.

Part IV includes documentation from some of these contemporary reconciliation efforts. But first, the Society has reminded itself and its partners in the various Jesuit works that reconciliation begins at home. The first text in Part IV is the entire single working decree from the 36th General Congregation, held in October of 2016. The decree is titled "Companions in a Mission of Reconciliation and Justice." Although relatively short, the decree springs from decrees of earlier General Congregations and from the Spirit of the founding document quoted above.

The text of Decree 1 is followed by a short reflection by the late Tom Stegman, SJ, a Scripture scholar who participated in the Congregation.

The final three texts in this Part represent efforts on the part of the Jesuits to engage in reconciliation projects for past institutional practice: Georgetown University's project with the North American Jesuit Assistancy to heal the terrible rift caused by selling African American slaves to raise money for the university in the 19th century; Canadian Jesuits' efforts to heal the long anguish caused by their treatment of Native Americans in their schools during the 19th and early 20th centuries, which included a visit and apology from Pope Francis in 2021; and a similar project in South Dakota to address the treatment of Indigenous students in their schools at Pine Ridge Reservation in the 19th and early 20th centuries.

Similar projects are being carried out around the world as the Society today continues to realize that helping others to reconcile begins at home. This ongoing work stands within the Scripture mandates laid down by Jesus to be merciful and loving. We forgive, and presumably are forgiven, an infinite number of times every day—seventy times seven times, according to the Gospel of Matthew. Ignatian spirituality, as a way of life, challenges Jesuits and partners alike to facilitate social healing, peace, and cooperation. In this chapter we see the importance of reconciliation at the heart of this way of life.

Eileen Burke-Sullivan

Companions in a Mission of Reconciliation and Justice

General Congregation 36

> All this is from God, who reconciled us to himself through Christ, and has given us the ministry of reconciliation.
>
> —2 Corinthians 5:18

The Society of Jesus has always sought to know and to follow God's will for us. This Congregation takes up that task again. We do so from the heart of the Church, but gazing upon the world "We know that the whole creation has been groaning in labor pains until now" (Romans 8:22). On the one hand, we see the vibrancy of youth, yearning to better their lives. We see people enjoying the beauty of creation.

We see the many ways in which people use their gifts for the sake of others. And yet, our world faces so many needs today, so many challenges. We have images in our minds of people humiliated, struck by violence, excluded from society, and on the margins. The earth bears the weight of the damage human beings have wrought. Hope itself seems threatened; in place of hope, we find fear and anger.

Pope Francis reminds us that "we are faced not with two separate crises, one environmental and the other social, but rather with one complex crisis which is both social and environmental."[1] This one

Decree 1 of the Thirty-Sixth General Congregation of the Society of Jesus.

1. *Laudato Si'*, 139.

crisis that underlies both the social and environmental crises arises from the way in which human beings use—and abuse—the peoples and goods of the earth.

This crisis has deep spiritual roots; it saps the hope and joy that God proclaims and offers through the Gospel, affecting even the Church and the Society of Jesus. Yet, looking at reality with the eyes of faith, with a vision trained by the *Contemplatio*, we know that God labors in the world.[2] We recognize the signs of God's work, of the great ministry of reconciliation God has begun in Christ, fulfilled in the kingdom of justice, peace, and the integrity of creation. GC 35 recognized this mission.[3] The letter of Father General Adolfo Nicolás on reconciliation[4] and the teaching of Pope Francis[5] have given this vision greater depth, placing faith, justice, and solidarity with the poor and the excluded as central elements of the mission of reconciliation. Rather than ask what we should do, we seek to understand how God invites us—and so many people of good will—to share in that great work.

Alone, we find ourselves humbled and weak, sinners. With the psalmist, we cry out, "Show us your steadfast love, O Lord, and grant us your salvation" (Psalm 85:7). But we experience joy in knowing ourselves as sinners who, in God's mercy, are called to be companions of Jesus, "For we are God's servants, working together; you are God's field, God's building" (1 Corinthians 3:9).

We are not the first to seek clarity concerning God's call. The meeting of the first companions in Venice is a powerful image, an important step in the formation of the Society (*Autobiography*, 93–95). There, the companions confronted the frustration of their plans to go to the Holy Land. This drove them to a deeper discernment of the Lord's call. Where was the Spirit drawing them? As they discerned new direction for their lives, they held fast to what they had already

2. The Contemplation to Attain Love, SE 236.
3. Cf. GC 35, D. 3, "Challenges to our Mission Today." In doing so, GC 35 built upon the message of GC 32, D. 4, n. 2. "The mission of the Society of Jesus today is the service of faith, of which the promotion of justice is an absolute requirement. For reconciliation with God demands the reconciliation of people with one another."
4. "Father Adolfo Nicolás Reply to Ex Officio Letters 2014," *Acta Romana Societatis* Iesu Vol. XXV (2014): 1032–1038.
5. Cf. *Evangelii Gaudium*, 226–230, 239–258 and *Misericordiae Vultus*.

found to be life-giving: sharing their lives together as friends in the Lord; living very close to the lives of the poor; and preaching the Gospel with joy.

They were priests, both learned and poor. For the First Companions, life and mission, rooted in a discerning community, were profoundly interrelated. We Jesuits today are called to live in the same way, as priests, brothers, and those in formation who all share the same mission. As we reflect and pray on each of these elements, we do so, knowing the intimate unity of mission, life, and discerning community, all afire with the love of Christ.

This Congregation finds consolation and joy in returning to these roots, this integral vision of who we are, as well as in the knowledge that there are many others who, like us, hear the call to labor with Christ. We return to those roots now, first to a discerning community, then to our life in faith, and finally to the mission that flows from both. The poverty of life and proximity to the poor of the first companions in Venice must mark our lives too, that poverty that engenders creativity and protects us from what limits our availability to respond to God's call.[6] Such poverty of life constantly calls us to reflect on how we can live more simply with less. We pray, too, to enter ever more fully into that great mystical tradition that our First Fathers bequeathed to us, ever a grace, ever a challenge. Finally, we insistently ask for the grace to know how we can share in the great ministry of reconciliation, knowing that, as Pope Francis reminds us, our response remains always incomplete.[7]

6. Constitutions [143, 159–160]. Our poverty is for us madre (Constitutions [287]) and muro (Constitutions [553]).
7. "Interview with Pope Francis," *Civiltà Cattolica*, 2013, III: 449–477.

A Discerning Community with Open Horizons

During their time in Venice, the companions were not always together; they were dispersed in order to fulfill many tasks. Nevertheless, it was at that time that they shared the experience of constituting a single group, united in following Christ, in the midst of the diversity of their activities. We Jesuits today are also engaged in a great variety of apostolates, which often demand specialization and a great deal of energy. If, however, we forget that we are one body, bound together in and with Christ, we lose our identity as Jesuits and our ability to bear witness to the Gospel (Constitutions [813]). It is our union with one another in Christ that testifies to the Good News more powerfully than our competences and abilities.

Thus, each of us should constantly desire that our own apostolic work develop, be stimulated, and helped to bear fruit, through the encouragement of our brothers. We always receive our mission from God in the Church, through our major superiors and local superiors, in the practice of Jesuit obedience, which includes our personal discernment.[8] If, however, our mission is not supported by the body of the Society, it risks withering. In our individualistic and competitive age, we should remember that the community plays a very special role because it is a privileged place of apostolic discernment.

The Jesuit community is a concrete space in which we live as friends in the Lord. This life together is always at the service of mission, but because these fraternal bonds proclaim the Gospel, it is itself a mission.[9]

In our Jesuit community life, we should leave room for encounter and sharing. This disposition helps the community become a space of truth, joy, creativity, pardon, and of seeking the will of God. Thus, community can become a place of discernment.

---

8. GC 35, D. 4.
9. CG 35 D. 2, 19, and D. 3, 41 and Father Peter-Hans Kolvenbach, "On Community Life," n. 2 and 10, *Acta Romana Societatis Iesu*, Vol. XXII (1998): 279–280, 288. Cf. CN, 314–330.

Communal discernment requires that each of us develops some basic characteristics and attitudes: availability, mobility, humility, freedom, the ability to accompany others, patience, and a willingness to listen respectfully so that we may speak the truth to each other.

An essential tool that can animate apostolic communal discernment is spiritual conversation. Spiritual conversation involves an exchange marked by active and receptive listening and a desire to speak of that which touches us most deeply. It tries to take account of spiritual movements, individual and communal, with the objective of choosing the path of consolation that fortifies our faith, hope, and love. Spiritual conversation creates an atmosphere of trust and welcome for ourselves and others. We ought not deprive ourselves of such conversation in the community and in all other occasions for decision-making in the Society.

In our world that knows too much division, we ask God to help our communities become "homes" for the Reign of God. We hear the call to overcome what can separate us from one another. Simplicity of life and openness of heart foster such mutual concern. Moreover, living together as friends in the Lord nurtures the vocations of our men in formation and can inspire men to enter the Society.

Of course, this disposition to attend to the Spirit in our relationships must include those with whom we work. Often they teach us this openness to the Spirit. Important discernments concerning mission are often enriched by their voices and their commitment.

It is critical to emphasize the continuing relevance of the real closeness of the first companions to the poor. The poor challenge us to return constantly to what is essential to the Gospel, to what really gives life, and to recognize that which merely burdens us. As Pope Francis reminds us: We are called to find Christ in the poor, to lend our voice to their causes, but also to be their friends, to listen to them, to understand them, and to embrace the mysterious wisdom which God wishes to share with us through them.[10] Such an attitude runs counter to the usual way of the world, in which, as Qoheleth

10. See *Evangelii Gaudium*, no. 198.

says, "the poor man's wisdom is despised, and his words are not heeded" (Ecclesiastes 9:16). With the poor, we can learn what hope and courage mean.

In our communities and apostolates, we hear the call to rediscover hospitality to strangers, to the young, to the poor, and to those who are persecuted. Christ himself teaches us this hospitality.

Men on Fire with Passion for the Gospel

Our First Fathers entered into such a rich discernment of God's call together because they had experienced the grace of Christ that set them free. Pope Francis urges us to pray insistently for this consolation that Christ desires to give.[11] Reconciliation with God is first and foremost a call to a profound conversion, for each Jesuit, and for all of us.

The question that confronts the Society today is why the Exercises do not change us as deeply as we would hope. What elements in our lives, works, or lifestyles hinder our ability to let God's gracious mercy transform us? This Congregation is deeply convinced that God is calling the entire Society to a profound spiritual renewal. Ignatius reminds us that each Jesuit must "take care, as long as he lives, first of all to keep before his eyes God" (Formula of the Institute of 1550, chapter 1). Thus, all the means that unite us directly with God should be more than ever prized and practiced: the Spiritual Exercises, daily prayer, the Eucharist and the Sacrament of Reconciliation, spiritual direction, and the Examen (Constitutions [813]). We need to appropriate ever more fully the gift of the Exercises that we share with so many, especially the Ignatian family and the Constitutions that animate our Society.[12] In a world losing its sense of God, we should seek to be more deeply united with Christ in the mysteries of his life. Through the Exercises, we acquire the style of Jesus, his feelings, his choices.

---

11. Address of Pope Francis to GC 36, 24 October 2016.
12. GC 35, D 6, n. 29.

At the heart of Ignatian spirituality is the transforming encounter with the mercy of God in Christ that moves us to a generous personal response. The experience of the merciful gaze of God on our weakness and sinfulness humbles us and fills us with gratitude, helping us to become compassionate ministers to all.[13] Filled with the fire of Christ's mercy, we can enflame those we meet. This foundational experience of God's mercy has always been the source of the apostolic audacity that has marked the Society and which we must preserve.

"Mercy," Pope Francis reminds us, "is not an abstraction but a lifestyle consisting in concrete gestures rather than mere words."[14] For us Jesuits, compassion is action, an action discerned together. Yet we know that there is no authentic familiarity with God if we do not allow ourselves to be moved to compassion and action by an encounter with the Christ who is revealed in the suffering, vulnerable faces of people, indeed in the suffering of creation (Cf. Matthew 25: 31–46).

On Mission with Christ the Reconciler

In preparation for the 36th General Congregation, Father General Adolfo Nicolás invited the Society to enter into a process of seeking to hear "the call of the Eternal King, and to discern the three most important calls that the Lord makes to the whole Society today."[15] Our provinces and regions, through the province and regional congregations, responded to this invitation. The call to share God's work of reconciliation in our broken world emerged often and powerfully. What GC 35 had identified as three dimensions of this ministry of reconciliation, namely reconciliation with God, with one another, and with creation, assumed a new urgency.[16] This reconciliation is always a work of justice, a justice discerned and enacted in local

---

13. Address of Pope Francis to GC 36, 24 October 2016.
14. Address of Pope Francis to GC 36, 24 October 2016.
15. Father Adolfo Nicolás, "Letter Convoking General Congregation 36," *Acta Romana Societatis Iesu*, Volume XXV (2014): 1096.
16. GC 35, D. 3.

communities and contexts. The Cross of Christ and our sharing in it are also at the center of God's work of reconciliation. This mission can lead to conflict and death, as we have witnessed in the lives of many of our brothers. While we speak of three forms of reconciliation, all three are, in reality, one work of God, interconnected and inseparable.

1st Call: Reconciliation with God

Reconciliation with God roots us in gratitude and opens us to joy, if we allow it. Pope Francis writes, "The joy of the Gospel fills the hearts and lives of all who encounter Jesus. . . . With Christ, joy is constantly born anew."[17] Announcing and sharing the Gospel continues to be the reason for the Society's existence and mission: that Jesus Christ be known, that he be loved in return, and that Christ's love be a source of life for all. He always remains the source of the joy and hope we offer to others. Thus, the Society must respond more decisively to the Church's call for a new evangelization, giving special emphasis to ministry to and with the young and with families. A special gift Jesuits and the Ignatian family have to offer to the Church and her mission of evangelization is Ignatian spirituality, which facilitates the experience of God and can therefore greatly help the process of personal and communal conversion. Pope Francis constantly affirms that discernment should play a special role, in the family, among youth, in vocation promotion, and in the formation of clergy.[18] Christian life is more and more personalized through discernment.

Proclaiming the Gospel takes place in many different contexts: a) Secularization is a major challenge for many cultures, calling for creativity particularly in attracting and initiating younger generations into the Christian faith. b) In an increasingly pluralistic world, interreligious dialogue in all its forms remains a necessity, one that is not always easy and that risks misunderstanding. c) In many parts of the

17. *Evangelii Gaudium*, 1.
18. *Amoris Laetitia*, 296–306.

world, the Society is called to respond to the challenge of believers abandoning the Church in the search for personal meaning and spirituality. d) Jesuits must continue to give importance to theological and scriptural studies by which we help people deepen their understanding of the Gospel in their diverse cultural contexts, with their hopes and their challenges. These studies should involve accompanying people from the depth of their spiritual traditions.

2nd Call: Reconciliation Within Humanity

Throughout our preparation for this Congregation as a universal body with a universal mission, we heard accounts of the shocking forms of suffering and injustice that millions of our brothers and sisters endure.[19] Reflecting on these, we hear Christ summon us anew to a ministry of justice and peace, serving the poor and the excluded, and helping build peace.

Among these various forms of suffering, three have appeared with consistency from many of our provinces and regions:

[26.] The displacement of peoples (refugees, migrants, and internally displaced peoples): In the face of attitudes hostile to these displaced persons, our faith invites the Society to promote everywhere a more generous culture of hospitality. The Congregation recognizes the necessity of promoting the international articulation of our service to migrants and refugees, finding ways of collaboration with Jesuit Refugee Service (JRS).

[27.] The injustices and inequalities experienced by marginalized peoples: Along with an enormous growth of wealth and power in the world comes an enormous and continuing growth of inequality. The present dominant models of development leave millions of people, especially the young and the vulnerable, without opportunities for integration into society.

19. GC 35, D. 2, n. 20.

Indigenous peoples and communities, like the Dalits and tribal groups in South Asia, represent a paradigmatic case of these groups. In many parts of the world, women especially experience such injustice. We are called to support these communities in their struggles, recognizing that we have much to learn from their values and their courage. The defense and promotion of human rights and integral ecology is an ethical horizon that we share with many other people of good will, who are also seeking to respond to this call.

[28.] Fundamentalism, intolerance, and ethnic-religious-political conflicts as a source of violence: In many societies, there is an increased level of conflict and polarization, which often gives rise to violence that is all the more appalling because it is motivated and justified by distorted religious convictions. In such situations, Jesuits, along with all who seek the common good, are called to contribute from their religious-spiritual traditions towards the building of peace, on local and global levels.

3rd Call: Reconciliation with Creation

Pope Francis has emphasized the fundamental connection between the environmental crisis and the social crisis in which we live today.[20] Poverty, social exclusion, and marginalization are linked with environmental degradation. These are not separate crises but one crisis that is a symptom of something much deeper: the flawed way societies and economies are organized. The current economic system with its predatory orientation discards natural resources as well as people.[21] For this reason, Pope Francis insists that the only adequate solution must be a radical one. The direction of development must be altered if it is to be sustainable. We Jesuits are called to help heal a broken world, promoting a new way of producing and consuming, which puts God's creation at the center.[22]

---

20. *Laudato Si'*, 139.
21. "Justice in the Global Economy: Building Sustainable and Inclusive Communities," *Promotio Iustitiae*, 121.
22. "Healing a Broken World," *Promotio Iustitiae*, 106.

The multifaceted challenge of caring for our common home calls for a multifaceted response from the Society. We begin by changing our personal and community lifestyles, adopting behavior coherent with our desire for reconciliation with creation. We must accompany and remain close to the most vulnerable. Our theologians, philosophers, and other intellectuals and experts should contribute to the rigorous analysis of the roots of and solutions to the crisis. Jesuit commitment in regions like the Amazon and the Congo Basin, environmental reserves that are essential for the future of humanity, should be supported. We should manage our financial investments responsibly. And we cannot forget to celebrate creation, to give thanks for "so much good we have received" (SE 233).

Toward the Renewal of Our Apostolic Life

All our ministries should seek to build bridges, to foster peace (see the Formula of the Institute of 1550, Chapter 1: "He should show himself ready to reconcile the estranged"). To do this, we must enter into a deeper understanding of the mystery of evil in the world and the transforming power of the merciful gaze of God who labors to create of humanity one reconciled, peaceful family.

With Christ, we are called to closeness with all of crucified humanity. With the poor, we can contribute to creating one human family through the struggle for justice. Those who have all the necessities of life and live far from poverty also need the message of hope and reconciliation, which frees them from fear of migrants and refugees, the excluded and those who are different, and that opens them to hospitality and to making peace with enemies.

The Congregation calls the entire Society to a renewal of our apostolic life founded on hope. We need more than ever to bring a message of hope, born of consolation from our encounter with the Risen Lord. This renewal focused on hope includes all our diverse apostolates.

We do not want to propose a simplistic or superficial hope. Rather, our contribution, as Father Adolfo Nicolás always insisted, should be characterized by depth: a depth of interiority and "a depth of reflection that allows us to understand reality more deeply and thus to serve more effectively."[23] To this end, Jesuits in formation should receive solid intellectual preparation and be helped to grow in personal integration.

Our educational apostolates at all levels, and our centers for communication and social research, should help form men and women committed to reconciliation and able to confront obstacles to reconciliation and propose solutions. The intellectual apostolate should be strengthened to help in the transformation of our cultures and societies.

Because of the magnitude and interconnectedness of the challenges we face, it is important to support and encourage the growing collaboration among Jesuits and Jesuit apostolates through networks. International and intersectoral networks provide an opportunity to strengthen our identity, as we share our capacities and local engagements in order to serve a universal mission together.

Collaboration with others is the only way the Society of Jesus can fulfill the mission entrusted to her. This partnership in mission includes those with whom we share Christian faith, those who belong to different religions, and women and men of good will, who, like us, desire to collaborate with Christ's reconciling work. In the words of Father General Arturo Sosa, Jesuits are "called to the mission of Jesus Christ, that does not belong to us exclusively, but that we share with so many men and women consecrated to the service of others."[24]

In all we do, we want to heed Pope Francis, who has urged us to promote dynamics of personal and social transformation. "What we need is to give priority to actions which generate new processes in society."[25] Prayerful discernment ought to be our habitual way of drawing closer to reality when we want to transform it.

---

23. Father Adolfo Nicolás, "Letter on Intellectual Formation", *Acta Romana Societatis Iesu,* Vol. XXV (2014): 926.
24. "Homily of Father," General Arturo Sosa, 15 October 2016.
25. *Evangelii Gaudium,* 223.

Aware of the urgency of the present moment and of the need to involve all the Society and its apostolates in responding to these calls, this Congregation asks Father General, working closely with the conferences and provinces, to develop clear goals and guidelines for our apostolic life today.

Conclusion

From Venice, Ignatius and his companions journeyed to Rome, there to give shape to the one apostolic body of the Society, and to launch an extraordinary missionary activity. They did so under the Roman Pontiff, who confirmed their charism. This Congregation has experienced a similar grace of confirmation, encouragement, and mission from Pope Francis.

The Holy Father emphasized that we should not be satisfied with the status quo of our ministries. He called us again to the *magis*, "that plus" which led "Ignatius to begin processes, to follow them through, and to evaluate their real impact on the lives of persons."[26]

In faith, we know that, amidst the difficulties and challenges of our time, God never ceases to labor for the salvation of all people, indeed of all creation. We believe that God continues his work of "reconciling the world to himself in Christ." We hear the urgent summons to join the Lord in caring for the neediest and to extend God's mercy to where injustice, suffering, or despair seems to thwart the divine plan. We pray for the courage and the freedom "to dare the audacity of the 'improbable,'" as we respond to God's call "with the humility of those who know that, in this service where the human engages all his energy, 'everything depends on God.' Now is the acceptable time! Now is the day of salvation!"[27]

---

26. Address of Pope Francis to GC 36, 24 October 2016. Cf. *Evangelii Gaudium* 223: "Giving priority to time means being concerned about initiating processes rather than possessing spaces."
27. (Original: English) 382.

Back to Fundamentals

Thomas D. Stegman, SJ

The first time I entered the newly renovated aula, the commissioned artwork immediately caught my attention. As Hung Pham points out in his own essay, [Ed. Note: This essay: "To Allow the Creator to Deal Directly with the Creature," is found in part III of this collection] the four painted panels—brightly hued in reds, oranges, and yellows—have subtle script near the bottom. Close inspection reveals that the writing is short phrases from *The Spiritual Exercises* (e.g., *en todo amar y servir*) as well as some citations from the New Testament. One of those citations, from Paul, proclaims the wonders of the "new creation" God has brought about through Christ (2 Corinthians 5:17).

As one who studies and teaches the Pauline letters, I have always been drawn to the fifth chapter of Second Corinthians, which contains some of Paul's most weighty theology. As the congregation progressed, I found myself reflecting more and more on the paragraph following 2 Corinthians 5:17—namely, 5:18–6:2—where the apostle Paul writes about God's work of reconciliation and the gift of the ministry of reconciliation to the church. In fact, Decree 1 is bracketed by the words at the beginning and end of this paragraph. Just beneath the title reads, "All this is from God, who reconciled us to himself through Christ, and has given us the ministry of reconciliation" (2 Corinthians 5:18). And the closing words of the decree are those of 2 Corinthians 6:2b: "See, now is the acceptable time; see, now is the day of salvation!"

Excerpt from "The Moment of GC 36 for Its Members" Edited by Hung T. Pham, SJ. *Studies in the Spirituality of Jesuits*, 49/3, Autumn 2017, Essay 10.

But more than quotations, it is the content of Decree 1 that evokes the wealth of material found in 2 Corinthians 5:18–6:2. In addition to its use of reconciliation as a leitmotif, the decree draws on Ignatius's beautiful image of God laboring on our behalf, and it sets forth God's invitation to us to participate in the work of reconciliation. In terms of the latter, the document alludes to Paul's use of *synergoi*—that is, to the divine empowerment to be "God's servant" (1 Corinthians 3:9, cited in footnote 8; cf. 2 Corinthians 6:1). Even more, Jesus's self-giving love on the Cross (cf. 2 Corinthians 5:21) as the paradoxical source of God's power undergirds much of what we participants prayed and reflected on, and what went into the decree.

These themes were prominent in Pope Francis's allocution to us early in the *ad negotia* phase of the congregation. [Ed. Note: The text of this allocution is located at the beginning of part II of this present collection.] It was striking to me how the pope called us back to the fundamentals of our spirituality. His appeal to allow ourselves to be moved by the love of Christ manifested on the Cross called to mind the colloquy of the First Week before the crucifix, especially the third question: What ought I to do for Christ in light of such love and mercy poured forth for me (SE 53)? Francis's counsel to pray intensely for the grace of consolation—for the love and joy that radiate from the risen Lord—was a reminder of one of his constant themes: the joy of the gospel. I cannot think of a more practical prayer. To beg for this grace is to pray to live each day with my will aligned more with God's; and, in so doing, to experience the joy and peace of God's Spirit. Of course, the gift is not just for our sake but is to be shared with others. As Francis poignantly reminded us, "Mercy is not an abstraction but a lifestyle consisting in concrete gestures."[1]

The call to the basics of our spirituality is also a summons to humility. Adolfo Nicolas modeled a salutary example of humility at the beginning of the congregation, as he related to us instances of diminishment he had recently experienced. The image of Father

1. "Address of His Holiness Pope Francis to the 36th General Congregation of the Society of Jesus."

Nicolas taking his seat among us in the aula, arranged in alphabetical order, after the vote that received his resignation was one I will never forget. So too was his decision, following the election of Arturo Sosa as Father General, to leave the aula—an act designed to give the congregation fuller freedom in our deliberations. Similarly, Decree 1 sets a tone of humility in the evocation of the meeting of the first companions in Venice. Rather than recall the vows at Montmartre, Ignatius's vision at La Storta, or the official founding of the Society, Decree 1 takes us to a moment when the first companions, having been frustrated in their attempt to go to the Holy Land, were vulnerable. They were led to rely even more on God's lead, which compelled them to more intense discernment of what the Lord was calling them to do.

In addition to the evocation of the first companions in Venice, Decree 1 sends out an important signal with its order of presentation. Notice that the document treats the theme of a discerning community before expounding on our life of faith, thereby giving prominence to our communal identity. Similar to the biblical perspective of Paul, the emphasis falls on community life and not on individuals. While Decree 1 was not written for the express purpose of giving flesh to Peter-Hans Kolvenbach's challenge to live Jesuit community as mission—a call taken up by GC 35—it does offer plenty of fodder for reflection on this topic. My hope is that we take this offer.

I presently live at the Saint Peter Faber Jesuit Community in Brighton, Massachusetts, which is connected with the Boston College School of Theology and Ministry (STM). The community is divided into eight small communities. The small community where I live has nine members, from seven different countries representing four continents. We are truly multicultural. But are we intercultural? And even more importantly, are we deepening our bonds as brothers in the Lord? The way toward such deepening is the spiritual conversation for which Decree 1 calls: "The exchange marked by active and receptive listening and a desire to speak of that which touches us most deeply."[2]

2. cc 36, d. 1, no. 12; 36th Gt'11cmi Cm1xnxatio11 Oornme11t, 3/16.

We have the opportunity to emulate the first companions—surely a diverse cast of characters!—in our commitment to one another, in sharing how the Lord is working in our lives, and in being joyful ministers of the gospel. Such a commitment, I hope, can go beyond weekly community meetings and permeate our lives together, as in dinner conversation.

The diverse makeup of the Faber Jesuit Community also offers an opportunity to bear witness to God's work of reconciliation among us. At our best, our ethnic, cultural, and socio-economic differences are not causes of division.[3] Rather, they are part of the rich mosaic of our unity-in-diversity that has its source of union in our spiritual resources, not least the Spiritual Exercises. To be frank, what most threatens to divide are differences across the theological spectrum, and especially around liturgy. But can we let our dedication to being true friends in the Lord—a dedication rooted in our identity as members of the Company of Jesus—trump the differences? Our participation in the ministry of reconciliation will be more authentic when we embody reconciliation among ourselves. Like charity, reconciliation begins at home.

So, too, does collaboration. Decree 2 acknowledges, while listing the challenges in collaboration, that a "particular difficulty can be the lack of genuine collaboration among Jesuits: individuals, institutions, communities, Provinces, and Conferences."[4] That is an acknowledgment that should give us reason to pause. The same decree calls for greater cooperation among Jesuits and our institutions through networking. Jesuit theology centers are a natural place for such cooperation to happen. In fact, there have already been some important initiatives. But there is so much potential to do more to enhance theological education in a global context. As the dean of the STM, I am challenged by Decree 2 to keep opportunities at the forefront of my prayer and thinking rather than get bogged down and discouraged by the obstacles and difficulties that naturally arise when discussing the practicalities involved.

---

3. On this point, see, for example, Galatians 3:28; 1 Corinthians 12:13.
4. CC 36, d. 2, no. 7; 36th General Congregation Decree 1, 2/23.

The art panels in the aula, with their fiery yellows, oranges, and reds, radiated energy, light, and warmth. The experience of GC 36 is one that will be etched in my heart for the rest of my life. I hope that we Jesuits allow the fruits of the congregation—especially Decree 1—to kindle within us the fire and love that animated the first companions in Venice. If we open our hearts to these graces, we will find ourselves becoming more effective instruments in God's ongoing work of reconciliation in bringing about the "new creation." Now is indeed the acceptable time.

An Apology Toward Reconciliation

Georgetown University Slavery Reconciliation Project

Ultimately, reconciliation requires relationship. To reconcile today, the [Georgetown] University community must know whom it seeks to reconcile with over this history and its legacy. That "who" can include many diverse people and communities. Much recent national attention has turned to the descendants of the slaves owned and sold by the Maryland Jesuits. The descendants, whose unprecedented outreach to the University has moved all of us so greatly, surely have a privileged role as witnesses to and participants in the University's pursuit of reconciliation. On our own campus, there are also the many whose experience of our community is fundamentally marred by estrangement, alienation, and hostility, sustained by persistent racism. The unrest on many campuses and in many communities over the past year gives evidence to how ubiquitous, profound, and enduring racial alienation and injustice remain in American society.

The University owes its own efforts toward reconciliation to all of these. Many of the recommendations made in the following section have as a goal the fostering of a relationship with the descendants and greater investment in solving the distinctively American racial injustice that scars our own University community. As the University works to develop its relationship with these groups, on and beyond

From "The Report of the Working Group on Slavery, Memory, and Reconciliation to the President John J. DeGioia of Georgetown University, Washington, D.C., Summer 2016"
[Editor's Note: Georgetown University and the North American Assistancy for the Society of Jesus have been working on a major project of reconciliation with descendants of African American slaves that Georgetown sold in the 19th century. This section is the final section of a longer working text.]

our campus, the Working Group recommends that the University offer a formal, public apology for its historical relationship with slavery. The Working Group believes that an apology from the University president offered jointly with the provincial superior of the Maryland Jesuits would be especially fitting, bringing together, as it would, the successors to the two officeholders who were the architects of the 1838 sale.

The Working Group finds an express apology proper for two reasons: first, because an apology is a precondition for reconciliation. The responsibility to apologize, moreover, belongs to the perpetrators; it is what perpetrators can do on their own initiative. They admit the performance of the deed, recognize that it was wrong, display regret, and pledge not to repeat the deed. While apologies often need repeating and this apology need not be thought of as the last, without an apology pursuit of reconciliation ends.

Second, a formal, spoken apology strikes the Working Group as appropriate because its absence rings so loudly. The University, despite the many ways that it has invested resources over the past half century to heal the wounds of racial injustice, has not made such an apology. While there can be empty apologies, words of apology, genuinely expressed, make a difference in the quest for reconciliation. Words along with symbolic actions, such as the naming of buildings, and material investments, such as the foundation of an institute for the study of slavery, work together in making apology a coherent whole. None of these components—words, symbolic gestures, and material investments—should be neglected. Again, the counsel of the descendants of the slaves, whose labor and value supported the University, should be sought out and weighted heavily.

The Working Group sees additional benefits from an apology and from conceiving the other recommendations as a form of apology: For example, apology offers a form of moral restitution to those who accept it. An apology can also inspire further discussion and debate, as can the decision not to apologize. Other universities have taken different routes in the past decade on the question of apologizing. For us, an apology is the truest response to our specific history and our core values. The Working Group foresees the University's apology fostering our ongoing process in productive ways. Finally, an apology becomes part of the history. An outright apology is not yet part of the history for the University. It ought to be.

By way of conclusion, we turn to the poignant words of President George W. Bush in 2003 at Gorée Island, a former slave-trading post in what is now Senegal. The president's lament portrays a general history that has a specific expression at Georgetown:

> For 250 years the captives endured an assault on their culture and their dignity. The spirit of Africans in America did not break. Yet the spirit of their captors was corrupted. Small men took on the powers and airs of tyrants and masters. Years of unpunished brutality and bullying and rape produced a dullness and hardness of conscience. Christian men and women became blind to the clearest commands of their faith and added hypocrisy to injustice. . . . My nation's journey toward justice has not been easy, and it is not over. The racial bigotry fed by slavery did not end with slavery or with segregation. And many of the issues that still trouble America have roots in the bitter experience of other times. But however long the journey, our destination is set: liberty and justice for all. (President George W. Bush, Gorée Island, Senegal, July 8, 2003)

That long and unfinished journey traverses the Hilltop (Georgetown University's historic main campus). Slavery—slave labor and the slave trade—is part of our history. All of us—students, alumni, faculty, staff, administration, and friends—are the heirs of this history, and all of us must make ourselves its humbled trustees. As a university community, we need to know, to acknowledge, and to absorb that history as part of what makes Georgetown what it is. We are, after all, slavery's beneficiaries still today. There can be neither justice nor reconciliation until we grasp that truth.

Meeting with Young People and Elders

Pope Francis

Dear Brothers and Sisters, good evening!
I greet the Governor General, and all of you, most heartily. I am happy to be here with you. I thank you for your words of welcome and for your songs, dances, and music, which I enjoyed greatly!

A short while ago, I listened to several of you, who were students of residential schools. I thank you for having had the courage to tell your stories and to share your great suffering, which I could not have imagined. This only renewed in me the indignation and shame that I have felt for months. Today too, in this place, I want to tell you how very sorry I am and to ask for forgiveness for the evil perpetrated by not a few Catholics who, in these schools, contributed to the policies of cultural assimilation and enfranchisement. *Mamianak* (I am sorry). I was reminded of the testimony of an elder, who spoke of the beautiful spirit that reigned in indigenous families before the advent of the residential school system. He compared those days, when grandparents, parents, and children were harmoniously together, to springtime, when young birds chirp happily around their mother. But suddenly, he said, the singing stopped: Families were broken up, and the little ones were taken away far from home.

Winter fell over everything.

Stories like these not only cause us pain; they also create scandal. All the more so, if we compare them with the Word of God and its commandment: "Honor your father and your mother, so that your days may be long in the land that the Lord your God is giving you"

Primary school in Iqaluit Friday, 29 July 2022.

(Exodus 20:12). That possibility did not exist for many of your families; it vanished when children were separated from their parents and their own nation was perceived as dangerous and foreign. Those forced assimilations evoke another biblical story, that of the just man Naboth (cf. 1 Kings 21), who refused to give the vineyard he had inherited from his ancestors to those in power, who were willing to use every means to snatch it from him. And we think too of the forceful words of Jesus about those who scandalize or despise even one of the little ones (cf. Matthew 18:6, 10). How evil it is to break the bonds uniting parents and children, to damage our closest relationships, to harm and scandalize the little ones!

Dear friends, we are here with the desire to pursue together a journey of healing and reconciliation that, with the help of the Creator, can help us shed light on what happened and move beyond the dark past. As a way of dispelling that darkness, now too, as in our meeting at the end of March, you have lit the *qulliq*. Not only did the *qulliq* give light amid the long winter nights, it also relieved the harshness of the weather by spreading heat. In this way, it was essential for living. Even today, this lamp remains a beautiful symbol of life, of a luminous way of living that does not yield to the darkness of the night. That is what you are, a perennial testimony to the life that never ends, a light that shines and that no one has been able to extinguish.

I am grateful for this opportunity to be here in Nunavut, within Inuit Nunangat. I tried to imagine, after our meeting in Rome, these vast places that you have inhabited from time immemorial and that others would consider inhospitable. You have come to love these places, to respect, cherish, and enhance them, passing on, from generation to generation, such basic values as respect for the elderly, genuine fraternity, and care for the environment. There is a beautiful and harmonious relationship between you and this land you inhabit, because it too is strong and resilient, and responds with brilliant light to the darkness that enshrouds it for most of the year. Yet this land, like every individual and every people, is also fragile, and needs to be cared for. Caring, teaching and learning how to care: To this task young people in particular, supported by the example of their elders, have been called! Care for the earth, care for your people, care for your history.

I would like now to address you, Inuit youth, the future of this land and the present of its history. I would like to say to you, in the words of a great poet: "That which you inherited from your fathers, must first be earned before it can become yours" (Goethe, *Faust*, Part 1: Nacht). It is not enough to live off the past; it is necessary to earn what was given to you as a gift. Do not be afraid, then, to continue listening to the counsels of the elderly, to embrace your past in order to write new pages of history, to be passionate, to take a stand before facts and people, to get involved! To help you make the lamp of your lives shine brightly, I too, as an elder brother, would also like to offer you three pieces of advice.

The first is: Keep walking upwards. You live in these vast regions of the north. May they remind you of your vocation to strive ever higher, without letting yourself get dragged down by those who would have you believe that it is better to think only of yourself and to use your time solely for your leisure and your interests. Friends, you were not made "to get by," to spend your days balancing duties and pleasures. You were made to soar upwards, towards the most genuine, true, and beautiful desires that you cherish in your hearts, to love God and to serve your neighbor. Don't think that life's great dreams are as unattainable as the sky above. You were made to fly, to embrace the courage of truth and the beauty of justice, to "elevate your moral temper, to be compassionate, to serve others and to build relationships" (cf. Inunnguiniq IQ Principles 3–4). To sow seeds of peace and loving care wherever you are; to ignite the enthusiasm of those all around you; to keep pressing forward and not to flatten everything out.

But, you might say, to live like that is harder than flying! Certainly, it is not easy, because there is a kind of hidden "force of spiritual gravity" that tries to drag us down, paralyze our desires, and lessen our joy. Keep thinking of the arctic swallow that in Spanish we call a "charrán." It does not let headwinds or sudden changes in temperature stop it from flying from one end of the earth to the other. At times, it chooses alternate routes, accepts detours, adapts to certain winds, but it always has a clear goal, and it always arrives at its destination. You will meet people who will try to discount your dreams, who will tell you to settle for less, to fight only for what is in your interest. Then you will have to ask yourself: Why do I need to go out of my way for what other people do not believe in? Or again: How can I "soar" in a world that seems constantly to be dragged down by scandals, wars, fraud, injustice, environmental destruction, indifference towards those in need, and disillusionment from those who should be giving an example? Faced with these questions, what is the answer?

Here is what I would tell you: Young people, you my brother, and you my sister, you are the answer! Not just because once you give up, you have already lost, but because the future is even now in your hands. The community that gave you birth, the environment in which you live, the hopes of your peers, of those who, without even asking, expect from you the irreplaceable treasure that you can bring to history: all these things are in your hands, because "each one of us is unique" (cf. Principle 5). The world you are living in is the treasure you have inherited: love it, even as God, who gave you life and its great joys, loved you and created all this great beauty for you. God never ceases to have confidence in you, not for a second. He believes in your talents. When you seek him, you will come to realize how the path he calls you to follow always goes upwards. You will realize this when you look up at the sky as you pray, and especially when you contemplate him on the Cross. You will come to realize that Jesus, from the Cross, never points his finger at you; he embraces you and encourages you, because he believes in you even at those times when you stop believing in yourself. So never lose hope, fight, give it your all, and you will not be sorry. Go forward on your journey, "step by step towards the best" (cf. Principle 6). Set the navigator of your lives on a great destination: upwards!

The second piece of advice is: Come to the light. When you feel sad or downcast, think of the *qulliq*: It has a message for you. What message? That you are meant to come into the light each day. Not just on the day of your birth, when it did not depend on you, but every day. Each day you are called to bring new light into the world, the light of your eyes, the light of your smile, the light of the goodness that you and you alone can bring. It cannot be brought by another. Yet, to come into the light, to be reborn, you need to fight each day against the darkness. For there is a daily clash between light and darkness, which does not take place somewhere out there, but within each of us. To follow the way of light requires courageous and heartfelt decisions to resist the darkness of lies. It means "developing good habits to live well" (cf. Principle 1), not to chase bursts of light that disappear quickly, fireworks that leave only smoke in their wake. These are "illusions, parodies of happiness," as Saint John Paul II said here in Canada: "There is perhaps no darkness deeper than the darkness that enters young people's souls when false prophets extinguish in them the light of faith and hope and love" ("Homily for World Youth Day," Toronto, 28 July 2002).

Dear brother, dear sister, Jesus is close to you and he wants to light up your heart, to make you come to the light. He said of himself: "I am the light of the world" (John 8:12), but he also told his disciples: "You are the light of the world" (Matthew 5:14). You too, then, are light for the world and you will shine all the brighter if you struggle to cast out the dark shadows of evil from your heart.

To do this, there is a skill that we have to acquire, one that calls for "overcoming difficulties and contradictions through a continuous search for solutions" (see Principle 2). It is the art of daily separating light from darkness. To create a good world, the Bible tells us, God began just like that, by separating the light from the darkness (cf. Gen 1:4). We too, if we want to become better, must learn to distinguish light from darkness. Where do we start? You can start by asking yourself: What are the things that first strike me as glittery and seductive, but then leave me with a feeling of deep emptiness? That is the darkness! What, on the other hand, is good for me and leaves a feeling of peace in my heart, even if it first calls me to give up certain conveniences and to master certain instincts? That is the light! And—I ask again—what is the power that enables us to separate the light from the darkness within us, that enables us to say "no" to the temptations of evil and "yes" to all that is good? It is freedom. Freedom does not mean doing everything I want and acting as I please. Freedom is not about what I can do in spite of others, but what I can do for others. Freedom is not total caprice, but responsibility. Freedom, along with life, is the greatest gift that our heavenly Father has given us.

Finally, the third piece of advice: Be part of a team. Young people do great things together, not alone. You young people are like the stars in the sky, which shine so marvelously in this land. Their beauty comes from the whole, from the constellations they make up, which give light and provide bearings in the nights of this world. You too, called to the heights of heaven and to shine here on earth, are made to shine together, in unison. Young people have to be allowed to congregate, to be on the move: They can't spend their days in isolation, hostage to a cell phone! The great glaciers in these lands make me think of Canada's national sport, ice hockey. How does Canada manage to win all those Olympic medals? How did Sarah Nurse or Marie-Philip Poulin get to score all those goals? Hockey combines discipline and creativity, tactics and physical strength; but team spirit always makes the difference; it is essential for responding to the unpredictability of every game. Teamwork means believing that, in order to achieve great goals, you cannot go it alone; you have to move together, to have the patience to practice and carry out complicated plays. Teamwork also involves making room for others, dashing out quickly when it is your turn, and cheering on your teammates. That is team spirit!

Friends, keep walking upwards, come to the light each day, and be part of a team! Do all this within your own culture and in the beautiful Inuktitut language. It is my hope and prayer that, by listening to your elders and drawing from the richness of your traditions and your personal freedom, you will embrace the Gospel preserved and handed down by your ancestors, and thus come to see the Inuk face of Jesus Christ. I bless you from my heart, and to all of you I say: *Qujannamiik!* [Thank you!]

Atoning for Sins Against Indigenous People Begins with Confronting the Past. Red Cloud Indian School Is Showing the Way.

Maka Black Elk and William Critchley-Menor, SJ

When Holy Rosary Mission was founded on the Pine Ridge Indian Reservation in South Dakota in 1888, many of the Jesuits and Franciscan sisters who established the mission learned the Lakota language. The missionaries believed this method of inculturation would be pastorally effective.

Ironically, in the boarding school they founded at Holy Rosary Mission, they prohibited native Lakota speakers from speaking their own language, following the policy of the federal government at the time. In so doing, the men and women religious became complicit in the destruction of the Lakota culture.

We—a Lakota Catholic Red Cloud alumnus and a white Jesuit in formation—are working directly on the Red Cloud Indian School Truth and Healing initiative to address this history.

From *America Magazine*, October 8, 2021.

A Traumatic History

The founding of Holy Rosary Mission was part of a much larger project of colonization ultimately engineered by the United States government. More than 300 boarding schools were funded by the government and often run by various Christian denominations. Like the boarding school at Holy Rosary Mission (renamed Red Cloud Indian School in 1969), these schools were places where aspects of indigenous culture were unwelcome and prohibited. The government's vision for the boarding schools was explained by one of their architects, General Richard Henry Pratt of the Carlisle Indian Industrial School in Pennsylvania, as a method of assimilation: "Kill the Indian, save the man."

To ensure the efficacy of this assimilation, the boarding schools relied on removing children from their families. While the church today preaches the sanctity of family life and the need for values and faith to be passed down in the family, in the 19th and 20th centuries in North America, the church participated in the process that systematically broke apart Native families.

One survivor from Holy Rosary Mission described the family separation as "detrimental" to the bond between parents and their children. "That's probably the most important thing they took away from us. . . . You lose that part of your culture. . . . I think you go around the rest of your life not knowing who you are."

Long hair was cut, given names were changed, and traditional dress was banned at most of these schools, including Holy Rosary Mission. "I found it very ironic," said a survivor of the mission about having his hair cut. "[They] told me one thing, and then they showed us Christ on the Cross who had long hair."

"We regret our participation in the separation of families and the suppression of Native languages, cultures, and sacred ways of life," said the Jesuit Conference of Canada and the United States in a statement last month. While these practices and our participation in such schools ended decades ago, their traumatic effects have continued to reverberate through the generations and are still very present with many today. Fundamental to these schools were structures and practices which forced Indigenous children to be separated from their families and prohibited these children from speaking their language and practicing their culture.

Indigenous Peoples' Day and Orange Shirt Day

Many Native peoples recognize the history of Indigenous cultures on two days every Fall. In addition to Indigenous Peoples' Day, which is celebrated this year on October 11 in the United States, many throughout Canada and the United States are beginning to commemorate the historical traumas suffered by Native peoples as a result of colonization every September 30, on what has come to be known as "Orange Shirt Day." Orange Shirt Day is named for Phyllis Webstad, a survivor of St. Joseph's Residential School in Williams Lake, British Columbia, who remembers wearing an orange blouse her grandmother had purchased for her on her first day of school.

"When I got to the Mission, they stripped me and took away my clothes—including the orange shirt!" recalled Ms. Webstad of the Stswecem'c Xgat'tem First Nation. "I never wore it again," she added. "The color orange has always reminded me of that and how my feelings didn't matter, how no one cared, and how I felt like I was worth nothing."

The tensions we experience at Red Cloud today stem directly from its foundations as part of a similar colonial project. The Jesuits came to Pine Ridge at the invitation of Chief Red Cloud, but the deleterious impacts of their assimilative efforts, made in conjunction with the United States government, are undeniably still felt—part of the reason that Orange Shirt Day resonates among the Native people of Red Cloud today.

As part of Orange Shirt Day commemorations this year, students at Red Cloud created a memorial using early 19th-century school desks they retrieved from our store. They painted the desks orange and invited the community to write on them, and also to offer memorials of flowers, fruits, and traditional medicines as a way to honor the estimated 6,000 children who died in Native American boarding schools across North America. From the very same desks students were once prohibited from speaking Lakota, our students wrote, in Lakota, words of remembrance and honor.

The Mission Today

Formerly an institution that systematically suppressed the Lakota language, Red Cloud Indian School is a Lakota language immersion school today. Lakota culture and sacred rites are also practiced and taught in our classrooms, and Native artists and culture are supported through our Heritage Center.

Yet the changes that have taken place at Red Cloud over the years can appear hollow—because our tragic past has not been adequately acknowledged. That is why we have embarked upon a truth and healing process modeled on the research of Dr. Maria Yellow Horse Braveheart, a psychologist who has studied the effects of generational trauma and pathways to healing. Dr. Braveheart lays out a four-pronged path to addressing this trauma: confrontation, understanding, healing, and transformation. It is our hope that this process will help us to acknowledge this damage and move our community towards collective healing.

At Red Cloud, we are now in the confrontation stage. This includes collecting the stories of survivors and facilitating frequent talking circles among our community to provide space to unpack this history and its impact on our present. Some survivors carry with them stories of pain; others carry fond memories and gratitude for their time at Holy Rosary. Their stories will help create a full picture of our history.

Confrontation has also meant initiating a community-wide process that will culminate in the use of ground-penetrating radar (G.P.R.) on our campus. It is already clear to us that in our historic cemetery there are graves that have lost their markers. This technology will help us determine the exact location of these graves and allow us to mark and memorialize them in a way that honors those buried there.

Confrontation has also spurred questions from students and educators for our classrooms and curriculum. What does it mean to teach American literature, for example, in an English department at a former boarding school where English was once mandated as a way to assimilate children into white culture?

An exploration of our Lakota-Catholic identity is also fundamental to the experience of confrontation. We are fully aware that some members of the Lakota community wish that Red Cloud was no longer a Catholic school. Yet there are Lakota people who wish Red Cloud would claim an even more vibrant Catholic identity. We believe that an essential component of confronting this past is facing these questions directly and at their deepest levels. No amount of balancing Lakota and Catholic spiritual practices by equal weight or mandate can address the fundamental issue of discomfort or anger toward Catholicism.

Red Cloud Indian School is ground zero, in many ways, for the long-needed intercultural and interreligious dialogue that seeks to address the tragic history of the Native American boarding school system. For Indigenous people, this is family history. We have grandparents who were in these boarding schools and can draw a straight line through trauma experienced across generations. For Jesuits, and other white Catholics, our spiritual lineage and privilege is tied directly to this history of colonization.

We are all wounded by this history. All people are affected by intergenerational trauma and experience themselves as both oppressor and oppressed.

Delving into this history probes both the mysteries of evil and of grace. We do not know yet what it looks like to be a decolonized Church. We hope, however, that by engaging the past and its legacy we can move toward collective healing and discover new pathways of relationship between Indigenous peoples and the Catholic Church.

V. Leadership and Mission

Part V Introduction

One of the more exciting areas of growth in Ignatian spirituality over the past several decades has resulted through a discourse with the fields of leadership studies and mission integration. Individuals formed through the Exercises and Jesuit education holding positions of influence in religious, educational, and secular fields sought to integrate personal values and faith experiences with their responsibilities and interests as leaders and executives.

As Vatican II encouraged congregations to return to their original founders' charism and purpose, scholars and practitioners of Jesuit ministries have brought forth new insights from the life and letters of Ignatius to suggest a particularly Ignatian style of leadership and administration. In 2005, Chris Lowney published the well-received *Heroic Leadership*, offering "best practices from a 450-year-old company that changed the world," which suggested principles of Ignatian spirituality applicable to the cultural and corporate mainstream.

The growth in scholarship on Ignatian spirituality took place in tandem with a growth in leadership studies, and eventually scholars and researchers explored merging the two fields. Concepts such as Ignatian decision-making, communal discernment, and mission integration became the foci of scholars and practitioners to enhance not only Jesuit apostolates, but also leadership throughout the public, private, and non-profit sectors. The establishment of the Loyola Institute for Spirituality in Orange, California, in 1997 is one example of a new type of pastoral ministry designed to "bring Ignatian Spirituality to people in their everyday lives" and blend principles of the Exercises with leadership development programming.

Initiatives grew throughout Jesuit apostolates and provinces, bringing Ignatian spirituality to new audiences, particularly Jesuit business school students, alumnae/i, civic and business leaders. Of course, these were not new audiences for scholars of Jesuit history, as Ignatius always intended for the Exercises to appeal to civic and economic leaders of his time. But what grew was a new synthesis of Ignatian history, including the spirituality and the Constitutions, the life of Ignatius, and the burgeoning fields of leadership theory and organizational development. New programs and publications proliferated in recent years to create a rich field of thought and praxis in Ignatian leadership.

The essays in Part V bring together some of the most recent explorations at the intersection of leadership studies and Ignatian spirituality from several vantage points. To begin, Sarah Broscombe in her article "What is Ignatian Leadership?" describes characteristics of the Ignatian leader such as humility, freedom, and a sense of direction, and suggests that a call to leadership is inherent to Ignatian formation. Michelle Wheatley asks the question, "What does the Ignatian leader *do*?" to introduce some very practical suggestions for creating workspace and organizational dynamics that allow an Ignatian vision to take shape. Jennifer Tilghman-Havens brings feminist and critical race theory into the conversation to suggest that Ignatian leadership is inherently liberatory for both the leader and those being led. Michele Murray poses the question, "Suppose we all presupposed?" to delve into the possibilities for applying the Presupposition of the First Week (SE 22) to leadership practices and interpersonal behaviors among colleagues. Debra Mooney suggests that in addition to caring for the whole person and caring for the apostolate, Ignatian leaders must care for themselves, a practice she terms *cura propria*, in order to lead from a place of hope. Part V closes with Kevin F. Burke's exploration of the mystical roots of Pedro Arrupe's leadership of the Society of Jesus to argue it was Arrupe's spiritual experiences, much like those of Ignatius, that grounded his courageous leadership.

In all, the reflections in this section were chosen to spark enriching and engaging conversations within Ignatian ministries on the spiritual dynamics of leadership, mission integration, and the person of the leader. Excellent endnotes in several of the articles point to suggestions for further reading.

Julia A. Dowd

What Is Ignatian Leadership?

Sarah Broscombe

What is your gut reaction when you hear the word "leadership"? For some, it evokes a tug of responsibility. Others switch off immediately—"I'm not a leader of anything"—or feel cynical: "Here we go again, corporate speak!" For others still there is a personal connection: "Ah yes, I remember that inspiring person who I would have followed into a burning building."

What makes Ignatian leadership special has something to do with the burning building reaction. And so it should. Ignatius of Loyola had something of the counterintuitive attractiveness of Jesus about him, and so should leaders within his sphere of influence. If there is a growing interest in the concept of leadership in general, and Ignatian leadership in particular, it is because our contemporary world (political, environmental, and social) has been a smorgasbord of good, bad, and absent leadership over the past few decades. Manifold crises face us, all of which cry out for brave, authentic leaders. This is urgent.

Leadership is so much more than being the boss. This is especially true for the Ignatian form of it, whereby leadership is not simply a subset of positional power, and the hierarchy is structured as a two-way, not a one-way street (each provincial steps back "down" after six years in office). It taps straight into vocation: Every Jesuit leads, well or badly. And the domain of Ignatian leadership does not stretch only as far as directors of Jesuit workplaces. As the Jesuits in Britain's online retreat, "31 days of Ignatius," so strikingly illustrated, everyone

From *Thinking Faith*, September 1, 2017.

shaped by an Ignatian education is formed to lead, whether they are in charge or not. If you are Ignatian, you are called to be aware of how you are leading in your life, and the impact of that on others.

I often hear Ignatian leaders characterized as empathetic, open to change, collaborative, and purposeful. But these are true of the best secular models, too. On a personal level, all excellent leaders need self-understanding, integrity, authenticity, and courage. Interpersonally, they must deploy good communication, motivation, inspiration, and empathy. Organizationally, they need to be strategic, visionary, purposeful, and mission-driven. But Ignatian leadership isn't simply generic good leadership seasoned with Jesuit jargon. The distinctiveness is more fundamental than that.

What distinguishes an *Ignatian* leader, then? Simple formulations will fall badly short, because "Ignatian Leadership" is not a coherent theory or a body of scholarship. It's a lived experience that immerses itself in the world, a disposition deeply rooted in the Spiritual Exercises and Jesuit history. I have heard Jesuits say, "You pick it up by osmosis," or, "Just live it." And I agree that it is irreducible to a neat formula. But for those new to Jesuit environments or attracted by what they have encountered and wanting to understand more deeply, some starting point is needed.

A recent eighteen-month Ignatian Leadership Program offered by the Conference of European Provincials faced some of these questions. We as a training team were mixed lay and Jesuit, and the participants came from twenty-two countries spanning a pretty broad conception of "Europe" (from Moscow to Lebanon, Portugal to Kyrgyzstan). This provided a rich melting pot of expectations and experiences. For me, it also helped to crystallize thoughts that have been forming gradually for the past decade or so. At this stage, I want to suggest five qualities typical of Ignatian leaders—typical either because they are linked to features distinctive to Ignatian spirituality, or because Ignatian teaching can nuance or enrich what we already know about leadership from other sources or our first-hand experience. These five are offered to provoke thought, definitely not in an attempt at comprehensiveness. But without any of them, I'd struggle to see leadership as Ignatian.

Humility

Ignatian humility is not about anxiously balancing your flaws and strengths, or comparing yourself to others, or self-abnegation (keeping your head down and your mouth shut). It is seeing your real self, truly and in proportion, in a world that is different because of Jesus' work; "If the gospel is true, then Christ has revealed potentials in the human condition for bringing good out of evil. . . . Moreover, only out of this sin and degradation can the full greatness of the redeemer be displayed."[1] Humility dares to look because it knows it is loved. It also dares to be humbled without believing the core of the self to be diminished by humiliation. False humility attacks a person's sense of dignity and worth. True humility frees us from the pressure of trying to earn worth. When Ignatius describes the third degree of humility in the Spiritual Exercises, he speaks of choosing poverty with Christ and choosing insults rather than honors (SE 167).[2] We choose differently not because we are addicted to self-sacrifice or self-abasement, and not because we are allergic to power, but because we love Jesus too much and want the journey with him too much to prefer ease, strength, and success.

Leaders operating with this humility, this sense of themselves as utterly loved sinners, will have different relationships. They will see themselves in proportion with their team, their organization and the purpose it serves. Ignatian leaders will view power differently; they will handle it carefully but not avoid it (Pope Francis exemplifies this beautifully).[3]

Humility supports authenticity, because it removes the pressure to be larger than life. It can help us carry the responsibility of leadership more lightly than leaders of the heroic, charismatic, and maverick stamp. Ignatian leaders are not threatened by others' brilliance, because they do not draw their legitimacy from being best

1. Philip Endean, "On Poverty with Christ Poor," *The Way* 47/1–2 (Jan/April 2008), 47–66.
2. Philip Endean, SJ's article on the third degree of humility is most helpful here.
3. James Hanvey, SJ's article on Pope Francis noted this humility in action from the first day of his papacy. See James Hanvey, "Because you give me hope," *Thinking Faith*, 30 April 2013.

at everything. They can surround themselves with teams of people who exceed their own skill. When this happens, humility is mutually reinforcing among those they lead.

Freedom

The second distinctive characteristic emerges from Ignatius's subtle teaching about freedom from inordinate attachments, a teaching that involves both a letting go and a letting come. There is an "indifference" (what Joe Munitiz, SJ, describes as "be[ing] prepared to wish to relinquish something out of love of God"—"prepared to wish to" seems to me a very helpful formulation) balanced by an "interior freedom"—a disposition that is open, unencumbered, and therefore able to welcome whatever comes.[4] This sounds attractive, but it is not easy. Many leaders have disordered attachments to aspects of their work or mission that are in themselves good. For example, have you encountered well-intentioned leaders whose drive towards a wonderful and worthy vision rides roughshod over warnings, or drives their team to exhaustion? Ignatian leaders need to grow in discernment of their own attachments, their own unfreedoms, and operate with a dynamism that is less train-like and more akin to flying. Their job is not to hurtle their organization along a predetermined track to a clear destination, but instead something more like following a flight path, constantly tuned in to radar, making micro-adjustments, ready for and unthreatened by change.

I would see the curiosity of the early Jesuits as a fruit of this freedom. "Living with one foot raised" is not just availability for mission; it shows a free *mindset* also. Ignatius and the early Jesuits are widely cited as masters of adaptation, perhaps partly to meet our own needs for role models of change management. Sometimes this adaptation was simply because they had got it crashingly wrong the first time.

---

4. Joseph Munitiz SJ, (trans), *St Ignatius of Loyola: Personal Writings* (London: Penguin Classics, 1996). See the glossary.

But certainly, Xavier's approach and attitude in India shifted in Japan.[5] Matteo Ricci's distinctive approach to inculturation in China also evolved through his experience there.[6]

Consolation

The third distinctively Ignatian quality I want to highlight is consolation. Secular leadership models ask leaders to inspire and motivate their teams. It would be inappropriate to request joy of them. One prevailing narrative is that we live in a VUCA world—volatile, uncertain, complex, and ambiguous—and the leader needs authenticity, agility, and resilience. All true. But the Christian narrative is one of resurrection. Moreover, in the Spiritual Exercises, Ignatius gives us ways to recognize the grace of consolation. In our life with God, in the joy of the Fourth Week of the Exercises, we earnestly seek and pray for this gift. Ignatian leaders imagine, even expect, that joy might somehow be present, to the point of becoming a decisive influence. They seek the Kingdom of Heaven in this VUCA world because the Resurrection means that sin doesn't win. Pope Francis chose this emphasis in his address to the 36th General Congregation of the Society of Jesus (GC 36) last year:

> In the Exercises, Ignatius asks his companions to contemplate "the task of consolation" as something specific to the Resurrected Christ. . . . Let us never be robbed of that joy, neither through discouragement when faced with the great measure of evil in the world and misunderstandings among those who intend to do good, nor by letting it be replaced with vain joys. . . . Joy is not a decorative add-on but a clear indicator of grace: it indicates that love is active, operative, present.

Ignatian leaders must hold hope, strategize with hope, and attend to "the task of consolation."

5. St. Francis Xavier, "Letter from Japan, to the Society of Jesus in Europe, 1552."
6. Nicolas Standaert, "Matteo Ricci: Shaped by the Chinese," *Thinking Faith,* 21 May 2010.

Sense of Direction

Vision and a clear sense of direction are vital for leading well. Many businesses struggle to articulate why they exist, because they usually look through the lens of what they do.[7] But a leader formed in the Ignatian tradition comes straight out of the "why," stated in the Principle and Foundation of the Exercises: "The human person is created to praise, reverence and serve God our Lord, and by so doing, save his or her soul." This, and the ubiquitous letters AMDG (*Ad majorem Dei gloriam*—"For the greater glory of God"), are attention-shifters, not straplines. Why are you leading? Because God is magnificent, and so focusing everything we do towards God's greater glory is sensible. Because the human person exists to praise, reverence, and serve God, and so can live joyfully, trustingly, because they know they are being saved. Ignatian leaders have their priorities right, and return to them frequently. Their gaze is on God, and the Principle and Foundation helps keep it there.

Discernment

Discernment—noticing "the movements felt in the heart and weighed by the mind"—is at the heart of the Ignatian way of proceeding.[8] I would see this as the crowning Ignatian quality; the one that integrates them all.

Leaders generally want to be wise; they don't all seek wisdom in the same places. Some strive to become a "thought leader." Others hone their intelligence and critical skills. Others constantly research and keep abreast of cutting-edge leadership theory. Ignatian leaders seek to be discerning. James Hanvey's article on Pope Francis's leadership puts it like this:

7. Simon Sinek's "Starting with WHY" TED talk is one of the most successful (and arguably influential) of all time, with about 34 million views.
8. Joseph Munitiz, SJ, *op. cit.*

> Discernment is a graced seeking—almost an aesthetic sense—for the movements of God's salvific action present in all our relational dynamics: formal and informal, personal or institutional, wherever our passive, receptive, and active agency is in play. Freedom is our obedience to the "gravitational force" and pattern of God's grace at work. . . . It is an operational wisdom that comes from knowing to whom we belong, where our heart really lies. It asks us to be attentive to the movement of the Spirit, both in the world and in ourselves, especially to be alert to whatever makes us deaf or distorts.[9]

An Ignatian approach to good decision-making in leadership involves more than calculating the benefits and losses entailed by different ways forward (itself one of the things that Ignatian jargon sometimes calls discernment). It involves a commitment to listen carefully to the different motivations at work in the organization, to the point that some decisions are ultimately based not on projected outcomes but rather on a sense that a certain way forward coheres with our sense of who we are under God, while the alternative does not.

Ignatian leaders pray, reflect, and discern in their personal lives in a way that naturally influences the culture of their workplace. A discerning organization will listen to its own experience differently. Quality of listening will rise; a kind of Godly tuning in of the radio together. Relationships between teams will enrich decision-making processes.

Discernment in common is a priority for the global Society of Jesus coming out of GC 36, so the next few years are going to be a rich ground of experimentation in growing discerning environments in Ignatian workplaces as well as Jesuit communities.

These five qualities manifest not in a defined common leadership style, but rather, in some unusual and shared aspirations. The personal, interpersonal, and organizational skills needed by every good leader are nuanced and enriched by these Ignatian qualities. Consolation, freedom, a clear sense of direction, humility, and discernment even

---

9. James Hanvey, SJ, *op. cit.*

make some of the skills easier to sustain. They act as compass bearings. And if the work is ultimately God's, then the leader's sense of responsibility can make a deep, freeing, and joyous shift.

All of this raises interesting questions for the future, too. As a layperson, I am intrigued by the ways in which leadership is different for a Jesuit and a layperson leading a Jesuit work. The latter are not called to be proto-Jesuits: The responsibilities are different, and I suspect the charisms are also distinct. Such questions confront those who design future Ignatian leadership courses, and call for a deep and fruitful collaboration between Jesuits and laypeople leading in real and difficult situations. The challenge will be not to reduce Ignatian leadership to a tidy theory with accompanying tools and practices. It is a disposition of mind, heart, and will. And I believe it's a distinctive way of incarnating the gospel in service of the world's need for true leadership.

What Does the Ignatian Leader Do?

Michelle Wheatley

"What are we supposed to *do*?"

This was a question I heard regularly during my time as a mission officer in a Jesuit university. It came from colleagues earnestly seeking to apply Ignatian principles in their work, but who felt unsure about what to do next. In many cases, they had already participated in formational programs or conducted their own study about the history of the Society of Jesus, Ignatian spirituality, and Jesuit education. Some had encountered the Spiritual Exercises. Others had long work experience in Jesuit contexts. They were inspired by Ignatian values and eager to participate and yet, still, they were searching for something. What?

Over time, through dialogue and accompaniment, colleagues elaborated on this desire for more. Themes emerged, such as the need for resources that attend to the increasing uncertainty and complexity of their work. Their most pressing mission questions were framed by adaptive rather than technical challenges, meaning tough issues related to identities, values, and commitments for which there was no single or obvious solution.[1] Additionally, they wrestled with how to talk about and integrate Jesuit values in different contexts, especially highly contentious or polarized ones. And they raised poignant

From *Jesuit Higher Education: A Journal*, 2023.

1. Ronald A. Heifetz, Marty Linsky, and Alexander Grashow, *The Practice of Adaptive Leadership: Tools and Tactics for Changing Your Organization and the World* (Brighton: Harvard Business Review Press, 2009), 19.

questions about personal, communal, and institutional integrity, particularly regarding ways that Jesuit institutions have themselves fallen short, bound up in unjust systems.

Without even more timely and practical preparation to integrate Ignatian values in organizational leadership, Jesuit identity ran the risk of remaining too abstract, rooted in the past, or confined to personal character formation. Given their questions about how to approach the complexities of institutional life in ways that advance mission, colleagues sought bridges between Jesuit wisdom and concrete personal, interpersonal, and systemic practices. Specifically, they desired ways of proceeding and contemporary strategies to operationalize the Ignatian vision across a wide range of responsibilities.

Recognizing and affirming that there are many ways to explore Ignatian leadership, including wonderful existing resources such as the Program for Discerning Leadership, the following reflections are humble contributions toward continuing to deepen reflection and practice among Ignatian leaders.[2] They are born from experiences, study, relationships, prayer, and a desire to be of help and hope. They seek to bring contemporary theories into conversation with meaningful resources in the Jesuit tradition, especially those of Saint Ignatius and the earliest companions. Ultimately, they aim to draw us more deeply into our inheritance as collaborators in Jesuit mission, calling on the discernment of those who have come before us but orienting us with urgency to listen and respond to the impelling Spirit, and one another, today.[3]

2. Program for Discerning Leadership, sponsored by the General Curia of the Society of Jesus in Rome, 2020. https://discerningleadership.org/.
3. Joseph F. Conwell, SJ, *Impelling Spirit: Revisiting a Founding Experience: 1539 Ignatius of Loyola and His Companions* (Chicago: Loyola Press, 1997), 416.

Begin with Purpose

Questions of purpose feature centrally in the Ignatian tradition. Throughout his life, Ignatius quested to develop his identity, an authentic spirituality, and a framework that would enable him and others to flourish in pursuit of union with God. Through attentiveness to his own experience, real presence to others in their spiritual journeys, and mystical encounters with the divine, Ignatius codified and refined a vision for human purpose in the Spiritual Exercises that has since become the foundation of all Jesuit endeavors. With precision, and deriving from this central vision, Ignatius and his companions included statements of purpose in their earliest foundational works.[4] This clarity was important because future decision-making hinged on an understanding of the goal. Ignatius encouraged companions to do, as much as possible, that which was more conducive to their purpose.[5] He provided extraordinary help, both personal and corporate, for choosing the better or more universal good in a variety of circumstances.[6] But this guidance assumed the desire of persons and unity of purpose in the Society, to fulfill the Jesuit mission as cultivated in the experience of the founders, expressed in key sources, and discerned over time.[7]

Today, Ignatius's discipline about naming purpose has been reinforced by popular wisdom and steady encouragement from contemporary sources.[8] However, we can easily take for granted that we have done enough to establish clarity about our goals, especially in the most complex systems. Our mission statements necessarily inspire us with bold aspirations, but do we have a shared sense of what

---

4. For example, see [21] of the Spiritual Exercises, [3] of the Jesuit Constitutions, and [7] of the Ratio Studiorum.
5. David L. Fleming, SJ, *Draw Me Into Your Friendship: A Literal Translation and a Contemporary Reading of the Spiritual Exercises*, (St. Louis: The Institute of Jesuit Sources, 1996), 26–27.
6. In addition to resources in the Spiritual Exercises, I appreciate this helpful commentary with references to the Jesuit Constitutions: Barton T. Geger, SJ, "What *Magis* Really Means and Why It Matters," *Jesuit Higher Education: A Journal*, Vol. 1, no. 2 (2012): 16, 18–19 https://epublications.regis.edu/jhe/vol1/iss2/.
7. John W. Padberg (Ed.), *The Constitutions of the Society of Jesus and Their Complementary Norms* (St. Louis: The Institute of Jesuit Sources, 1996), 316–317.
8. For example, Simon Sinek's, "Starting with WHY," https://www.ted.com/talks/simon_sinek_how_great_leaders_inspire_action; or Stephen R. Covey's "Begin with the End in Mind" from *The 7 Habits of Highly Effective People: Powerful Lessons in Personal Change* (New York: Fireside Catholic Publishing, 1989), 96–144.

the words mean in practice? Does our vision orient us toward the right activities? If we participate in larger traditions and structures, does our work contribute to the bigger picture while honoring the unique creativity and integrity of our people?[9] Do members of our communities, representing different roles and identities, see how they contribute to a larger, common project? Are priorities understood in such a way to empower decision-making, ingenuity, and initiative?

Cultivating shared vision, whether among a small group or throughout a complex institution, can be a daunting task, especially when time is short and stress is high. However, this work may also unleash tremendous creative potential as a community negotiates who it is called to be and what it hopes to accomplish. As Ignatius would remind us, establishing a clear goal is an essential first step toward answering questions about what we should be doing and what we need to decide next. If questions persist, reclarifying purpose is an important place to start.

Practical Ideas

- Develop, refresh, or reaffirm mission statements, vision statements, community values, and strategic plans.
- Where multiple purposes exist, prioritize them.[10]
- Document key stories and case studies that demonstrate mission and values in action, and share them widely.
- Honor exemplars of mission in the community.
- Commission or receive proposals for artwork, photography, theater, dance, and more to creatively express mission and values.
- Create conversation spaces to envision goals in detail.
- Find ways to share joy in the work.
- Identify structures that support mission and structures that do not.[11]

---

9. I appreciate the references to creative loyalty from Arturo Sosa, SJ, in his address: "The university as a source of a reconciled life" at the World Meeting of Universities Entrusted to the Society of Jesus in Bilbao, Spain, July 2018, https://www.sjweb.info/documents/assj/2018.07_SOSA_The-university-as-a-source-of-a-reconciled-life_LOYOLA.pdf, 8–9.
10. Heifetz, Linsky, and Grashow, *Adaptive Leadership*, 227.
11. Heifetz, Linsky, and Grashow, 56.

- Pinpoint persistent questions and disagreements about strategy for deliberation and clarification.
- Identify and explicitly name cross-purposes when they emerge among groups or in the organization.

Empower Adaptation

One could assume that with such rigor in identifying purpose, Ignatius would be uncompromising about how to reach it. However, he deliberately left room for the mysteries of discernment, enabling different pathways toward realizing the Jesuit vision. In the First Principle and Foundation, he even cautioned against a disordered attachment to any single "gift of creation," acknowledging that various realities have the potential of leading toward the same goal of deeper relationship with God.[12] In each circumstance, the objective is the same, but the approach varies, revealing a firm commitment to purpose but openness to different tactics.[13]

This balance of structure and flexibility has profoundly shaped the identity and mission of the Society.[14] In the preface to the first edition of the Jesuit *Constitutions*, the author comments on Ignatius's wisdom in recognizing that different approaches to work and ministry would be needed in different contexts.[15] If Jesuits were to be fruitful in accompanying people all over the world, their corporate structures could not interfere with their ability to perceive and respond to God's invitation. These companions, after being formed in the mission, vision, and values of the Ignatian way, would need empowerment to use their own adaptive capacities: deep attentiveness to realities within and around them; thoughtful sense-making through the affect and intellect; and loving action in collaboration with others and the

---

12. Fleming, *Draw Me Into Your Friendship*, 26–27.
13. I am drawing here from the expression "steady in purpose, but flexible in strategy" from Gil Rendle, *Journey in the Wilderness: New Life for Mainline Churches* (Nashville: Abingdon Press, 2010), 23.
14. Chris Lowney's comments on Jesuit ingenuity speak to this dynamic in *Heroic Leadership: Best Practices from a 450-Year-Old Company That Changed the World* (Chicago: Loyola Press, 2003), 29; 127.
15. Padberg, *Constitutions of the Society of Jesus*, xvi. It is noted that the author of the preface is likely Father Pedro de Ribadeneira.

Holy Spirit to bring about God's deepest desires for the world. This discernment, when cultivated through regular exercises like the Examen, facilitates creative and reflective practice.

As present-day Ignatian companions, we still live and work in different contexts, including ones that are progressively complex and increasingly unpredictable. We, too, rely on our capacities for adaptation, particularly by paying close attention to our experiences, drawing meaning from our observations, choosing next steps, and then starting the cycle over again. Scholars and practitioners have referred to these iterative cycles with different names and models, but often with steps or questions such as What? So What? Now What?[16] Orienting ourselves to this kind of ongoing inquiry and action is especially important when engaging our biggest and more complex challenges, as we may need to take a step and assess the result before we can understand which actions need to follow.[17]

Building adaptive capacity among colleagues and communities is as essential in Ignatian work today as it has ever been. The scaffolding for such empowerment includes freedom for colleagues to determine best pathways toward purpose; mechanisms to reflect on experience, share feedback, and evaluate work; and nimble systems that allow for course corrections when needed. Designing organizations and communities to reflect this balance of structure and flexibility can take additional time and care at first, but with tremendous effect as people and teams become fully alive and activated in their work.

Practical Ideas

- Build time directly into work schedules and structures for reflection, thinking, and/or prayer.
- Create tools and rituals to ask powerful questions about experiences and environments, individually and across teams and organizations.

---

16. I am referring here to the Adaptive Action method by Glenda Eoyang and Royce Holladay in *Adaptive Action: Leveraging Uncertainty in Your Organization* (Stanford: Stanford University Press, 2013), 30.
17. Eoyang and Holladay, 32.

- Pay special attention to patterns.[18]
- Analyze bright spots and successes for clues about best practices.[19]
- Identify content experts who can help make sense of observations.
- Differentiate the types of challenges you are facing (and their components) as either adaptive or technical, so you can design appropriate action plans.[20]
- Define rules that empower people and teams to make their own decisions.[21]
- Clarify roles and which decisions can be made at different organizational levels (decision continuum.)[22]
- Offer gestures of care and support to acknowledge the fatigue and discomfort that may occur while navigating complex and uncertain work.

Embrace Tension

A nuance of adaptation in the Ignatian tradition is an invitation to hold together realities that some might deem incompatible. As William Barry, SJ, and Robert G. Doherty, SJ, have described it, the spirituality of the Jesuits emerges directly from such tensions. For example, Jesuits were missioned to be both contemplative and active; sophisticated and humble; passionate and indifferent; worldly and countercultural; invested and available; inventive and receptive.[23]

---

18. Eoyang and Holladay, 43–46. This section provides some guidance for identifying patterns by looking into similarities, differences, and connections.
19. This is an "appreciative" approach, drawn from Diana Whitney, Amanda Trosten-Bloom and Kae Rader, *Appreciative Leadership: Focus on What Works to Drive Winning Performance and Build a Thriving Organization* (New York: McGraw-Hill Education, 2010), 27.
20. Heifetz, Linsky, and Grashow, *Adaptive Leadership,* 19–20. This resource provides practical help for tackling challenges with existing expertise (technical) and orienting people to a change process (adaptive).
21. Eoyang and Holladay, *Adaptive Action,* 96.
22. Barry Johnson, *Polarity Management: Identifying and Managing Unsolvable Problems* (Amherst: HRD Press, Inc.: 2014), 189.
23. William Barry, SJ, and Robert G. Doherty, SJ, *Contemplatives in Action: The Jesuit Way* (New Jersey: Paulist Press, 2002), 4–5.

These tensions infuse Jesuit contexts, and companions in the Ignatian way are invited to navigate similar polarities as they discern which path will better lead to their goal.

However, organizationally, it may not be possible to lean in both directions at the same time, or when making one specific decision. Therefore, naming polarities and orienting people and teams toward the work of navigating them is critically important.[24] For example, are we encountering a tension between tradition and innovation? Between the needs of a person and the needs of a community? Between structure and flexibility? Between contemplation and action? Which side do we need to affirm right now, and why?

Framing the polarities in our work enables us to collaborate in maximizing the gifts of each pole. Through ongoing management, people and communities can discern when it is time to favor one direction or another, appreciating that both sides are needed over time to fulfill the ambitious Ignatian vision. Furthermore, this approach provides opportunities to honor and value the advocates within our teams and organizations who remind us to pay attention to the other side of various polarities.

In leadership, we regularly encounter tensions that cannot ultimately be resolved. And, as we find in the Ignatian way, such polarities are needed to help us stay adaptive in pursuit of our purpose. Navigating tension as a "way of proceeding" challenges us to stay attentive and expand our thinking beyond either/or binaries. If we remove the expectation to eliminate tensions, and instead orient ourselves to embrace and navigate them, we open possibilities for even richer discernment and more complex accomplishments ahead.

Practical Ideas

- Identify and prioritize key polarities in the work.[25]
- Engage colleagues in acknowledging the upsides and downsides of each pole.[26]

---

24. This extraordinary resource gives structure to the work of navigating polarities. See Johnson, *Polarity Management*.
25. Johnson, 82.
26. Johnson, 38.

- Determine the current state for the group or organization in managing these polarities.[27]
- Design processes for making shifts from one side to another when needed.
- Find humor in the tension when possible.
- "Protect troublemakers," meaning withstand pressure to dismiss voices of dissent, alternative perspectives, courageous questions, and uncomfortable observations that help the group achieve a more comprehensive perspective.[28]

Create Cultures of Discernment

One of the key tensions in the Ignatian tradition is between the personal and communal, and the opportunities and challenges that come from striving to share life and work in community. Ignatius and the first companions took seriously the question about whether they should, in fact, become one mission body as a religious order, recognizing that such a decision would come with associated commitments and practices.[29] To maintain "unity of mind and heart" when dispersed in various apostolic activities, and to exercise co-responsibility for the life of the Society, would require active engagement from each person as well as a certain relational dynamic among them.[30] These companions modeled for us a profound connection between life, mission, and rootedness in discerning communities, an ideal of the Ignatian way.[31] In Joseph F. Conwell, SJ's extraordinary work on the experiences of the founders, he painted a compelling portrait of the spirituality and mentality that enabled those first companions to be "bold, daring, innovative, creative, passionate, and filled with a sense of urgency."[32] They had deep faith that the Holy Spirit was active in

---

27. Johnson, 116.
28. Heifetz, Linsky, and Grashow, *Adaptive Leadership*, 167.
29. Conwell, *Impelling Spirit*, 13.
30. Padberg, *Constitutions of the Society of Jesus*, 319.
31. "Documents of General Congregation 36 of the Society of Jesus," Society of Jesus, January 2017, https://jesuits.eu/images/docs/GC_36_Documents.pdf, 17.
32. Conwell, *Impelling Spirit*, 416.

each of their lives and in their Company as a whole, and therefore a sincere freedom and commitment to listening, within their own hearts and around them in the world. Conwell wrote:

> The Company remains the work of the Spirit and of the Company, and as such it remains the responsibility of the whole Company. The Company comes into being through discernment, by being open to and trusting in the movements of the Impelling Spirit, and only through discernment can it fulfill its purpose. . . . Discernment, in turn, takes place only in an atmosphere of prayer and of trust, of daring to trust in God and to trust in one another, of daring to trust that the Spirit reveals the direction to go and guides the Company along the right path.[33]

Such a vision invites and challenges us to consider the foundations we have created for our contemporary discernment. How have we cultivated shared vulnerability and trust among our teams? How have we honored the unique insights, identities, and experiences of our people? How free and safe do members feel to share what they see and know? How responsible does each person feel for the journey of the community? How does conflict become an opportunity to advance shared understanding? How do we create opportunities to listen deeply to one another and to the signs of our times?

These foundations take time to build and do not suddenly appear when a discernment question arises. Proactive, formative work to build strong relationships, make time for honest and deeper sharing, and express hopes and fears is a powerful investment toward creating cultures in which revelations about a path forward become possible. Sometimes, this work requires reassurance that tangible outcomes will emerge, even if the process gets messier before it becomes more orderly. In a healthy discerning culture, the push and pull of ideas and perspectives, combined with a genuine interest in learning from one another, will advance both tasks and relationships in service to the ultimate purpose.

33. Conwell, 416.

Practical Ideas

- Find images and examples that illustrate what you hope your discerning community will look like at its best.[34]
- Identify and find opportunities to collaborate with wise people, whose presence and insight help nurture cultures of discernment.[35]
- Employ tools to build up psychological safety among groups and organizations.[36]
- Intentionally cultivate trust through consistent behaviors that lead to a willingness to be vulnerable.[37]
- Create structures for giving and receiving feedback.
- Listen for sharing *underneath* the sharing, such as underlying hopes, fears, assumptions, or competing commitments.[38]
- Utilize a model for discerning together, such as The Social Discernment Cycle.[39]
- Encourage adaptability among colleagues when working together with people who have different styles.
- Make and sustain commitments to diversity, equity, inclusion, and belonging.[40]

---

34. For example, I like the image of the "Community of Truth" (contrasted with the "Objectivist Myth of Knowing") from Parker J. Palmer in *The Courage to Teach* (San Francisco: Jossey-Bass, 2007), 102–109.
35. Sosa, "The University as a Source of a Reconciled Life," 5. He writes that "Wisdom exists through its embodiment in wise people . . ."
36. A valuable resource with a practical tool kit is Amy C. Edmondson's *The Fearless Organization* (New Jersey: John Wiley & Sons, Inc.: 2019), 159.
37. A definition of trust and associated resources that I appreciate comes from Megan Tschannen-Moran, *Trust Matters: Leadership for Successful Schools,* 2nd ed. (San Francisco: Jossey-Bass Publishers, 2014), 19.
38. A tremendous resource for harnessing the power of communication: Robert Kegan and Lisa Laskow Lahey, *How the Way We Talk Can Change the Way We Work (*San Francisco: Jossey-Bass Publishers, 2001).
39. Elizabeth Liebert, *The Soul of Discernment: A Spiritual Practice for Communities and Institutions* (Louisville: Westminster John Knox Press, 2015).
40. There are many important resources to support this work. From an organizational leadership perspective, I appreciate Abeni El-Amin's chapter called "Improving Organizational Commitment to Diversity, Equity, Inclusion, and Belonging," 2022, https://scholars.fhsu.edu/cgi/viewcontent.cgi?article=1014&context=management_facpubs.

- Be courageous when facing the most challenging discernment questions, especially those that require transformation within the community or organization to more fully reflect the Jesuit vision of justice.

So, what does the Ignatian leader *do*?

The four suggestions offered here—begin with purpose, empower adaptation, embrace tension, and create cultures of discernment—are all oriented toward supporting us in the kind of attentiveness, active engagement, and collaboration that enable us to discover our path together. With intentionality, Ignatian leaders can frame and guide processes in which people and communities join in purpose and take steps forward, even in the face of complex or unsolvable dilemmas. In the best cases, such journeys lead to an impression that the collective is greater than its parts, the experience was meant to be, and Ignatian leadership is, in the end, ultimately about a spiritual sense of being led.

Saint Ignatius and the original companions handed on incredible resources that have changed lives and transformed the world for almost 500 years. Perhaps most significantly, they modeled the quest, as persons, companions, and corporation, to listen and respond to God's Word in all their activities. Their journey may give us confidence that with similar commitments and practices, and drawing on the wisdom available to us now, we, too, can experience the graces of striving toward the Ignatian purpose. However, their example also reminds us that we must embrace the challenges and invitations of our present-day discernment questions as we claim our co-responsibility for animating and adapting the Ignatian tradition today.

Our work may confront us at times with uncertainties and complexities that seem beyond us. We may be asked to adapt or change in ways that feel scary or impossible. However, the resources gifted to us in the Ignatian tradition are infused with an enduring sense that we have what we need, if only we would listen to one another and the impelling Spirit who is as present to us now as to Ignatius.[41] In this way, the question of what to do is given back to us, as we discover together how we will choose to respond.

41. Conwell, *Impelling Spirit*, 416.

Ignatian Leadership for Love and Liberation

Jennifer Tilghman-Havens

Each morning, I open my news app and see headlines that reveal a society deeply conflicted about the meanings of leadership, gender, race, faith, and justice. Recent narratives offer ample opportunity to experience the "desolation" that Ignatius honored as an instructive part of the spiritual life: climate disasters that threaten homes and lives; an epidemic of anxiety and depression among young people; grasps for power and control by global leaders; outdated civic and ecclesial structures that resist the influence of the feminine; discrimination against LGBTQIA+ people; attempts to deny the existence of systemic racism; and threats to the foundations of democracy. These narratives cry out for creative, diverse new models of leadership that honor each person's dignity, attempt to right the wrongs that have caused (and still cause) suffering, and bring vision towards a future of hope. Yet most popular books on leadership rely on the outdated assumption of the white male manager aiming at a narrow vision of success. Popular thinking about leadership often fails to satisfy the deeper human hunger for a guidance toward a more humane, sustainable, and just world in which each person can strive toward what Ignatius called "the end for which they were created."[1]

From "Ignatian Leadership as a Mechanism for Human Liberation: 'What's Love Got to Do with It?'" *Jesuit Higher Education: A Journal*: Vol. 12: No. 1, Article 8.

1. Ignatius of Loyola, *The Spiritual Exercises of Saint Ignatius*, ed. T. Corbishley (New York: P.J. Kennedy, 1963).

The Anglo-Saxon root of the word *leader* is *laedon*, which means "to take with you, as on a journey," and *ship* comes from the Gothic *schaeppen* or "to shape something of value." St. Ignatius embodied the kind of leadership that guided others on a creative journey toward the Jesuit ideal of the *magis*: The greater, deeper good, rooted in the values of the Gospel. Theologian Bryan Massingale describes the *magis* as a "holy restlessness"—a deep, aching desire for more truth, more justice, and more humanity, to heal the fractures of our world. Ignatian leaders can offer a needed balm for our societal wounds in guiding people and institutions toward the greatest goods: equity, justice, truth, and liberation for all. Leadership guided by Ignatian wisdom cultivates freedom, honors the affect and intellect, centers people on the margins, discerns from deep self-knowledge, and demonstrates love through deeds.

As we engage with each of these aspects of leadership, I invite you, dear reader, into a dynamic tension that is worthy of illuminating explicitly. Both the Ignatian wisdom tradition and the vast majority of contemporary leadership theories emerge out of a primarily white, male, Western framework, without explicitly claiming that standpoint.[2] This article's exploration of Ignatian leadership attempts to take seriously the identity of the leader as a key influence on how a leader chooses to engage with others. Too often the dominant white male perspective goes unnamed yet profoundly influences contemporary considerations of leadership. Kimberle Crenshaw called this "the peril of perspectivelessness."[3] If effective leadership aims to heal the divides that plague our local, national, and global community, then leaders of dominant gender, race, and class (including myself) must examine unearned privilege in order to actively lead organizations toward greater justice. Because the range of complicity by leaders in our historical and current societal injustices is vast, leadership models must take seriously the leader's positionality, inviting examination of

2. Sandra Harding, "'Strong Objectivity': A Response to the New Objectivity Question," *Synthese* 104, no. 3 (1995): 331–349, https://link.springer.com/article/10.1007/BF01064504.
3. Kimberle Crenshaw, "Toward a Race-Conscious Pedagogy in Legal Education," *National Black Law Journal* 11, no. 1 (1989): 1.

one's participation in both the shadow and light side of our collective history and one's embodiment of both the "imbedded oppressor" and the "imbedded oppressed."[4]

In this paper, I attempt to bring to the Ignatian tradition and to considerations of leadership an explicit focus on identity and privilege, in order to respond to the call of Pedro Arrupe as he instructed alumni of Jesuit universities in his 1973 address: We must notice injustice and bring to it "an attitude not simply of refusal but of counterattack against injustice."[5] Therefore, you may notice an implicit or explicit invitation to discern how your identity and positionality might influence how you enact leadership. This invitation emerges out of the rich tradition of contemplation in action, a dynamic that feels ever more important for leaders amidst the challenges and complexity facing organizations today.

Cultivates Freedom

Ignatian spirituality upholds the ideal of interior freedom. This is not personal freedom, as Americans often conceive of it, as a right or entitlement. This core Ignatian tenet is a much deeper, interior process to examine and detach from where we have become unduly defined by material assets, titles, occupations, honors, privileges, the praise of others, or particular locations.[6] St. Ignatius believed that attuning to God's call requires detachment from possessions and security in order to be free to respond with generous and loving attunement to the difficult and beautiful realities of the world. Ignatius's First Principle and Foundation in the Spiritual Exercises proposes the radical idea that we make ourselves indifferent to or detached from "health rather than sickness, riches rather than poverty, honor rather

4. Shann Ferch, *Forgiveness and Power in the Age of Atrocity: Servant Leadership as a Way of Life* (Lanham, MD: Lexington Books, 2012).
5. Pedro Arrupe, "Men and Women for Others," *Commitment to Justice in Jesuit Higher Education* (Baltimore, MD: Apprentice House, 2011), 1–19.
6. Kevin O'Brien, *The Ignatian Adventure: Experiencing the Spiritual Exercises of St. Ignatius in Daily Life* (Chicago, IL: Loyola Press, 2011).

than dishonor, a long rather than a short life . . . so that we ultimately desire and choose only what is most conducive for us to the end for which God created us" (SE 23). Cultivating interior freedom can feel different for people of different identities as they embrace a radical openness to God's movement within the self and within the realities of another person's experience. When leaders of historically dominant identities notice attachments to privilege, cultivating interior freedom beckons them to be "detached from their own interests . . . to assume whatever is the greater good."[7] A leader with a marginalized identity may find interior freedom through seeing clearly their worthiness and refusing to renounce or undervalue themselves. Interior freedom "is the human possibility to grow as persons in gratuitous relationship with others, seeking the greater good of all."[8] An Ignatian leader who cultivates interior freedom in turn allows others to be freer, more authentic, and more fully human.

How does one develop interior freedom as an Ignatian leader? Ignatian leaders of dominant identities can practice placing themselves in the productive discomfort felt when one detaches from ego and de-centers oneself in order to see through the eyes and experiences of another. Ignatius would caution those with positional power to be wary of creating distance between themselves and others by insulating themselves from authentic mutual engagement. It has been said that Ignatius welcomed people into his office with the phrase "May you be at home here." One practice that can aid the development of interior freedom is for the leader to regularly invite honest feedback from others. Leadership scholars suggest that healthy leaders create psychological safety that allows others to speak freely their needs, critiques, and constructive feedback, without fear of retribution.[9] The role of the leader is to listen fully to the feedback, to be transparent about what they discover, and to disclose their plan for growth and

---

7. Adolfo Sosa, "On Discernment in Common," Address to the Whole Society, 27, accessed May 22, 2023, https://www.educatemagis.org/documents/official-letter-by-fr-general-arturo-sosa-sj-on-discernment-in-common/.
8. Sosa.
9. Matt Kincaid and Doug Crandall, *Permission to Speak Freely: How the Best Leaders Cultivate a Culture of Candor* (Oakland, CA: Berrett-Koehler Publishers, 2017).

change in response.[10] An Ignatian leader with interior freedom creates psychological safety for others to share what is on their minds and hearts by enabling them to voice ideas, seek feedback, provide honest critique, collaborate, take risks, and experiment, all with the aim of both individual and organizational growth and transformation. By creating space for others to share honestly, leaders become interiorly freer from complacency, self-centeredness, bias, expectation, and habit as they open themselves to the reality of the people whose lives they influence. This cyclical process creates fertile ground for true humility that liberates leaders from misconceptions about themselves while also liberating others to authentically offer their ideas, insights, and experiences without risk of retribution.[11] Coupled with personal reflection and prayer, the Ignatian leader engages in deep listening, radical receptivity, and a stance of welcoming diverse perspectives to nurture their interior freedom, for the transformation of heart and mind.

Honors the Affect and Intellect

Ignatian spirituality values the integration of the head and the heart. In the Ignatian worldview, emotional awareness accompanies intellectual analysis.[12] Ignatius is known for founding institutions that pursued intellectual excellence, but he also believed in paying attention to affectivity, or the "interior motion" that moves one toward or away from God. Ignatius was often moved to tears in his prayer and in community with his "companions in the Lord." As the Ignatian worldview honors affectivity and intellect, it also seems to encourage a reintegration of the lost or suppressed feminine, which has traditionally

10. Christos G. Coutifaris and Adam M. Grant, "Taking Your Team Behind the Curtain: The Effects of Leader Feedback-Sharing and Feedback-Seeking on Team Psychological Safety," *Organization Science* 33, no. 4 (2022): 1574–1598.
11. Amy Edmondson, "Psychological Safety and Learning Behavior in Work Teams," *Administrative Science Quarterly* 44, no. 2 (1999): 350–383, https://web.mit.edu/curhan/www/docs/Articles/15341_Readings/Group_Performance/Edmondson%20Psychological%20safety.pdf.
12. Wilkie Au and Noreen C. Au, *The Discerning Heart: Exploring the Christian Path* (Mahwah, NJ: Paulist Press, 2006).

been associated with nurturance, tenderness, and empathy. Ignatius embodied a full embrace of societally inscribed "masculine" and "feminine" leadership characteristics, as he integrated within himself the fullest spectrum of human affect, intellect, and activity. The Spiritual Exercises of St. Ignatius are evidence of this integration, as they incorporate both traditionally masculine and feminine elements, guiding retreatants to explore their emotive responses, develop an interior life, and to find ways to care for and love others.[13]

How does an Ignatian leader integrate affect and intellect? Leadership that employs necessary critical thinking can integrate critical *feeling* as well. Steger and Wahlrab describe critical thinking as not just an analytical skill about how things are, but also a reflection on "how they might and should be."[14] Johann Wolfgang von Goethe, the German poet, playwright, and critic, similarly argued that science should entail the rigorous engagement of observation and thinking, but also animate faculties such as feeling, imagination, and intuition. Science, as Goethe understood and engaged it, "has as its highest goal the arousal of the feeling of wonder through contemplative looking."[15] In the Spiritual Exercises, Ignatius encouraged the use of imagination as a way to enter Scripture more deeply through a "composition of place" to discern how God might be inviting the retreatant to deeper awareness of one's calling. Ignatian leaders offer opportunities to imagine new possibilities using both the head and the heart as a way to discover the *magis* as they face decisions about resources, time, or attention.

Ignatian leadership can be enhanced by "emotional intelligence," which is the capacity to reason about one's affectivity, and for emotion to enhance thinking. Emotional intelligence invites an individual to "monitor one's own and others' emotions, to discriminate among them, and to use the information to guide one's thinking and actions."[16] Studies show that when emotional intelligence is

13. Maria Prieto Ursúa, "Feminine Psychological and Spiritual Clues to the Spiritual Exercises," *The Way* 59, no. 1 (January 2020): 90–102.

14. Manfred Steger and Amentahru Wahlrab, *What Is Global Studies?: Theory & Practice* (New York, NY: Routledge, 2017).

15. Jeremy Naydler, *Goethe on Science* (Great Britain: Floris Books, 2000).

16. John D. Mayer and Peter Salovey, "The Intelligence of Emotional Intelligence," *Intelligence* 17, no. 4 (1993): 433–442.

cultivated, organizations shift to being more responsive to the needs of their people, especially those without positional power.[17] As Ignatian leaders honor the illumination of both thought and feeling, they notice "movements felt by the heart and weighed by the mind," become more fully human, and allow those around them to also become more themselves, towards a greater good.[18]

Centers People on the Margins

If the world-affirming stance of Ignatian spirituality sees God as potentially found in all things, where does a leader focus his or her particular energies? This is where the Jesuit commitment to faith and justice aligns with Catholic social teaching and the Jesuit Universal Apostolic Preferences: Ignatian leaders make a "preferential option" to attend to those on the margins. Ignatian leaders prioritize the needs of those without access and power. For example, while the Ignatian tradition upholds the human dignity of all lives, Ignatian leaders recognize that the lives of black brothers and sisters—diminished through enslavement, mass incarceration, segregation in schools, and countless unjust killings—not only matter but deserve a commitment to reparation. Jeanette Armstrong echoes this principle as she describes decision-making in her Native Okanogan community. She states, "From our point of view, the minority voice is the most important voice to consider, in terms of the things that are going wrong, the things that we're not looking after, the things we're not being responsible toward."[19] An "option for the poor" aligns with this Okanogan practice, urging Ignatian leaders to continuously assess how a decision—economic, political, or social—will impact those most oppressed by systems and structures. Ignatius's own story

17. Jin Woo Chang, Thomas Sy, and Jaepil Neil Choi, "Team Emotional Intelligence," in *Research Companion to Emotion in Organizations*, ed. Charmine E. J. Härtel, Wilfred J. Zerbe, and Neal M. Ashkanasy (Cheltenham, England: Edward Elgar Publishing, 2012), 273–286.
18. Sarah Broscombe, "What Is Ignatian Leadership?," *Thinking Faith* (September 1, 2017), https://www.thinkingfaith.org/articles/what-ignatian-leadership.
19. Jeanette Armstrong, "Human Relationship as Land Ethic," YouTube, published December 19, 2014, https://www.youtube.com/watch?v=qwNoX3MNisE.

exemplifies this principle. Ignatius's injury invited him to reconsider his priorities: Ignatius had lived an early life of unexamined privilege, and the "cannonball moment" broke through his unawareness, inviting him to consider how he might disentangle himself from the oppressive systems of which he was a part. As he lay down his sword and gave away his finery at Monserrat, he relinquished his security, opting to live alongside beggars whom others had cast aside. Throughout his ministry, Ignatius served people in need. The Jesuit Catholic tradition emphasizes solidarity with those on the margins as core to a life of faith.

What does centering people on the margins look like in an Ignatian leader? There is a Haitian proverb that says, "We see from where we stand." Ignatian leadership invites leaders of historically privileged identities to take a stand with the historically underprivileged and to inquire what others experience: If I am a man, how do my decisions affect women? If I am a person who identifies as white, how are people of color impacted by how I inhabit my role? If I am able-bodied, how might my colleagues with limitations be freed from restrictions? If I am a citizen or straight or cis-gender or wealthy, how can I take the standpoint of immigrants, LGBTQIA+ and trans folx, and individuals in poverty? Building upon feminist scholar Peggy McIntosh's seminal work,[20] Ijeoma Oluo speaks and writes about the importance of assuring the flourishing of others: "Every time you go through something, and it's easy for you, look around and say, 'Who is it not easy for? And what can I do to dismantle that system?'"[21] St. Irenaeus believed that the "Glory of God is the human person fully alive."[22] Ignatian leaders are animated to act for justice so that God's glory be made manifest through "fully alive" human beings.

20. Peggy McIntosh, "Unpacking the Invisible Knapsack," *Peace and Freedom* 49 (1989): 10–12.

21. Ijeoma Oluo, "I Am Drowning in Whiteness," *National Public Radio*, October 1, 2017, retrieved from https://archive.kuow.org/news/2017-10-01/ijeoma-oluo-i-am-drowning-in-whiteness.

22. Irenaeus, *St. Irenaeus of Lyons against the Heresies*, Vol. 1, ed. John J. Dillon (The Newman Press, 1992), 420.

Discerns from Deep Self-knowledge

Ignatius developed a process of discernment that entails prayerful decision-making through a deep reflection on one's affect, experiences, and relationships in order that one might live in greatest alignment with God's calling. Practices that foster self-knowledge are crucial to discernment. Self-awareness creates conscious space for reflection on one's identity, history, emotional responses, assumptions, and unconscious biases, giving rise to continuous growth, transformation, and ethical decision-making. Ignatius invites retreatants in Week One of the Spiritual Exercises to know one's self as deeply loved by God and also mired in human sin. This understanding of the self challenges us to trust our belovedness while also noticing the ways we have caused harm. Robert Greenleaf, originator of the Gospel-inspired model for Servant-Leadership, recognized that entering into self-awareness can produce disturbances as leaders move "below the level of conscious intellect" to notice the biases inherited by our culture and our families which healthy leaders need to "unlearn."[23] Greenleaf writes, "Awareness is not a giver of solace—it is just the opposite. It is a disturber and an awakener. Able leaders are usually sharply awake and reasonably disturbed. They are not seekers after solace."[24] Discomfort, guilt, or pain sometimes arises for people of historically dominant identities as they engage in critical self-awareness about their participation in the sins of colonization and racism. Perhaps this experience is an example of the kind of Ignatian desolation that, through God's grace, urges one toward a more authentic self. Like Ignatius, Greenleaf recommends that leaders remove what blinds us from the truth of ourselves, even to the point of choosing to lose "what must be lost," akin to Ignatius's discernment to forfeit his sword and finery. Ignatian leaders with historically advantaged identities may discern that they are called to adopt anti-racist or feminist practices that require sacrificing the comforts of privilege and power. White, anti-racist author Robin DiAngelo suggests that as white

23. Robert Greenleaf, *Servant Leadership: A Journey into the Nature of Legitimate Power and Greatness* (New York: Paulist Press, 1977), 41.
24. Robert Greenleaf, *Servant Leadership*, 41.

people awaken to the realities of white privilege and racial inequality, they must build "capacity to sustain the discomfort of not knowing, the discomfort of being racially unmoored, the discomfort of racial humility."[25] Although uncomfortable, awakening to the truer self gives consolation as it directs our focus beyond ourselves, inspiring us to actively work toward the racial justice that we know is needed for God's glory to be realized. Ibram Kendi challenges leaders by suggesting that those who discern not to adopt an active anti-racist or anti-sexist stance are actually choosing to uphold white supremacy and patriarchy; there is no "neutral" ground.[26] Deep discernment, rooted in self-awareness, interior freedom, and a commitment to center people on the margins, helps leaders take courageous and potentially transformative action for good.

What does discernment look like for Ignatian leaders? Leaders first must carve out intentional time and space for reflection. Ignatian discernment emerges out of a lived commitment to notice God's call through one's lived experience. Leaders discern what are the experiences, thoughts, and actions that lead them toward God (consolations) or away from God (desolations). Ignatian discernment in a context of racial and gender inequity also invites reflection on how one's social identity impacts others, so that leaders gain clarity about when to claim their wisdom and voice and talent (especially if it has been historically undervalued) and when to use their power to lift up the skills and talents of others. Oluo invites discerning leaders to "check their privilege" by critically reflecting on their participation in systems. She counsels: "When we are willing to check our privilege, we are not only identifying areas where we are perpetuating oppression, but we are also identifying areas where we have the power and access to change the system as a whole."[27] Ignatian leaders continually discern how to create equity by challenging the system of historical dominance and assess when to give space for marginalized voices. As a white woman, I am called to discern in every space I inhabit when to notice and disrupt the dominance of whiteness and when to offer

25. Robin DiAngelo, *White Fragility: Why It's So Hard to Talk to White People About Racism* (Boston, MA: Beacon Press, 2018), 14.
26. Ibram X. Kendi, *How to Be an Antiracist* (New York: One World/Ballantine, 2019).
27. Ijeoma Oluo, *So You Want to Talk About Race* (New York: Seal Press, 2018).

an underutilized feminine perspective to unsettle sexist assumptions. The aim of self-reflection is a discernment towards a leadership identity that actively seeks opportunities to disrupt and correct inequitable systems so that, in the tradition of great educator Paolo Freire, both the oppressed and oppressor may find liberation.[28]

Demonstrates Love through Deeds

Howard Gray described Ignatian spirituality as "self-awareness" leading to "self-donation."[29] Ignatius believed that good discernment leads us to offer self-giving, generous love modeled by Jesus. Pedro Arrupe, too, highlights the centrality of love in the work for justice: "To be just, it is not enough to refrain from injustice. One must go further and refuse to play its game, substituting love for self-interest as the driving force of society."[30] Ignatius, Gray, and Arrupe challenge Ignatian leaders to discern how they will manifest love as they encounter the earth and its people. bell hooks gives depth and fullness to the concept of love, defining it as a combination of "care, commitment, knowledge, responsibility, respect and trust," each of which must be experienced together in order for the receiver to experience love.[31]

Ignatius famously said that "love ought to be put more in deeds than in words."[32] What does it look like for Ignatian leaders to demonstrate this love? The Ignatian leader takes well-discerned action born of contemplation, to ensure that people (and the earth) feel cared for, both through *cura personalis* ("personal care of individuals") and *cura apostolica* ("care of the work" or, "care for the whole"). hooks's and Ignatius's insistence that love must be made manifest in concrete action aligns with leadership research showing that when

---

28. Paolo Freire, *Pedagogy of the Oppressed*, trans. Myra Ramos (London: Sheed and Ward, 1972).
29. Howard Gray, SJ, "Ignatian Spirituality," *Ignatian Spirituality Reader*, ed. George Traub, SJ (Chicago: Loyola Press, 2008), 61.
30. Arrupe, "Men and Women for Others," 6.
31. bell hooks, *All About Love: New Visions* (New York: William Morrow, 2000).
32. David Fleming, SJ, *Draw Me into Your Friendship: The Spiritual Exercises: A Literal Translation and a Contemporary Reading* (St. Louis, MO: Institute of Jesuit Sources, 1996), 174.

leaders embody processes of positive affirmation, commitment, acts of trust, and truth-telling, not only do people feel cared for, but the organization as a whole outperforms expectations.[33] In their interactions with others, healthy leaders consistently affirm those around them, lifting up the contributions of others and expressing genuine appreciation, aiming for a ratio of 5:1. For every one piece of constructive feedback, a healthy Ignatian leader will offer five extensions of appreciation, respect, enthusiasm, empathy, validation, apology, or humor, which unsurprisingly has proven to significantly improve leader-member relationships and team effectiveness.[34]

Corporately, demonstrating care could include the following practices: giving voice to hidden stories at the intersections of race, gender, class, sexuality, ethnicity, and nation to aid mutual understanding and compassion;[35] analyzing the practical, everyday practices within organizations that create barriers for women, people of color, members who identify as LGBTQIA+ or differently abled; establishing proactive hiring and promotion processes that seek out diverse candidates; facilitating practices for personal and collective reflection; holding anti-bias trainings for all stakeholders of the organization; creating policies that support work/life balance, family responsibilities, health, and community engagement; creating community partnerships across previously uncrossed barriers; committing to seeking ongoing reconciliation and reparations with individuals and communities impacted by the organization; and creating space for imagination about how our organizations can better prioritize marginalized communities and the earth.[36] This is how love can manifest in organizations with the guidance of rooted Ignatian leaders. Importantly, the Ignatian leader also creates space to care for self, through contemplation, time with beloved companions, and Sabbath rest.

---

33. Kim Cameron, *Positive Leadership: Strategies for Extraordinary Performance* (San Francisco: Berrett-Koehler Publishers, 2012).
34. Fakir Mohan Sahoo, "Human Emotion: Towards Developing Guidelines for Application," *Vilakshan: The XIMB Journal of Management* 11, no. 2 (2014): 91–102.
35. Evangelina Holvino, "Intersections: The Simultaneity of Race, Gender and Class in Organization Studies," *Gender, Work & Organization* 17, no. 3 (2010): 248–277.
36. Jennifer Tilghman-Havens, "The Will to (Share) Power: Privilege, Positionality, and the Servant-Leader," *The International Journal of Servant-Leadership* 12, no. 1 (2018): 87–128.

Ignatian Leadership toward Love and Liberation

Civil, corporate, ecclesial, educational, and family systems cry out for leaders that cultivate freedom, honor the affect and intellect, center people on the margins, discern deeply, and demonstrate love through deeds. Ignatian leaders can turn our beautiful and broken society toward the healing and justice it so desperately needs. The ultimate aim of Ignatian leadership is liberation—from structures and systems that have served to benefit some at the detriment of many, and liberation for the flourishing of all, especially those who have been bound by their race, gender, or identity. Liberatory Ignatian leadership, rooted in Ignatian spiritual wisdom, frees leaders who are historically advantaged from toxic whiteness and masculinity, and frees BIPOC (black, indigenous, and other people of color) folks and women from unjust and oppressive systems, ushering them into full participation at all levels of organizations. Ignatian leaders trust that the path toward this *magis* is paved with humility and courage as they guide others toward the beloved community and the Reign of God through which all creation can flourish when each of us commits to the liberation of all of us.

A New Ignatian Virtue Necessary for Promoting Justice: *Cura Propria*

Debra K. Mooney

In the Ignatian Year (May 20, 2021–July 31, 2022), Superior General Fr. Arturo Sosa, SJ, called all Jesuits and companions in the Ignatian family to continue in the "service of faith and promotion of social justice" and advance on the four Universal Apostolic Preferences 2019–2029 (UAPs). This challenge is made amidst a lifting global pandemic, which certainly makes the charge especially difficult.

I know. While in the depths of the lockdown with no vaccine in sight, I had the wonderful privilege of facilitating campus leaders in weekly gatherings at which we deeply reflected upon the UAPs and considered our leadership in light of each of them. As we were discussing the 3rd Preference, *To accompany young people in the creation of a hope-filled future*, one of my colleagues burst out, "If we are going to help our students feel hopeful, then *we* need to be hopeful. We need to be models!"

I think her insight is quite profound and much weightier than it may appear; and we all know that she is right. As the colloquial sayings state: "You can't take care of anyone else unless you first take care of yourself" or "You can't give what you don't have." So, unless we, first, take care of ourselves, we can't effectively move on the UAPs and (1) show the way to God, (2) walk with the poor and the outcasted, (3) accompany young people, or (4) care for our earth.

This article is adapted from a statement offered at the virtual Commitment to Justice in Jesuit Higher Education conference on June 8, 2021, and appeared in *Conversations on Jesuit Higher Education*, online edition, September 5, 2021.

Conversely, when we are thriving, our deepest humanity radiates and we can effectually be in compassionate service and solidarity with others.

At the present time, personal care and attention are essential. Although we are leaving the COVID-19 pandemic world, social scientists have stated that we are entering a psychological pandemic. A snapshot of college students revealed that 95% had mental-health struggles specifically associated with the pandemic. The symptoms include loneliness, anxiety, depression, inattention, and unhealthy eating, sleeping, and physical activity; 20% have had a friend or family member die. Globally, 32% of college students desire more well-being and mental-health resources from their institution.

Moreover, faculty and staff are similar to students. A survey conducted by the American Council on Education in the autumn of 2020 found that the top concern of university presidents, from a list of eighteen, was the mental health of students (70%), next was the mental health of faculty and staff (60%). According to the U.S. Census Bureau, 36% of adults report feeling anxious, up from only 6% before the pandemic.

With this psychological pain, how can we be the hopeful and hope-filled models our students need us to be? Feeling as we do, how can we meet Fr. Sosa's call to address "the large and complex problems like equity and inclusion for those who have been excluded because of race, gender, or sexual orientation"? How do we muster the courage to ask necessary justice questions and, as the late Fr. Walter Burghardt, SJ, invited us, truly take a *long loving look at the real*?

Jesuits and companions in the Ignatian higher education family are familiar with *cura personalis* (Latin, meaning "to care for the whole individual person") and with *cura apostolica* (meaning "care for the ministry or institution"). In this difficult time, I propose a new Ignatian virtue for effective justice advocacy and education: It is *cura propria*, or "care for oneself."

As I was noodling on this concept of self-care, I consulted my friend and colleague, a professor of Classics, Dr. Shannon Byrne; *propria* is what she considered the best Roman noun and adjective declension/paradigm, matching to *personalis* and *apostolica.* More importantly, she exclaimed, "If *ever* there was a time we needed a *curia propria*, it's now!"

After sharing my concept of *cura propria* in a presentation at the Commitment to Justice in Jesuit Education Conference, Fr. Daniel McDonald, SJ, Midwest Provincial Assistant for Higher Education, contacted me to discuss the importance of this value. He noted that when St. Ignatius Loyola emphasized the values of *cura personalis* and *apostolica*, "it came at the light of his time and perhaps a disordered idea of self-abnegation, humility, and service-for-the-other."

In fact, Ignatius had a period of depression and guilt regarding his former (vain) life, which included self-denial of adequate food, shelter, and clothing, before his spiritual and vocational conversion was completed. This cultural pressure towards maladaptive selflessness also impacted St. Francis Xavier, a fellow founding member of the Society of Jesus. He experienced depression as a young adult and, at the time of his death, was known to be lying "exhausted" and spent from compulsively working and excessive fasting on the shores of an island off mainland China, his aspirational destination. (To be clear, this extreme deprivation is not the religious custom of fasting and atonements enacted to strengthen one's faith and relationship to the divine.)

Unfortunately, similar normative standards exist today. Too often, attention on personal care and wellness is perceived as selfishness, self-absorption, even narcissism. This socio-cultural stronghold is why I consider *cura propria* a moral good and a contemporary virtue for post-pandemic well-being and service to others. In light of the history of the early founders, and with the current societal circumstances, Fr. McDonald agrees that there is essential value to *cura propria*; "Much wiser today is that we take care of ourselves in order to serve, in order to share in the sufferings of others, in order to become genuinely humble."

I believe that in "reading the signs of the times," loving care for oneself should be our (new) Ignatian "way of proceeding." Consequently, I offer four Ignatian tools for *curia propria* and the strength to build a community of people characterized by love, mercy, equality, and equity.

1. Identify Daily Gratitude

Research finds that when we focus on gratitude we experience many benefits. Intrapersonally, we are happier and more optimistic. Interpersonally, we are more empathic and forgiving, helpful and compassionate. Physically, we are more likely to stick to an exercise plan, get good sleep, and choose healthy foods. And spiritually, when we attribute the daily uplifts and blessing to the transcendent or divine, then we are "seeking to find God in all things"—the foundation of Ignatian spirituality.

2. Find Inspiration

Inspiration literally means "divine influence and breathing" or "God-breathed." So when we are inspired, we are encountering the divine. And when we are inspired we are likely to *be* inspiring.

3. Be Patient

Fr. James Martin, SJ, shared an important message he received from the late Fr. Daniel Berrigan, SJ, a leading peace activist. When people asked him how many times he'd been in jail, his response was "not enough." Fr. Martin offered the advice that he received from Fr. Berrigan when he asked for ways to cope with a specific advocacy setback. Fr. Berrigan's response was surprising given how radical he was known to be. His advice to Fr. Martin was: Remember that you're in it "for the long haul." This message is a good reminder that justice advocacy and education work are commitments; like a marathon, such work is not a moment.

4. Daily, Engage in an Ignatian Examen

This Ignatian prayer helps us to identify gratitude, to find inspiration and God, and to be patient. In short, it is imperative that we care for ourselves in order to have the spiritual, psychological, and physical well-being necessary to be social justice educators, advocates, allies, and promoters. In other words, to fully express our commitment to justice and to living the UAPs in a post-COVID-19, psychological pandemic, we can collectively demonstrate *cura personalis* and *apostolica* by forwarding *cura propria.*

Suppose Leaders Presupposed?

Michele C. Murray

During a particularly contentious period on the campus where I work, I began carrying a pocket-sized reminder of the conditions for right relationship, especially during disagreement. Beside a picture of St. Ignatius of Loyola, I had typed the words of the Presupposition. During difficult clashes of perspective, I would take out the cheat sheet I had created and remember to assume good intentions, to give others the benefit of the doubt, and to ask good questions when I was tempted to automatically dismiss or negate another's idea or perspective.

Understood colloquially as "the Ignatian plus-sign," the Presupposition is St. Ignatius's first instruction to spiritual directors and retreatants in his singular contribution to Christian spiritual life, the *Spiritual Exercises*. In the version translated by George E. Ganss, SJ (Ignatius & Ganss, 1992, p. 31), the Presupposition reads:

> It should be presupposed that every good Christian ought to be more eager to put a good interpretation on a neighbor's statement than to condemn it. Further, if one cannot interpret it favorably, one should ask how the other means it. If that meaning is wrong, one should correct the person with love; and if this is not enough, one should search out every appropriate means through which, by understanding the statement in a good way, it may be saved.

From *Conversations on Jesuit Higher Education*, March 2023.

These are rather straightforward instructions for the spiritual director and retreatant to seek and maintain mutual respect: Be eager to see the good. Ask clarifying questions. Correct with love. Endeavor toward mutual understanding.

In the context of giving and receiving the Spiritual Exercises, the Presupposition is a reminder that God is at work, communicating directly and offering insight. In cooperating with God, it seems that the least the director and retreatant can do is to assume good intentions on one another's part. In my own experience as an exercitant, the generous listening and patient probing of my spiritual director only enhanced what I was understanding as God's work within me. Indeed, receiving and giving the benefit of the doubt also opened my eyes and my heart to the ways in which God was at work within others as well. There was a holiness in the director-retreatant relationship that was based on mutual respect and openness, and I found it easier to seek and find what was good and true in the other's statements and suggestions.

Alas! As one spiritual director told me, "Even Jesus had to come down from the mountain." Meaning that, as the Spiritual Exercises were coming to a close for me, my task was to seek and find that same quality of holiness, or right relationship, within my everyday encounters. In the context of everyday life, that direction, like the tenets of the Presupposition, proves to be deceptive in its simplicity.

In a world where zero-sum debate and argument are reflexive, where those who hold differing viewpoints are immediately viewed with suspicion, and where mutual vulnerability and dialogue are far from mainstays in daily interactions, applying the Ignatian plus-sign is often a difficult, and sometimes insurmountable, task. The Presupposition requires that we sidestep the conventions of persuasion and declaration in favor of generosity and curiosity. This is more challenging than it seems at first blush. In environments where there are winners and losers in any discussion, the advice to "put a good interpretation on a neighbor's statement" may feel like a disadvantage. It probably is if the goal is to win an argument at all costs. But if the goal is to understand one another's point of view, the

Presupposition opens the way to healthier relationships at home and at work, more effective collaboration, and, perhaps, more imaginative problem-solving.

Admittedly, the principles of the Presupposition are a more comfortable fit for the space and purpose of a directed experience of the Spiritual Exercises. In retreat mode, perhaps more so than in our daily lives, we are predisposed toward some of the spiritual habits that make it easier to adopt and apply the Ignatian plus-sign. In order to assume good intentions and pursue right relationship, the Presupposition asks us to enter spiritual direction with humility, lean into generosity of thought, listen deeply and attentively, and ask questions for clarity and understanding. Imagine what it might look like to practice these postures of the Presupposition at home and at work.

Humility. In some ways, to be humble is to admit to one and all that we do not know everything, and, moreover, that most times we don't know what we do not know. To be sure, in a knowledge economy the proposition of confessing to not knowing creates an uncomfortable level of vulnerability. Yet there is power in welcoming the insight of others, allowing others' expertise to shine, and learning something new and unexpected. Facing the limits of our own knowledge and experience can also help us to be gentle and forgiving when others reach the edges of theirs. Suppose we all entered conversations eager enough to learn that we allow ourselves to be vulnerable and say, "I don't know"?

Generosity. Generous thinking helps us ground ourselves in the knowledge that each and every person is beloved of God. The Presupposition calls us deeper into this reality and to accept that our conversation partners are good people who, just like us, are doing the best they can with what they have. My mother used to encourage me with these words: "Remember that we are all God's children; no one is better than you, and you are no better than anyone else." In some ways, my mother's wisdom mirrors St. Ignatius's directive to be eager to see the good. As James Martin, SJ, observed, "We expect others to judge us according to our intentions, but we judge others according to their actions."[1] Instead, suppose we all decided to give to others the same benefit of the doubt, the same allowance for complexity, that we give ourselves or that we expect others to give us?

Deep and Attentive Listening. Of all the habits required to faithfully apply the Ignatian plus-sign, deep and attentive listening is most elusive for me. Almost on a daily basis I find myself listening, not for understanding, but for positioning and rebuttal. If I am not trying to think several steps ahead of whoever is speaking, I am attending to email or the morning news or some other "important" task. Judging from what I observe in my workplace and in my home, I am guessing that I belong to a community of poor listeners. Usually there is safety in numbers, but in this case, being one of the pack only contributes to a larger problem. In taking attention off the speaker, whether a family member or a colleague, and putting it on our own business, not only are we missing the person's meaning and creating the circumstances for miscommunication, but we are also showing the type of disrespect that leads to unhealthy relationships. Suppose that, instead of multitasking, we all gave each other the attention we deserve? Suppose that, instead of looking for fissures to exploit in another's perspective, we all looked for and called attention to what is true and beneficial?

Questions for Clarity and Understanding. Occasionally it happens that someone offers a perspective replete with error such that there is little to salvage, let alone offer as beneficial. In these circumstances, Ignatius was clear: Correct with love. However, before arriving at that point, Ignatius was also clear that the first step is to ask for clarity. Questions, as my friend and colleague, Tim O'Brien, SJ, observed, create a spacious way of interacting that opens the door to possibility. If we are assuming good intentions on the part of our conversation partner, we are also allowing that we may have misunderstood what was said. The well-placed question for understanding both guards against unnecessary confusion and provides the conversation partner enough space to correct course gracefully. Questions for clarity and understanding are a much more humane approach to situations that would otherwise end in conflict or impasse. Whereas

1. James Martin, SJ, *The Jesuit Guide to (Almost) Everything,* (New York: Harper Collins, 2010), 235.

statements and declarations close off possibility, questions open us. Asking thoughtful questions, rather than "questioning," can also shift momentum in a discussion and create space for new perspectives to emerge. Suppose we all suspended judgment long enough to ask questions as a way of seeking understanding?

Humility. Generosity. Deep and attentive listening. Questions for clarity and understanding. These are the tools and habits I associate with the Presupposition. They allow me to slow down and assume that others have good intentions just as I hope they assume good intentions of me. These are the tools that encourage me to seek clarification rather than jump to conclusion. And these are the tools that help me to correct wrong statements with the same love and respect I hope to receive.

Even with my homemade card to aid me, however, applying the Ignatian plus-sign in daily life can be enormously challenging. I'm grateful that one of St. Ignatius's insights was that God labors throughout all the nooks and crannies of our lives. So I continue trying to presuppose. By no means am I great or even good, but I am learning. . . . And I know God is at work amid the learning. When I am practicing and making strides, I can sense the difference the Presupposition makes in the quality of interactions at home and at work, and I experience silhouettes of the same grace I experience in the midst of spiritual direction. The spirit of competition and self-absorption gives way to cooperation and generosity. In Ignatius's words, consolation is more abundant than desolation. The reverse is also true. When the Ignatian plus-sign eludes me (or when I elude it), I find myself more troubled by the quality—or lack thereof—of my interactions with others. Even when I am the only one in the room playing by the rules of presupposing and trying to apply the Ignatian plus-sign in my everyday, God's grace is present. When others presuppose too, God's grace feels multiplied. I want to live in a world of God's infinite grace, and so I wonder: Suppose we all presupposed?

The Ignatian Roots of Arrupe's Mysticism

Kevin F. Burke, SJ

In 1965, just months before the conclusion of the Second Vatican Council, Fr. Pedro Arrupe, SJ, assumed the duties of Superior General of the Society of Jesus. In the sixteen years that followed he led the Jesuits through the most profound renewal in their history, a renewal called for and modeled by Vatican II itself. His own remarkable life story prepared him well to lead that renewal. Then, in late summer 1981, Fr. Arrupe suffered a devastating stroke that left him partially paralyzed and left his speech severely impaired. No longer able to physically carry out his duties as Superior General of the Society of Jesus, he sought to resign his office. However, the Society had to wait two years before it could convoke the 33rd General Congregation in 1983, at which time it accepted his formal resignation as General and elected his successor, Fr. Peter Hans Kolvenbach. In his final address to his brother Jesuits, an address he himself dictated but left to one of his closest advisors to read, he said:

> More than ever, I now find myself in the hands of God. This is what I have wanted all my life, from my youth. And this is still the one thing I want. But now there is a difference: the initiative is entirely with God. It is indeed a profound spiritual experience to know and feel myself so totally in His hands.

From "Introduction: A Mysticism of Open Eyes," in *Pedro Arrupe, Essential Writings* (New York: Orbis Books, 2004), 26–34.

How did Pedro Arrupe come to speak this way? What spiritual experiences planted and nourished his confidence in God? And what can we learn from him? What gift does he offer us today? What word of hope in response to our most urgent longings?

We refer to Arrupe as a mystic, but this designation can be highly misleading. For one thing, he never used this category to speak of himself or his own experiences in prayer. He refused to be drawn into a cult of personality because he understood too well the dangers of spiritual pride. He also knew that labels such as mystic, guru, holy man, or saint are often used to pigeonhole people of faith, to domesticate their words by creating a distance between their example and the lives of "ordinary people." For another thing, Arrupe really did not see himself as special. While he did speak openly about the graces he received during his lifetime, whenever he himself became the focus of conversation, he drew attention precisely to his ordinariness and above all to his faults, failures, and sins. Like all true spiritual giants, he seemed unaware of his distinctive spiritual gifts. He considered himself a simple man utterly bereft but for the grace of God. Speaking of such souls, the poet Denise Levertov observes:

> They know of themselves nothing different
> from anyone else. This great unknowing
> is part of their holiness. They are always trying
> to share out joy as if it were cake or water,
> something ordinary, not rare at all.[1]

Understanding Arrupe as a mystic runs into a further problem, one created by the tendency to over-identify mystical experience with miraculous visions, spectacular interior dramas, and otherworldly transports. Not every mystical experience involves visions per se, and not every mystic withdraws from the world. Arrupe's life manifested the practical, apostolically oriented mysticism that flows from St. Ignatius's Spiritual Exercises. Likewise, his spiritual life assumed

1. Denise Levertov, "Translucence," in *This Great Unknowing: Last Poems* (New York: New Directions, 1999), 48.

the contours of Ignatius's mystical itinerary. As a way of elaborating this latter point, I draw attention to several key moments in the life of Ignatius, and Arrupe's reflections on them.

Like Arrupe, Ignatius Loyola lived during a time of social upheaval and massive cultural transformation. He was born in 1491 in the Basque region of Northern Spain and died in Rome in 1556. He thus lived through the early stages of the Protestant Reformation and the conquest of the Americas. This was the age of the printing press and the earliest recorded circumnavigations of the globe, the dawn of the modern era. All this affected Ignatius, but he was marked at least as much by the piety and structures of medieval courtly life, and his own early training as a courtier and a knight. The turning point in his life occurred in battle in 1521 while defending a fortress near the town of Pamplona. A cannonball shattered his leg, and during his excruciating convalescence, he began to notice within himself the movements of different spirits and a desire to go on pilgrimage to Jerusalem once he had recovered his strength.

The first part of Ignatius's pilgrimage led him to the town of Manresa, where he withdrew to a cave and lived a life of extreme austerity for the better part of a year. As his interior movements grew in intensity, he engaged in a range of "spiritual exercises," including fasting, examining his conscience, going to confession, and meditating on the Gospels. These experiences in prayer formed the basis of a spiritual program focusing on conversion and discernment that eventually grew into his most important written work, *The Spiritual Exercises*.[2] In his *Autobiography*, Ignatius attests that the main actor in the drama that unfolded in Manresa was God. Moreover, he experienced God as his teacher. "During this period God was dealing with him in the same way a school teacher deals with a child

2. Ignatius Loyola, *The Spiritual Exercises of Saint Ignatius*, trans. and ed. by G. Ganss (St. Louis: Institute of Jesuit Sources, 1992). The *Spiritual Exercises* provides a detailed method for the practice of a spirituality of discipleship rooted in the Gospels. It attempts not to describe but to facilitate an encounter with God, and to draw one into a living experience of God's presence and action. In order to distinguish the written text of the *Spiritual Exercises* from the act of doing the Spiritual Exercises (or directing another who is doing them), the former appears in italics and the latter does not.

while instructing him."[3] At Manresa, Ignatius experienced the most dramatic interior lesson of his life. It happened one day while he was meditating near the banks of the Cardoner River.

> As he sat there the eyes of his understanding were opened and though he saw no vision he understood and perceived many things, numerous spiritual things as well as matters touching on faith and learning, and this was with an elucidation so bright that all these things seemed new to him.[4]

Ignatius goes on to comment that he learned more on that one occasion than in all the other experiences of his life added together. The experience involved a kind of "seeing," though not in the sense of ocular vision. It was a spiritual illumination—the opening of "the eyes of his understanding." This was the grace that Arrupe sought when he prayed: "Grant me, O Lord, to see everything now with new eyes . . . Give me the clarity of understanding that you gave Ignatius." In his essay on the Trinitarian logic of Ignatius's mysticism, he offers further commentary on the essence of this grace.

It is an infused intellectual illumination about the Divine Essence and the Trinity of Persons in a generic way and, more concretely, about two of its outwardly directed operations: the Creation and the Incarnation. Ignatius is brought into the Trinitarian intimacy and finds himself an illumined spectator of the creation and incarnation in a Trinitarian context.

Ignatius experienced many other mystical graces, but alongside the illumination at the Cardoner River, one in particular stands out: his vision in the chapel at La Storta while on his way to Rome in 1537 with Diego Lainez and Pierre Favre. To this momentous event he dedicates only a one-sentence description in his *Autobiography*: "One day, a few miles before reaching Rome, while praying in a church, he felt a great change in his soul and so clearly did he see God the Father

---

3. Ignatius Loyola, *A Pilgrim's Journey: The Autobiography of Ignatius of Loyola*, trans. Joseph N. Tylenda, SJ (Wilmington, Delaware: Michael Glazier, 1985), 35–36.
4. *A Pilgrim's Journey*, 39. Arrupe quotes this passage in his essay, "The Trinitarian Inspiration of the Ignatian Charism." Note that Tylenda's translation cited here differs from the translation used in the official English text of Arrupe's essay.

place him with Christ, His Son, that he had no doubts that God the Father did place him with His Son" (*A Pilgrim's Journey*, 113). Although Ignatius gives us but the bare outlines of his vision, his companions later supplied a fuller picture of it:

> As Ignatius entered the chapel he felt a sudden change come over him, and while he was praying he had a remarkable vision. He saw God the Father together with Jesus, who was carrying His cross. Both Father and Son were looking most kindly upon him and he heard the Father say to the Son: "I wish you to take him as your servant." Jesus then directed His words to the kneeling pilgrim and said: "I wish you to be our servant." This was exactly what Ignatius had always wanted. Then he heard the Father add: "I will be favorable to you in Rome." This was God's answer to Ignatius's frequent prayer that he be placed next to Mary's Son. Leaving the chapel and continuing his way to Rome, Ignatius did not know whether he would meet success or persecution, but he knew that God would be with him.[5]

Arrupe, in line with the biographers of Ignatius and the leading historians of the Society of Jesus, focuses on the essential point of the vision: "Ignatius, creator of this apostolic group and bearer of the virtual charism of the Society whose existence is assured at that very moment, is received as the servant of Jesus and of the Father in Jesus." La Storta is the summit of Ignatius's mystical experiences. It links the life-changing illumination of the Cardoner to his life's vocation. He is called to be a companion of Jesus carrying his Cross. Within two years of La Storta, Ignatius and his first companions begin a new religious order. Because of the inspiration of La Storta, Ignatius will insist that this new society take the name of Jesus. The vision at La Storta thus links the mysticism of Ignatius to the essential charism of the Society of Jesus. Not surprisingly, both Arrupe and GC 32 find in La Storta the touchstone of the Society's renewal as an apostolic order. The latter expresses this succinctly.

---

5. Joseph Tylenda, "Commentary," in *A Pilgrim's Journey*, 113. Tylenda draws on the testimony of Diego Lainez; see *Monumenta Historica Societatis Iesu*, Vol. 73 (Madrid/Rome: 1951), 133.

> What is it to be a Jesuit? It is to know that one is a sinner, yet called to be a companion of Jesus as Ignatius was: Ignatius, who begged the Blessed Virgin to "Place him with her Son," and who then saw the Father himself ask Jesus, carrying his Cross, to take this pilgrim into his company.[6]

The heart of Ignatian spirituality—the spirituality that so deeply formed Pedro Arrupe—appears between the poles of these two great mystical experiences in the life of Ignatius. The Cardoner generates the spiritual program of conversion, discernment, and vocation outlined in the Spiritual Exercises. La Storta further specifies the content of this conversion, discernment, and vocation in the lives of Ignatius and his companions. Theirs is an apostolic life focused on mission and praxis, a mysticism of discipleship that follows Jesus carrying his Cross, a spirituality of service with a particular sensitivity for suffering. This spirituality appears in historical continuity with the mysticism of St. Francis of Assisi, one of Ignatius's spiritual heroes. A contemporary historian of spirituality, Ewert Cousins, refers to this broad Franciscan-Ignatian current in the history of Christian spirituality as a "mysticism of the historical event." Cousins writes, "Just as in nature mysticism we feel united to the material world, so in this form of mysticism we feel part of the historical event—as if we were there, as eyewitnesses, participating in the action, absorbing its energy."[7] The movement into historical events that we see in Francis's erection of the Christmas crèche or his desire to imitate and follow the poor Jesus, appears in Ignatius's vision at La Storta—his identification with Jesus carrying his Cross—and in many of the key contemplations of the Spiritual Exercises. This mysticism stands alongside, not in competition with, other paths along the mystical way. At the same time, it broadens the notions of "mystic" and "mysticism," providing an alternative to spiritualities that are predominantly interior and otherworldly. Rather than moving away from history into the realm

6. "Jesuits Today," 401.

7. Ewert Cousins, "Franciscan Roots of Ignatian Meditation," in *Ignatian Spirituality in a Secular Age*, ed. George Schner, SJ (Waterloo, Ont.: Wilfrid Laurier University, 1984), 60.

of the timeless, rather than turning one's back on human society and journeying into the inner expanses of one's own soul, the historical mystic turns toward God revealed in history and society.

Here, then, we see the essential elements of Pedro Arrupe's mysticism of open eyes. The German theologian, Johann Baptist Metz, coins this image to speak of the following of Jesus and the spirituality of the beatitudes. It corresponds closely to the biblical category of "poverty of spirit." Indeed, it seems to evoke the mysticism of Jesus himself as the synoptic Gospels portray him. Metz writes:

> In the end Jesus did not teach an ascending mysticism of closed eyes, but rather a God-mysticism with an increased readiness for perceiving, a mysticism of open eyes, which sees more and not less. It is a mysticism that especially makes visible all invisible and inconvenient suffering, and—convenient or not—pays attention to it and takes responsibility for it, for the sake of a God who is a friend to human beings.[8]

It is a mysticism that makes visible all invisible and inconvenient suffering, a mysticism that pays attention and takes responsibility, engaging this broken world in order to find there its God. It is a mysticism of dangerous memory—Auschwitz for Metz, Hiroshima for Arrupe, the *memoria passionis, mortis et resurrectionis Jesu Christi* for all Christians—in which the mystical and the political are radically engaged and correlated.[9] Arrupe shows us that historical reality itself opens our eyes to the One who transcends that reality. He acknowledges that it was reality that opened his eyes. For example, while celebrating Mass early on the first morning after the atomic bomb destroyed Hiroshima, he turned to face a mangled, bleeding, uncomprehending congregation of survivors: *"I saw before my eyes many wounded, suffering terribly."* Some years later, after celebrating Mass amidst the appalling poverty of a Latin American slum, a "big

8. Johann Baptist Metz, *A Passion for God: The Mystical-Political Dimension of Christianity*, trans. J. Mathew Ashley (New York & Mahwah, NJ, 1998), 163.
9. For Metz's notion of "dangerous memory," in particular his understanding of the Passion, Death, and Resurrection of Jesus as a dangerous memory, and his understanding of the mystical-political structure of Christian faith, see *Faith in History and Society* (New York: Seabury, 1980); "The Future in the Memory of Suffering," in J. B. Metz. & J. Moltmann, *Faith and the Future* (Maryknoll, N.Y.: Orbis, 1995), 3–16.

fellow, whose fearful looks could have inspired fear," invited Arrupe to his home in order to express his thanks by sharing with the Jesuit General the only thing he had: a great view of the setting sun. *"Señor, see how beautiful it is!"* In both instances Arrupe saw reality and he saw *through* reality. He saw both the suffering and the beauty. He saw the tragic depths of our mortal poverty and the transcendent depths of our immortal destiny. He lived and prayed with opened and open eyes. This is his gift to us.

VI. Adaptations

Part VI Introduction

From the early days of the Society of Jesus, an openness to non-Catholics and non-Christians as students and collaborators marked the culture-embracing orientation of Jesuit schools. Though these schools were deeply Catholic in their theology and sacramental imagination, their Catholicity was also expressed in the belief that God was active and present "in all things" and, by extension, in all people.

Today, among those connected with Jesuit works there is a renewed interest in how the Spiritual Exercises inform and undergird what we do. From classroom pedagogy and parish identity to discernment practices among university leaders, those laboring within Jesuit institutions are (re)turning to the Exercises as the common inspiration and language for our work. The Exercises are the reclaimed portal to our mission and meaning—the charism (i.e., gift of the Spirit) that has been entrusted to the Society and its companions for the benefit of the people of God. In short, they ground all Jesuit apostolates and make them distinctive.

Among the caveats associated with the Spiritual Exercises is that they must be experienced to be understood. A mere reading of Ignatius's text amounts to little more than the review of a retreat director's handbook. They are prose rather than poetry and on their own do little to inspire. It is the mutually illuminating texts of the scriptures and of one's life that give the Exercises their impact.

In one sense, Ignatius and his companions began adapting the Exercises very early in Jesuit history. Offering what began as a roughly thirty-day retreat in shorter forms or guiding some people through only the first Week of the retreat were but a few of the flexible practices employed to meet individuals in the crux of their reality. The faculty, staff, students, and alum of Jesuit institutions today are religiously complex and diverse on many levels. The sixteenth-century,

Catholic, male, European context of Ignatius may not be immediately translatable to their experience, but there remains something deeply attractive and life-giving at the heart of his spirituality.

It is humbling to read about the variety of adaptations that thoughtful spiritual directors have undertaken to make the Spiritual Exercises widely accessible to God's people. In some cases, this involves new interpretations of Ignatius's original text or the creation of a fresh pastoral theology in an Ignatian key. More frequently, directors share recommendations for reinterpreting elements of Ignatian spirituality to speak explicitly to the experiences of women, LGBTQIA+ persons, couples, refugees and migrants, seniors, those in twelve-step programs, persons with physical disabilities or neuro differences, those experiencing homelessness, and a host of other realities.

In Part VI we offer three selections, each of which addresses a specific consideration for adapting the Exercises. In doing so, we remain deeply aware that there are infinitely more questions to explore.

Adaptation and the Ignatian Way

The second volume of *An Ignatian Spirituality Reader* seeks to present fresh, new material that was not available for publication in Volume I. In rare circumstances, however, an article of timeless value and relevance to the topic simply cannot be overlooked. The late Rev. Philip Endean, SJ's incisive essay "How Far Can You Go? Ignatius's Exercises, Fidelity, and Adaptation" explores the balance between adherence to the text of the Exercises, practical applications by Ignatius, and the unvarnished life of the retreatant. His fearless articulation of the questions surrounding adaptation may provide encouragement for some readers and elicit criticism from others. Endean presents an image of the Exercises in which "freedom and flexibility are the norm" rather than the exception. His essay addresses adaptation for individual retreatants but is also a useful backdrop for discussing the religious and spiritual pluralism of colleagues serving in Jesuit institutions today. It sets the table for considering both articles that follow.

A Feminist View

Dr. Elizabeth Liebert presents a feminist perspective on the Exercises through an essay titled "The Spiritual Exercises and Gender." Liebert, one of the editors of *The Spiritual Exercises Reclaimed: Uncovering Liberating Possibilities for Women,* builds on the efforts of that groundbreaking book by exploring how interpretive principles for adapting the Exercises for multi-religious and even non-religious audiences (though she ultimately finds this latter attempt wanting) can be instructive for adapting the experience in light of gender as well. A second, expanded edition of *The Spiritual Exercises Reclaimed* has now been published, and we recommend it as a companion to this essay, which offers an important window into an insufficiently explored aspect of the Ignatian tradition, and its application for today.

A Multi-Religious View

If the Exercises are our common foundation, then how can non-Catholics, non-Christians, and non-believers encounter them honestly, without minimizing the centrality of Jesus or, conversely, infringing upon the retreatant's religious freedom? Are non-Christian faculty and staff in Jesuit institutions simply exempt from access to the tradition that so animates every Jesuit work from higher education to advocacy?

Experience tells us that the Spiritual Exercises resonate at a basic level with people of varying religious backgrounds, or of no religious identification, because they tap deeply into human chords of commonality. Who among us has not experienced a desire to be known and still loved, and to give ourselves meaningfully and generously to others? Who has walked through life untouched by suffering? And who has not undergone an awakening or epiphany that reconnects us to the world and ourselves? These currents flow through the life of Christ, shaped by Ignatius into a retreat that is inarguably Christocentric and, at the same time, profoundly insightful about the "spirits" that invite, tempt, console, and accompany every person seeking a richer inner life. The question is, can we, as companions in mission, share a common language and experience of the Ignatian charism when we come from radically different relationships with the person of Christ?

We offer here an excerpt from Dr. Erin Cline's thoughtful book *A World on Fire: Sharing the Ignatian Spiritual Exercises with Other Religions*. Cline's piece addresses the preliminary question of what motivates Jesuits and their Ignatian companions to share the Spiritual Exercises with non-Christian partners. She outlines some of the theological and spiritual dissonances between Ignatian spirituality and various non-Christian traditions, especially those of Hinduism, Buddhism, and Confucianism, which are her areas of expertise. From this foundation Cline introduces the topic of "Jesuit Norms for Choice of Mission and the Exercises." The connection between sharing the Exercises in an adapted form with non-Christian partners and the fundamental inspiration of Ignatius to "help souls" is at the center of her argument.

Conclusion

The purpose of an Ignatian retreat—and of Ignatian spirituality as a whole—is to lead an individual to greater freedom, so that they can discern an increasingly loving and self-giving direction in their lives. Surely this invitation can be extended to all of us in some form. We are charged with stewarding the gift of the Exercises that God bestowed upon the Church through Ignatius and extending it to others in respectful, reciprocal ways. It is admittedly delicate and sometimes fraught work. But, in a world riven by religious division, the Ignatian way—our shared way—can be one contributor toward healing and wholeness.

Stephanie Russell

How Far Can You Go? Ignatius's *Exercises*, Fidelity, and Adaptation

Philip Endean, SJ

How Far Can You Go? is the title of a satirical novel by the English Catholic writer, David Lodge. Wittily, affectionately, all too accurately, he traces how a group of Catholic university students in London, who first met in the 1950s, experienced the upheavals in the Church over the two subsequent decades. The question in the title "How far can you go?" sums up the scrupulosity common in preconciliar Catholicism, at least in the English-speaking world.

Reading the novel is a powerful experience for British Catholics above a certain age because it plays on our ambivalences. We know that the religious anxiety so common among the pious a generation ago was just silly. Yet still, deep down, it can exert a captivating force on us. There is still something in us, however enlightened we may be or think ourselves, that wants to be told how far we can go in matters religious—even when it comes to giving the Ignatian Exercises.

When we look at the wide range of ways in which retreat facilitators now use Ignatius's text, the "How far can you go?" question can all too easily surface. This essay has a subversive purpose. The question about Ignatian authenticity is an important one, deserving a considered answer, and I will try to offer at least the beginnings of one. Yet we will never be true to Ignatius unless we recognize that he is above all a teacher of freedom and confidence. If it is anxiety that

From "How Far Can You Go? Ignatius's Exercises, Fidelity, and Adaptation," *Review of Ignatian Spirituality* 29, no. 1 (Spring 1998): 35–49.

drives our concern for authenticity, if our questions are legalistic worries about "how far can you go," then there are still deep levels of ourselves, however enthusiastic our love for Ignatius, that have never appropriated his message.

Ignatius's Text and Current Practice

If we look at how, at least in the English-speaking world, the eight-day retreat is currently practiced, we see a range of different ways in which the process draws on the Ignatian sources. Sometimes we seek to recapitulate Ignatius's whole process, from the Principle and Foundation to the Contemplation to Attain Love. On other occasions, we choose just one week of the Exercises that seems to meet our need or devotion in this particular year. Other approaches are looser. Many of us have made or given retreats based on particular themes, for example the approach to discipleship typical of one of the four Gospels, or the insights arising from a psychological tool such as the Enneagram. Then there are some retreat-givers who are happy to let the retreatant set the agenda, giving guidance in response to whatever comes up. Ignatius's text here functions merely as a resource: it is there in the background for both retreatant and facilitator to draw on as appropriate, but in no way does it determine the retreat's structure.[1] Once we move beyond the eight-day retreat, adaptation becomes yet more varied in form: various kinds of Exercises in daily life, of Eighteenth Annotation retreats, of programs of guided prayer.

The last thirty years have seen an enormous expansion in the ministry of the Exercises. Those who make them and give them come from a far wider range of Christians—by no means all Roman Catholics—than the traditional circle of Jesuits and other Ignatian religious. The

1. This piece originates from a weekend seminar which, together with Fr. Michael Ivens, I led in October 1997 for the staff and associates of Loyola Hall Jesuit Spirituality Centre, near Liverpool, England. It is based on my closing input, and depends on ideas and insights shared throughout the weekend by the various participants. In particular, the above typology of different kinds of eight-day retreat derives from a presentation given by Fr. Ivens at the seminar. The consensus emerged that all three approaches could be legitimate, and that it was a mistake to proscribe any one of them.

experience of such people throws new light on the text, enabling us to see in it significances previously hidden from us. Ignatian courses of spiritual direction are launching people into the world as spiritual directors who, a generation ago, would not even have known what a spiritual director was.

Our overall reaction to these developments is one of exhilaration, a sense of the Spirit of God working through the Exercises in creative and unprecedented ways. Moreover, it seems to be primarily in human need, and only secondarily in the Ignatian text, that we seem to be encountering this Spirit. This paper emerged from a weekend seminar titled "The Spiritual Exercises and the Shorter Retreat." As the participants shared what they hoped for from the regular retreats they themselves made, they said much about their need for ongoing discernment, about finding modes of prayer appropriate to particular situations, about the need to be listened to and taken where they were. No one, however, seemed particularly concerned to get an annual exposure to the Two Standards.

And yet a niggle remains. Can sensitivity to spiritual need here and now really serve as the only indispensable criterion for determining what is authentically Ignatian? Those same participants shared a sense that something more, somehow, needed to be said; that limits, of some kind, needed to be re-established. Sensitivity and careful listening are important qualities, indeed the most important qualities, in a retreat-giver. They may lead us to adapt the text radically. But not just anything can count as an Ignatian retreat. There has to be a distinction between legitimate adaptation and inauthentic deformation, albeit a distinction that honors the full range of what we are now discovering and does not foreclose too many options too quickly. The next sections attempt to articulate such a distinction, taking as a starting-point Ignatius's legislation in the Jesuit Constitutions for how formed Jesuits should pray.

Rules and Their Limits

There is, in fact, nothing new about our concern. In his seminal history of the Ignatian Exercises, Ignacio Iparraguirre sees that the same issues were arising for the second and third generation of Ignatian retreat-givers:

> There was a serious problem which urgently needed solving. The problem was that St. Ignatius used to leave wide scope for the director. He indicates the material for meditation [sic], points out the goal towards which one is meant to aspire, gives norms for the difficult steps, but then, after these and other specifications, still leaves wide range for the spiritual guide's initiative. In order not to become disorientated within this wide range of possibilities left by St. Ignatius, people asked, from the first years, for the drawing up of a directory which would regulate these aspects The most serious uncertainties turned on whether it was against authenticity to add, change, complement or fill out the meditations—and, if it was not, to what extent and according to what criteria could these changes be made?

The difficulty lay in the text itself. Ignatius insisted that his particular provisions not be taken too seriously or literally—a fact which his followers, keen to idolize him and anxious for the security of a fixed norm, found hard to accept:

> On the one hand, the Founder's book appeared as a hallowed object, the object of sublime veneration. It seemed a sacrilege to touch anything, however minimal, that formed part of it. On the other hand, its flexible character, the different kinds of cases which it envisaged, and above all the fact that one could not put it into practice blindly or mechanically, but only in a living way, from person to person—all this necessitated, not its modification (because the text itself repeatedly stresses the need for adaptation, adaptation that is one of the

> most characteristic features of the method), but certainly an accommodation to persons, different in each case, according to the diverse circumstances.[2]

For Iparraguirre, the Directory solves the problem: it laid down a set of rules about when adaptation could and could not occur.

Here is not the place to assess whether Iparraguirre's account of the Directory's function is historically accurate. We must, however, insist that the question we are facing cannot be addressed by drawing up further rules, over and above those left us by Ignatius. In principle, God's Spirit is free. Every retreatant is unique and unprecedented. It is, therefore, simply impossible to specify in advance what "adaptation" is going to be legitimate or necessary. Ignatius's Exercises are sensitive to human need and individuality in a way that disallows such an approach. We have to address the issue on another basis.

Ignatius, Prayer, and Regulations

At this point Ignatius can help us. He did not, to my knowledge, ever explicitly address the question of how far the Exercises could be adapted, but he did write some wise legislation about the prayer life of trained Jesuits, and the principles implicit in this material can be applied more widely. Ignatius presupposes that the long period of testing and training can assure us that those admitted to the Company are "spiritual persons," able to "run along the way of Christ our Lord." "Because of this," he continues:

> . . . it does not seem good to give them any other rule in matters concerning prayer, meditation and study, or in the bodily practices of fasting, vigils and penances, other than that which discriminating charity will dictate to them.

2. Ignacio Iparraguirre, *History of the Exercises of St. Ignatius, Vol. 2: From the Death of St. Ignatius to the Promulgation of the Official Directory*, 1556–1599 (Bilbao and Rome: El Mensajero del Corazón de Jesús, 1955), 324–325.

Ignatius then adds a proviso, to which I shall return in a moment, before saying as much as he is prepared to say in the way of rules:

> Only this will be said in general: that care should be taken both that the excessive use of these things not weaken bodily strength so much and take up so much time that these do not suffice for the spiritual help of our neighbors in accordance with our institute, and, equally and conversely, that one not desist from them so much that the spirit becomes cold and the low human passions are enkindled. (Constitutions VI.3.1 [582], translation mine)

Ignatius says that his men should pray neither too little nor too much, while studiously avoiding any pronouncement on what that amounts to in particular cases. Such a strategy can help us with our contemporary problem. We are struggling with two principles or values that appear to be in some sort of tension. If we stress fidelity to the Ignatian text, we sound all too easily—despite our best intentions—as though we want to force all our retreatants through a program. On the other hand, if the spiritual need of the person in front of us is the only basis of our response, then what we are offering as an Ignatian retreat can lose any distinctive identity. Before long, we find ourselves asking the question how our purportedly Ignatian spiritual guidance differs from any other kind of spiritual direction, or indeed from straightforward secular counseling.

My proposal is modest, but not insignificant. We cannot, in principle, give an exhaustive account of which procedures are authentically Ignatian, but we can proceed more negatively. We can characterize some approaches as clearly not authentically Ignatian. It would not be Ignatian were we to neglect completely the experience and circumstances of the person making the retreat. It would not be Ignatian were we to proceed as though the Ignatian text in particular, and the Christian tradition in general, were of no relevance whatever for what happens in the retreat. Any Ignatian procedure must be open both to the text and to the possibility that the God whose Spirit gave rise to that text may be performing a new deed as a new retreatant encounters it.

This formulation, of course, leaves open the nature of the balance between these two factors. But such open-endedness is an Ignatian virtue. The nature of the interplay in any specific case is itself a matter of charism, of discernment, of following the leadings of the Spirit as best one can in particular situations. To echo the Ignatian text referred to above: It is presupposed that trained retreat-givers will be sensitive to the call of Christ in their own experience and in that of others. It therefore does not seem sensible to lay down any precise rules about when they should follow Ignatius's text literally and when and to what extent they should feel free to adapt. They should simply follow the lead of "discriminating charity."[3] In other words, they should go with their sense, under the guidance of God's love, of the differences between particular situations. Only this can be said in general: on the one hand they should not follow the written text so slavishly that they cease to respond to the particular needs of their neighbors; on the other, they should also not neglect the text so much as to risk losing contact with Ignatius's inspiration.

Balances in Retreat-Giving

This approach offers, I hope, encouragement and reassurance to those of us who find ourselves giving Exercises, of a sort, in very new situations, and adapting the method radically. Sometimes we worry about the liberties we take with the text, but we also know that a stricter procedure would not work and therefore continue, with an uneasy sense of guilt, to proceed anyway. If the suggestion just made is correct, we can afford to relax. Provided we are regularly asking two sorts of question—"What does the text say?" and "What is this situation demanding?"—and taking the answers to both seriously, then we are not in principle misguided. Obviously, we can all grow in skill at reading situations in the light of the Gospel and in God's grace. Obviously, too, some of us are more sensitive, experienced, and

3. The English Jesuit jargon for this phrase, "discreet charity," seems to me seriously to obscure an important aspect of its meaning.

generally competent in these matters than others. But any anxiety we may have that there is something intrinsically or systematically wrong in our attempts to adapt Ignatius's pedagogy is probably overscrupulous.

There are also implications for the general question of how far retreatants should be left to themselves and how far they should be given, or allowed, specific input. The question arises in various contexts. Should we allow, or encourage, retreatants to read books during the retreat? Should they be given talks in a group? How, if at all, should we tailor the liturgical homily to the retreatants' situation? Opinions differ among experienced retreat-givers on questions like these. In my own retreats over the years, I have benefitted from directly opposing policies. Sometimes, however, these have been presented as "the right Ignatian way," as though Ignatius himself would never have countenanced an alternative. The more relaxed approach to Ignatian authenticity I am suggesting here enables us to accept a diversity of approaches on such issues. Ignatius's Exercises engage us at our most personal and intimate, but Christian personality and Christian intimacy are defined and specified by the word of the Gospel, as mediated through the tradition and the community of believers. Therefore, no authentic Ignatian procedure can afford to exclude, programmatically, confrontation with the Word of God; no authentic Ignatian procedure will ever neglect the fact that persons must receive that word in freedom, with the question of what it means for them left open generally to the leading of the Spirit. Again, the balance to be struck between those two considerations will itself be a matter of tentative discernment, and of charism.

The Importance of Consultation

If we seek criteria for the truly Ignatian in terms of the characteristics which any authentic procedure must exhibit, the above is the most that can be said, and it is not very much. There is, however, a further important point, one centering not on what we decide to do, but on how we decide to do it. Although Ignatius declines to lay down detailed prescriptions for how trained Jesuits should pray, he does insist that decisions in this sphere be taken in consultation. "Discriminating love" may be the only guideline for judging an individual companion's needs, but its use is not to be left exclusively to the individual. Decisions are made, rather, "with the confessor always being informed, and, if there is doubt as to what is appropriate, the Superior as well."[4] Ignatius does restrain individual freedom, but by an insistence on interpersonal contact, not by setting objective limits.

Again, Ignatius's teaching on Jesuit prayer can be transposed to the issue concerning us here: when and how far to adapt the text of the Exercises to the needs of individual retreatants. In principle, there is no limit to our freedom to adapt; we should be as bold and creative as the situation demands. Nevertheless, the retreat process, however intimate it may be and however much confidentiality must be respected, occurs in communion with the wider body of believers. In modern terms, the retreat-giver's creativity will always be supported by what, in English-speaking countries, we call pastoral supervision. "Adaptation," particularly in unusual or unfamiliar situations, should occur "with the supervisor always being informed, and, if there is particularly strong uncertainty, some other wise and spiritual person as well."[5]

The term *supervision* can mislead. It is not, or not primarily, a matter of the supervisor instructing, evaluating, or restraining the retreat-giver. The practice has grown out of the recognition that the retreatant's conflicts can set off a similar process in the retreat-giver, a process which the retreat-giver needs to discern. For this task, support and guidance are often helpful. Ethical problems obviously arise regarding the retreatant's confidentiality, but not insoluble ones.[6]

In reaction to the legalism of the recent past, modern writing on Ignatius has sometimes presented him almost as a spiritual anarchist. The truth being exaggerated in such accounts is that Ignatius normally

---

4. *Constitutions*, 300.
5. George E. Ganss, SJ, *The Spiritual Exercises of St. Ignatius: A Translation and Commentary* (Chicago: Loyola Press, 1992), 26–29.
6. The practice obviously has its roots in the best practice of contemporary psychotherapy and counseling, which recognizes how the relationship between supervisor and counselor often mirrors that between counselor and client. For further information, consult the relevant article in any standard dictionary of pastoral care or psychotherapy, e.g., John P. Millar, "Supervision, Pastoral," in *A New Dictionary of Pastoral Care*, edited by Alastair V. Campbell (London: SPCK, 1987), 272–273.

locates final authority not in written law but in the judgment of wise persons. Thus the General of the Company of Jesus is given authority to dispense from the provisions of the Constitutions, "with the power of discrimination [*con la discreción*] that the eternal Light will give him." In such cases, dispensation appears as what the law's authors would actually have intended, had they foreseen the circumstances (Constitutions IX.3.8 [746]).[7] The same applies when dealing with the prescriptions of Spiritual Exercises: "adaptation" is not an arbitrary, capricious process but a matter of discriminating judgment, often aided by informed second opinion. Jesuit culture has frequently fostered a defensive individualism regarding pastoral practice—an individualism that Ignatian authenticity may require to be unlearned.

Decloistering the Ignatian

This paper has been written for givers of Ignatian Exercises worried about how their adaptations sometimes feel rather far removed from Ignatius's text. Its principal aim has been to reassure and build confidence. Every retreat-giver can obviously hope to grow in sensitivity to God's Spirit. But no one who is so concerned about authenticity as to work through a paper like this is likely to be an Ignatian deviant.

The request, however, which led to this paper being written emerged from a certain anxiety, an anxiety worth probing. Underlying it, I suspect, is a sense that somewhere in history, perhaps in a cloud hovering over Manresa, or in manuscripts hidden within the walls of the early Jesuit novitiate in Rome, there still remain perfect Spiritual Exercises, of which anything we do here and now is a more or less defensible "adaptation." The very idea of adaptation suggests a pristine norm which can, in response to circumstances, be changed, but which in an ideal world would remain unsullied.

7. On Ignatius's understanding of the superior, see Peter Knauer, "The Interior Law, Our Way of Proceeding in the Lord" and "The Constitutions: Towards a Hermeneutics of the Constitutions—Insights from Constitutional Theory," *CIS Review of Ignatian Spirituality*, 65 (Autumn 1990), 29–38; and Philip Endean, "The Draughthorse's Bloodlines: Discerning Together in the Ignatian Constitutions," *The Way Supplement*, 85 (Spring 1996), 73–83.

Ignatius's guidelines for prayer, however, imply something rather different. There, freedom and flexibility are the norm; it is the fixed structure that is the exception to the principle—if also, paradoxically, an application of it. The structure is imposed only in those situations where it is conducive to freedom.[8]

Under the anxiety about Ignatian authenticity may lie a sense, mostly unacknowledged, that the normative Ignatian Exercises are those made at the outset of their religious lives by new recruits to the Jesuits and to other Ignatian institutes. This sense needs to be exorcized. In this review, Maria Clara Bingemer has recently drawn attention to how laypeople can and do make the authentic Exercises, and to how the concepts and traditions we inherit (including some from Ignatius himself) prevent us from recognizing that reality.[9] Yet even to put the matter in those terms still implies that the experience of vowed religious is somehow the norm, one to which—to our surprise?—we discover that some non-religious, "lay" women and men somehow conform. It is no derogation of priesthood or consecrated life to say that our theology, particularly our implicit and unreflected theology, must get beyond the clericalism latent in such a mindset.[10] If we can achieve that, then the anxiety this paper addresses may, if not vanish, certainly appear in a different, more manageable and less paralyzing form.

"Can it be really Ignatian, when faced with a retreatant still struggling with painful memories of childhood abuse, to omit or attenuate what Ignatius says about the Third Mode of Humility?" When we ask ourselves a question like that, we need to reflect on what the word *Ignatian* means. Even now, many of us would instinctively say that *Ignatian* denotes one particular approach to the Christian life.

---

8. Constitutions VI.3.1.A [583]: "If with some people it is thought appropriate to give them a set amount of time to prevent them exceeding or falling short in spiritual exercises, the Superior will be able to do this. So too regarding the use of the other means, if he judges definitively that one or other of them should be used without it being left to the discretion of the individual, he will proceed in accordance with what God our Lord will lead him to understand as being appropriate, and it will be for the one under him to accept with complete devotion the order which is given him." (Translation mine.)
9. Maria Clara Bingemer, "Perfection in Whatever State of Life: Ignatian Spirituality and Lay Holiness," *Review of Ignatian Spirituality*, XXVIII, iii, no. 86 (1997): 39–56.
10. See further Leonard Doohan, *The Lay-Centered Church: Theology and Spirituality* (Minneapolis: Winston Press, 1984); Philip Endean, "The Double Priesthood of All Believers: Not the Theology of the Laity," *The Month*, 20 (1987): 250–256.

Implicitly we contrast it with alternatives—alternatives we cannot but call names like "Carmelite," "Benedictine," "Augustinian," and "Cistercian." Some things, it seems, are all very well in other legitimate Christian spiritualities, but they will not do if we are purporting to live by the Ignatian Exercises.

It is, however, a mistake to allow such a way of thinking to influence our vision now, when the Exercises are being made in a far wider range of life situations than ever before. There is more to Christian spirituality than the experience of vowed religious, and more to Ignatian spirituality than the experience of Jesuits. Yet the mistake is also understandable: It is going to take us time to realize that Christians at large (let us avoid that patronizing word "laypeople") have a genuine spirituality in their own right, and not merely as honorary appendages to one or other of the great religious orders.

Revisioning Ignatius's Distinctiveness

Once we make this acknowledgment, then we look at the distinctiveness of Ignatius in a new way. Ignatius obviously did found a new form of consecrated life, and devoted the major part of his energies to promoting it. Moreover, he saw Spiritual Exercises as a powerful means for gaining recruits to his new company. But this is not the only, nor the most important, significance of the Exercises. They also represented a turning point in the history and self-understanding of the Christian Church as such. "Finding God in all things" and being "contemplative in action" are not characteristics of one particular way of being Christian, one way contrasting with alternatives. On the contrary, they articulate, quite simply, aspects of what it is to be Christian. No more, but also no less. Ignatius's achievement is not to contribute a new doctrine or theology but to synthesize the traditional message in an unprecedentedly creative way, matching perhaps the great cultural movement we call the Renaissance. Towards the end of his life, the great German Jesuit theologian Karl Rahner wrote a whimsical piece, in which he imagined what Ignatius, speaking from heaven, would say now to a contemporary Jesuit. Near the beginning,

Rahner's Ignatius insists that he had no ambition but to proclaim the word of the Church as it had always been proclaimed: ". . . and yet I thought—and this opinion was true—that I could say what was old in a new way."[11]

It follows that Ignatian spirituality is not a simple alternative to other spiritualities. Rather, it articulates something fundamental to any lived experience of God. Other Christian spiritualities—say, for example, that of John of the Cross—should be read by the Ignatian family not as alternatives to our way of proceeding but as complements. John of the Cross articulates in more detail particular areas of human spiritual experience; conversely, Ignatius distills from John's experience dynamics common to any lived experience of the God of Jesus Christ. It does not make sense to talk of non-Jesuits or non-Ignatians finding God only in some things.

Revisioning Ignatian Authenticity

The theoretical and pastoral issues raised here are, of course, vast and they deserve much fuller treatment.[12] But if the claims I have just been making are even remotely correct, then they must affect how we think about Ignatian authenticity. The worry or concern that provoked this paper may need to be formulated in different, more inclusive terms.

Of course it is important that we use Ignatius's Spiritual Exercises well, in a way that mediates their full power. Of course we must present them with sensitivity to Ignatius's charism, and take care not to distort their fundamental reality. What, however, this amounts to may be less a matter of what is anything specifically Ignatian than an issue about simply what constitutes authentic pastoral care. With the

11. Karl Rahner, "Ignatius of Loyola Speaks to a Modern Jesuit," in *Ignatius of Loyola;* with a Historical Introduction by Paul Imhof (London: Collins, 1978), 11–38, at 11. (Translation amended.)

12. I hope, in a sequel to this article, to present some more historical material originally prepared for the Loyola Hall seminar. In this, I suggest how a less Jesuit-centered approach might enable us to use in a new and more helpful way the standard source material on Ignatius's Spiritual Exercises and their early practice.

enormous growth in training programs for spiritual directors, obvious questions arise regarding the competence of those who emerge, and about mechanisms for accreditation. However, when problematic cases arise, the issue is not, I suspect, that the people concerned, though competent Christian ministers, do not know much about Ignatius. The difficulty is rather that people who have gone through a short training program may simply lack pastoral competence and experience in a much more general and straightforward sense.

To ask questions about authentic Ignatian procedures presupposes some notion of what counts as authentically Ignatian. We need to unlearn, at the level of gut instincts, the idea that Jesuits are the normative Ignatians. Ignatian spirituality consists in a distillation of the Christian message as a whole. At least in its fundamentals, it can be of value and relevance for those following any form of Christian life whatsoever. The question of authenticity in the Ignatian Exercises is ultimately identical with the more general question of what counts as authentic Christian ministry. Is it appropriately consonant with tradition? Is it sensitive to God's ongoing self-disclosure in people's experience? Out of the vast range of contemporary "applications" of the Exercises, none, surely, fails this double test outright and in principle. As long as they are striving towards the God ever present in human need, experience, and circumstance, they are on the way to being authentically Ignatian.

Revisioning the Ignatian *Magis*

How Far Can You Go? is at times a riotously comic novel, but the reality it evokes was in some ways grim: a Catholic culture dominated by restrictive rules, where only clerical opinion counted. The question also refers to how far some of the novel's characters depart from the Catholicism of their youth as that culture collapses. Yet one of the factors provoking that collapse was a sense that God's presence with us is far more widely diffused than that culture could ever imagine. God is present in all "the joys and hopes and the sorrows and anxieties of people today, especially of those who are poor and afflicted."

Moreover, holiness is not the prerogative of one sector within the Church; on the contrary, "all the faithful . . . are called to the fullness of the Christian life," and it is "one holiness" that is "cultivated by all who are led by the Spirit of God."[13]

The very idea of adaptation suggests a standardized pattern. Ignatius's Exercises, however, offer not a blueprint but a resource for dialogue between the Christian tradition and the whole gamut of human experience. If, at any level of ourselves, we are asking, "How far can you go?" then we are still trapped within a dependence that we need to unlearn. For the truth is that we can never go far enough. Ignatian spirituality is, famously, about the *magis*, about a God of the more, the greater. Narrow Jesuit cultures sometimes trivialized this rhetoric, using it to exhort the young to macho exploits in the divine service. If, however, we see Ignatian spirituality as a distillation, simply, of Christianity, then the *magis* appears as a sense of how God is always to be sought as one greater than our present projects or imaginings. The quest for God's presence in human history, the discovery of God's disposing in the whole range of human experience, can never end. There is always further to go.[14]

---

13. *Gaudium et Spes*, n. 1; *Lumen Gentium*, n. 40, 41.
14. This piece has been influenced by two recent articles of Joseph Veale: "Manifold Gifts," *The Way Supplement*, 82 (Spring 1995), 44–53; "Saint Ignatius Speaks about 'Ignatian Prayer,'" *Studies in the Spirituality of Jesuits*, 28/2 (March 1996): 1–31.

The Spiritual Exercises and Gender

Elizabeth Liebert, SNJM

Ignatius's *Autobiography* and other source documents clearly reveal that the Spiritual Exercises came together in their earliest form in a context of spiritual conversations between Ignatius and women of Manresa, Alcalá, and Barcelona.[1] Only after Ignatius moved to Paris as a student do the women seem to disappear from his pastoral conversations as recorded in the *Autobiography*. During his student days in Paris, Ignatius met those men who would become his lifelong companions, grounded them in the Spiritual Exercises, and together they discerned their call to place themselves at the service of the pope and live by a common rule of life.

This essay was originally presented orally at the Symposium on Mystagogy in the Spiritual Exercises, at Manresa, Spain, on June 13, 2022, and subsequently published (in Spanish) among the Symposium papers. English version used with permission.

1. Martin Palmer, John Padberg and John McCarthy, *Ignatius of Loyola: Letters and Instructions* (St. Louis: Institute of Jesuit Sources, 2006), ix, indicates that Ignatius wrote more than 6,800 letters, collected in twelve volumes of the *Monumenta Ignatiana*. The first extant letter after his conversion is a 1524 letter of spiritual direction addressed to Agnès Pascual in which he urges Agnès always to go forward, avoiding everything that is a hindrance; thus, temptations will have no power over her (ix, 3).

Women didn't really disappear, however. Ignatius constantly engaged in spiritual conversations in person and by letter with women of various classes and social locations.[2] As women experienced the spiritual and apostolic charism of Ignatius and other early Jesuit leaders, desire for closer affiliation with the Jesuits began to surface. Some women wanted to start a group of female Jesuits, while others wished to be incorporated into the existing Society. Much of the appeal of the Jesuits for women focused on the opportunity to live a religious life in the world.[3] Several women, namely Isabel Roser, an early supporter of Ignatius, of whom he says, "For to you I owe more than anyone in this life," her maidservant Francisca Cruillas, and Lucrezia da Bíadene actually took vows after Roser appealed directly to Paul III for permission to do so.[4]

When Roser showed up in Rome with this intention firmly lodged in her mind, Ignatius put her in charge of the administration of the House of Martha, a ministry to "wayward" women already begun by the Jesuits and supported financially by Roser and her companions. Relatively soon, however, the relationship between Ignatius and Isabel soured, and, after eventually reconciling with Ignatius, she returned to Spain. Ignatius sought and received from Pope Paul III permission to release Isabel and her two companions from their vows. He then resolved to have no women in the young but rapidly growing Society of Jesus (despite later relenting on the secret membership of Juana of Spain, the only woman to die under vows). Ignatius formalized this

---

2. See Hugo Rahner, ed. *St. Ignatius Loyola: Letters to Women* (New York: Herder and Herder, 1960) for the range of conversations and letters that Ignatius carried on with women. Rahner selects and comments on the letters by category rather than chronologically, yet his treatment clearly indicates that his correspondence with women continued up to the end of his life. Among secondary sources see Philip Caraman, SJ, *Ignatius of Loyola: A Biography of the Founder of the Jesuits* (New York: Harper and Row 1990), especially chapters 5–8. For a more detailed narrative of Ignatius's dealings with women in this early period during which the Exercises took form, see José Ignacio Tellechea Idígoras, *Ignatius of Loyola: The Pilgrim Saint* (Chicago: Loyola University Press, 1994), 171–264. He includes several direct quotations, often from second generation testimonies gathered as part of Ignatius's canonization process, that reveal how Ignatius interacted with the women, especially in Manresa and Alcalá and indicate that he gave them spiritual exercises similar to those recommended in the Eighteenth Annotation. To one, Maria de la Flor, it is clearly recorded that he gave a longer version of his exercises, during which Ignatius spoke with Maria daily for a short time over the period of a month (Caraman, 64).
3. Charmarie Blaidell, "Calvin's and Loyola's Letters to Women: Politics and Spiritual Counsel in the Sixteenth Century," in *Calviniana: Ideas and Influence of John Calvin*, ed. by Robert Schnucher (Kirksville, MO: Sixteenth-Century Journal Publishers, 1988): 238.
4. Hugo Rahner, *St. Ignatius of Loyola: Letters to Women*, 265.

decision in 1547 with a petition to Paul III to free the Jesuits for all time from the spiritual direction of women who wish to put themselves under vow to one of their number.[5]

What can we make of these snippets of Ignatius's life? How might we move from then to now in how we understand gender and the Spiritual Exercises? What might a hermeneutics of gender reveal?

Gender: To What Does the Term Refer?

A shared understanding of gender provides the foundation to launch this discussion. The World Health Organization offers the following definition:

> Gender refers to the characteristics of women, men, girls and boys that are socially constructed. This includes norms, behaviors and roles associated with being a woman, man, girl or boy, as well as relationships with each other. As a social construct, gender varies from society to society and can change over time. Gender interacts with but is different from sex, which refers to the different biological and physiological characteristics of females, males and intersex persons. Gender and sex are related to but different from gender identity. Gender identity refers to a person's deeply felt, internal and individual experience of gender, which may or may not correspond to the person's physiology or designated sex at birth.[6]

This definition clearly represents a contemporary understanding of gender. Ignatius's understanding would necessarily have been embedded in the cultural assumptions about the roles of men and women of his time, the constraints of class, the economics of his early itineracy and of the young Society, his educational level, and so on.

---

5. Tellechea Idígoras, *Ignatius of Loyola*, pp. 472–74.
6. World Health Organization, "Gender and Health," https://www.who.int/health-topics/gender#tab=tab_1. Accessed February 14, 2022.

With this basic understanding of gender, what general principles of adaptation might guide either contemporary directors or contemporary interpreters of the Exercises in their task of developing useful hermeneutics around gender?

Two Contemporary Examples of Adapting the Exercises

Two contemporary American authors, Roger Haight, SJ, and Erin M. Cline, take on the issue of appropriately adapting the Spiritual Exercises for unusual audiences; Haight does so for seekers of no particular religious practice but who still seek spiritual depth, and Cline seeks appropriate adaptation for persons of religions other than Christian.[7] Examining their principles of adaptation can assist us in the task of appropriate adaptations for contemporary women.

Haight developed his interpretative strategy experimentally. He first became intimately acquainted with his audience. In his case, the audience was a group of students at his institution, which is a liberal Protestant seminary with a strong orientation toward social engagement and is centrist in doctrinal and theological issues. It has a pluralistic student body representing many Christian traditions, from Roman Catholics to Unitarians, Christians affiliated with no denomination, some persons belonging to other religions than Christian, and some belonging to no religion at all. In other words, this group contains persons who may differ substantially from the usual group that finds its way to the Spiritual Exercises.

After deeply immersing himself in this group, he set an appropriate goal for presenting the Exercises to this varied constituency. He concluded that, rather than "press people into Christian service," his language for the outcome of the Fourth Week, the goal would simply be to make Jesus available to spiritualities of various kinds.

---

7. Roger Haight, SJ, *Christian Spirituality for Seekers: Reflections on the Spiritual Exercises of Ignatius Loyola* (Maryknoll, NY: Orbis Books, 2012) and Erin Cline, *A World on Fire: Sharing the Ignatian Spiritual Exercises with Other Religions* (Washington, DC: Catholic University of America Press, 2018).

Next, he listened carefully to the language used by this diverse group and attempted himself to use language that would communicate with them rather than bombard them with Ignatian terminology.

Finally, and crucially, he needed to shift any aspect of the Exercises in such a way that it could be rooted in common human experience, and therefore imaginable from multiple perspectives, rather than in some explicit dimension of Christian faith or particular group of Christians. Haight found that an authentic appeal to common human experience did give the practices involved a striking relevance and opened up new dimensions of the story of Jesus.[8]

These four steps—becoming deeply immersed in the situation of those making the Exercises, committing to make Jesus available to them, framing the dynamics of the Exercises in their language and sensibilities, and rooting the Exercises in common human experience—can also provide a hermeneutic for the director of the Exercises where the retreatant is female. In fact, Haight's principles of adaptation do broadly honor Ignatius's directives in Annotation 15 not to lean or incline in any direction but serve like a pointer on a scale at equilibrium and allow the Creator to deal directly with the creature and the creature with the Creator.

Erin Cline, however, critiques Haight's principles of adaptation as so broad that they can describe almost any kind of self-help or self-cultivation practice such that the result is not necessarily Ignatian at all. Cline's principles of adaptation, though developed as part of her project for sharing the Spiritual Exercises with persons of non-Christian religions, explicitly attempt to preserve the unique heart of the Spiritual Exercises. Among her general principles, I have selected five, and then focused them directly on issues of gender and the Exercises.

Seek to remove any stumbling block that prevents the retreatant from entering into the retreat. Given Ignatius's initial directives for making the Exercises profitably, particularly Annotations 15 and 18–20, it is clear that Ignatius encourages the director to just this kind of commitment.

8. Haight, *Christian Spirituality for Seekers*, xi–xv. Haight develops his adaptation of Ignatian dynamics and language in chapter 2, discusses how to adapt the logic of the Exercises in chapter 3 and touches on some other key issues of interpretation that the Exercises present his [18] specific audience in chapter 4.

Ignatius provides a very broad set of exercises that he regularly offered women and men who were not (at least not yet) ready to make the full Exercises in either the enclosed (Annotation 20) or non-enclosed (Annotation 19) versions.

One example of a stumbling block for many women within the Exercises themselves is the masculine imagery for God used throughout. Listen to the words of this retreatant:

> As a woman who is a victim and survivor of incest at the hands of my father, I found it difficult to relate with God as Father. The image of Father God made me more than uncomfortable; it made me angry. I felt Father God betrayed me. I gave up on God and became an agnostic for seven years. Yearning for something deep within me drew me back to a need for a spiritual dimension in my life. However, I continued to struggle with God as Father. The thought of God as Father made me sad. I hurt too much to go there. I just stayed with Jesus. Then, through the guided retreat, I was introduced to Sophia, the God of Wisdom—nurturing, compassionate, and unwavering in her love for me and for all of creation. A block was removed, a door opened as vast as the eye could see and deep enough to reach the recesses of my heart. She with Jesus nurtured me, gave me courage to enter into the depth of my pain, and gradually begin the healing process.[9]

Another retreatant, a Mennonite woman, recalls that the Call of the King held little attraction for her. But, while praying through the Exercises, the image of Jesus as king on his throne was transformed. She shared that Jesus got off the throne and put on an apron and asked her to serve others with him. This made his call extremely attractive.[10] In this case, the exercise was presented as Ignatius offered it, with the Spirit working through the retreatant's prayer. The director's role here is to discern the authenticity of this movement and, if sensing the Spirit's work, to nourish this movement in the retreatant.

9. Maria McCoy, "Ignatian Spirituality and Christian Feminism," *The Way* 54 (2) April 2015, 91–106. This retreatant is quoted on 96–97.
10. McCoy, "Ignatian Spirituality and Christian Feminism," 103.

Update the historical and culturally anachronistic aspects of the Exercises. This task, particularly with respect to gendered communication and reception, is an ongoing challenge given each interpreter's own commitments and blindness with respect to gender. The delicate balancing act, however, comes both in the principle of selection (is this point necessary in the dynamic of the Exercises?) and in the degree of adaptation (does the proposed adaptation actually obliterate the intent or essential movement of the Exercises, or does it make it accessible in a way that the original text no longer does?). The line between appropriate adaptation and essential dynamics is frequently both highly subjective and subtle to discern.

In adapting the Exercises for Lutheran retreatants, for example, Brandon Peck used as his criterion the foundational Lutheran commitment that Scripture must ground all prayer and spiritual practice. Hence, he substitutes, in place of Jesus' appearance to Mary after the Resurrection (SE 218–225), Jesus' appearance to Mary Magdalene in John 20:1–18.[11] What, one wonders, would happen if individual women (and men) were instead offered the choice to pray with Ignatius's original Exercise?

Another example, though a gender neutral one and therefore appropriate for all retreatants, is to ground the biblical texts upon which the Contemplations are based in contemporary exegetical insights and interpretations. It is also possible to follow one evangelist consistently through the original text of the Second and Third Week contemplations instead of alternating the evangelists according to how Ignatius imagined the story might have unfolded. This way of proceeding engages each Gospel on its own terms, otherwise obscured when Gospels are alternated thematically. Another version of this selective substitution is to focus on texts where women appear significantly. The Second Week lends itself to such substitution.

Adapt as lightly as possible for each individual, maintaining a mean between challenge and adaptation. It is not only possible but often tempting to adapt away a particular growth point. Just because a retreatant

11. Brandon Peck, "A Lutheran Adaptation of the Spiritual Exercises of St. Ignatius," paper submitted for SP4042 Spiritual Exercises in Context, Jesuit School of Theology of Santa Clara University, 2018.

does not have any devotion to Mary, for example, does that mean that the Triple Colloquy should be rewritten to omit the colloquy with Mary? Is it better to support the retreatant in her attempt to form a relationship with Mary through the Exercises? How might a director assist?

Use discernment about what and how much is adapted. Every adaptation, no matter its size, should flow from discernment: Does the proposed shift assist this person to meet and deepen her relationship with her Creator and Lord? To deepen her discipleship? To desire spiritual freedom? To examine her deepest desires for how they might speak to her of God's desire for her? To choose a path of greater discipleship?

Add supplemental resources as helpful tools for bridging the experience of the one making the Exercises to the more foreign aspects of the Exercises. This principle, like the others, is highly subjective. What additional reading or experiences might make entering into a given part of the Exercises more possible or more productive for this woman? Finding these resources can be a mutual investigation.[12]

Cline's final general principle applies directly to her project of adapting the Exercises across religious traditions. She encourages her readers to engage in careful comparative work with the tradition of the retreatant to set the stage for any adaptation. In developing a hermeneutic of gender, the necessary comparative work occurs via immersion in current feminist scholarship and the experience of women from a variety of contexts. Such comparative immersion does, in fact, help create appropriate bridges that women can use to cross fruitfully into the world of the Spiritual Exercises.[13]

One more interpretive principle, intersectionality, which arose in the context of race, has immediate, direct, and often catastrophic ramifications in the situation of women.[14] Intersectionality points to the interconnected nature of social categorizations such as race,

12. Cline, *A World on Fire*, 4–111. This appropriation of Cline's interpretive principles appears in Elizabeth Liebert and Annemarie Paulin-Campbell, *The Spiritual Exercises Reclaimed: Uncovering Liberating Possibilities for Women*, 2nd ed. (New York: Paulist Press, 2022), xvi–xvii.

13. Liebert and Paulin-Campbell, *The Spiritual Exercises Reclaimed*, 2nd ed. (New York: Paulist Press, 2022).

14. Legal scholar Kimberlé Crenshaw coined the term in 1989, in response to white middle-class views that dominated "second wave" feminism. See, for example, Grace Ji-Sun Kim and Susan M. Shaw: *Intersectional Theology: An Introductory Guide* (Minneapolis: Fortress Press, 2018), 1.

class, and gender, as they overlap and influence one another and result in complex and interdependent systems of discrimination and disadvantage. For example, in many cultures, simply being a woman is a distinct disadvantage in terms of voice, power, economic opportunity, educational access, and so on. Being a woman of color in a white dominated society greatly compounds the disadvantage, and that compounding continues if that woman of color is a single mother working a low-wage job without access to childcare, living in substandard housing in a dangerous neighborhood controlled by gangs.

Depending on what the interlocutor sees as key, one might highlight the interaction among race, education, sexuality, ability, age, class, language, culture, ethnicity, religion, citizenship, and so on, in terms of their impact on gender. All these identity markers are both constructed and fluid, and their relative importance can change, given the perspective of the interlocutor. Indeed, gender itself is a constructed and fluid category only adequately assessed within the insights of intersectionality.[15]

Returning to the World Health Association's definition of gender, we can see immediately the implication of intersectionality on our understanding of gender:

> Gender is hierarchical and produces inequalities that intersect with other social and economic inequalities. Gender-based discrimination intersects with other factors of discrimination such as ethnicity, socioeconomic status, disability, age, geographic location, gender identity, and sexual orientation, among others.[16]

---

15. Elizabeth Liebert, "Interior Motions from a Female Perspective," *Studies in Spirituality* 31 (2021): 73. See also Ali Chavoshian and Jun Eun Sophia Park, who alert us to the deep power of language in "Listening Not in Spiritual Direction: A Lacanian Inkling," in *Presence: An International Journal of Spiritual Direction* 25 (June, 2019): 8: "When a subject speaks, it is impossible for her to be free from the frame of language, embedded as the subject is in a culture family relationships and a society," and Joohyung Lee, "The Discerned Choice for East Asian Christian Spirituality: Korean Approach," in his Ph.D. dissertation submitted to the faculty of the Claremont School of Theology, 2015, especially chapter 1, in which Lee clearly illustrates the intersectional connection between culture and gender, though he does not isolate gender as his primary category.
16. World Health Organization, "Gender and Health," https://www.who.int/health-topics/gender#tab=tab_1. Accessed February 14, 2022.

The ramifications, either positive or negative, multiply with each intersection.

Taking intersectionality seriously, then, means that, just as the experiences of men cannot serve as the norm for experiences of women, neither can the experience of an individual director serve as the single lens on the experiences of women. Nor can the experiences of any single woman with the Exercises serve as a basis for generalization to other women. Each person who comes to the Exercises, either as the one making the Exercises or as the one directing them, is absolutely unique, and the Exercises will take root in each person uniquely.

Foundational Principles for Adapting the Exercises with Respect to Gender

With these interpretive principles and definitions in place, what can we now say about the Spiritual Exercises and gender? Six foundational principles follow.

1. If we expand the horizon in which we view the Exercises to include the experience of women, we can recognize the participation and influence of a company of women in Ignatius's time imbued with an Ignatian vision, lived out through the world of women, and influencing the larger milieu. These women, and the countless women through the centuries who have offered and received the Spiritual Exercises, challenge all of us to creatively adapt the Spiritual Exercises to include women's perspectives. This work is both timely and urgent.
2. The history of the Exercises reveals the world of women as a place of revelation, further enabling us to discover God in all things—even the daily minutiae of women's lives, then and now. This assumption may seem obvious

to contemporary persons, but it was not always so. Take women's concrete lives seriously as a theater for God's action through the Spiritual Exercises.

3. Since God's Revelation can occur in the gendered experiences of women, inclusive discernment is essential in the inevitable struggle to make choices that lead to spiritual freedom. Any scan through the history of the Exercises reveals the enormous formative influence of social structures and the barriers created by class, race, gender, and religions both on Ignatius and on the women with whom he interacted. Such barriers create pockets of power and powerlessness, systems of domination and subordination, and situations of inclusion and exclusion that still plague us today. No longer can women's desires and actions be ignored in any movement toward social transformation toward the reign of God—and toward the received interpretation of the Exercises.
4. Class is inevitably intertwined with power, and power partially determines the degree to which the fruits of the Spiritual Exercises can be actualized in the world. Women of various classes participated in differing ways in the ministry of the Spiritual Exercises and early apostolates of the Jesuits. Class not only determined the degree to which women participated in apostolic ministries, but also influenced the mode of reception of certain texts and images of the Spiritual Exercises. Definite class assumptions occur in the imagery of the Exercises in that they presume, perhaps unconsciously, upper-class women and men. While contemporary persons in some societies may be tempted to dismiss class distinctions as irrelevant, we still encounter ranking systems by gender, ethnicity and race, education, professional expertise, and socioeconomic status—the new and hidden class structure. Can the current practice of the Spiritual Exercises accommodate and even welcome diversity in these areas? That is, will the Exercises continue to have the potential to liberate both women and men for new possibilities?

5. Right relationships are essential to mission. The tendency to limit women's potential by consciously or unconsciously accepting the cultural stereotypes of women is clearly visible in Ignatius's dealing with women. Ignatius, and often even the women themselves, are caught in assumptions about women's subordinate status and role. As the women in Ignatius's sphere of influence constantly grappled with the impact of his message in their lives, it caused conflict, challenge, ambiguity, struggle, liberation, desire for God, conversion, and suffering. Yet the historical data also provides examples of women helping Ignatius, and Ignatius facilitating the gifts of women for the common mission. How do we foster that same liberation today?[17]
6. The mutuality expressed in the Presupposition (SE 22) certainly extends to gender. Companions, especially if they are male, need to convey implicitly and explicitly their willingness to learn from and at times be challenged by their female retreatants, and particularly by the gender non-conforming among them. It is now readily accepted in many parts of the world that women may offer the Exercises, but have we also intentionally encouraged non-binary persons to prepare to accompany others?[18]

Practical Attitudes and Actions

With these interpretive principles in mind, we can further inquire about practical attitudes and behaviors for those who guide women in the Exercises. These recommendations apply equally to male and female guides.

17. These first five implications are treated more extensively in Liebert and Paulin-Campbell, *The Spiritual Exercises Reclaimed*, 2nd ed., chapter 2.
18. Liebert and Paulin-Campbell, *The Spiritual Exercises Reclaimed*, 2nd ed., chapter 3.

- *Know yourself.* Actively work on self-knowledge. Know the things and persons that matter to you. Know your strengths and weaknesses. Ask for the grace to become aware of your blind spots. Own your besetting sins. Be aware of how God works with you. Ask also for the grace to see yourself as a deeply loved sinner, the key grace of the First Week of the Exercises. The more you know yourself and your own interior motions, the less likely you will be to project yourself onto the one you are accompanying.
- *Act out of humility.* Take each woman (and man) as unique in God's eyes. Start with the assumption that you do not, and cannot, know what *this* woman senses, feels, thinks, and values, nor can you know how God and she interact, what God desires for her, her unique vocation, etc. All these things are to be discovered in the dynamic of the relationship between each woman and her Creator and between her and her guide.
- *Take Annotation 15 with absolute seriousness.* To allow the Creator and Lord to deal directly with this woman, "do not lean or incline in any particular direction, but rather, standing by, like the pointer of a scale in equilibrium, allow the Creator to deal immediately with the creature and the creature with its Creator and Lord."
- *Allow Annotation 18 to take root as appropriate.* Adapt the Spiritual Exercises to the disposition of the person who desires to make them, that is, to her "age, education, and ability." But be especially alert to your assumptions about the values attached to age, education, and ability, as well as to gender, mindful of the compounding forces revealed in intersectionality. Exercises other than those that Ignatius offers in the full (Annotation 20) Exercises are not less good. The Exercises that "work" for this woman become her Spiritual Exercises. This flexibility of attitude and practice takes constant monitoring, lest we promote one version of the Exercises over the Exercises that meet this person where she is. Ignatius offers a very pragmatic principle here: Give

those making the Exercises as much as their circumstances will allow; likewise, give them whatever will provide them with greater help and progress.

- *Listen contemplatively,* giving deep attention to the singular person you are engaged with, trying to see that person as God sees her. Use all that you are to try to make an empathic connection while at the same time bracketing all that you are so that it does not obscure the unique person in front of you, a delicate dance that takes constant monitoring. Contemplative listening is itself a deep spiritual practice and one that those who guide the Exercises need to internalize and practice assiduously.
- *Check what you think you hear and see if the speaker verifies or nuances or contradicts your perception.* Let her lead you into a greater and clearer sense, for herself as well as for you, of who she is and how God is working uniquely with her.
- *Attribute the best intentions to your seeker as illumined in the Presupposition* (SE 22). Ask what she means, stay alongside her even in her critiques, her anger, her sadness. Try to "save," that is, to hold, to honor her comments and her perspective as deeply as possible.[19]

Clearly, these attitudes and commitments apply to any person who assists others through the Exercises and any person making the Exercises, yet they are critical in the gendered hermeneutics of the Exercises.

Conclusion

There are surely other ways to approach the topic of gender and the Spiritual Exercises. For example, one could trace Ignatius's devotion to Our Lady, beginning with his early life in Loyola and the surrounding towns; Mary's significant role in Ignatius's developing

19. Liebert and Paulin-Campbell, *The Spiritual Exercises Reclaimed*, 2nd ed., chapter 3.

understanding of his call as he narrates it in the *Autobiography* (10, 13, 17) and the extant sections of his spiritual diary where it is clear that much of his prayer on the Constitutions is either addressed to or in the context of his devotion to Mary; Mary's appearances in each week of the Exercises, especially the Colloquy to our Lady and the non-biblical but deeply intimate exercise in which we are invited to imagine Jesus' appearance to Mary immediately after the Resurrection (SE 218–225).[20] Sustained reflection from an intersectional feminist perspective will surely yield further fruit that can speak to our times.

Yet another way to unpack the issue of gender and the Exercises is to search out and analyze the reported responses that women have to various exercises and to the Exercises as a whole. For example, Julia Dowd's research on Spiritual Exercises as made by women faculty, staff, and administrators at Jesuit universities in North America and interpreted through a feminist lens revealed that many women had prayer experiences through the Exercises that challenged the traditional symbols and theology of their faith. Through the Exercises, these women discovered Mary, Jesus, and God as liberating characters and forces that oppose and challenge traditional justifications of women's subordinate position in clerical and patriarchal systems.[21] Annemarie Paulin-Campbell's work with women directors in South Africa also shows unique patterns for women, and further illustrates the intersection of gender and culture.[22] More studies in this vein await study and comment and theory building around gender and the Spiritual Exercises.

Yet even this brief attempt at developing a hermeneutics of gender and the Spiritual Exercises reveals that gender is indeed a rich vein with much still to be mined in order to feed our growing understanding of the Spiritual Exercises and their implication for today. The final words come from the Mennonite woman whose transformed image of Jesus as King appeared earlier:

---

20. Liebert and Paulin-Campbell, *The Spiritual Exercises Reclaimed,* 2nd ed., 192–195.

21. Julia Dowd, "Gathering the Graces: Women, the Spiritual Exercises and Jesuit Education," DMin dissertation submitted to the faculty of the Pacific School of Religion, 2018.

22. Annemarie Paulin-Campbell, "The Impact of the Imaginal and Dialogical (Relational) Processes in the Spiritual Exercises on Image of Self and Image of God in Women Making the Nineteenth Annotation Retreat," Ph.D. dissertation submitted to the University of KwaZulu-Natal, South Africa, 2008.

> Some years ago, when I contemplated "the women who stayed at the cross," I prayed with Sophia and these women who stayed and had a profound sense of joining the "great feminine heart" that could choose to be up close to the suffering . . . of Jesus . . . and the world. I continue to feel Sophia's energy to STAY to engage the sorrow of the world, to feel empowered and not paralyzed.[23]

May we have the sensitivity to issues raised by intersectional perspectives on gender so that we too stay highly focused on how God is at work in each woman we companion in the Exercises and on how the Spirit wishes to work through a wide variety of women interpreters and guides for the Spiritual Exercises.

23. McCoy, "Ignatian Spirituality and Christian Feminism," 105.

Jesuit Norms for Choice of Mission and the Exercises

Erin Cline

In his 2009 address in which he urges us to explore how the Exercises can be appropriated by non-Christians, Father Adolfo Nicolas stresses a number of broader Jesuit aims. Among these are the norms for choice of mission outlined in chapter 7 of the *Constitutions of the Society of Jesus*, which guide Jesuits as they consider establishing or continuing work in particular areas and which Nicolas paraphrases as follows:

> (1) helping souls, that is, helping people; (2) the greater glory of God; (3) going where there is greatest need; (4) searching for the *magis*, that is, for what exceeds mediocrity and moves toward excellence, going beyond what has already been achieved; (5) taking on works, also, where no other workers are present or available; (6) moving sometimes to controversial frontiers of action or knowledge, even breaking settled boundaries; (7) undertaking works that promise a more universal good and a deeper reach of contact; and (8) creating or joining communities of solidarity in seeking justice.[1]

I would like to focus on these norms because there are good reasons to think that a number of them are pertinent to the question of whether the Exercises should be offered to members of other faith

From *A World on Fire* (The Catholic University of America Press, 2018).

1. Adolfo Nicolas, SJ, "Companions in Mission: Pluralism in Action," Mission Day Keynote Address, Loyola Marymount University, Los Angeles, California, February 2, 2009, https://www.xavier.edu/jesuitresource/online-resources/addresses-and-keynotes/index, 82.

traditions. Accordingly, considered alongside the aims and purposes of the Exercises, they can serve as a helpful guide in sorting out whether this practice might be an appropriate part of the Jesuit mission today. To begin with, the potential of the Exercises for helping souls or helping people who are not Christians is worth considering. Much depends here on what we regard as "helping." If the Exercises deepen the faith of a Muslim, a Buddhist, or a Hindu, even though it is not Christian faith, does this constitute "helping souls"? It might be helpful to consider some specific examples. A Zen Buddhist might make the Exercises, perhaps in a heavily modified form, and believe that she has had a direct experience not of God or Jesus but of the ultimate emptiness of the universe—including the fact that there is no such thing as the soul. If this reaffirms her Buddhist faith and she is able to live out her faith by showing greater compassion to others as a result of making the Exercises, has her soul been helped? (And does it matter if she denies that she has a soul?) A Hindu might make the Exercises and believe that in the course of the Exercises he has encountered the Hindu deities Kali and Shiva; perhaps he also encountered Jesus but regards him as an avatar (or incarnation) of Vishnu. His Hindu faith is deepened and he discovers his vocation as a result of making the Exercises. Has his soul been helped?

There are good reasons to think that both Christian inclusivists and Christian exclusivists could agree that these do constitute cases of "helping souls," although their reasoning would differ. Inclusivist and exclusivist are among the most prominent 20th-century approaches to the question of how Christian theology should view other religions. Christian exclusivists are united by their belief that God is revealed exclusively in Jesus Christ (*solus Christus*) and that only those who profess Christ—who hear the Gospel (*fides ex auditu*) and confess it in their hearts—can be saved.[2] In contrast, inclusivists hold that Christ is the normative revelation of God but that salvation is possible outside of the explicit Christian Church (including, for

2. Exclusivists hold a variety of different positions on issues such as whether God elected some for salvation and others for damnation, and on whether the opportunity to confess Christ must take place before death. For a helpful overview of these differences, see Gavin D'Costa, "Christian Theology of Religions," in *The Routledge Companion to Modern Christian Thought*, ed. Chad Meister and James Beilby (London: Routledge, 2013), 662.

some inclusivists, through other religions) although this salvation is always from Christ. In various forms of inclusivism, then, we find solus Christus without the *fides ex auditu*.[3] So a Christian inclusivist, who might for instance believe that non-Christians sometimes encounter God and experience Christ's love without knowing that it is Christ—and who maintains that there can be salvation outside of Christianity, even though this is always the work of Christ, even if the person is unaware of it—should have no trouble maintaining that giving the Exercises to these non-Christians may be a way to help souls. For the inclusivist, the Buddhist and the Hindu described above have both, in fact, experienced Christ's love through the Exercises, even though they are unaware that it is Christ. They misunderstand (and thus misdescribe) their experience, but the outcome is good: they both go on to lead better lives, both by the standards of their own religious tradition and by Christian standards, even though they did not convert to Christianity, and their religious views did not become more Christian. The inclusivist is content to consider their fruits, with fruits understood primarily in ethical terms: the kind of lives they are leading, the sort of people they are. These fruits might look precisely the same for a Christian who made the Exercises and found that her faith was deepened, and that she is more patient and caring towards others as a result. For the inclusivist, the difference is that the Christian knows that this is due to Christ.

On the other hand, a Christian exclusivist, who maintains that conversion is necessary for salvation, could also maintain that these souls have been helped, but the exclusivist will be less satisfied with purely ethical fruits. The exclusivist will also contend that they have been helped because through the Exercises the person has been exposed to the Gospel and has thus been moved closer to conversion. The exclusivist is not satisfied with the inclusivistic view that some people will experience Christ but call that experience by another name; the exclusivist's goal is for the person to recognize that she is

3. If one moves further down the theological spectrum from inclusivism, one finds pluralism, which jettisons the uniqueness of Christianity entirely. Pluralists hold that all religions are or can be paths to either the one divine reality or plural divine realities; Christ is one revelation among many different and equally important revelations. For an overview of different forms of pluralism and inclusivism, see D'Costa, 661–62.

having an encounter with God in Christ and to profess Christ. In this way, having correct beliefs matters a good deal more to the exclusivist than to the inclusivist, especially correct beliefs concerning one's understanding of one's religious experiences.

The exclusivist's concerns can help us recognize a series of important questions about members of other faith traditions who might make the Exercises. First, in what ways and to what extent do the exercitant's beliefs about what she is doing matter? If one of the purposes of the Exercises is to deepen one's relationship with God, does it matter if one does not believe that has happened? Do we feel differently about giving the Exercises to the Zen Buddhist who does not believe in any God, and the Hindu, who does? While we might be comfortable saying that the Buddhist has in fact encountered God but that she mistakenly understands this as "emptiness," would we be equally comfortable saying that she has deepened her relationship with God without knowing it (and without even believing in God)? Is it possible for a person to deepen her relationship with God if she doesn't believe in God? Or must a person believe in God in order for us to speak meaningfully of her having a relationship with God? It is important for monotheists who are interested in other religions to understand that not all members of other religious traditions conceive of their religious experience in terms of a relationship; many Zen Buddhists, for instance, deny that their experience of reality is of a relationship. Instead of experiencing a presence or having an encounter with the divine, they experience the true nature of reality as empty.

Overall, I think most inclusivists and exclusivists could agree that giving the Exercises to members of other faith traditions such as the Buddhist and Hindu described above can be a way of "helping souls," because these individuals can become better people both by Christian standards and by the standards of their own traditions, and perhaps also—and this would be especially important for the exclusivist—because the experience might move them toward a full recognition of God in Christ.

In addition to "helping souls," a number of the other norms for choice of mission in chapter 7 of the *Constitutions* are helpful for thinking about why giving the Exercises to members of other faith traditions may or may not be central to Jesuit works. For instance, "searching for the *magis*, that is, for what exceeds mediocrity and moves toward excellence, going beyond what has already been achieved" is worth our consideration. The Exercises have long been given to Catholics and now are widely given to other Christians as well; they are an extraordinarily powerful way of experiencing the Gospel, and this has proven to be true for Christians of many different theological orientations. In what way might Jesuits "go beyond" in giving the Exercises? One way of answering this question is to consider who else might find them meaningful, which is of course precisely what Father Nicolas asks us to do. Giving the Exercises to members of other faith traditions is one way of searching for the *magis*. The norms for choice of mission are remarkably clear, as well, that Jesuits should be "moving sometimes to controversial frontiers of action or knowledge, even breaking settled boundaries" and also "undertaking works that promise a more universal good and a deeper reach of contact." Giving the Exercises to members of other faith traditions is certainly a way of moving beyond settled boundaries and seeking a more universal good by bringing the Exercises to new communities.

These are themes that resonate deeply with the address of Pope Benedict XVI to the 35th General Congregation of the Society of Jesus in 2008 when Father Nicolas was elected Superior General. In his speech Pope Benedict called upon Jesuits "to reach the geographical and spiritual places where others do not reach or find it difficult to reach. These words of Paul VI have remained engraved in your hearts: 'Wherever in the Church, even in the most difficult and extreme fields in the crossroads of ideologies, in the front line of social conflict, there has been and there is confrontation between the deepest desires of man and the perennial message of the Gospel, there also there have been, and there are, Jesuits.'"[4] Today's obstacles "are not so much the seas or the long distances as the frontiers that, due to a mistaken or superficial vision of God and of man, are raised between faith and human knowledge, faith and modern science, faith

4. Benedict XVI, *Address of His Holiness Benedict XVI to the Fathers of the General Congregation of the Society of Jesus*, Vatican Web site, February 21, 2008, https://www.vatican.va/content/benedict-xvi/en/speeches/2008/february/documents/hf_ben-xvi_spe_20080221_gesuiti.html.

and the fight for justice."[5] He stressed that the Church is in urgent need of people to stand on those frontiers in order to witness and help to understand that there is in fact profound harmony between faith and reason, between evangelical spirit, thirst for justice, and action for peace. Only thus will it be possible to make the face of the Lord known to so many for whom it remains hidden or unrecognizable. This must be the preferential task of the Society of Jesus. Faithful to its best tradition, it must continue to form its members with great care in science and virtue, not satisfied with mediocrity, because the task of facing and entering into a dialogue with very diverse social and cultural contexts and the different mentalities of today's world is one of the most difficult and demanding.[6]

Pope Benedict concluded by calling upon Jesuits to "reserve a specific attention to the ministry of the Spiritual Exercises," noting that they are "the fountain of your spirituality and the matrix of your Constitutions, but they are also a gift that the Spirit of the Lord has made to the entire Church: It is for you to continue to make it a precious and efficacious instrument for the spiritual growth of souls, for their initiation to prayer, to meditation, in this secularized world in which God seems to be absent." Pope Benedict notes, further:

> In a time such as today, in which the confusion and multiplicity of messages, the speed of changes and situations, make particularly difficult for our contemporaries to put their lives in order and respond with joy to the call that the Lord makes to every one of us, the Spiritual Exercises represent a particularly precious method to seek and find God in us, around us, and in everything, to know his will and put it into practice.[7]

Pope Benedict's remarks about the importance of going to the frontiers, with all of their social and cultural diversity and all of their confusion, have been echoed not only by Father Nicolas but by Pope Francis, who extends this work to theologians:

5. Benedict XVI.
6. Benedict XVI.
7. Benedict XVI.

> Teaching and studying theology means living on a frontier, one in which the Gospel meets the needs of the people to whom it should be proclaimed in an understandable and meaningful way. We must guard against a theology that is exhausted in academic dispute or one that looks at humanity from a glass castle. . . . Let the theology that you elaborate therefore be rooted and based on Revelation, on Tradition, but also correspond with the cultural and social processes, in particular difficult transitions.[8]

Careful theological reflection on the practice of giving the Exercises is an instance of theology that fits this sort of description, for the question of why and how we ought to give the Exercises to members of other religious traditions is not only very practical but surely marks one of these "difficult transitions." Yet Pope Francis insists, "Your place for reflection is the frontier. Do not fall into the temptation to embellish, to add fragrance, to adjust [the conflicts] to some degree and domesticate them. Even good theologians, like good shepherds, have the odour of the people and of the street and, by their reflection, pour oil and wine onto the wounds of mankind."[9]

In order to achieve such ends, Father Nicolas has stressed the importance not only of Jesuits sponsoring works but of Jesuits becoming companions and co-workers in someone else's work: "Yet even when they are co-workers in someone else's mission, Jesuits (alone or in groups) choose it because of its resonance with their own deepest sense of mission."[10] Throughout Jesuit history, he argues, Jesuits saw themselves as co-workers and companions with non-Christians, "with all men and women of good will—men and women with a good heart." He goes on to point out:

> While Jesuits bring their own distinctively Catholic, Christian identity to whatever work they join, they know that others' projects are not always conceived explicitly in Christian or even religious terms. They

8. Francis, *Letter of His Holiness Pope Francis to the Grand Chancellor of the "Pontifica Universidad Catolica Argentina," For the 100th Anniversary of the Founding of the Faculty of Theology*, Vatican Web site, March 3, 2015, https://www.vatican.va/content/francesco/en/letters/2015/documents/papa-francesco_20150303_lettera-universita-cattolica-argentina.html.
9. Pope Francis.
10. Nicolas, "Companions in Mission: Pluralism in Action," 82–83.

> join such projects, with the identities that are their own, because they see deep consonance between the non-religious mission and their own criteria for mission. Similarly, they ask members of other religious traditions or simply men and women of good will to join in their own sponsored works without, in any way, asking of them that they deny or negate their own identities in the common work.[11]

I want to tease out a couple of dimensions of what Father Nicolas is highlighting here. He contends that it is possible to be faithful to one's own religious identity and tradition—and even further the mission of one's faith—while engaged in projects that are not rooted in one's tradition. One looks for areas of agreement between missions, and as he goes on to point out, we should not see "mission" here as suggesting proselytism but as "clarity about goals and the strategies to achieve them." He mentions that Jesuits have run schools (e.g., in Muslim countries) where they explicitly promised that they would not try to convert anyone. Father Nicolas goes on to discuss the decree promulgated at Jesuit General Congregation 34 (held in 1995), normative for the whole Society of Jesus, titled "Cooperation with Laity in Mission," which called on Jesuits to "foster an attitude of readiness to cooperate, to listen attentively, and to learn from others," being "men for others" and "men with others."[12] He quotes Fr. Peter-Hans Kolvenbach's 2004 reaffirmation of the commitment enunciated at GC 34: "We Jesuits need to be not only friends and companions of the Lord and each other, we must be friends and companions of our partners in mission."[13] Indeed, Father Kolvenbach (Superior General of the Society of Jesus from 1983 until 2008) has made clear that this vision of human solidarity is grounded in the vision that is articulated at the Second Vatican Council:

11. Nicolas, 83.
12. Nicolas, 84–85.
13. From Peter-Hans Kolvenbach, "Cooperating with Each Other in Mission," Address at Creighton University, Omaha, Nebraska, October 7, 2004, quoted in Nicolas, "Companions in Mission: Pluralism in Action," 85.

> One is the community of all people, one their origin, for God made the whole human race to live over the face of the earth. One also is their final goal, God. God's providence, manifestations of goodness, and saving design extend to all people, until that time when the elect will be united in the Holy City, the city ablaze with the glory of God, where the nations will walk in God's light.

The council continues:

> [T]he Church therefore exhorts her sons and daughters, that through dialogue and collaboration with the followers of other religions, carried out with prudence and love and in witness to the Christian faith and life, they recognize, preserve and promote the good things, spiritual and moral, as well as the socio-cultural values found among these people.[14]

Kolvenbach highlights the four dialogues recommended by the Pontifical Council for Interreligious Dialogue and Congregation for the Evangelization of People—which were adopted into the Society of Jesus' way of proceeding at GC 34—one of which is "The dialogue of religious experience, where persons, rooted in their own religious traditions, share their spiritual riches, for instance, with regard to prayer and contemplation, faith and ways of searching for God or the Absolute."[15] While this is labeled a "dialogue," the language here—which refers to the "sharing of spiritual riches" with regard to prayer and contemplation—suggests more than just describing how we pray, which is something Jesuits have already done throughout their history. Father Nicolas points out that GC 34 "stressed that

---

14. Paul VI, *Nostra Aetate, Declaration on the Relation of the Church to Non-Christian Religions*, Vatican Web site, October 28, 1965, https://www.vatican.va/archive/hist_councils/ii_vatican_council/documents/vat-ii_decl_19651028_nostra-aetate_en.html.

15. *Documents of the 34th General Congregation of the Society of Jesus: The Decrees of General Congregation Thirty-Four, the Fifteenth of the Restored Society and the Accompanying Papal and Jesuit Document*, ed. John L. McCarthy, SJ (Saint Louis: Institute of Jesuit Sources, 1995), Decree 5, "Our Mission and Interreligious Dialogue." Kolvenbach's views on these aspects of the vision articulated at the Second Vatican Council and on the Society of Jesus' way of proceeding can also be found in Peter-Hans Kolvenbach, "The Service of Faith in a Religiously Pluralistic World: The Challenge for Jesuit Higher Education," in *A Jesuit Education Reader*, ed. George W. Traub, SJ (Chicago: Loyola Press, 2008), 168–71.

ecumenism is a new and essential way to be Catholic today and that interreligious dialogue—between Christians and those of non-Christian religions or those of secular faith—should be made a Jesuit apostolic priority."[16] He goes on to discuss Decree 6, "Collaboration at the Heart of Mission," the follow-up document from GC 35, which states, "We are enriched by members of our own faith, but also by people from other religious traditions, those men and women of good will . . . with whom we labor in seeking a more just world."[17] Father Nicolas adds, "It should not cause surprise that Jesuits, whose originating charism dictates that they attempt to discern and find God present and laboring in all things, might also try to find that same God working in and present to all persons, whatever their identities, traditions, cultures or religions."[18] He stresses that GC 35's document on collaboration reflects the reality that Jesuits "engage with Buddhists, Jews, Hindus, Moslems or even agnostic co-workers in their own works," and he quotes the document's conclusion: "The Society desires strong relationships in mission with as many collaborators in the Lord's vineyard as possible."[19]

The allusion to Luke 10:2 is interesting to consider in light of the concerns of this book. Jesus sends the first seventy-two disciples out on mission saying, "The harvest is plentiful, but the laborers are few; therefore ask the Lord of the harvest to send out laborers into his harvest" (Luke 10:2, *NRSV*). There is a strongly inclusivistic tone to Father Nicolas's use of this passage, and also in the way he weaves together and stresses the importance of particular documents from GC 34 and GC 35. He highlights the connection between ecumenism and interreligious dialogue, maintaining that Jesuits should partner not only with other Christians but with those of other faith traditions as well. He further stresses that the goal is not conversion but the achievement of our shared mission and values, and the deepening of our awareness of the way in which God works in and is present to all traditions, cultures, and religions. He argues that all of this is central to what the Constitutions say about how Jesuits should choose their

16. Nicolas, "Companions in Mission: Pluralism in Action," 85.
17. Nicolas, 86, quoting GC 35, d.6.3.
18. Nicolas, 86.
19. Nicolas, 87, quoting GC 35, d.6.24.

missions. Given that this discussion precedes his remarks about the prospect of sharing the Exercises with non-Christians, it seems clear that this endeavor, for Father Nicolas, is a way of being faithful to the mission of the Jesuit order. Indeed, not only is it possible to share the Exercises with members of other faiths, in his view; it is essential to do so.

What Father Nicolas says about the Exercises in relation to other traditions leaves the door open to a number of possibilities. In his speech he quotes Father Kolvenbach: "We Jesuits owe it to our partners to remain rooted in the graces of the Spiritual Exercises and to find ways to make this apostolic resource available to those with whom we cooperate in mission."[20] What does it mean "to make the Exercises available"? The most straightforward interpretation would seem to be to give the Exercises to them, but whether this would mean giving the full and complete Exercises is unclear. Father Nicolas does not specify any of this in his subsequent remarks. Rather, he writes that "[w]hile the Spiritual Exercises of Ignatius Loyola are radically Christo-centric, centered on the core notion of discipleship and the Kingdom of God, experience and the testimony of non-Christians suggest that important elements of the Spiritual Exercises, especially those concerned with spiritual freedom, equipoise and discernment, can be fruitfully appropriated even by non-Christians."[21] Here he reaffirms the Christocentric nature of the Exercises and does not seem to envision adapting them in ways that move beyond the "core notions" he mentions. His claim that "important elements" of the Exercises can be "fruitfully appropriated" by non-Christians may suggest something other than giving the full and complete Exercises to non-Christians: It might mean drawing out particular elements of the Exercises—especially those elements concerned with spiritual freedom and discernment—for non-Christians. This could be an 18th Annotation retreat or it could be something still different; precisely what he thinks might be done with those elements of the Exercises—how they might be "appropriated" by members of other faiths—isn't clear.

20. Nicolas, 87; quoting Kolvenbach, "Cooperating with Each Other in Mission."

21. Nicolas, "Companions in Mission: Pluralism in Action," 87–88.

In his speech, he goes on to say that "the Spiritual Exercises can be shared by non-Christians. Even though Christ is at the heart of the full experience of the Exercises, it is also true that their structure involves a process of liberation—of opening to new horizons—that can benefit people who do not share our life of faith."[22] Again, his remarks here suggest that he may not have in mind the "full experience" of the Exercises for members of other faiths, since he contrasts this with the structure of the Exercises, a structure that he says can benefit those who do not share our faith. It is not clear what he means when he refers to the "structure" of the Exercises, though. He goes on to say that in Japan—where he taught systematic theology for more than thirty years and served as Provincial before becoming Moderator of the Jesuit Conference for East Asia—non-Christians would sometimes ask if they could make the Exercises, but he does not specify how he responded to this request, only that it "triggered a reflection, and it is one that we need to continue. What are the dynamics in the Exercises that non-believers might make their own to find wider horizons in life, a greater sense of spiritual freedom?"[23] When Father Nicolas refers to "dynamics" here, it is not entirely clear what he means. He may be referring to various movements or phases felt within a person who is praying through the Exercises, or to the different exercises or dimensions of the Exercises. Is Father Nicolas suggesting the possibility of giving parts of the Exercises to non-Christians? Or by "make their own" does he mean to suggest something broader, such as creating a new set of meditations or contemplations that are inspired by the Exercises but designed to help individuals to make choices grounded in their faith? Much rests on which "important elements" or "dynamics" one thinks could be helpful to members of other faiths, and what it means to "appropriate" the Exercises and "make them their own."

The lack of clarity on these matters makes it unsurprising that Father Nicolas's remarks have been cited not only by those who believe the Exercises should be given to members of other faiths (who understandably tend to read these remarks and ask, "What

22. Nicolas, 88.
23. Nicolas, 88.

else could he mean other than giving them the Exercises?"), but also by those who argue against the view that the Exercises should be given to non-Christians. William Reiser, SJ, for instance, writes that "Fr. Nicolas's language is careful. He speaks of the 'Ignatian experience,' particularly with its emphasis on each person being led by God; he does not refer to the determinate Christian experience that lies beneath the Exercises."[24] As Reiser points out, the LMU speech was not the first time that Father Nicolas spoke of these matters. About a year before being elected superior general, he gave an interview in which he noted that there has been some discussion of whether the Exercises could be presented to non-Christians and how this might occur, saying:

> The question is how to give the Ignatian experience to a Buddhist. Not maybe formulated in Christian terms, which is what Ignatius asked, but to go to the core of the experience. What happens to a person that goes through a number of exercises that really turn a person inside-out. This is still for us a big challenge.[25]

Again, the language here is unclear. What does it mean to "give the Ignatian experience" to someone? What is "the core of the experience"? Father Nicolas here seems to be raising the question of what is at the core of the Exercises or the transformative element—the element that "turns a person inside-out."

There have been a variety of thoughtful responses to these remarks. Francis Clooney, SJ, writes:

> Fr. Nicolas's insights bring to mind my own experience in Kathmandu in the mid-1970s, when I was teaching at St. Xavier's High School, a boarding school in which almost all the students were Hindu and Buddhist. It was the custom, as in Jesuit schools here in the United States, for the senior students to go away on weekend retreats, and

---

24. William Reiser, SJ, "The Spiritual Exercises in a Religiously Pluralistic World," *Spiritus* 10 (2010), 135.
25. Michael McVeigh, "Profile: Father Adolfo Nicolas," *Province Express, A Newsletter of the Australian Jesuits,* January 22, 2008, https://web.archive.org/web/20080122063407/http://www.express.org.au/article.aspx?aeid=2305.

> even when the students were not Christian, the Exercises were still at the core of reflections on the world, sin, our responsibilities, and the power of making a choice for God in human life.[26]

Clooney talks about drawing upon stories from the Hindu and Buddhist traditions during these retreats, noting that "in such stories lies a way to God, for God does not spurn the small openings that appear when we discover, in what we've long heard and seen, that God has already been with us." It is noteworthy that Clooney, like Father Nicolas, uses monotheistic language here; Father Nicolas says in the above-cited interview that "the Exercises are about letting God guide people." He gives no indication of the view that the Exercises should be adapted in the kind of non-theistic terms that we saw in Haight's discussion. Yet Clooney goes further than Nicolas in acknowledging precisely where the challenges lie:

> The Spiritual Exercises turned out to be a key to a rich range of spiritual exercises, the choice for Christ shedding light on the supreme value of giving God first place in one's life and practice. I am sure that this kind of venture will be somewhat worrisome for some of us—for is not companionship with Jesus, contemplation on his life and a choice for him, at the very core of the Exercises? Surely yes, and there is not much value in recasting them as a generic form of self-reflection. . . . Yet it is also clear—from my brief experience, but more importantly as validated in the ministry of Jesuits throughout Asia, that the gift of the Exercises—like the gift of Jesus himself—can be given and received in multiple ways, with an abundance that cannot be restricted to the properly normative ways already well known in the Church and the Society of Jesus.[27]

26. Francis X. Clooney, SJ, "Inside-Out with Fr. Nicolas," *America Magazine*, Feb. 3, 2008, https://www.americamagazine.org/content/all-things/inside-out-fr-nicolas.
27. Clooney.

VII. Imagination and Creativity

Part VII Introduction

One of the most important characteristics of Ignatian prayer is the use of imagination. Ignatius recommends practices of meditation, consideration, and contemplation as ways for humans to open themselves to the work of God's Spirit, who prays within the bodied spirit of the human person. Each of these practices requires the person of prayer to both remember past experiences and to mentally or emotionally "try on" some experience that is suggested by a story—written or told orally—a painting, a dance or play, a landscape or cloudscape, or any number of other opportunities to think about and feel within oneself something that is not an ordinary part of one's life moment. Imagination is necessarily formed by education, attitude, and knowledge granted through all kinds of studies and forms of understanding. To think of imagination as formless is to accept a non-human perception that lacks the rational capacity of humanity. Emotion alone does not form imagination, nor does rationality alone. Rather, the gift of human imagination is a complex blending of all the forms—intellectual, memory-based, and sensate by which we discover the other, the world, and ourselves. At its best, imagination is an informed human knowing that leads into the discovery of God and God's desires for us, which become the ground for true discernment about what makes us joy-filled and fully human. In other words, the right use of creativity and imagination enable us to receive God's will (which Jesus describes as his daily bread—that which keeps him alive) and to act upon it meaningfully.

Ignatius's early studies in Paris focused on arts and letters, the subject fields of literature, history, the arts, and rhetoric, prior to his more advanced studies in philosophy and theology. In these studies, he apparently felt confirmed in the importance of both imagination and human creativity for more perfectly grasping the truth about his inner life, the existence and creativity of God, and the importance of understanding how people of diverse ages, genders, races, cultures, and religious traditions grew more fully human through engagement with truth, beauty, and goodness.

Ignatian spirituality, ordered toward relationship, is shaped by the right use of creative talent toward service of the physical world and all the life within it. Those who stand on the margins of acceptance in various cultures are often deprived of the truth, beauty, and goodness; thus their poverty is often so much more than financial. It is a poverty of spirituality that brings despair and lack of joy or peace.

From the earliest days of the Jesuit education mission, the creative arts and imaginative humanities have been central dimensions of developing fully human students. Other Jesuit works are similarly infused with the talent and skill of stirring the imagination and awakening creativity. These dynamics manifest in a wide range of actions, from preaching and the celebration of the sacraments to direct service on behalf of political power for the voiceless and creating welcome for the undocumented.

In Part VII of the *Reader* we wanted to include examples of such imagination and creativity. As with other Parts, we are presenting texts that invite readers to dig more deeply and find some of the lasting contributions to the long list of fine arts including poetry, film, storytelling, photography, theater, dance, musical creation and performance, sculpture, painting, crafting, and to the longer list of forms of literature, psychology, history, anthropology, symbology, theology, and other subjects that fall under the umbrella of studies in humanity and art today. Wherever humanly created beauty can be discovered we will find imagination and creativity being well served.

In the first article Tom Lucas, SJ, writes very clearly about the long appreciated link between the Spiritual Exercises and art. Next, Bert Daelemans, SJ, writes of the wound of Ignatius (from the cannonball strike at Pamplona) in art. In the third article, Holly Schapker starts a conversation about the importance of art surrounding students. Joshua Hren follows with a discussion of the Jesuit influence (not easily discerned by everyone) on one of the great contemporary novelists, David Foster Wallace, in his final and unfinished novel. Tim McEvoy brings to focus the importance of an imagination informed by knowledge that science, history, and other scholarship brings to focus. McEvoy's article provides an excellent opportunity to see how easily the imperial behavior of anachronistic thought and imagination assumes attitudes that harm the heritage of persons and skew the information of other times as much as it can dominate persons of our own time. Part VII concludes with a reflection by Eric Immel, SJ, on an experience of imagination in his own prayer.

Creativity and imagination inspire new ways of discovering ourselves, others, and God, but they are aspects of a larger whole that they enrich and are enriched by.

Eileen Burke-Sullivan

The Spiritual Exercises and Art

Thomas Lucas, SJ

> Dateline: Paris, 1686. In the Jesuit college on the rue St. Jacques, rehearsals for the August ballet and play are in full swing. Onstage, Hercules slays monsters. Offstage, a killer is on the loose. And the Siamese ambassadors, on their way to see Louis XIV, are coming to the college show. Charles, the young Jesuit rhetoric teacher—and ballet producer—trying to do his job, keep his vows, and stop the murders, falls into the net of the first Paris police chief.

So begins the teaser for Judith Rock's 2010 novel *The Rhetoric of Death*. In this delightful historical whodunit and the three brisk page-turners that follow it, Rock, a dance historian by training, evokes the rich tradition of theater, dance, the arts, and intrigue at the Jesuit Collège Louis-le-Grand in 17th-century Paris. Young Charles du Luc introduces the modern reader to the long line of Jesuit artists and their colleagues—composers, dance masters, scene painters, and artist-architects—who used to and continue to use and teach the arts in our educational institutions.

Although Ignatius Loyola didn't have an artistic bone in his body, he bequeathed to the Jesuit order and its institutions a sensibility, an appreciation for the revelatory power of the imagination that was a breakthrough in the Western spiritual tradition. Unlike so many earlier spiritual writers who warned against fantasy or the use of images, Ignatius in his Spiritual Exercises encourages retreatants actively to use their imaginations as well as their intellects. While a

From *Conversations*, March 2015.

few of the exercises are analytic or content-driven, the most important are exercises of the imagination: "contemplations" of the life of Jesus wherein the retreatants enter the scene with eyes and ears and heart open. They begin with a visual composition "made by imagining the place." And each day ends with an application of the senses: "To see the persons with the imaginative sense of sight . . . to hear what they say or could say, to smell and to taste . . . to touch with the sense of touch . . . always seeking to derive some profit from this" (SE 122–126). Ignatius thus connects the spiritual realm to the concrete world of the retreatant's sensory experience with all its symbolic and metaphorical furnishings. In short, those making the exercises are taught to trust their imaginative experience. No stranger himself to the uncharted and sometimes confusing places to which such trust can lead the untrained, Ignatius moreover laid out a simple yet effective check mechanism for the overactive imagination in his rules for discernment.

Less than a decade after the opening of the first Jesuit college for lay students at Messina in 1548, *Fabulae Eruditiae* (learned, if somewhat fractured fairytales) were being performed there. Even before Ignatius's death in 1556, full-scale plays were being performed with his blessing at Rome's flagship Collegio Romano and at the Jesuit college at Ingolstadt, Bavaria.

The 1586 version of the *Ratio Studiorum*, the Jesuits' uniform educational code, recognized the dual value of performance for the young as training in poise and memory: "Our students and their parents become wonderfully enthusiastic, and at the same time very attached to our Society when we train the boys to show the result of their study, their acting ability, and their ready memory on the stage." From these beginnings, a rich and complex tradition of plays grew up in Jesuit colleges around the world: Twice each year, and sometimes more frequently, from Vilnius to Cuzco, from Goa to Manila, the work of the colleges gave way to vast spectacles that filled the courtyards and theaters of the colleges.

Youngsters declaimed bowdlerized Latin and Greek reworkings of ancient classics and Christian stories composed in doggerel verse by overworked scholastics like Charles du Luc. Dramatic intervals between the recitations, called *intermedes*, were filled with spirited dance numbers that inspired modern ballet practice, and their *son e lumière* extravaganzas were the 17th- and 18th-century equivalents of Industrial Light and Magic productions. Fireworks imported from the missions in China, flying students hoisted aloft on ropes and pulleys, and pet dogs pulling chariots filled with allegorical virtues and vices portrayed by little Benoit or Juan Pablo added visual interest. Important court composers such as Marc-Antoine Charpentier and Jean-Baptiste Lully provided the scores; royal ballet masters such as Pierre Beauchamps and Jesuit Fr. Joseph Jouvancy provided the choreography. Indeed, Jesuit theorists and historians produced five of the most important early treatises on ballet at the Collège Louis-le-Grand.

This tradition—150,000 plays performed across the world over the first two centuries of Jesuit education, and countless more since the 19th-century restoration of the order after its suppression—was about more than entertainment, fun, and games. Theater, dance, and visual spectacle were not considered as ends in themselves but were seen as useful educational tools that formed morally astute citizens and socially competent persons who could comport themselves in public in a convincing way. They learned to sing and play instruments in church and on the stage. They were given the social tools to become presentable gentlemen, and, in the case of many, the opportunity to rise from their lower-middle-class origins into higher status.

Although what we now call studio arts were not formally taught, applied arts were part of the program: Students learned to sketch, construct, and paint trompe l'oeil scenery and were given practical lessons in rudimentary engineering so that their confreres flying above the stage on painted clouds would not crash.

The ribbon surrounding the MGM lion reading *Ars Gratia Artis*, "Art for the Sake of Art," would have been incomprehensible to Charles du Luc and his fellow professors. That 19th-century formulation, variously attributed to Théophile Gautier, Benjamin Constant, and Edgar Alan Poe, is profoundly at odds with what might be characterized as the "instrumental" view of the function of the arts in the early Jesuit tradition.

From the very beginning, the Jesuits used the arts for persuasion. They built grand and beautiful churches and imposing college buildings, recruited artists to join the order, and employed a stable of some of the best lay musicians, architects, and artists of the early modern and baroque periods. Gian Lorenzo Bernini was a close friend of Jesuit General Gian Paolo Oliva, and Carlo Maderno designed the Basilica of St. Ignatius at Loyola in Spain. Rubens was a devout member of Jesuit sodalities. Yet it would be a serious mistake to consider the Society's interest in the arts as a mere aesthetic oddity or concern for making the *bella figura*. The arts were seen as means to an end, never an end in themselves: concrete, visible, and audible ways to come into contact with the invisible and inaudible realm of spirit.

The 1814 restoration of the Society of Jesus and its schools after the trauma of the suppression (1773–1814) saw the Jesuits return as shell-shocked survivors of PTSS. In the half-century leading up to the suppression, the order's schools had become locked into traditions and habits of mind that made it difficult, if not impossible, for them to adapt to the times with the same agility that marked the early years of Jesuit education. With the restoration, old customs were revived, old styles of pedagogy were resurrected, and old artistic styles that looked backwards and not to the present were embraced anew. Novelty was eschewed at all costs and with it a kind of benign philistinism came to rule in the Jesuits' approach to the arts. Nothing too beautiful, nothing too lavish, and nothing too daring was allowed. Following the fortress mentality of the institutional Church in the aftermath of the French Revolution and throughout the 19th and into the mid-20th centuries, caution was the watchword. For all practical purposes, no great art was inspired by or came out of Jesuit institutions, with the exception of the brilliant and tortured verse of English Jesuit Gerard Manley Hopkins. His work was unappreciated and unpublished during his short and painful life. Summarizing the attitudes of the age he wrote sadly, "Brilliancy does not suit us."

So where does that leave us, in the second decade of the 21st century? Our institutions, both universities and colleges, have adopted modern curricula and have forgone the antique classical rigors of the

Ratio Studiorum. While theater and music survived the suppression, the visual arts are a fairly recent addition to the offerings in many of our schools. Clearly, the notion that art is and must be instrumental is not generally accepted in the culture at large and in our art departments. The arts, visual and performing, are often the first target when budget cuts loom on the horizon. The less benign philistinism of our present age often enough considers the arts as charming if irrelevant and unprofitable remnants of bygone times.

Toward the end of his life and in the midst of much doubt and depression, Hopkins grappled with this same question in his sonnet "To What Serves Mortal Beauty." His answer could be the beginning of a discussion for us as educators in the Jesuit humanistic tradition:

> To what serves mortal beauty '—dangerous; does set dancing blood—
>   the O-seal-that-so 'feature, flung prouder form
> Than Purcell tune lets tread to? 'See: it does this: keeps warm
> Men's wits to the things that are; 'what good means—where a glance
> Master more may than gaze, 'gaze out of countenance.
> Those lovely lads once, wet-fresh 'windfalls of war's storm,
> How then should Gregory, a father, 'have gleanèd else from swarmed
>   Rome? But God to a nation 'dealt that day's dear chance.
> To man, that needs would worship 'block or barren stone,
> Our law says: Love what are 'love's worthiest, were all known;
> World's loveliest—men's selves. Self 'flashes off frame and face.
> What do then? how meet beauty? 'Merely meet it; own,
> Home at heart, heaven's sweet gift; 'then leave, let that alone.
> Yea, wish that though, wish all, 'God's better beauty, grace.

"See: it does this: keeps warm / Men's wits to the things that are, what good means . . ." Hopkins reminds us that beauty, as expressed in art or in the elegance of a quadratic equation or a DNA helix or the sunrise, opens the heart to the deepest levels of our human experience: to ask the profound questions about meaning, value, goodness, dignity, and, ultimately, hope.

The multicultural milieu of the 21st century is, of course, radically different from that of baroque Europe or 19th-century England's "Commonwealth of Christendom." Our formerly all-male, mostly

Catholic institutions now serve diverse and transcultural populations. As art historian Hans Belting characterizes it, in former times art served religion; in these modern days, at least in major capitals, the "religion of art"—*ars gratia artis*—erects museums that overshadow and strive to displace the cathedrals of old.

While our culture and our institutions have moved beyond the understanding that art must ever and always be instrumental, art continues to remind us that ultimate questions need to be asked. University arts programs have the advantage of being able to present those questions in a bewildering variety of non-linear, post-didactic, pebble-in-the-shoe ways.

For those who are believers, beyond that reminder is the hope of "God's better beauty, grace"; for all, art challenges us with questions that can serve as antidotes to the paralyzing cynicism of "whatever." As Hopkins insists, this is dangerous business, countercultural in the extreme. "Merely meet it; own / Home at heart, heaven's sweet gift; then leave, let that alone." The answers, art teaches us, are not what matters. The questions do.

The Wound of Ignatius in Art

Bert Daelemans, SJ

Íñigo de Loyola was a proud man who saw great things for his future. He imagined a life filled with adventure, fame, and riches—dreams of life at court and all the honors that accompanied it. Those dreams came to an end in 1521 when, badly wounded and subjected to an excruciating convalescence, Ignatius was transformed in a process of gradual self-discovery, grace, and conversion. It is no surprise that the structure of the Society of Jesus, and the formation of her members, closely mirrors Ignatius's journey to a life of service. The question we should be asking is this: On the anniversary of his injury and conversion, will we focus only on Ignatius's spiritual conversion, or will we truly honor his literal embodiment of vulnerability—the embodiment that founded the Society of Jesus—by finding strength in fragility?

As members of a Body, we are encouraged to place ourselves under the banner of the vulnerable God, the Lord who chose a humble and beautiful place to call his own (SE 144). This is the Christ of Glory, who, in the celebrated Portal of Glory in Santiago de Compostela, unashamedly shows his wounds—that is, vulnerability—as the way of salvation. By choosing vulnerability as the way, Ignatius does not distance himself from his Lord, nor does the Society that walks in his wake.

Originally published in *Jesuitas. Revista de la Provincia de España de la Compañía de Jesús* (n. 148, Summer 2021).

Vulnerability is not *identified* with fragility: It is fragility *accepted*. Vulnerability is the capacity to be wounded. There is a path from fragility to vulnerability. From Loyola's bed, a vulnerable pilgrim emerged. Perhaps vulnerability is just another name for glory, as we pray in the Eucharistic Prayer: *Transform our fragile body into a glorious body like yours*. Perhaps vulnerable is only God and vulnerability is a divine art, handled by the saints with fluency and ease.

The worst and the best of ourselves can emerge from our wounds: A hurtful and violent word, which is nothing more than fragility wrapped in noise and rage, or a courageously vulnerable wound that, without hurting or making noise, is the one thing capable of connecting with another: with connecting to *their* wound. There, in the depth of another person, the encounter is celebrated.

Recall Michael Buckley's famous words of encouragement to Jesuits preparing for priesthood: "Are you vulnerable enough to be a priest? That is, do you have enough faults and failures, trials and weaknesses? What do I mean by weakness? Not sin, but the opposite."[1]

> Weakness is the experience of a peculiar vulnerability in the face of suffering, of a deep sense of inadequacy. . . . The strength of our priesthood lies precisely in the weakness that seems to threaten it. . . . Weakness is a profound relationship between us and others. It is also the context for the Lord's epiphany; it is the night in which He appears. The Eucharist can only penetrate our lives if it has been broken and distributed.[2]

The bronze working of Canadian sculptor William McElcheran (1927–1999), *San Ignatius the Pilgrim*, is a fine reflection of this relationship. It is a work of art that represents Ignatian vulnerability because it focuses not only on the bodily wound from Pamplona but also conveys an interior struggle: simultaneously drawing the attention of the viewer both deeper and to the surface.

1. Michael Buckley, "Because Beset with Weakness," from Robert E. Terwilliger and Urban T. Holmes (eds.), *To Be a Priest: Perspectives on Vocation and Ordination* (New York: Crossroad, 1975), 129.
2. Buckley, 129.

In this sculpture, Ignatius moves forward. Always with one foot in front, always on the way, both outwardly and inwardly. He defines himself as a pilgrim: The way opens up, step by step. He is not alone, although it may seem so: He tenderly bends his face to meet others, to raise spirits and help souls, contemplative in action, anchored in movement. He wears only a cloak to protect himself from the elements: He goes, vulnerable, to where he does not know; *he follows the Spirit, he does not go ahead of him . . . wisely ignorant, with his heart simply set on Christ.*

Always bent, not straight and unperturbed, but humbly leaning, ready to meet, attentive and with a keen ear. Always available, head uncovered. *And many have leaned on your inclination*, as Jesuit poet Greg Kennedy beautifully expresses in a sonnet-oration. Always on the move, always attentive to the motions, discerning: *Many anchor their calm in your movement.* If this inclination were the expression cast in bronze to speak of your vulnerability, would that we could exclaim: *Many have followed you on your path of the vulnerable.* Many have found support in this inclined gait, more flexible than rigid intransigence and more resistant than soft permissiveness, solidly *grounded in an equally pilgrim God.*[3]

At the base of this inclination is the wound of Ignatius, not only the one of Pamplona, but the most interior and lasting one, the *incurable* one, the one that kept him always inclined and on that path both interiorly and exteriorly. After being cured, the great existential wound that he must face is that of voluntarism and narcissism. He wants to go to Jerusalem, but in the way he wants, by mortifying himself. An exhausted body is the only thing he earns in his eagerness to imitate the saints.

Ignatius does not close himself in his wounds. In his fragility, God meets him. The wound of scruples opens a new path for him, from voluntarism to availability. Integrating his sufferings makes him more available: He chooses and turns this fragility towards another, in an apostolic and fraternal way. God frees him from his ego, making him a free and generous person. It is the difference between becoming a

---

3. Savour the sonnet in its original language at: https://ignation.ca/2018/07/31/st-ignatius-pilgrim-sonnet-statue/.

saint by oneself and letting oneself be molded by God: Ignatius discovers what it is to be imperfect, a saint with cracks and weaknesses. He becomes more sincere and humble.

In this sense, the sonnet speaks of *Jerusalem always moving away*: Destiny is certain and changing, like the horizon. Ignatius discovers that Jerusalem is not where he wants it to be but is in the *magis*. It is part of vulnerability not to have clarity; not to carry his own "Jerusalem" with him as an untouchable and unshakable treasure, but to place the point of gravity always outside himself. Ignatius does not remain *immobile on the roadside* (Mario Benedetti), but gets wet and gets down to work, because *love must be put more in deeds than in words* (SE 230).

A significant detail of the statue is the letter that has become one with his body, a sign of his intimate and fraternal connection despite the distance among companions on the road, spread over the innumerable frontiers of the world. His vulnerability is *apostolic* and fraternal. He knows he is sent as an apostle, pushed by the Spirit and fundamentally *unarmed* (even "naked" according to the Syriac term). From the bed of Loyola to the *camerette* of Rome, the laborious transformation from the voluntarist Íñigo, who hides and forgets his fragility, to the vulnerable Ignatius, who chooses it as a way and a portal of encounter, took place.

Let me end on a personal note. For years, I have been approaching the theme of vulnerability, although it was never as clear as during my tertianship in Alaska. This year, marked by the pandemic, I have been able to deepen it in a group exhibition of contemporary art at the O Lumen space in Madrid, collaborating with a Dominican and four artists whose work I find particularly lucid and hopeful in highlighting the inherent strength in fragility, showing that pilgrim and apostolic vulnerability is something universal that connects us to one another.

Available and Willing

Holly Schapker

Seven years ago I completed the Spiritual Exercises under the guidance of Darrell Burns, SJ. One can do the Exercises without departing for an extended retreat and instead make them while going on in one's everyday life. That is what I did. I practiced them daily and met with my director once a week. This changed my whole perspective on life and, most particularly, on my artwork. Before my experience of the Exercises, I was a traditional landscape painter, concentrating on developing my skills and hoping that my art would be successful by looking the way I wanted it to look. Being so focused on the outcome brought a lot of strife because I was trying to control the end result. The Spiritual Exercises helped me understand that I am not the sole creator of my work but a co-creator with God. I now listen to my work and allow it to give me the answers. I stay open in the creative process with a trust that all has a purpose, even the mistakes, twists, and turns, and that the end result is exactly as God intends it to be.

As I got to know St. Ignatius, I was surprised by how much I related to this man who lived at the turn of the 16th century. I was inspired to create a series of paintings based on his life and spirituality. I named these works *Adsum* because that is the Latin word for Mary's response when Gabriel asked her to have the son of God. It means, "I am here and completely available and willing to serve God." The Spiritual Exercises moved me closer to that point.

From *Conversations*, March 2015.

The Third and Fourth Weeks of the Spiritual Exercises deal with the Crucifixion and then the Resurrection of Christ. I realized that a God who can make something as ugly and horrible as what happened in the Passion at Calvary into something beautiful can make anything I offer him into something beautiful as well. I discovered that my insecurities regarding my talents were blocking my creativity. Comparing my skills to other artists' is a futile, masochistic habit. I relinquished these character defects to the Black Madonna just as St. Ignatius did with his sword as a statement that he would thereafter become a pilgrim for God. This is one of the best things I ever did for myself and my creative process, as it knocked those self-defeating thoughts out of the studio. This surrender allowed me to let go of others' expectations of me as an artist, and, rather than compare myself to other talented artists, I now express art in my own unique way.

Ignatius Loyola's Spiritual Exercises continue to be alive in my life today. All those old paintings, which I considered a failure because I could not resolve them, now have new life. I see answers and beauty in those old paintings, and it's a joy to paint on them. Each painting session begins with an acknowledgment of God's grandeur and an offering up of my work for God's purpose. I am now more interested in the process than concerned with the results.

Because of the Spiritual Exercises, I experience more moments in my studio that seem like a practical holy experience. There is an intersection in the creative process where my heart is guiding my hands and I experience timelessness as I am in the present moment, filled with love. Although there was a great deal of pain and frustration before I experienced this, I bow to all my struggles and the Spiritual Exercises that brought me to this point of understanding.

David Foster Wallace's Denomination of Joy

Joshua Hren

> We—under our own nihilist spell—seem to require of our writers an ironic distance from deep convictions or desperate questions, so that contemporary writers have to . . . make jokes of profound issues.
>
> —David Foster Wallace (Review of Joseph Frank's *Dostoevsky*)

> Irrelevant Chris is irrelevant only on the subject of himself?
>
> —David Foster Wallace (notes for *The Pale King*)[1]

David Foster Wallace strung gallows humor throughout much of his unfinished novel *The Pale King*. A short section titled "I.R.S. Worker Dead for Four Days" queries "why no one noticed that one of their employees had been sitting dead at his desk for four days before anyone asked if he was feeling all right."[2] The deceased's supervisor supplies the painful punch line: "He was very focused and diligent, so no one found it unusual that he was in the same position all that time and didn't say anything."[3]

Something to Do with Paying Attention, a standalone novella culled from *The Pale King*'s 1,100 pages, is decidedly not devoted to bureaucracy's banal hilarities. Instead, it renders the improbable-but-believable

From *America*, October 2022, 56–58.

1. "Feodor's Guide: Joseph Frank's Dostoevsky," David Foster Wallace, *Village Voice*, https://www.villagevoice.com/feodors-guide-joseph-franks-dostoevsky/.
2. David Foster Wallace, *The Pale King: An Unfinished Novel* (New York: Back Bay Books, 2012), 29–30.
3. Foster Wallace, 29–30.

reformation of "Irrelevant" Chris Fogle, a self-described 1970s "wastoid" who discovers his calling to the I.R.S. when he mistakenly wanders into a DePaul University tax class taught by a "fearful Jesuit."[4]

The priest summons his students to a new species of valor found within the invisible army of I.R.S. accountants. Here, stripped of fanfare or histrionic pomp, heroic feats are accomplished by "you, alone, in a designated workspace. True heroism is minutes, hours, weeks, year upon year of the quiet, precise, judicious exercise of probity and care—with no one there to see or cheer."[5]

In the wake of his own father's horrific accidental death on a Chicago Transit Authority train, the restless Fogle finds solace and direction through the priest, the "first genuine authority figure I had ever met."[6] The priest was someone who proved that "real authority was not the same as a friend or someone who cared about you, but nevertheless could be good for you. . . . Such authority, though not 'democratic' or equal . . . could have value for both sides."[7]

Judith Shulevitz of Slate considers Fogle's experience "the most unusual conversion experience in confessional narrative," and she may be right.[8]

But Wallace weighs down the graceful arc of conversion, making us wonder whether grand retellings of impactful past events are reliable or driven by self-delusion. The text is tempered by contrapuntal tensions; almost constantly the reader is pulled in two directions—sincere belief and resigned skepticism—inducing a kind of elevated attention.

Wallace deliberately parallels "Irrelevant" Chris Fogle's own dramatic reorientation with the conversion story of his college roommate's girlfriend. "Fervent Christians," Fogle claims, "are always

---

4. David Foster Wallace, *Something to Do with Paying Attention* (New York: McNally Editions, 2021), 4, 86.
5. Foster Wallace, 106.
6. Foster Wallace, 102.
7. Foster Wallace, 102.
8. Judith Shulevitz, "Why David Foster Wallace Couldn't Finish," Slate, https://slate.com/culture/2011/04/david-foster-wallace-s-the-pale-king-the-irs-boredom-and-an-unfinished-novel.html.

remembering themselves as . . . lost and hopeless and just barely clinging to any kind of interior sense of value or reason to even go on living before they were 'saved.'"[9]

According to the roommate's (nameless) girlfriend, prior to her conversion, she too was a "wastoid." Listless, one day she wandered into an evangelical service just as the preacher announced that "there is someone out there with us in the congregation today that is feeling lost and hopeless and at the end of their rope and needs to know that Jesus loves them very, very much."[10]

In her shared dorm lounge, the girlfriend describes her spiritual rehabilitation, her certainty of being unconditionally known and loved. Fogle pushes back, reminding her that "pretty much every red-blooded American" during the "late Vietnam and Watergate era felt desolate and disillusioned and unmotivated and directionless and lost."[11] To him the preacher's proclamation that someone in the congregation "is feeling lost and hopeless" dovetails with a drugstore horoscope, whose "universally obvious" prophecies exploit that "special eerie feeling of particularity and insight. . . . Most people are narcissistic and prone to the illusion that their problems are uniquely special."[12]

Here, just as Fogle's college-age sneering reaches the high point of demystification, his grown-up, retrospective self questions the motives of his youthful, knee-jerk nihilism. In hindsight, Fogle concedes, he "actually liked despising" the convert, a sport that sharpened his own cynicism and delivered the dopamine rush of feeling "superior to narcissistic rubes like these two so-called Christians."[13]

Like a latter-day Augustine looking back at adolescence, "Irrelevant" Fogle finds that he, though a "feckless" failure, was somehow "nearly always the hero of any story or incident I ever told people," something that "makes me almost wince now."[14] But the central question that the novella leaves artfully unanswered is whether Fogle's own

---

9. Foster Wallace, 81.
10. Foster Wallace, 82.
11. Foster Wallace, 83.
12. Foster Wallace, 83.
13. Foster Wallace, 80.
14. Foster Wallace, 84.

"conversion" from nihilist to the accountant was founded on premises as vulnerable as those advanced by the "so-called Christian." Fogle's arc, too, opened on the "lost and hopeless."[15] Wasting away slouched on a couch, spinning a soccer ball on his finger while watching *As the World Turns*, Fogle became lucidly cognizant of the world turning around him, of people "with direction and initiative" who didn't squander hours readjusting the antenna with hopes of siphoning televisual treats.[16]

"Whatever a potentially 'lost soul' was, I was one—and it wasn't cool or funny," says Fogle. At once he knew, "sitting there, that I might be a real nihilist," a condition defined by being "in a way, too free, or that this kind of freedom wasn't actually real—I was free to choose 'whatever' because it didn't really matter."[17]

Then Fogle stumbles across the Jesuit lecturer (that the Jesuit is a substitute teacher underscores the chance nature of the encounter). A priest whose hands help turn unleavened bread into the Light of the World, he is also an expert on advanced taxation, combining in one person both the secularly dull and the sacrosanct sublime. While Wallace describes the Jesuit as "pale in a way that seemed luminous instead of sickly," the priest's focus is entirely this-worldly.[18]

A Ciceronian orator of impressive stature, the priest displays the "same burnt, hollow concentration" as veteran soldiers who have seen "real war, meaning combat." The A/V projector in the dimmed DePaul classroom lights his face from below, "which made its hollow intensity and facial structure even more pronounced."[19] With absolute poise, the Jesuit delivers a "hortation" of haunting, exhilarating pathos. Accounting, a supposedly soul-crushing job that demands submission to incalculable boredom, is, he insists, the site of "true heroism."[20]

15. Foster Wallace, 81.
16. Foster Wallace, 96.
17. Foster Wallace, 98.
18. Foster Wallace, 88.
19. Foster Wallace, 90.
20. Foster Wallace, 105.

True, "no one queues up to see it."[21] True, "there is no audience."[22] But "enduring tedium over real time in a confined space is what real courage is."[23] This is because, declares the priest, "the less conventionally heroic or exciting or adverting or even interesting or engaging a labor appears to be, the greater its potential as an arena for actual heroism, and therefore as a denomination of joy unequaled by any you men can yet imagine."[24] Souls "called to account" spend their lives "serv[ing] those who care not for service but only for results."[25]

This peroration marks a high point in the novella: After that the story keeps at bay any unconditional celebration of Fogle's "calling." It does not glorify the vocation of the I.R.S. employee. Fogle's own sentiments eerily echo those of a traditional religious convert. He concludes that "much of what the father said or projected"—about the liberating "loss of options," about the "the death of childhood's limitless possibility"—"seemed somehow aimed directly at me."

In establishing an affinity between the novella's two conversion narratives, Wallace juxtaposes the emotional subjectivism of the girlfriend's fundamentalism with a distinctly Catholic devotion to reasoned truth. ("Please note," the priest clarifies, "that I have said 'inform' and not 'opine' or 'allege' or 'posit.'")[26] If Fogle finds authentic authority and ethical self-abasement within the structures of the I.R.S., though, he lacks the reliably transcendent religious categories by which the pale kingdom he enters must be measured. The fateful speech gains persuasive power from the priest's cadence and "carriage" rather than his priestly collar.[27] Does Wallace thereby mean to alert us to the distance between moral and spiritual conversions? The Jesuit's diagnosis of Fogle's false freedom is absolutely accurate, but does he unduly spiritualize secular work? When "Irrelevant" Chris

21. Foster Wallace, 106.
22. Foster Wallace, 106.
23. Foster Wallace, 105.
24. Foster Wallace, 107.
25. Foster Wallace, 108.
26. Foster Wallace, 104.
27. Foster Wallace, 88.

Fogle enters the Service in search of the Jesuit's promised "denomination of joy unequaled," he seems destined to come up short, as only the beatific vision could bestow such peerless bliss.[28]

Celebrating "Irrelevant's" deliverance from "wastoid" nihilism, moved by a priest's perfectly-pitched hard truths, we yet have reason to fear that during the happy holidays, Fogle wears a face akin to the "exhausted and disheveled" I.R.S. recruiter who appears late in the book.[29] In the novella's final, mysterious metaphor, the recruiter receives the aspirant Fogle's filled-out forms with "the exact kind of smile of someone who, on Christmas morning, has just unwrapped an expensive present he already owns."[30] To the posthumous end, Wallace animates our attention: What rich gift does the recruiter already possess, and does it write off—in the balance sheet—his bedraggled appearance?

28. Foster Wallace, 107.
29. Foster Wallace, 136.
30. Foster Wallace, 136.

Ignatius and the Stars

Tim McEvoy

The image of Ignatius gazing in wonder at the stars is one that seems to endear him to many people today. It appears frequently in modern biographies and personal portraits of him, especially where authors want to evoke Ignatius's incarnational spirituality and mysticism. It has also been captured in art. These references often carry romantic overtones, such as Michael Paul Gallagher's affectionate description of him as "the mystic on the balcony."[1] Since the rediscovery of his *Autobiography*, *Spiritual Diary* and other early sources, Ignatius's stargazing, like his copious tears, seems to have struck an emotional chord with people, evoking a softer and more soulful saint than the rather austere pin-up of the Counter-Reformation commonly encountered prior to Vatican II.[2]

There is something attractive and mysterious about Ignatius's relationship with the stars and our privileged glimpses of him at night, lost in contemplation of them. It is not surprising, then, that his stargazing is usually a keynote of the more human and appealing revisionist image of Ignatius, which reveals the depths of his affectivity, his intimacy with God the Creator, and even his eco-mysticism, as has been argued recently.[3] However, while our imaginative and

From *The Way*, April 2021.

1. Michael Paul Gallagher, 'Ignatius of Loyola,' in *Spiritual Stars of the Millennium*, edited by Selina O'Grady and John Wilkins (London: Bloomsbury Continuum, 2001), 64.
2. See chapter 5, "Ad Majorem Dei Gloriam," in James Martin's *My Life with the Saints* (Chicago: Loyola, 2006).
3. See Hedwig Lewis, *St Ignatius Loyola: Retrospective—Perspective—Reflective* (Anand: Gujarat Sahitya Prakash, 2006), chapter 1.

affective engagement is to be encouraged, we need to be careful not to enlist Ignatius's stargazing too eagerly as evidence of his proto-modernity.

I would like to explore here what happens to our imaginings when we consider Ignatius's relationship with the stars with more historical distance and look at the night sky, alongside Ignatius, through the lens of medieval cosmology.

Whatever the resonances with us today, the stars clearly meant something to Ignatius himself, and his lifelong habit of contemplating them was noted by those closest to him. The first reference to it occurs in his own words, as recorded by the Portuguese Jesuit Gonçalves da Câmara, as he describes the latter end of Ignatius's recovery in Loyola in late 1521 to early 1522.

> Part of that time he would spend in writing, part in prayer. And the greatest consolation he used to receive was to look at the sky and the stars, which he did often and for a long time, because with this he used to feel in himself a great impetus towards serving Our Lord. (*Autobiography*, n. 11)

Ignatius's great longing at this time was to be on his way to Jerusalem, imitating Saints Francis and Dominic, and it was the stars that consoled him in his time of impatient waiting. The passage above goes on immediately to say: "He often used to think about his intention, wishing he was already completely well so as to begin on his way." We might imagine Ignatius, with his itchy feet, longing for the road and the skies above Jerusalem. What was it about gazing up at the night sky that consoled him so much at this time, we might wonder—so much more, we are told, than his writing and other prayer experiences during this fertile spiritual period in his life. What caused him to feel interiorly such "impetus" to serving God?

It is perhaps worth mentioning that his idol St. Francis was also a noted stargazer, as his friend and first biographer Thomas of Celano confirmed: "Who would be able to narrate the sweetness he enjoyed while contemplating in creatures the wisdom of their

Creator . . . while he gazed upon the stars and the firmament?"[4] It is tempting to think that Ignatius was in some way influenced in his behavior by his strong affinity with Francis—whose own dreams of military success had been checked by illness and who later in life experienced eye-sickness "for continual weeping" during prayer, a phenomenon that also affected Ignatius. But if Ignatius was aware of this aspect of St. Francis, he did not get it from his reading material in Loyola Castle.[5]

The most frequently cited reference to Ignatius and the stars is from his time in Rome, some two decades later as he approached the end of his life. By now he was Father General of the burgeoning Society, largely tied to his desk as an administrator and no longer free to wander the roads of Europe beneath the stars. Each night, on the balcony of the Jesuit residence, it is said that he would look up in reverence at the stars and silently shed tears.[6] It is a moving and intimate picture that seems to have originated from the first official biography of Ignatius, by a Jesuit who knew him well at this time. Pedro de Ribadeneira makes clear in his account that Ignatius's star-gazing habit—which began at the time of his conversion at Loyola—remained with him for the whole of his life.

> . . . because many years later, already an old man, I would see him on a rooftop, or in some high place, from where he could see the horizon and a large part of the sky, fixing his eyes on it. And after some time spent in rapture and amazement, he would come to himself, moved,

4. Thomas of Celano, "First Biography of St Francis," n. 81, translated by Placid Hermann, in *Writings and Early Biographies: English Omnibus of the Sources for the Life of St Francis*, edited by Marion Habig (Chicago: Franciscan Herald, 1983), 295.
5. The most likely "life of the saints" read by Ignatius at this time is a vernacular version of the widely diffused Legenda Aurea by Jacobus de Voragine, which has no mention of the stargazing episode in its account of Francis: see José Ignacio Tellechea Idígoras, *Ignatius Loyola: The Pilgrim Saint*, translated by Cornelius Michael Buckley (Chicago: Loyola, 1994), 120; *The Golden Legend: Lives of the Saints*, translated by William Caxton, edited by George V. O'Neill (Cambridge: CUP, 1914).
6. See MHSJ FN 4, 746–748; Pedro de Ribadeneira, *The Life of Ignatius Loyola*, translated by Claude Pavur (St Louis: Institute of Jesuit Sources, 2014), 5.1.15; and Kevin F. Burke and Eileen Burke-Sullivan, *The Ignatian Tradition* (Collegeville: Liturgical, 2009), xxxv.

> and with tears pouring from his eyes because of the great delight that his heart felt, I would hear him say: "Oh, how vile and low the earth seems to me! When I look at the sky, it is manure and garbage."[7]

This was a pattern of behavior, of prayer, which had stayed with Ignatius since the earliest days of his conversion and which seems to have consistently consoled him and drawn him closer to his Creator and Lord. But what do we imagine was going on for Ignatius in his contemplation of the night sky? What do we make of his tears and delight, or his striking words, if Ribadeneira's memory is to be relied upon?

Ignatius's stargazing obviously leaves room for some interpretation and projection, which is perhaps encouraged by its evocativeness. We can too easily picture the scene for ourselves and be tempted to step clumsily into his mental or emotional space. One corrective to this which is easily forgotten is historical distance. Since we can all think of ourselves looking up at the night sky, we imagine that all people in all times and places have always looked at it the same way. But looking is an intensely subjective activity that is also shaped significantly by society and culture over time. As L. P. Hartley famously put it in his novel *The Go-Between*: "The past is a foreign country: they do things differently there." Perhaps there is a need to recover some of Ignatius's foreignness to us in that regard if we are to begin to appreciate the place of the stars in his imagination?

For those of us living in the early 21st century, it is difficult to gaze at the night sky without our looking being influenced by two important filters that would have been absent for Ignatius: our knowledge of modern science and cosmology, and our very modern sensibility towards the natural world in general following the Romantic movement of the late 18th and early 19th centuries. Both

7. "Porque muchos años después, siendo ya viejo, le vi yo estando en alguna açutea, o en algún lugar eminente y alto de donde se descubría nuestro emisferio y buena parte del cielo, enclavar los ojos en él; y a cabo de rato que avía estado como hombre arrobado y suspenso y que bolvía en sí, se enternecía; y saltándosele las lágrimas de los ojos (por el deleite grande que tení su coraçón), le oía dezir:—Ay quán vil y baxa me parece la tierra, quando miro al cielo, estiérco y vasura es" (MHSJ FN 4, 95, translated by the author and Marta Gil de Sola Bellas). It is interesting to note that the Spanish is much more revealing in this instance than the more abridged Latin version of Ribadeneira's text, recently translated into English by Claude Pavur.

of these are so embedded in the way we look at, feel, and talk about nature or creation today that they can easily avoid detection, and we risk unwittingly projecting them backwards on to our ancestors who lived, thought, and contemplated in quite a different mental universe.

The differences in scientific outlook are easier for us to grasp, but it is also easy to overlook the significant shift in attitudes towards creation influenced by the Romantic movement, with its cult of sensibility and new notion of the "sublime," whose vestiges we still carry around with us today.[8] For example, our modern way of looking at, say, a mountain range or great waterfall—evoking language of wonder and awe in us—is quite different from how the same features would have been taken in by people of Ignatius's generation, who are more likely to have framed their experience as terror or even revulsion. Nature tourism and our modern sense of appreciation of much of the natural world did not emerge until the early industrial age.

It would be a mistake and an anachronism, then, to superimpose on to Ignatius much later and more familiar ways of seeing the night sky, such as the "admiration and awe" towards the "starry heavens above" of an Immanuel Kant, writing in 1788, or the breathless "Look at the stars! look, look up at the skies!" of Gerard Manley Hopkins in 1877.[9] Kant's famous passage, taken in context, not only exemplifies fairly well the quite recent sense of the sublime, but it also illustrates an already modern cosmology, post-Copernican and post-Newtonian. His admiration and awe come from his sense of smallness and insignificance in relation to the vastness of the universe, gazing above himself.

---

8. See Duncan Heath and Judy Boreham, *Introducing Romanticism: A Graphic Guide* (London: Icon, 2010).

9. Two things fill the mind with ever new and increasing admiration and awe, the oftener and the more steadily we reflect on them: "The starry heavens above and the moral law within": Immanuel Kant, "Critique of Practical Reason," in Kant's *Critique of Practical Reason and Other Works on the Theory of Ethics*, translated by Thomas Kingsmill Abbott (London: Longmans Green, 1879), 376; Gerard Manley Hopkins, "The Starlight Night," in Hopkins: *Poems and Prose* (London: Everyman, 1995), 24.

> A countless multitude of worlds annihilates as it were my importance as an animal creature, which after it has been for a short time provided with vital power, one knows not how, must again give back the matter of which it was formed to the planet it inhabits (a mere speck in the universe).[10]

Ignatius, living in a very different age and seeing through quite different filters, might have experienced similar emotions but they would have been for quite different reasons.

Ignatius was possessed of a thoroughly medieval imagination, which applies to his stargazing as much as to his images of God, his penchant for chivalry or his views on hell, with which we might be more familiar. Although he lived during a period of dramatic change in Europe—as printing brought about an information revolution and the effects of global exploration, economic and political expansion, and religious reform had their impact on people's lives in myriad ways—there was still much in his time that remained the same. A man or woman from Europe in the 1520s or 1550s looking up at the night sky saw much the same ordered, earth-orbiting universe as his or her ancestors of a hundred or even three hundred years before, and Ignatius would have been no exception.

It is very easy to caricature what such people believed they saw—and medieval cosmology in general—as absurdly naive and inaccurate, perhaps even at odds with the astonishingly prescient spiritual insights of somebody such as Ignatius, which we might think emerged in spite of the intellectual and scientific limitations of his day rather than from within their framework. But to do so is not only unfair—taking advantage of our hindsight—it also does a disservice to what was a complex, multifaceted, and highly adaptive worldview, and ends up just repeating the anti-medieval propaganda of the founding figures of modern science much later in the period.[11]

---

10. Kant, "Critique of Practical Reason," 376–377.
11. See Anthony Grafton, *New Worlds, Ancient Texts: The Power of Tradition and the Shock of Discovery* (Cambridge, MA: Harvard University, 1995), 7.

Although a contemporary of the great Polish astronomer Nicolaus Copernicus, Ignatius would almost certainly have lived, like the vast majority of his contemporaries, in complete ignorance of the new heliocentric theory that Copernicus published, reluctantly, in the year of his death, 1543.[12] Ignatius certainly would not have been rocked to the core by that theory—even in the unlikely event that he had come across it, as a mathematical model being debated by specialist academics. The immediate impact of *On the Revolutions of the Heavenly Spheres* was nowhere near as revolutionary as its title, or popular history, likes to claim.

Owing in part to its prologue—where the theory was presented as a hypothesis, not as fact—Copernicus's work did not attract much controversy, and the Church had no trouble accepting it initially as another contribution to the debate and reform of classical cosmology, still dominated by Ptolemy's Almagest and the physics of Aristotle.[13] In fact only a tiny handful of academics read it, and full-scale debate in Europe over the potentially huge and destabilizing implications of heliocentrism did not erupt until decades after Ignatius's death, a turning point being the appearance of an apparently new star in the Tycho supernova of 1572. In Spain, there was only one recognized Copernican while Ignatius was still active, and Copernicus's text was only included in the astronomy curriculum at the University of Salamanca in 1561.[14] Galileo's wider publication of the theory and his tussle with Rome were even further off on the horizon.[15]

When it comes to his stargazing, then, we have to set Ignatius firmly beneath the geocentric medieval firmament. So, what would men and women of Ignatius's day imagine they saw when they looked up at the night sky? How might that have affected Ignatius's looking?

---

12. Before 1543 Copernicus's theory remained in manuscript and the topic of private discussion only: see Euan Cameron, "The Power of the Word: Renaissance and Reformation," in *Early Modern Europe: An Oxford History* (Oxford: OUP, 2001), 79.
13. Initially accepted by the Church, it was only placed on the Index in 1616 when Catholics joined a wave of Protestant opposition in Europe to the heliocentric theory: Grafton, *New Worlds, Ancient Texts*, 112–115.
14. See Victor Navarro Brotons, "The Reception of Copernicus in Sixteenth-Century Spain: The Case of Diego de Zúñiga," *Isis*, 86/1 (March 1995), 52–55.
15. Cameron, "The Power of the Word," 81.

Standing on the surface of the earth—at once the very center and the very lowest point in the entire cosmos, in an absolute sense—looking up (again in an absolute sense), they would have seen the harmonious heavenly spheres above them. While down on earth all was change and decay, below the moon's orbit, up above, the stars could be observed turning in changeless perfection. The seven mobile planets, fixed in their transparent, crystalline spheres, stacked one upon the other in their separate orbits—Moon, Mercury, Venus, Sun, Mars, Jupiter and Saturn—and beyond this, there was the canopy of the fixed stars, or *Stellatum*, the last visible place between humanity and the dwelling place of God. Stargazers would look up and see the dome of heaven itself directly above them—a place beyond space and time yet full of God, light, and love—almost as we would look up at the vast vault of a cathedral. It was perceived in terms of height, not, as for us, distance. "The medieval world is vertiginous," as C. S. Lewis once wrote.[16]

Did Ignatius experience a sense of vertigo when he gazed at the stars from his balcony? What was it like for him to contemplate, high above him, the threshold of heaven itself which, in the influential imagery of Dante, "has no 'where' other than the mind of God. The love that makes it turn is kindled there, so, too, the powers it rains. Brightness and love contain it in one ring."[17] His place in the cosmos felt quite different, in a real and spatial sense, from how we might experience our own. The heights of the heavenly spheres above him were vast, but not infinitely vast, distances away. Where we might lose ourselves in the unimaginable dimensions of the ever-expanding universe, Ignatius's cosmos was much more stable, intimate, and less perplexing. As the medievalist Lewis put it: The "space" of modern astronomy may arouse terror, or bewilderment or vague reverie; the spheres of the old present us with an object in which the mind can rest, overwhelming in its greatness but satisfying in its harmony.[18]

---

16. C. S. Lewis, *The Discarded Image: An Introduction to Medieval and Renaissance Literature* (Cambridge: CUP, 1964), 98.
17. Dante, *Paradiso*, Canto 27, 109–112, in *The Divine Comedy*, translated by Robin Kirkpatrick (London: Penguin, 2012).
18. Lewis, *Discarded Image*, 99.

What light does all this cast upon Ignatius's greatest consolation and delight in spending long hours gazing heavenwards? For him this was no mere metaphor. His gaze took him upwards to the visible, finite limits of the universe, beyond which, he knew, was the throne of his divine majesty. It is hard for us to imagine what that experience must have felt like.

It is perhaps worth returning to the striking words attributed to Ignatius by Ribadeneira: "Oh, how vile and low the earth seems to me! When I look at the sky, it is manure and garbage."[19] On first sight, they might seem difficult to reconcile with the Ignatius many of us claim to know and even love. The man who learnt to see and serve God in all things discarding the earth as sordid rubbish? Perhaps, on further reflection, we might come to see his heartfelt exclamation as reflecting something of what was expressed by St. Paul in Philippians 3:8—next to Christ all else was worthless. But there is something else going on here as well and though we might recoil at it, we should not explain it away as mere hyperbole: the Augustinian or dualistic overtones that were also ingredients in Ignatius's imaginative universe.

In Ribadeneira's reading of Ignatius's stargazing, the contemplation of God's goodness and beauty in the heavens above—the realm of unchanging perfection—put into stark contrast his own smallness and sinfulness as an earthly creature below, confined to the sublunar realm of impermanence and imperfection. He would look attentively at the night sky for so long:

> . . . because its external appearance, and the consideration of what is within the heavens and above them, was a great stimulus and incentive to him to disdain all the transitory and changeable things that are below them, and inflamed more his love for God.[20]

19. Though it has gone out of style today, this was once one of Ignatius's better-known catchphrases, often appearing, with some variation, via the abbreviated Latin version of Ribadeneira's text: "Heuquam sordet terra cum coelum aspicio!" ("Alas, how sordid is the earth when I look at the sky!"). It appears frequently in pious nineteenth-century literature and is referenced in *Tellechea Idígoras*, Ignatius of Loyola, 149.
20. MHSJ FN 4, 95.

How do we reconcile and hold in tension these different dimensions of Ignatius in our imagination? The world-spurning and heaven-seeking with his deeply embodied, incarnational spirituality? Somehow we need to hold this strange, old cosmological dimension in place alongside Ignatius's mysticism and profound awareness of the immanence of God in creation—the God who caused him to weep tears of delight and consolation. After all, Ignatius was a 16th-century mystic who was able to hold these in tension himself, even if we might struggle to. His cosmology may even have been a help to contemplation rather than a hindrance, as we moderns tend rather arrogantly to assume. For all its absolute and morally charged "ups" and "downs," his was a spiritually soaked universe that was fundamentally orientated towards heaven.

This brings us lastly to another piece of mental furniture that Ignatius would have carried around with him, probably unconsciously: the ancient theory of "sympathies" and "antipathies." Everything in the medieval universe—whether spiritual or physical—had its rightful place and naturally inclined to it, was drawn to it, by a sort of homing instinct. Since the soul came from heaven, our desire for God and godliness was simply a natural inclination of like for like, kind for kind: one thing being drawn back to its rightful place almost as if by magnetic force. Our restless hearts longed for their resting place in God, as Augustine expressed it.

What applied to the human soul equally applied to the physical universe, including the heavenly bodies, and vice versa; the language of *drawn* and *desire* could be employed in a non-figurative sense for both. In this world-view, as C. S. Lewis expresses it, there was "continuity between merely physical events [in our eyes] and our most spiritual aspirations."[21] Dante was not just being poetic when he ended his *Paradiso* by describing how "my will and my desire were turned, as wheels that move in equilibrium, by love that moves the sun and the other stars."[22]

21. Lewis, *Discarded Image*, 94.

22. Dante, *Paradiso*, Canto 23, 143–145.

In Ignatius's day, long before Newton and the theory of gravity, there was no sense of reality being governed by mathematical laws: Love was the driving force of the universe. While this may be a leap of faith for a modern—a spiritual or mystical insight into the heart of reality—for Ignatius it was also a self-evident scientific fact. What else but the love of God could attract and move objects even as large as the sun: the same love that drew and moved him. The stars that Ignatius gazed on were no mere balls of gas but God-created, God-desiring spirits: fellow creatures, as St. Francis would have recognized them also, with a character and charism of their own.

What do we make of this stargazing Ignatius? When we add some of the foreignness, the strangeness, back onto his looking at the stars, their place in his imagination takes on a different dimension from what we might at first expect. The question, perhaps, for us is: Do such differences discourage or enliven our own imaginative engagement with Ignatius and the stars?

As Ignatius reminisced to da Câmara, "the greatest consolation he used to receive was to look at the sky and the stars, which he did often and for a long time, because with this he used to feel in himself a great impetus towards serving Our Lord" (*Autobiography*, n. 11). Was this "impetus," we might wonder, recognized by him as a natural inclining of his soul? The same love that moved the stars was moving him heavenwards, homewards, inflaming his heart and drawing him on in reciprocal love to the greater glory of God: the origin and destination of his soul. As Ignatius looked up at the sky and wept, he knew that what lay behind and beyond his vision was the source that drew both him and the stars ever onwards, from where "all that is good and every gift descends from on high" (SE 237). The motions of the heavenly bodies and the interior motions he felt in his own body were not unrelated but macro- and microcosmic levels of the same phenomenon: the drawing of the creature home to its loving Creator.

Touching Jesus' Cloak: Imaginative Prayer in Action

Eric Immel, SJ

The following reflection is part of our "Jesuit 101" series, celebrating the Ignatian Year. This piece helps us dive deeper into Ignatian Contemplation. To learn more about this form of prayer, check out our explainer article: "Jesuit 101: Ignatian Contemplation, Encountering God Through Our Imagination."

The sand-colored rocks along the Atlantic shoreline at Eastern Point Jesuit Retreat House stand twenty feet tall over frigid waters, simultaneously sharp and rounded with a slight shimmer in sunlight. At points, the rocks fold into each other and make what I can only describe as nature's recliner, the perfect place to sit in silence, listen to waves, and imagine Portugal somewhere across the seemingly infinite horizon of ocean.

The day was cold, but still warm for January. Strong wind lingered from the prior day's nor'easter. Waves crashed violently into the rocks, sending sprays of diamond-like droplets into the air. White clouds piled high in front of an azure sky. I lounged in an unbreakable La-Z-Boy, cast my eyes upward, and breathed deeply. I offered a prayer of preparation and opened my Bible to Mark 5:21–43. After I read the passage slowly, noticing the narrative, I closed my eyes. Where to?

From *The Jesuit Post*, "Jesuit 101," November 2021.

I stared into the gold-trimmed mirror and hastily covered my face and arms with clean bandages. I cursed the doctors who couldn't heal my suffering, and I cast my frayed, dirty dressings into the corner with the others. I had to leave now—there was a commotion rising in the streets, and I suspected it was the healer. I prayed, maybe he'll notice me today . . . maybe I won't get pushed aside this time.

When I found the crowd, people were jamming the intersections, pushing forward toward the narrow road the healer and his companions walked along. I always had an advantage in these kinds of crowds—once people saw the dark stains appearing across my covered arms and face, they scattered like roaches suddenly exposed to light. I hugged a wall, and with the buffer people afforded me, made it to the narrow road. The healer was just ten feet ahead of me.

I cried out, "Healer! Healer!" But, he didn't turn. I pushed closer, still crying out, but my weak, ever-exhausted voice was drowned by the crowd. I was so close—just a foot or two behind him. My hands shook with desperate anticipation. A large body slammed into me from behind, and as I reached out to break my fall, my fingers found the edge of his cloak. My knees hit the ground hard, and I rolled to my side. The crowd began to trample over me. I began to cry from the pain of footfall above, brushing against my arms and face and breaking open my slowly healing skin. Please, I prayed. No.

As quickly as that prayer came, a warmth flooded my entire body, and the crowd stopped moving forward. The healer had called out, but I couldn't make out his words. Then again: "Who touched my cloak?"

My heart froze, but the spreading warmth beckoned me to rise. "I touched your cloak, healer. I'm so sorry, but I was falling and had nothing to catch myself on, and the crowd overwhelmed me, and I—"

"Sister." He cut me off, his voice deep and strong and full of light. "Your faith has healed you. Go in peace, and be freed from your suffering." He turned, not unkindly, but quickly, and moved along his way. I stood for a long moment, and people around me stared. They still only saw me, covered as I was. But I knew I was changed.

I made my way home, tingling, almost floating along. I stood before my mirror. I unwrapped myself. My skin was clear and pure. I ran a finger along my opposite arm, and goosebumps spread across my entire body. I looked into my own eyes, filled with tears, and felt beautiful.

One way to consider this moment is that it all happened in my head. I made it all up. And, in a sense, I did. I don't identify as a woman. I came to find out later that her hemorrhages were not a kind of leprosy—the image I had in mind was historically and exegetically inaccurate. Curious about the gold-trimmed mirror, I googled them and learned that mirrors like the one I imagined weren't popularized until well after Jesus' time. The buildings and streets don't really exist anywhere in the world, and the face—my face in the contemplation—didn't belong to a real person. Jesus' voice didn't really sound that way, and the Gospel didn't say that the woman was falling and caught Jesus' cloak on the way down, only to be momentarily trampled.

But then again.

When I opened my eyes after this moment of prayer, my whole body was filled with warmth, in spite of the cold rocks beneath me and the whipping wind of a cool January day. I imagined my own face, and while I was used to seeing eyes filled with uncertainty and diminished self-worth, I saw instead someone beautiful and worthy and whole. I saw someone who had been trampled before but who knew how to rise. I saw Jesus, my friend and companion, smiling at me and loving me.

The risk of this kind of prayer, perhaps, is that we fear dishonoring the true narrative of sacred scripture, or that our imaginations run a little too wild, or we create for ourselves something inauthentic to the true person of Jesus.

Be at peace with these fears. We must believe that God guides us in imaginative prayer, that in practice the picture becomes clearer, and that in sharing the faith of Jesus revealed in scripture, we come to know him deeply and authentically. As a friend once said, let good things run wild.

The gifts of imaginative prayer are endless, but here I point out just two. First, we can grow in relationship with Jesus. We can see him. We can hear his voice speaking to us. We can watch what he does, and how he does it, and who he does it for.

Second, we can grow in relationship with ourselves. My prayer that day helped me name that I still had questions about my worth and my beauty. My prayer helped me realize that I had not yet moved beyond some of the deep hurts in my life. My prayer gave me an experience of what wholeness feels like, and how Jesus could help.

Thank you, I said to Jesus.

You're welcome. He said back. Now—where to next?

VIII. Ignatian Spirituality and Anti-Racism

Part VIII Introduction

Even after hundreds of years, the Spiritual Exercises of St. Ignatius of Loyola remain relevant in their adaptability to address the modern world's ills. The tenets of Ignatian spirituality continued to provide sturdy grounding tools for individuals and communities when society belched from its gluttonous meal of colonialization and slavery. The themes throughout the Exercises buttressed my faith in God as I endured the fallout that unfolded in June 2020 after the murder of George Floyd—one of many recent murders of African Americans at the hands of law enforcement. While the collective silence from the Church was deafening during this time, rather than feeling emotionally inept and unworthy to address what I saw in the early months of the 2020 pandemic, the Spiritual Exercises gave me a place to land in response to society's imposing grip of injustices against people of color.

The liberative clarion call of the Spiritual Exercises embodies *imago Dei* and serves as a malleable roadmap to meet people wherever they are on their journey. The authors of this compendium creatively showcase this adaptability of Ignatian spirituality in addressing the psychological, educational, and social damage that racism births. They creatively introduce practical methods for initiating a call to action on college campuses, within parishes and communities of faith, and in families. Ignatian spirituality cries out to humanity as a means to exercise personal and collective responsibility in dismantling racism and its tentacles found in every corner of our societal structure. The resources noted herein are offered to expand our understanding of Ignatian spirituality in such a way that it compels our core spirituality to respond to the suffering *imago Dei* in all people and to find God's call in all aspects of the human experience.

Lori Stanley

The Jesuit Spirituality of Martin Luther King Jr.

Marcia Chatelain

In the summer of 1967, *Ebony* magazine readers were offered a rare and deeply personal look into the life of Dr. Martin Luther King Jr. The esteemed leader had dispensed with his suits and ties—the standard uniform for mass meetings and court appearances. An elegant photo spread captured King in swim trunks, pajamas, and slippers. King was at rest. Surrounded by the natural beauty of Ochos Rios, Jamaica, and unknowingly in the penultimate winter of his life, King's time away from his multiple responsibilities to the freedom movement revealed an intimate portrait of a leader in transformation.

Although *Ebony* titled the somewhat breezy feature "MLK's Tropic Interlude," the reporter noted that despite King modeling his life after Gandhi, the pastor failed to devote any great portion of his time to "leisurely reflection." The frequently overworked and exhausted King agreed and the article concluded that "nobody deserved a vacation more than MLK." King used his time on the telephone-free estate to complete the draft of his final book, *Where Do We Go from Here: Chaos or Community?* which was published the following summer.

In presenting the two possibilities for the global future in the book's title, King presented the solution to growing militarism, escalating racial unrest, and deepening levels of poverty: togetherness. Despite his partial isolation in Jamaica, King's mind was always fixed on the strength and the radical potential of human connection,

From *America Magazine* on January 18, 2021.

from the crowds that marched behind and beside him to the scores of people whose hearts were transformed by the images of protestors assaulted while at prayer.

Many of us today may not be able to understand King's commitment to nonviolence or his unshakeable focus on the beloved community. In a year in which most of this year's celebrations of the King holiday will be convened virtually and apart, due to the scourge of COVID-19 and with a heightened vigilance due to the most recent rash of white supremacist attacks on the U.S. Capitol and statehouses across the country, King's vision is woefully out of focus.

As an educator routinely tasked with teaching the U.S. civil rights movement or invited to reflect on King's legacy for the annual holiday, I often return to King's retreat in Jamaica because it set in motion the pivotal eleven-month period between the appearance of *Where Do We Go from Here* and his final oration, delivered the day before he was assassinated on April 4, 1968. In thinking of this period in King's life, I am reminded of St. Ignatius Loyola's eleven months in Manresa, Spain. For Catholics, particularly those who find great wisdom and hope in the life of St. Ignatius, King provides us numerous examples of how Ignatian spirituality can be lived and modeled outside of the church.

In the same way that nearly a year of contemplation allowed St. Ignatius to bequeath Catholics a roadmap for faith in *The Spiritual Exercises*, King provided keys to understanding the complexity of realizing racial justice and defined the moral grounds in which this work could happen in *Where Do We Go from Here*. The collection of essays answered timely questions about the direction of the civil rights movement, the roots of Black radicalism, and highlighted the importance of economic justice to ending his "three evils"—racism, excessive materialism, and militarism.

While in Jamaica, King undoubtedly reflected on how he would communicate the urgency of his nascent Poor People's Campaign, which would include advocacy for a $12 billion investment in universal basic income, a federal jobs guarantee program, and fair, affordable housing. The leader most likely meditated on how he would make a weary public empathize with victims of police brutality. He probably prayed for the courage to continue to speak out against a growing American military presence in Vietnam and knew that these actions would alienate some of his veteran allies and the president of the United States.

King's time in Jamaica was drastically different from Ignatius's cave, but both men found themselves needing to turn inward to feel the graces that would inspire their hearts and their pens to share how God was working through them in moments of personal strife. I often wonder if King's time gazing upon the Ocho Rios Bay imbued him with confidence in the next phase of his journey, in the same way that encountering the Cardoner River gave Ignatius tremendous clarity.

It is hard to relate to the King that is rightfully memorialized in voluminous biographies and artful documentaries. Yet we are able to return to King's writings and speeches, and when paired with a review of *The Spiritual Exercises*, we can sharpen our gaze and our resolve to do justice to these compatible visions. Both provide us inspiration in seemingly opposite models, which are both necessary to identify and repair our fractured world: Ignatius's mystic experience and King's most humble revelations of faith; Ignatius's great emptying of ego while alone and King's luminous spirit in front of many. In 1959, King wrote: "My call to the ministry was neither dramatic nor spectacular. It came neither by some miraculous vision nor by some blinding light experience on the road of life. Moreover, it did not come as a sudden realization. Rather, it was a response to an inner urge that gradually came upon me."[1]

The slow and gradual process of King's life reminds us that our own purpose requires patience, moments of retreat, and ultimately a return to ourselves and others to build community. King's Ignatian spirit impressed itself on those he loved and cared for, and for many of us who never knew him personally. It is particularly fitting that in the foreword to the revised edition of *Where Do We Go from Here*, his widow, the activist Coretta Scott King, described her late husband as having "toiled vigorously to offer discerning leadership." King's many discernments throughout his life and in his final year were declared

1. King, Martin Luther, Jr., Letter to Joan Thatcher, August 1959, https://kinginstitute.stanford.edu/king-papers/documents/my-call-ministry.

in the last minute of the last speech he gave before his death. While delivering an address that assessed the history of human struggle, called for economic solidarity with striking sanitation workers, and recounted his many near-death experiences, King shared the greatest desire of his life:

"Like anybody, I would like to live a long life—longevity has its place. But I'm not concerned about that now. I just want to do God's will."[2]

2. Martin Luther King, Jr., "I've Been to the Mountaintop," April 3, 1968, https://archives.ubalt.edu/bsr/articles/king%20speech.pdf.

Racism and the Gift of Sorrow

Becky Eldredge

Last year as I listened to people in spiritual direction, on virtual retreats, and in conversations with friends, colleagues, and neighbors, I became acutely aware that many of us are holding a deep sorrow about the long suffering of our Black brothers and sisters. God broadened my awareness this past year as I watched Black friends and colleagues' grief reach a depth that makes my heart ache as I write these words. One colleague shared with me, "George Floyd's death was the straw that broke the camel's back for me. I don't feel safe anymore." Another friend shared how afraid she was for her children to be out playing in her neighborhood for fear of what people may assume about her kids.

I heard their words and pain, and I hear them now still. I am aware, too, that as a white mother this is a suffering that I will never experience. This *does not*, however, give me permission to ignore the pain of an entire community of people who are crying out. Their sorrow is real. The sorrow that wells up in me is real as well. I feel God urging me, and all of us, to pay attention to the grace of sorrow rising within us. The deaths of George Floyd, Breonna Taylor, Elijah McClain, Ahmaud Arbery, Tamir Rice, and many other Black victims killed unjustly, bring racism back to our collective consciousness and vividly remind us that racism never went away.

From *Jesuits Magazine*, Fall 2021, Central and Southern Province, vol. VIII, no. 3, pages 10–12.

During the First Week of *The Spiritual Exercises of St. Ignatius*, there is a kind of sadness that God allows us to feel as we pray about evil and sin in the world and ask for God's mercy. It is a sadness that wells in us as we are awakened to sin in our lives and in the world. This sadness calls forth in us an urge to change. *This is the grace of sorrow.* Grace defined theologically is a gift from God that helps us come to new insights about ourselves, God, and each other. Sorrow is a gift from God that can aid us in understanding suffering in ourselves and in others.

Sorrow as defined in Ignatius's rules of discernment is spiritual consolation. It is the Holy Spirit awakening us to something that is keeping us individually or collectively from fully loving others and God.

What Do We Do When We Feel the Grace of Sorrow?

We acknowledge the grace the moment we feel it. God is with us in a real, palpable way. When we are moved to tears because of our own sin or due to the suffering of others, we are sitting in a moment seeped with the Holy Spirit's presence. Right now, I feel the Holy Spirit begging us to acknowledge the sorrow we feel as we hear our Black brothers and sisters cry from the pain of racism.

Aren't we being invited to notice how an entire race does not feel fully loved? Aren't we being challenged to ask ourselves: Are we loving as Christ loves? Isn't the Holy Spirit inviting us to see the rippling effects of the sin of racism in our world?

I feel we are being challenged to notice our own bias, evaluate our behaviors that contribute to systemic racism, and discern what our actions can be to bring about change.

It can be painful to notice and name our sorrow. As humans we tend not to want to acknowledge our faults. Sometimes, too, it is hard for us to sit with the suffering of others. Sorrow can also bring a sense of helplessness as we realize how hard it is to change anything by ourselves. The grace of sorrow also brings to light our dependency on God, our need for God's mercy and help. We are not alone in naming our sorrow.

St. Ignatius offers us a prayer tool, the Triple Colloquy, to help us name our sin. This prayer tool invites us into a colloquy, or conversation, with Mary, Jesus, and God to awaken us where we contribute to sin in the world. I offer us this Triple Colloquy to pray with our role in racism.

We go to Mary first and ask her to go to her son and ask for these graces for us:

- *To know deep down the sin of racism and the rootedness of this sin in my life and in the world.*
- *To have a deeply felt understanding of how I contribute to the sin of racism.*
- *To recognize any moments that have kept me from loving my Black brothers and sisters in the way God loves them.*
- *To experience a deep desire to amend my life and my actions and turn away from all that contributes to the sin of racism.*

After we speak to Mary, we go to her son, Jesus, and ask him for these same three things. Then we go to God and make these same three requests.

I believe that praying the Triple Colloquy will help us acknowledge our role in the sin of racism, confront our personal bias and behaviors, and increase our desire to be part of the solution to eradicate racism.

Once We Acknowledge Our Sorrow and Sin, What Do We Do with It?

St. Ignatius invites us to take our sorrow and sin directly to Christ in prayer. In prayer, we can honestly talk to God about what we are noticing and the sorrow we feel. As we bring our sorrow to Christ, God enters what we are feeling and brings mercy.

God longs to free us from our own sinfulness. God also longs to enter our hurt, brokenness, and pain in order to heal us.

Some of our pain is due to our own sinful capacity as humans. Sometimes the brokenness we experience is not caused by us or our actions but is simply the result of life's journey and the risk of being in relationships. Sometimes what we feel is the ripple effect of another person's choices. Sometimes our sorrow is the result of our listening to the wrong voices and forgetting who we are.

Bringing our sorrow to God allows God to enter into what we are feeling; it also invites us to discern how we are being invited to call forth change in ourselves and in the world. St. Ignatius offers us a prayer tool that helps us bring our sorrow to God and discern our response: the Colloquy with Christ on the Cross.

Imagine Christ our Lord suspended on the Cross before you, and converse with him about what emerged as you prayed the triple colloquy on our role in racism. Then ask him these three questions to help guide your discernment as to what you are being called to do:

What have I done for Christ? What am I doing for Christ? What ought I do for Christ?

We go to Christ crucified and speak honestly to him with whatever comes to our mind and ask Christ to guide our steps and actions to change our bias and behaviors. We ask Christ to show us what our response might be right now to confront and help eradicate racism in our world.

I urge us to not ignore the sorrow we are hearing from our Black brothers and sisters and the sorrow we might also be feeling. I invite us to go to our inner chapels and pray so we can listen and discern our response. Prayer always sends us outside ourselves and leads to action that is generous in spirit. It spurs us beyond ourselves to take part in God's mission and to love others as God loves them.

May the gift of sorrow we feel be offered to God to eliminate the sin of racism in our world today.

How to Use Ignatian Spirituality for Anti-Racism and Racial Justice

Mary J. Lomax-Ghirarduzzi

Ignatian Spirituality and Diversity

In March of 2012, I led a series of university dialogues on Ignatian Spirituality and Diversity to spotlight the importance of diversity and inclusion at a Jesuit, Catholic university. Serving as the Vice Provost for the University of San Francisco's (USF) Office of Diversity Engagement and Community Outreach, we teamed up with the Office of Human Resources and University Ministry to sponsor this professional development conversation to frame diversity, equity, and inclusion as a moral imperative informed by our Jesuit Catholic mission and identity. Bringing together distinguished religious thinkers and diversity education teachers, the purpose of the series was to discuss Ignatian spirituality and diversity by examining how racial justice, cultural inclusivity, and cultural humility are critical parts of a campus culture where students, staff, and faculty continue to learn and examine our individual and collective biases and assumptions as we commit to the Ignatian principle of *magis*—of being and doing More.

Looking back now, I realize just how much we were ahead of the time as an urban-situated campus, as we understood fundamentally that the university could not imagine the fullest expression of the mission without understanding what diversity, equity, and inclusion

From *Alpha Sigma Nu Magazine*, October 1, 2020.

means in the context of Ignatian spirituality. Amid civil unrest with the deaths of George Floyd, Breonna Taylor, and Ahmaud Arbury, a long overdue reckoning on race in America is happening. This reckoning has captured the attention of people who have not thought deeply about race until recently. Seizing this moment is critical to fulfill our Jesuit Catholic mission as there is an urgency buoyed by the demands of marginalized people that institutions have a responsibility to address racial inequalities and a duty to understand what racial justice means in the context of their works.

As I have spent the past few months coaching my own young adult Black children on how to manage their fear and frustration about racism as well as my own Black students at USF, I believe that Ignatian spirituality has taken on a new meaning as a way to understand racism and how to do better for students of color experiencing racial injustice. As a Black executive woman and Black mother working in Jesuit higher education, I know we must do better for their futures.

All of this brings me back to the original framing questions that informed the 2012 Ignatian Spirituality and Diversity dialogue series at USF. Led by Sonny Manuel, SJ, professor of psychology, I knew the combination of his clinical training and important work at the intersections of psychology, faith, and multiculturalism along with his spiritual work with underserved communities uniquely qualified him to begin the discussion. For such a time as this, I would like to offer the same framing questions we used from our 2012 discussion series to all members of the Jesuit higher education community to further examine the role and purpose of Ignatian Spirituality in the current state of rampant racial injustice:

1. What is the intersection of the Jesuit university mission and diversity, equity, and inclusion? And how can the tools of Ignatian spirituality inform how we address racial injustice to make a difference?
2. What are the tenets of Ignatian spirituality that are connected to diversity, equity, and inclusion?
3. How does Jesuit education's core values and beliefs embrace people of diverse backgrounds? When and how has Jesuit education been exclusionary?

4. What are the beliefs, behaviors, and spiritual practices that inform and embrace diversity, equity, and cultural inclusiveness?
5. And finally, how does one's life story inform their approach to diversity, equity, and inclusion in the Jesuit educational tradition? What are the desolations associated with personal and institutional narratives that have led to racial injustice?

Responding to an unprecedented call to address the enduring harms of structural racism in Jesuit works and in society, we must assert the link of our Ignatian spirituality to a faith that does justice. This means that we recognize the harm committed to Black, Indigenous, and People of Color (BIPOC) by individuals and institutions and take responsibility for that harm. We especially need our white allies who are institutional actors in Jesuit higher education to use their platforms for the purposes of understanding what anti-racism is and clarify its relationship to racial injustice.

An Ignatian Call to Action

Ignatian spirituality provides a framework for people of conscience who believe that God has a plan for everyone to prosper. Ignatian spirituality also gives us a framework for understanding racism as a sin that can exist only within structures of power, privilege, and oppression. Focusing on the needs of marginalized and vulnerable communities on our campuses is an Ignatian call to action. We hold these Ignatian spiritual gifts to help us dissolve the desolation of guilt and shame and confront the institutionalized evil of racism:

- Seek to find the divine in all things—in all peoples and cultures, in all areas of study and learning, in every human experience;
- See life and the whole universe as a gift calling forth wonder and gratefulness;

- Give ample scope to imagination and emotion as well as intellect;
- Cultivate critical awareness of personal and social evil, but point to God's love as more powerful than any evil;
- Empower people to become leaders in service, men and women for others, becoming whole persons of solidarity, building a more just and humane world.

Once we employ our Ignatian tools of understanding for the purposes of racial justice, our institutions will become platforms for transformative change where individual actors can labor to end all forms of structural racism where we live, where we work, and where we do business.

Disrupting Whiteness in Jesuit Institutions

Anti-racism is the active process of identifying and challenging racism by changing systems, organizational structures, policies and practices, and attitudes to redistribute power in an equitable manner. Anti-Black racism is a two-part formation that both strips Blackness of value (dehumanizes), and systematically marginalizes Black people (Center for the Study of Social Policy). When we say that Black lives matter, we are talking about the ways in which Black people are deprived of basic human rights and dignity. It is an acknowledgement that Black poverty and genocide are forms of state violence and the fact that the lives of Black people—not all people—exist within these conditions is consequence of state violence (Alicia Garza, co-founder of Black Lives Matter).

Disrupting whiteness is essential racial justice work. To do so takes courage and a commitment to bear the witness of others while uncovering one's own complicity and lack of awareness. Hearing the experiences and truths from those who have been marginalized, excluded, and whose dignity has been left behind, is an act of Ignatian solidarity; we see the divine in others as God's love through us.

Disrupting whiteness means cultivating an awareness of the stories of people who are different from your own. Disrupting whiteness means empowering BIPOC through one's power, privilege, and resources so they, too, can reach their highest potential. Disrupting whiteness means seeing the divine in Black students, faculty, and staff.

As we prepare for the work ahead to address racial injustice, we can take the critical step of reflecting and unpacking whiteness through an anti-racist lens by answering these questions: What is my role in enacting anti-racism? Do I understand what that means? Why is it important that people have said for years that Black lives matter? Why do some people insist on saying, Well, don't all lives matter? Am I one of those individuals? What is my understanding of the historical context and experiences of BIPOC, whom I have been called to serve? What might I need to unlearn that I was taught? What do I believe about race? What do I need to do now to take advantage of this time that God has given us? And, how is God calling me to be a person for others during this racial pandemic? The good news is that we have inherited a spiritual tradition that has equipped us to disrupt whiteness and guided us to push through difficult conversations and revelations.

Jesuit institutions must do better now and not later. As we begin the start of another academic year, my hope is that we will engage our *magis* to root out everyday forms of institutional racism for my children, for our students of color, and for our colleagues of color. Now is the time to muster our collective courage, to be responsive to the demands of racial justice with a sense of urgency, to answer the call from people everywhere, to commit ourselves to Black lives on our campuses. May we each learn how to call upon Ignatian spirituality to do this work and frame our humble yet earnest response in a climate of injustice to stop the effects of institutional racism for the greater glory of God. If we do this work, we are truly living the mission.

What Dr. King and St. Ignatius Taught Me about Discernment and Anti-Racism

Ken Homan, SJ

> *I have a dream that my four little children will one day live in a nation where they will not be judged by the color of their skin but by the content of their character.*
>
> —Martin Luther King Jr.

Like many Americans, I grew up with an inadequate understanding of Dr. Martin Luther King, Jr. In Catholic grade school, we heard snippets of the "I Have a Dream" speech and offered vague prayers for racial harmony during February. In high school, I began hearing classmates' whispers aimed at undermining his legacy. In college, MLK Day meant committing to peace and service. Not until graduate school did I gain a fuller understanding of his teachings, actions, and legacy.

I recently read Dr. King's book *Where Do We Go from Here?* It has shaped my understanding of Ignatian spirituality and its relationship to racial justice. Here are three lessons that MLK and Ignatius taught me about discernment and anti-racism.

From *The Jesuit Post* on January 18, 2021.

Discernment and Freedom

What is freedom? It is, first, the capacity to deliberate or to weigh alternative. . . . Second, freedom expresses itself in decision. . . . A third expression of freedom is responsibility. . . . The immorality of segregation is that it is a selfishly contrived system which cuts off one's capacity to liberate, decide, and respond.[1]

King's words on freedom sound quite like those of Ignatius. Ignatius spoke of freedom as being opposed to disordered attachments. We must cast off our attachments in order to freely discern God's call. Doing so enables us to make decisions true to the Gospel.

It is a disappointment with the Christian church that appears to be more white than Christian, and with many white clergymen who prefer to remain silent behind the security of stained-glass windows.[2]

Ignatius and MLK rightly identified fear as one of the greatest disordered attachments. A longing for a sense of security inhibits a movement toward God and justice. Elizabeth Eiland Figueroa states that "this clutching does not allow much space for God. Fear tells us that if we lessen our grip, chaos will ensue."[3] I constantly see arguments against racial justice, reparations, and liberation framed in terms of possibly dangerous consequences or an allied group not perfectly aligning to Church teaching. These arguments desperately cling to power and comfort, hiding behind the security of stained-glass windows.

In the Spiritual Exercises, Ignatius has the retreatant pray about three categories of people. Each has acquired a significant amount of wealth (not necessarily by wholesome means) and desires to part with it to save their soul. The first postpones until their death, deeming other things more important. The second rationalizes and deceives themself into believing that God wants them to keep their wealth. The third asks to be free from the attachment to the wealth, to do with it whatever God asks.

White privilege and white supremacy are particularly insidious because the attachment is often to comfort, social standing, or claims of social innocence with no awareness of their connection

1. Martin Luther King Jr., *Where Do We Go from Here: Chaos or Community?* (Boston: Beacon Press, 2010), 104.
2. King Jr., 36.
3. Full text available at https://www.ignatianspirituality.com/freedom-from-fear/.

to whiteness and racism. Attachment to white privilege and white supremacy leads to an inauthentic faith. They are not open to the power of God's justice. For me as a white man, Ignatian anti-racism means I must learn to recognize my unfreedoms regarding racism.

Vociferously Reject Heresy

The greatest blasphemy of the whole ugly process [of slavery] was that the white man ended up making God his partner in the exploitation of the Negro. What greater heresy has religion known? Ethical Christianity vanished and the moral nerve of religion was atrophied. This terrible distortion sullied the essential nature of Christianity.[4]

In 1554, Ignatius wrote an emphatic letter on heresy to Peter Canisius. He states that the success of heretics was due to negligence of those, particularly the clergy, who should have taken action to prevent false teaching. He encouraged the publication of pamphlets and easy-to-use print materials to combat heresy. Centuries later, American Jesuits published thousands of pamphlets aimed at evangelization and defeating perceived theological enemies such as communism. We rarely, however, took on the heresy of racism with the same zeal.

Racism is a faith. It is a form of idolatry. . . . In its early modern beginnings, racism was a justificatory device. It did not emerge as a faith. It arose as an ideological justification for the constellations of political and economic power which were expressed in colonialism and slavery. But gradually the idea of the superior race was heightened and deepened in meaning and value so that it pointed beyond the historical structures of relation, in which it emerged, to human existence itself.[5]

Racism became an American ideology and became embedded in white Catholic faith. In recent years, we white Catholics have begun making strides to address this heresy. I wonder what would happen, though, if we Jesuits and all of our institutions were to

4. King Jr., *Where Do We Go from Here?*, 79.
5. King Jr., 79.

give anti-racism the same or more attention that we give to other priorities. Doing so would fit perfectly within our guiding Universal Apostolic Preferences.

Discernment Leads to Action

But declarations against segregation, however sincere, are not enough. The church must take the lead in social reform. It must move out into the arena of life and do battle for the sanctity of religious commitments.[6]

The fruit of discernment is action. Bad discernment leads to actions that simply confirm our attachments. For example, I regularly encounter people arguing against action on racial injustice by using quotes from Dr. King's "I Have a Dream" speech. Like most historic figures, both Dr. Martin Luther King, Jr. and Ignatius Loyola face the danger of softened, misused, and abused legacies. In their lifetimes, they demanded bold action.

The practical cost of change for the nation up to this point has been cheap. The limited reforms have been obtained at bargain rates.[7]

Discernment demands concrete steps and actions. We Jesuits have begun making some important changes, such as researching our participation in slaveholding and being in dialogue with the descendants of individuals who were enslaved. Dr. King makes several suggestions that Jesuits, our institutions, and our colleagues could pursue: using our significant purchasing power to demand changes from businesses; clergy collaboration to demand racial and labor justice; and, most importantly, organizing.

Strong discernment and anti-racism are responses to God's love and action in the world. They demand the *magis,* a full commitment to God's liberating action. Pursuing this liberating action asks us to cast aside disordered attachments, seek truth and authentic teaching, and take bold action. Ignatian discernment and anti-racism ought to spur us to a transformation of ourselves and our communities.

6. King Jr., 105.
7. King Jr., 5.

Remembering George Floyd with a Steadfast Commitment to Racial Justice

Christopher Kerr

Today, May 25, 2021, marks the one-year anniversary of the murder of George Floyd. "I can't breathe, I can't breathe" were the words he uttered over twenty times while being held face down on the ground for nine minutes and twenty-nine seconds.

Floyd's death propelled the U.S. more deeply into a racial reckoning. Indeed, the last year has further compelled the Ignatian family to grapple with the legacy of racism in our own network through accountability, action, and, as people of faith, discernment and prayer.

We work within an Ignatian and Catholic landscape that historically, and even today, is often complicit in the sin of racism, both implicitly and explicitly. We know that in working for racial justice, we will, at times, fall short and make missteps, but to fulfill our faith-based social justice mission rooted in the Gospel, we must make this a priority.

Sunday, the Catholic Church celebrated the Feast of Pentecost, commemorating Jesus breathing on his disciples the power of the Holy Spirit. In his breath, he offered his followers a breath that had the potential to change the world—a breath of hope, a breath of peace, a breath of love, a breath of justice. As we commemorate the unconscionable loss of George Floyd, whose breath was taken

From *Ignatian Solidairty Network* blog, May 25, 2021.

away—are we committed to responding to the Pentecost Gospel? Are we willing to be people of love, of peace, of hope, and of justice? What will each of us do to build a society where no one's breath is stolen?

We invite you to explore some of the ways that the Ignatian Solidarity Network and others in the Jesuit network have worked to advance anti-racism in the past year. Please use and share these resources as we work together to respond to the call to dismantle systemic racism, reimagine policing in our communities, and build a more just and equitable society.

We continue to hold in our prayers the family of George Floyd and all who continue to be victimized and traumatized by the impacts of systemic racism.

Please contact Ignatian Solidarity Network at https://ignatiansolidarity.net/resources/ to access a collection of resources on racial justice.

The Ignatian Witness to Truth in a Climate of Injustice

Bryan N. Massingale

In an address in 1980 to the Roman Rota, a chief legal court in the Catholic Church, Pope John Paul II cited a 17th-century maxim: "Truth is the basis, foundation, and mother of justice." He thus highlighted the often-noted connection between the pursuit of justice and the quest for truth. For example, the many "truth and reconciliation" processes undertaken in the aftermath of severe social traumas, such as in South Africa and Rwanda, are vivid reminders that healing estrangements between peoples and establishing right relationships between social groups can only be premised upon an honest acknowledgment of the harms committed or tolerated against others. Communal and national honesty are the prerequisites for effective reconciliation and a just society.

By any measure or reckoning, the pursuit of racial justice is still, in the words of the African American poet Langston Hughes, "a dream deferred." In a report published in the summer of 2016, a United Nations commission investigating the situation of African Americans in the United States forthrightly concluded:

From *Conversations on Jesuit Higher Education*, Vol. 52, Article 3. (2017).

> Despite substantial changes since the end of the enforcement of Jim Crow and the fight for civil rights, a systemic ideology of racism ensuring the domination of one group over another continues to impact negatively on the civil, political, economic, social, and cultural rights of African Americans today.

What accounts for this disturbing persistence of racial injustice, manifested in almost every area of our national life, including gross disparities in criminal justice, education, poverty rates, and health-care services? Why, despite years of protest and agitation, do we as a nation find ourselves locked in a seemingly endless cycle of racial recrimination, resignation, and even despair? I offer two reasons: first, a persistent belief in an ideology of "personal responsibility"; and second, the profound, pervasive, and perhaps even willful ignorance of the majority of white Americans about the history that has led to and fuels our current impasses and divisions.

The Mantra of "Personal Responsibility"

One manifestation of the current ideology of "personal responsibility" was given at Marquette University by Ben Shapiro, a noted young conservative activist and provocateur. His presence on campus was the subject of a great deal of controversy, as a student group timed Shapiro's lecture to coincide with Marquette's annual "Mission Week" celebration of its Ignatian charism and Jesuit ideals. It was especially problematic given the university's chosen theme for 2017—"Racial Justice and the Call of the Church"—and the title of Shapiro's address, "Can You Handle the Truth?" I decided to attend his speech, which he delivered in a packed lecture hall to an audience of overwhelmingly white male students.

Once one gets past the caustic *ad hominem* polemics that peppered Shapiro's address, his position can be summarized in the following moves:

- There was a time when institutionalized racism existed in the US, but that was forty to fifty years ago. (Note that he isn't sure exactly when it ended, nor did he give a historical marker for its demise.)
- Therefore, systemic racial injustice is no longer a reality.
- Shapiro acknowledges that there are individual racists, that is, people who do bad things and discriminate because of racial bias.
- But society as a whole isn't intentional in putting down or holding back people of color.
- Thus, for people of color, it is now all up to them. At the core of his argument is a plea for personal responsibility. "Life is what you make of it" was a mantra repeated several times. In fact, he declared that if you follow three rules, you are virtually guaranteed to achieve middle class status: (1) Finish high school. (2) Don't have children out of wedlock. (3) Get a job.
- Left unsaid explicitly but assumed throughout his presentation: If you don't get ahead, if you don't make it, it's your own fault. To think otherwise is to succumb to a "psychology of victimhood" and to allow oneself to be defeated, because there are no longer any systemic obstacles to one's progress.
- More pointed conclusions follow from this line of thinking: We, as a society—and especially white people—have no obligation to help anyone, because all of the systemic obstacles and barriers to individual advancement have been eliminated and eradicated.
- Therefore, most of all, but left unsaid: If straight white men have a disproportionate share of society's goods and benefits, it's because they've *earned* them by being more intelligent, virtuous, and responsible than other groups.

I dwell on Shapiro's argument and views because he is not an aberration. His presentation of this worldview is but an exaggeration of a typical point of view present among many Americans, especially white Americans. His line of thinking explains why so many white people, and especially white Christians and Catholics, are so anemic and tepid in their engagement with issues of racial justice. They believe society is now a level playing field. Therefore, notwithstanding a few bad apples—of *both* and *all* races—black failure and racial disparities are due to personal irresponsibility, laziness, and lack of effort.

Let us consider a concrete example of how this insistence upon the demise of systemic racism and assumption of personal responsibility plays out. Such thinking explains in great measure the apathy or indifference of white Christians toward police violence and misconduct in our society, especially as these are experienced by communities of color and protested by the movements for Black lives. A recent Public Religion Research Institute report related how over eighty percent of black Christians believe that police-involved killings of black people are part of a much larger picture of racial injustice. However, an almost equal number of white Christians believe the opposite, holding that such deaths are mainly isolated incidents with no connection to one another. (Seventy-one percent of Catholics hold this view.) Indeed, white non-Christians are more likely than white Christians to see a systemic problem.

In other words, white Christians are among the least likely to believe that there is a systemic race-based problem with policing in our country. They admit that bad things happen. But these are "isolated incidents"—that is, the fault of a few renegade individuals—not events that point to deeper systemic faults in the institutions of our society. The majority of white Americans, it would seem, hold that racial injustice is no longer a pressing issue in society; it is, rather, at most, an episodic aberration committed by some bad people.

A Pervasive (Willful) Ignorance of Truth

Yet, note how the widespread acceptance of an ideology of personal responsibility—put more colloquially, the mentality of "it's their/your own damn fault"—is abetted by a pervasive ignorance of the real history of racial injustice in our country. (Recall how the first and necessary move made by Shapiro is a declaration that systemic institutional racism has been eradicated.) African American religious scholar Eddie S. Glaude, Jr., states that "willful blindness" to our history allows so many to "absurdly believe . . . that black social misery is the result of hundreds of thousands of unrelated bad individual decisions by black people across this country."

One of the best independent assessments of the lack of accurate knowledge of our nation's racial history comes from the United Nations' investigation of our racial practices referred to earlier. It notes that most Americans have not been and are not being taught the true history of the country's complicity with what it called the "crimes against humanity" that were perpetrated upon communities of color, especially African Americans. Two of its findings are especially pertinent.

- In particular, the legacy of colonial history, enslavement, racial subordination and segregation, racial terrorism, and racial inequality in the United States remains a serious challenge, as there has been no real commitment to reparations and to truth and reconciliation for people of African descent. Contemporary police killings and the trauma that they create are reminiscent of the past racial terror of lynching. Impunity for state violence has resulted in the current human rights crisis and must be addressed as a matter of urgency.
- There is a profound need to acknowledge that the transatlantic trade in Africans, enslavement, colonization, and colonialism were crimes against humanity and are among the major sources and manifestations of racism, racial discrimination, Afrophobia, xenophobia, and related intolerance. Past injustices and crimes against African Americans need to be addressed with reparatory justice.

Note how this report relates that ignorance of our past compromises our ability to cope with present-day racial injustices, which are the enduring manifestations of an unacknowledged and actively avoided past. Glaude concurs, opining that being "willfully ignorant" of our history of racism "has consigned so many black people to poverty with little to no chance of escaping it." Thus, it comes as no surprise that the U.N. task force, in its recommendations for a more racially just society, concluded: "Consistently, the school curriculum in each state should reflect appropriately the history of the transatlantic trade in Africans, enslavement and segregation."[1] In short, telling and facing the truth of our tragic past is an essential part of achieving justice in the present. What Canadian Jesuit philosopher Bernard Lonergan called the "flight from understanding" is a major contributing factor to the racial apathy and indifference that result from a race-based ideology of personal responsibility.

The Ignatian Witness to Truth

What, then, are the challenges and opportunities of this state of affairs for Jesuit higher education in the United States? What does it mean for Jesuit campuses to be "sanctuaries of truth" in the midst of so much injustice, denial, and willful ignorance? What does the summons to fidelity to our mission entail in such circumstances?

First, a reclaiming of and recommitment to the fundamental inspirations and values of the Society of Jesus. One of the lasting memories of my undergraduate theology courses at Marquette was studying the book *The Faith that Does Justice*. It was a compilation of articles written by Jesuits in the mid-1970s, reflecting on how the promotion of justice was an essential part of Christian faith. I no longer remember

1. See *Strategic Action Plan: Report of the Secretary-General's Task Force on Addressing Racism and Promoting Dignity for All in the United Nations Secretariat*, New York, December 2021, https://hr.un.org/sites/hr.un.org/files/sap_final_report_0.pdf.

the specifics of the articles. But the title arrested me then and inspires me still. It was the first time that an explicit connection was made between my belief in God and my hunger for justice.

I then discovered that this deep connection is a fundamental Jesuit conviction, first articulated in 1975 during the 32nd General Congregation and then reaffirmed repeatedly since, most notably in 2000 at Santa Clara University by then Father General Peter-Hans Kolvenbach. His words are powerful and prophetic:

> Since Saint Ignatius wanted love to be expressed not only in words but also in deeds, the Congregation committed the Society to the promotion of justice as a concrete, radical but proportionate response to an unjustly suffering world. Fostering the virtue of justice in people was not enough. Only a substantive justice can bring about the kinds of structural and attitudinal changes that are needed to uproot those sinful oppressive injustices that are a scandal against humanity and God.

Therefore, a first step for Jesuit campuses is a forthright and public commitment to this legacy of seeking justice as a vital component of our identity and mission—a commitment that is not just rhetorical but effective. How do we come to see ourselves as custodians of sacred trust, "the service of faith through the promotion of justice," that has been committed to our care? How do our campuses continue to inspire new generations of young people, captivating them with book titles, courses, experiences, and witnesses that show them the deep connection between love of God and justice for their neighbors?

To put this first step negatively: If, in the midst of a society scarred by racial injustice, Jesuit colleges and universities are not forthright witnesses of "concrete, radical but proportionate responses" to unjust suffering, then we fail to embody what makes us unique among institutions of higher education. And if we are no different from any other college or university, especially lower-cost competitors who can offer just as valuable an educational product, then we have no reason to survive—and in all likelihood, we will not.

Second, we must acknowledge that we have much to learn and to "un-learn" about our racial (and racist) history. Malcolm X once said, "Untruths have to be untold. We have to be untaught before we can be taught, and once untaught, we ourselves can unteach others." He thus stated the implication of his belief that injustice in America is sustained by a not accidental strategy of miseducation and omission. The bottom line is that most of us have been taught many half-truths and untruths about our nation's dealings with communities of color.

If "truth is the basis, foundation, and mother of justice," then an important contribution of Jesuit higher education toward a racially just society is fostering a deeper and truer knowledge of this nation's legacy of racial animus and privilege. Our curricula should ensure that no one graduates from our institutions without a sustained engagement with the reality of racial injustice. This is wholly and entirely consistent with our institutions' mission to discover and disseminate knowledge. This leads to a pressing question: How do our curricula both reflect and respect the intellectual contributions of the majority of the human race? For we cannot fulfill the mission of discovering and disseminating knowledge of the human condition if, by omission or silence, we ignore, downplay, or disparage insights and knowledge arising from the majority of humankind.

Third, we must accept that solidarity with the racially "other" means living in the midst of human conflict. I teach courses that focus on race, white supremacy, and religious complicity. Students are often bewildered, confused, and dismayed as they encounter new knowledge, question previously held beliefs, and face the uncomfortable truth that religious leaders have not always been agents of social justice. Sometimes they express their discomfort in less than mature ways. And, as this winter's controversy at Marquette demonstrated, fostering honest engagement with racial privilege generates intense and often passionate resistance. Radical responses to unjust suffering, what Father Kolvenbach detailed as a core component of Jesuit higher education, will generate not only sincere misunderstandings but also polemical counterattacks. The road to a just society must go through the path of social conflict.

Institutions, because of their instincts for self-preservation, are inherently averse to conflict and risk. Yet, the unique nature of institutions founded upon an Ignatian charism demands a different and even counter-intuitive approach. There is no other way we can be faithful to our mission of truth in the midst of social injustice.

To paraphrase the insight of Martin Luther King, Jr., the ultimate measure of our institutional integrity is not where we stand in times of convenience and comfort but where and how we stand in times of challenge and controversy.

At the very least, we must make it absolutely clear—effectively and not only rhetorically—that intolerant words, actions, or postings will not be tolerated on our campuses. Students, staff, and faculty of color must not only know this but also feel it as an existential commitment from the highest levels of the university. How we engage the controversies of witnessing truth in a climate of injustice will often be a matter of deep discernment. Yet the commitment to doing so, and accepting the inevitable risks that such a stance entails, are the acid tests of fidelity to our Ignatian values.

Finally, we must become beacons of hope. The promotion of truth inherently undermines ideological appeals to "personal integrity" that evade the demands of justice. It necessarily generates obstacles and resistance. Yet, this is consistent with the spirit of the Spiritual Exercises as those who engage them move from a contemplation of the suffering Jesus to an encounter with the risen Christ. The Resurrection is not an escape from conflict. Rather, it summons us to engage conflictual reality in light of a new experience: an experience of being loved beyond death. This fills one with the courage to struggle for a justice founded on truth, in the words of St. Ignatius, "not counting the cost." Because no cost is too great in the light of such great love.

In teaching about racial justice and white supremacy, I have learned that it is important to leave students with a sense of hope. This is not the facile optimism that maintains that good always prevails over evil, and sooner rather than later. But it is the hope that believes that good ultimately (though not always) prevails, and often at a great price. This is the hope to which the Ignatian Exercises lead us. It is the only hope that is adequate in the face of the long and bitter struggle that racial justice requires. It is an important contribution that our institutions, each in their own way, can offer to our fellow citizens.

The "service of faith." The "promotion of justice." The "quest for truth." Witnessing to the inherent links between these realities in concrete and radical ways is the summons of Jesuit higher education in the midst of unjust racial suffering.

An Examen for White Allies

Maddie Murphy

It is no secret that racism is a long-lasting and dangerous major sin and violence within American society. Unspeakable actions that negatively and systematically impact people of color persist in our society: the racial violence leading to the murders of Black individuals, the continued destruction of Indigenous lands, the separation and marginalization of families and individuals seeking asylum at our border. It has felt spiritually overwhelming to face the racism that some of us may have convinced ourselves was long gone. It is challenging to recognize that while progress has been made in this country, we are nowhere near being a just, or even safe, country for people of color.

I must admit that I, when faced with the immensity of racism in this country, have chosen to check out at moments rather than lean in as an ally, or have failed to realize because of my privilege that these seemingly "new" actions of racism are in fact not new but have been happening for centuries. My own privilege has allowed me to not be conscious of these actions, but rather has allowed me to cling to my chosen ignorance. While it is a privilege for white folks to be able to "check out" of some of these difficult and challenging conversations, actions, and movements, it is essential for us to lean away from

From *Ignatian Solidarity Network* blog on June 3, 2020.
[Editor's Note: A slightly different version of this reflection was originally published in December 2018 as part of ISN's JV Reflects series, in partnership with Jesuit Volunteer Corps and Jesuit Volunteer Corps Northwest.]

apathy, cynicism, and passive, complicit ignorance—and lean into a vocation that we as human beings and people of faith and justice are called to become: racial allies in a society steeped in white supremacy. I can find ways in which I have used my power, privilege, and resources to benefit and support my clients of color, just as I can shamefully find ways in which I have ignored or abused my privilege. I am not proud of these moments. Although it would be easier for me to ignore them and move on, part of being a racial ally is in the presence and awareness and self-education of these moments. Truly, reflecting on my actions and how I take from and make space for people of color is an incredibly Ignatian thing to do.

Ignatian spirituality invites us to become contemplatives in action, to view the way in which we can be in this world. It asks us to be aware not only of the world around us but of how we move, act, and love within it. Being an ally for racial justice asks us to do the very same thing—that is, to reflect and be aware of the systemic racial oppression our society is built upon, and how we not only benefit from it, but on how we can use our power and privilege to dismantle it and support people of color. In short, it asks us to be present and put in the work.

It is not only civilly important for me, but morally and spiritually imperative that I reflect on the ways my whiteness supports or challenges racism—in my daily thoughts, words, and actions. Thus, I have reworked the traditional Ignatian Examen to be used as a tool for white folks hoping to act as racial allies. A common version of the Examen is as follows:

Become aware of God's presence
Review the day with gratitude
Pay attention to your emotions
Choose one feature of the day and pray from it
Look forward to tomorrow.

Below is my adaptation of an Examen for white allies in our Ignatian family:

1. Become aware of God's presence.

Think about the God of the oppressed, the true and loving God. Think about the people God called her own. Remember that the people She sought to protect, the people She pulled prophets from, were the poor and marginalized of society.

Reflect on the poor and marginalized of today's society—who do you see? Remember God's love for them by seeing them, and how you are called into God's love by loving them and resisting the systems, thoughts, and institutions that seek to prevent love and community. Remember there is no room for racism in love.

Reflect on the systems that seek to keep us from loving one another. Recognize that God's own face is reflected in the faces of the marginalized of our society. God's face is in a Brown, Jewish carpenter's, just as much as it is in the Black American woman's, or in the forgotten American Indian's, or in the faces of the family of color seeking asylum from violence and political unrest.

Find God in all things and all people—especially those whom racism seeks to divide us from through hate, discrimination, and systemic institutionalized oppression.

2. Review how you used your white privilege today.

If a person of color was telling you their experience, did you listen with openness and compassion? Or did you argue, ignore, or interrupt?

In your place of work/service, did you use all available resources to make things culturally sensitive for your coworkers or clients, or did you assume American Western whiteness as the status quo?

Did you reflect on the land you stand on, on the rights you have that our justice system sees as racial privileges?

Did you speak up when a white friend/relative/coworker said or acted in a problematic way, or did you choose silence over action?

Allow yourself to remain present in all reflection—in the moments you are proud of your actions, but especially in the moments where you are not. Do not shy away from examples of your need and capacity for growth and love.

3. Pay attention to your emotions.

In reflecting on how you utilized your privilege today, identify your feelings. Is there shame, anger, discomfort, fear, or hatred? Are there prejudices you hold that you are becoming aware of? Are there parts of your day when you felt confused, not sure whether something you said, did, or heard was problematic or oppressive?

However uncomfortable, sit with the discomfort; lean into it and begin to educate yourself from the actions of the day. Write down things you wish to learn more of, or journal about the challenges of allyship. Do not push away from your emotions; they are key in addressing white privilege and white supremacy.

4. Choose one moment of the day when you used your privilege to either make or take space from people of color. Reflect on that moment.

Find one moment from the day in which you can find your white privilege at work in either an oppressive or just way. If it was something you are proud of, then take the moment to recognize and hold gratitude for the improvement and the opportunity you took to choose love and unity over divisiveness.

Pray for the courage, insight, humility, and self-awareness to continue to grow as a white ally for racial justice.

Recognize the need and call for more growth and education. If it is a moment in which you abused your privilege, focus on what prejudices, notions, or structures were influential in your action. Reflect on how that moment was harmful and divisive. Brainstorm ways to work towards restorative racial healing in the future.

Pray for guidance, perseverance, and awareness for the future.

5. Look forward to tomorrow.

Reflect on ways you can move closer towards allyship. Are there social justice groups or organizations asking for white allies that you can join or give support to? Are there books, articles, or other forms of media on race that you can turn to for education? Are there white folk in your life with whom you may need to have uncomfortable conversations on race?

Make conscious, practical, and intentional action plans to use your power to help dismantle racism. Be prepared to translate this spiritual work into concrete, physical actions. As St. Ignatius says, "Love is shown more in deeds than in words."

Racism is a violence that manifests within minds, souls, actions, institutions, and systems, making itself a place within our history, present, and—unfortunately in soon-to-be-seen ways—even our future. It is a penetrative, infectious violence that, even after years of social justice actions, protests, and victories, continues to persist. There is much to be done to resist and dismantle racism. Part of what we can do as white folks is to make space within our moral and spiritual lives for continuous reflection, honesty, and self-improvement. It is on us to put in the work—physically, mentally, and spiritually—to educate ourselves and position ourselves to be better allies, and, most importantly, to help us love better. The root of racism is hate, and we are not called to hate, but to love.

Today, I believe that, for white allies, love should be like allyship: listening, humility, self-education, reflection, and consistent social justice action. It is hard work, but it is also essential work we all have the capacity to perform.

As the poet Rupi Kaur says in her book *The Sun and Her Flowers*:

To hate is such a lazy thing
But to love
Takes strength
Everyone has
But not all are
Willing to practice.

A Doorway to Racial Healing

Patrick Saint-Jean, SJ

The Jesuits are known for being an intellectual and academic order, but Ignatian spirituality reaches past the mind, connecting with both the emotions and actions. In the Spiritual Exercises, Ignatius makes this clear when he asks us to pray about three categories of people. All three individuals have acquired significant wealth and now, concerned about God's expectations, they believe they should part with their money. The first person, however, postpones doing anything until the hour of her death; she is too focused on the concerns of this world to have time for spiritual matters. The second person rationalizes that God wants him to keep his wealth; intellectually, he believes that his money belongs to God but is unwilling to incarnate this value in his real-life world. Finally, the third person prays to be free from the attachment to wealth; this person allows God to use the money for the benefit of God's community on earth.

This exercise has direct application to white privilege and systemic racism. Like the first and second individuals, we may be unwilling to see that our attachment to our material comforts has a connection to racism—or that our participation in systemic racism has a spiritual component. We either postpone taking any kind of action against racism, or we rationalize away the call to take part in anti-racist work. But as my Jesuit brother Ken Homan wrote, "Attachment to white privilege and white supremacy leads to an inauthentic faith.

Excerpt from *The Crucible of Racism: Ignatian Spirituality and the Power of Hope* (Maryknoll, NY: Orbis Books, 2002), chapter 5.

They are not open to the power of God's justice."[1] Ignatius calls us to work for justice actively in collaboration with God. As a Jesuit, I live and breathe Ignatian spirituality. It has become the doorway through which I see possibility in a world that is broken by racism. It empowers me to trust in a better future. Despite its human flaws, the Society of Jesus is a vehicle of justice. It maintains its roots in the teachings of Ignatius, affirming that we are all friends in the Lord. Living in the Jesuit community, I have experienced firsthand honest, healthy friendships with people who share my commitment to work for justice.

But I am not writing this book only for other Jesuits to read. As Ignatius himself taught, this is a spirituality that is available to everyone; you do not have to join the Society of Jesus to practice Ignatius's practical approach that integrates emotions with intellect, contemplation with action, and love of God with love for other human beings.

No one can claim to be immune to racism; its patterns are indelibly imprinted on our thoughts and actions. But Ignatius insisted that we are "lovable sinners" who can be changed by the love and grace of God. Ignatian spirituality is about possibility thinking. It refuses to be confined by societal expectations; it looks past appearances. It perceives a deeper reality, and that reality becomes a call to action. This requires a conscious choice on our part.

Be alert, Ignatius taught. Be aware. Pay attention to wherever you find the presence of God. See the divine presence in those who are different from you and in those who are suffering from poverty and societal injustice. Don't overlook any brother or sister, because everyone—no matter how dissimilar to you they may seem—carries the image of God. To ignore the experience of any part of the human family is to ignore an aspect of God.

Awareness is the process by which we open ourselves to divine love. This intentional awareness is the hallmark of Ignatian spirituality. Through awareness, we step out of our selfish fears and into the security of God's love. In doing so, we lose our self-absorption and become more aware of the needs of others.

---

1. Ken Homan, SJ, "What Dr. King and St. Ignatius Taught Me about Discernment and Anti-Racism," *Jesuit Post*, January 18, 2021, https://thejesuitpost.org.

Awareness is the foundation of anti-racism. It empowers us to see the possibilities that lead to justice.

Invitation to Discernment

Harriet Tubman, the great abolitionist, is often quoted as saying, "Every great dream begins with a dreamer. Always remember, you have within you the strength, the patience, and the passion to reach for the stars to change the world."[2] Ignatian spirituality believes that God speaks to us through our deepest desires, the dreams that inspire us to work for a better future. Use this Examen as an opportunity to focus on your dreams.

Become aware. Take a quiet moment to become aware of the dreams that motivate your life.

Now ask yourself:

Are my dreams fueled by my ego or by compassion?

Review your life with gratitude. Ask yourself:

What dreams has God already fulfilled in my life?

What new dreams might God be calling me toward?

Look forward. Working to make a dream come true is always a risk. I dream of a more just world for people of color, and I am taking a risk by opening myself to you through this book, inviting you to join me in the spirit of togetherness.

Ask yourself:

Am I willing to let go of my self-interest in order to experience the suffering of others?

What risks am I willing to take on their behalf? Can I dare to dream a bigger dream, one that encompasses the needs of others?

2. It turns out that there is no historical evidence that Harriet Tubman actually spoke or wrote these sentences. However, we do know that dreams were important in her life, and they helped to inspire her to take action on behalf of her people.

Prayer

Lord, Jesus Christ, who reached across the ethnic boundaries between Samaritan, Roman, and Jew, who offered fresh sight to the blind and freedom to captives, help us break down the barriers in our community, enable us to see the reality of racism and bigotry, and free us to challenge and uproot it from ourselves, our society, and our world. Amen.[3]

3. John Bucki, SJ, Social Justice Resource Center, https://socialjusticeresourcecenter.org/prayers/racism/.

IX. Care for Our Common Home

Part IX Introduction

During the rise of the popular ecological movement of the last seventy-five years, Saint Francis of Assisi emerged as a Christian hero in the face of a perceived myth that Christians were not concerned about the material world. Both elements of this myth—the so-called Christian scorn for creation and Francis's lonely battle for its care—are false. Certainly, Francis expressed love for the natural world and extolled God's glory imprinted upon nature in his prayers and poetry, but caring for the survival of the natural world was no more uniquely his contribution than was his gratitude for its reflection of divine goodness.

Like Saint Francis, who was Ignatius's great hero among the saints, Ignatius was as deeply affected by the cosmos as medievalists were. From Ignatius, however, we don't examine the affection he had for nature. Rather we look to the methods of prayer and discernment that he taught as ground for moral decisions about the use of the material world for our own profit or aggrandizement. It is right decision-making that clearly illuminates the imperative of care for our common home.

Rapidly changing conditions within the natural order, which serve as harbingers of disaster if not attended to, require thoughtful consideration of their causes. In this, the practice of Examen and the work of discerning God's will have led Pope Francis, following his predecessor popes for the past seventy years, to recognize the common causes for violent harm caused by humans fighting within our own hearts, fighting among each other, and fighting the notion of a God whose desires are more important than our own. In every case the concept of desire for power and control has caused every human to contribute to the systematic destruction of the created order.

Reading the "signs of the times" as called for by the Second Vatican Council of the Catholic Church in the previous century, the Jesuits and their partners in Ignatian mission determined that care for our common home—that is, creation itself—requires a preferential concern in our apostolic works for at least the next decade. As a "Universal Apostolic Preference," care for our common home has challenged all persons engaged in Ignatian spirituality to attend to this critical project of restoring health and healing to our broken physical world (see Part I of this *Reader* for texts that describe the full outcomes of the UAP discernment process). Some texts in earlier chapters include this topic within a larger context (see Julia Dowd's essay "In Our Bones" in Part II, for example), but selections for Part IX of this volume focus principally upon the relationship between Ignatian spirituality and the preference of care for our common home.

Karin Botto's short article integrates the topic of Ignatian leadership (more expansively addressed in Part V) with the ecological conversation called for by the fourth UAP.

Joseph Carver addresses Ignatian spirituality, with its appreciation of the incarnation of God in human flesh and time, sacramental appreciation, the human context within the natural order, and the prayer of the Spiritual Exercises, as means for entering a conversation with the earth that expands our ability to make just and moral decisions on behalf of the natural world.

Paul Younger's article, written from a perspective of worldwide efforts to restore ecological balance, offers a means for understanding Pope Francis's encyclical letter *Laudato Si'* in light of the preparation for and the practice of Ignatian Spirituality.

Part IX, and the *Ignatian Spirituality Reader, Volume II*, end with Pope Francis's prayers for reconciliation among persons, with the natural order, and with God that conclude the encyclical *Laudato Si'*. We share the final phrases of that prayer to focus our hopes as we begin this concluding section.

> O Lord, seize us with your power and light, help us to protect all life, to prepare for a better future, for the coming of your Kingdom of justice, peace, love and beauty.
>
> Praise be to you! Amen.

Eileen Burke-Sullivan

Ignatian Spirituality and Ecology: Entering into Conversation with the Earth

Joseph Carver

The earth, in all its wonder and diversity of creatures, is in crisis, and responding to this crisis will require every ounce of our willingness, skill, creativity, and commitment. Any contemporary theology that claims to address the ecological crisis will need to be a theology that understands the human person as part of the natural world. My assertion is that committed Christians have a particular role in the environmental movement because of our understanding of both the Incarnation and communion. A communal theology, which takes seriously the incarnational grounding of our human identity, transforms humanity's relationship to the natural world and inspires an enriched approach to the ecological movement. I would argue that the sacramental tradition of Catholicism, and especially Ignatian spirituality, offers unique points of entry into ecological spirituality and thus the restoration of creation. When the great themes of Christian theology, such as covenant and Incarnation, are brought to our contemporary understanding of ecology, with an attitude that is critical yet respects the beauty and depth of both disciplines, they raise our ecological vision from one of mere materialism to one of reconciliation, re-creation, and ultimately resurrection.

In what follows, I do not pretend to offer the full realization of what will come from this meeting of Ignatian Spirituality and an ecological imagination, but I hope to offer a few initial approaches.

From *Jesuit Higher Education: A Journal*, January 2015: Volume 4, Number 2, Article 10.

The tradition of Ignatius provides a foundational dimension to the spirituality of the contemporary Church. In examining aspects of this spirituality, I hope to show how both its incarnational grounding and the character of kinship (communion of subjects) may act as means to understand and encounter God as Creator, thus allowing our "kinship" with the earth and all of creation to inform our encounter with the Incarnate Christ.[1] Ignatian spirituality demands a critical awareness of the environment in our daily lives, moving us from a sense of mere stewardship of the earth to a deeper committed covenant of membership in the order of creation. One manifestation of this deeper covenant is found in a eucharistic ecology that both emerges from the tradition and is imaged in Ignatian spirituality.

This view is not simply instrumental but sacramental: the very relational quality of God as actualized in creation. Such a perspective recognizes that we are engaged in a relationship with the incarnate God, and, therefore, must see ourselves as kin with all creation, both biologically and spiritually. The model and movements of the Ignatian Examen serve as a tool for persons to enter the conversation through this transformative practice. The world can no longer sustain the dichotomies of spirit versus matter or ecology versus spirituality. The responsibility is ours—perhaps especially those of us graced by the gift of Ignatian spirituality—to reconcile these opposites for the life of the world. This demands an ecological conversion and commitment, by which we address the current environmental crisis with a fresh recognition of our kinship to the created order. A newfound communion can enable us to overcome abstraction and to know the bonds of heaven to earth, of spirit to matter.

---

1. We live in a broken world (the 1999 Jesuit document on ecology states that Ignatius affirms a "three-fold relationship of subjects" between God, humans, and the rest of Creation), *Promotio Justitiae* 70 (1999), 21. In his address to Arrupe College in Harare, Father Kolvenbach insists that these three relationships are "so closely united that a person cannot find God unless he finds him through the environment and, conversely, that his relationship to the environment will be out of balance unless he also relates to God." "Our Responsibility for God's Creation," August 22, 1998, address at the opening of Arrupe College.

Applying the Spiritual Exercises: A Way of Commitment

In the Spiritual Exercises, we find a basis for both a creation-centered and resurrection-centered approach to ecological spirituality. The fullest expression of this approach is found in the Contemplation to Attain Divine Love. However, there are several key meditations that assist in sensitizing us to the ecological issues of our time. Ignatius's view of Christ as "Eternal Lord of All things"[2]—a resurrection-centered approach—addresses the polarization of human transformation over against the redemption of creation. To argue that Ignatius was focused on the transformation of the natural world would be anachronistic; however, it is clear that for him creation is the place for salvation.

Indeed, it is within the wonder of creation that we begin to comprehend Ignatius's mystical principle of "finding God in all things." At the beginning of the Exercises, we experience God through creation around us, and we are moved spontaneously "to praise, reverence, and serve." In the third rule of discernment, Ignatius indicates that we cannot know God apart from creation. He presents consolation as "an interior movement . . . aroused in the soul, by which it is inflamed with love of its Creator and Lord, as a consequence, can love no created thing for its own sake, but only the Creator of them all" (SE 316). The movement toward indifference (i.e., relating freely) in the Principle and Foundation, the Meditation on the Incarnation, and the Meditation on the Two Standards assist in increasing our ecological awareness.

2. This phrasing is drawn from the Kingdom Meditation.

The Principle and Foundation: An Invitation to Relationship

Ignatian indifference in the Principle and Foundation does not imply a lack of concern for the natural world; in fact it is meant to cultivate understanding of "the end for which we are created" (i.e., compassionate awareness and gratitude for life with God). As the retreatant acknowledges her own creaturehood before God, there is an increase in knowledge of her role in that self-same creation. The language and instrumental focus on creation can certainly be read in an anthropocentric manner; however, throughout the Exercises, Ignatius makes it clear that creation is both a resource from God as well as an avenue to God. Indeed, he emphasizes that God is both dwelling in all creation and co-laboring with us in creation. We must remember that the Principle and Foundation exists as a starting point, set within the larger dynamic of the Spiritual Exercises, the goal of which is always greater interior freedom.[3] Thus, Ignatian indifference is not a matter of not caring for the things of creation, but rather relating freely to them. The goal of the Exercises is a spiritual journey toward ever-greater freedom. It is no accident that Ignatius asks retreatants to begin to clarify the relationship between themselves and creation. The theological anthropology operative in the Exercises emphasizes humanity's ability to discern both God's ongoing labor in and through creation, as well as God's invitation for persons to cooperate in God's divine work.

Ignatius specifically invites retreatants to marvel at the heavens, the sun and moon and all the stars, the earth with its plants and animals, and to consider how these created things sustain, nourish, and protect us. They keep us alive even when we ignore God and refuse to praise the divine majesty; when we shut ourselves off in isolation and refuse to serve God; when we abuse and misuse creation (SE 23). It becomes clear to retreatants that God's plan for creation requires specifically discerned choices and delicate precision. The other beings within creation are companions helping us attain the fullness of relationship with God. In fact, humans are given a share in God's authority, a real part

3. Roger Haight's recent article, "Expanding the Spiritual Exercises," *Studies in the Spirituality of Jesuits*, 42, no. 2 (Summer 2010): 1–43, expands on this and other points of creation spirituality.

in establishing, maintaining, healing, and restoring creation. Other beings of creation are companions to us, helping us attain the fullness of relationship with God. "For human beings there is no authentic search for God without an insertion into the life of Creation, and, on the other hand, all solidarity with human beings and every engagement with the created world cannot be authentic without a discovery of God."[4] Throughout the First Week of the Spiritual Exercises, retreatants become intimately aware that they are involved in the processes of sin at work in the world. The possibility of participation in the social and structural sins of consumption and greed mentioned in the introduction, though at first distant and impersonal, becomes all too real. It is incumbent upon the retreatants, therefore, to discern their own complicity with such structures and thus to increase their ecological awareness and sensitivity.

The Nativity and the Incarnation: A Way to Intimacy with Creation

In the Second Week of the Exercises, the meditations on the Incarnation and the Nativity, like the Principle and Foundation, offer us an opportunity to raise our ecological sensitivity. Ignatius presents the contemplations on the Incarnation and Birth of Jesus as "models for all the other contemplations."[5] He directs retreatants to enter the life of Jesus directly. "With the inner eyes of the soul" retreatants imagine the road from Nazareth to Bethlehem, the size of the cave, and the persons they encounter. (Note: although Ignatius invites an encounter with the "holy persons," there is also an opportunity to encounter the road or to become other parts of creation as the scene is composed; never is a retreatant limited to only human roles in the contemplations.) Each contemplation, like the Eucharist, becomes an

4. Peter Hans Kolvenbach, SJ, Discourse to GC 34, 6 January 1995.
5. See Adolf Haas, "The Mysticism of St. Ignatius," in *Ignatius of Loyola: His Personality and Spiritual Heritage*, ed. Friedrick Wulf (St. Louis, MO: Institute of Jesuit Sources, 1997), 188.

encounter with both creation and the divine. The encounter becomes thereby a sharing in the transformation of the elements of creation, and indeed the universe as well.

While the Nativity Meditation focuses retreatants' attention on the historical events within creation, the Meditation on the Incarnation focuses on the divinity of Christ and the mystery of the Trinity. Ignatius does not intend to present a theological formulation for the unity of creation in God, as his focus is always human salvation. However, it is clear that his vision encompasses the whole of creation in all its concreteness. In fact, it is precisely through the Incarnation Meditation that Christ participates in and draws creation "back to God." Creation is therefore the place to experience God's redemptive love. At this point, it is difficult to overlook the resonances with Paul's letter to the Colossians. "He is the image of the invisible God, the firstborn of all creation; for in him all things in heaven and on earth were created, things visible and invisible, whether thrones or dominions or rulers or powers—all things have been created through him and for him" (Colossians 1:15–16). Because Jesus shares identity with God, he shares the same relationship to creation as God. Therefore, it is clearly appropriate to say that the earth is Jesus' and everything in it belongs to Jesus. Thus our failure to care for and protect creation is an affront to God. Creation clearly shares in the effects of the sinfulness of humanity, but it also shares in Jesus' divinity.

Jesus became human, a carbon-based life form, participating in creation, exchanging food and cells, and sanctifying life, blood, and even the very air we continue to breathe.

The Two Standards: A Way to Awareness

The Meditation on the Two Standards (SE 136) leads retreatants into an understanding of both Christ's identity and virtue, as well as the deceits and strategies of Satan leading us to "riches, honor, and pride." As noted above, it is not difficult to see the implications of our greed and consumptive pattern related to the earth's natural resources. Whether we examine water, food consumption (beef in particular), oil, building materials, land use, waste production, or energy—an unsustainable pattern emerges. However, when we apply the interconnectedness revealed in an ecological worldview to the Meditation on the Two Standards, the issues of greed and consumption become frighteningly clear:

- As many as 3.1 billion people on the planet struggle to survive on less than two dollars a day, and more than 1 billion people lack reasonable access to safe drinking water.
- Americans constitute 5% of the world's population but consume 24% of the world's energy. On average, one American consumes as much energy as two Japanese, six Mexicans, thirteen Chinese, thirty-one Indians, 128 Bangladeshis, 307 Tanzanians, or 370 Ethiopians.
- Americans eat 200 billion more calories per day than necessary, enough to feed 80 million people, and Americans spend $30 billion a year on diet programs, while millions of people around the world starve to death.
- Producing one pound of wheat requires twenty-five gallons of water with modern Western farming techniques. Producing one pound of beef requires 5,214 gallons of water.
- In matters of commercial energy consumption: One person in the industrialized world = ten people in the developing world.
- Worldwide, 1.2 billion people do not have access to clean water. Americans flush 6.8 billion gallons of water down their toilets every day. Each day, nearly 10,000 children under the age of five in Third World countries die as a result of illnesses contracted by use of impure water.[6]

In choosing the Standard of Christ, we are reminded of his simplicity, humility, and way of finding God in the natural world. Knowledge of this standard leads to awareness, to love, and to worship. Following the Standard of Christ reminds us that God "labors and works for us in all creatures on the face of the earth." A retreatant finds the Creator "in all things" and "not in spite of created things as if they were hiding from him as behind a veil, or even with their help, as if

6. Worldwatch Institute, "Annual Report 2014: Vision for a Sustainable World."

they had only instrumental value. He is one with them in relationship with God which God lovingly established for us in union with our environment."[7]

Contemplation to Attain Divine Love

In the Fourth Week, Ignatius calls us to a new life in Christ, and no matter how many times I read the words above, I cannot help but be consoled by God laboring on my behalf. As with the Principle and Foundation, Ignatius asks retreatants to consider how God dwells in creation. Spending time praying in and with creation fosters a communal consciousness and a growth in kinship and responsible action. Just as it is clear that we can harm creation from great distances, whether through the worldwide impact of coal-fired plants in China or destructive oil spills in the Gulf of Mexico, so too we can heal and restore creation from great distances. As we grow in our awareness of our interconnectedness, we become more sensitive to the impacts of our consumerist behaviors and their global effects. If we drive less, eat lower on the food chain, use toxic materials sparingly or not at all, watch for signs of stress on ecosystems, use renewables, and do nothing that will degrade the water supply, then we are part of the earth protecting itself. All of these opportunities have a cumulative effect in a closed earth system, allowing us to participate in the resurrection of the planet.[8]

Thirty years ago, on May 18, 1980, Mount St. Helens erupted and destroyed over 200 square miles of mature forest. A massive landslide reduced the mountain's summit by 1,300 feet, and in less than three minutes, ecosystems were obliterated. I recall walking through the visitors' center and viewing a screen to see thousands of downed trees, scattered like matchsticks over an area that looked as

7. Kolvenbach, "Our Responsibility."

8. The insights shared in this section were inspired by conversations with Dr. Janet Ruffing and Dr. Trileigh Tucker, and expanded upon in "Ecology and the Spiritual Exercises," *The Way* 43, no. 1 (2004): 7–18.

though it had been strip-mined. Now, three decades later, the blast zone is once again teeming with life, amazing visitors and scientists alike. Resurrection!

The eruption of Mount St. Helens destroyed so much that we often overlook how much has been resurrected: an entirely new ecosystem. What was a fifteen-story wall of mud and volcanic material, travelling at more than 300 miles per hour down a mountainside, is now 130 new ponds, two new lakes, and thousands of creatures. The ash and debris unleashed by the eruption clogged streams, seeps, and hollows, trapping rain and groundwater. The result? Ponds replete with algae for tadpoles and aquatic salamanders to eat, stoking populations. The fern and lupine lush in flower and leaf have helped build the soil quickly. Gophers that survived the blast underground have proven surprisingly important, forcing up nutrient-rich soil from below the ash, with the added benefit of providing migratory tunnels for toads. Alder have returned, hosting scores of blackbirds with their tuneful songs. Some animals, such as the northwestern salamander, continue to adapt, keeping their gills and living their entire lives as aquatic animals rather than moving into the rich undergrowth and soil of a mature forest they would normally inhabit as adults.

Thirty years later, hiking over Windy Ridge, as Spirit Lake comes into full view, one encounters an ecosystem teeming with croaking, blooming, singing, soaring, darting, swimming, and chewing life. What began 40,000 years ago on an eroded surface of still older volcanic and sedimentary rocks, the youngest of the major Cascade volcanoes has been transformed in three short decades. It is not restoration, renewal, or recovery. It is an entirely new ecosystem.

Lessons from Giving the Exercises

It is not surprising that when retreatants are asked where they "find God," they most often respond, "in nature." Never have I heard: "in a clear-cut forest," "a polluted river," or "an over-crowded city." We are drawn to God in creation, just as we are drawn to healthy community. As a retreat director, understanding how individuals pray in creation is a great help toward understanding their relationship with God, and this offers insights into where and how consolation is working in their prayer.

On the Oregon coast a short time ago, as I sat with a retreatant, it was clear to me that he was spinning. He was immersed in day six of the Third Week of the Exercises, preoccupied not with Christ but with the intensity of Christ's suffering, speaking again and again of the gruesomeness of the contemplations. As we came to the end of our session, I invited him to place Christ in the tomb by the end the day. He agreed. Though rarely so directive in accompanying a retreatant, holding on to my piece of gneiss—I felt compelled by the Spirit. I invited him to consider imagining himself as the tomb in the contemplation. Again, he agreed. When we met late the next day, he tearfully said four words: *"Christ rose within me."* Deeply consoled and joyful, he went on to recount the powerful contemplation he had experienced as Christ's tomb.

A resurrection-centered approach to the environment begins with God moving us toward the realization of his love in all created things. The paradox of love resides at the very center of the gospel and at the core of the Exercises. The center of Ignatius's spiritual experiences is the awareness of Christ's divine love present and at work in the world. Therefore, finding God at work in creation for Ignatius does not begin with that creation and then ascend by some form of purification of the senses, but rather begins in God and moves into and through creation. Developments since the era of high scholasticism have not fundamentally changed such an understanding of the basic mystery of God's relationship to creation. Teilhard de Chardin, for example, thought it his life work to reintegrate spirituality with the earth. He accomplished much toward that end; however, his thinking concludes by subsuming all material creation within human transformation. As he writes: "In a convergent universe, every element finds its fulfillment, not directly in its own perfection, but in its incorporation into the unity of a superior pole of consciousness in which it can enter into communion with all others. Its worth culminates in a transmutation into the other, in a self-giving excentration."[9] Or again, he reflects on "the end of the world; the overthrow of equilibrium, detaching the mind, fulfilled at last, from its material matrix, so that it will henceforth rest with all its weight in God's Omega."[10] These and other passages indicate that Teilhard saw the universe as being subsumed into human fulfillment in Christ.

The Spiritual Exercises are written entirely from the point of view of Christ as "Eternal Lord of all things," as well as the humble self-emptying servant. The split between human transformation and the redemption of creation seems to result from a separation of humans from the world or an overly rationalized approach to the final transformation (as in Origen's and Teilhard de Chardin's view). If transformation is accomplished by God's self-emptying and resurrecting love, and love preserves the "otherness" of the other and does not simply subsume it, there would be no reason to deny the self-emptying and resurrecting of the universe as the place where humans (and Christ as human) can contemplate the immensity and diversity of God's creativity, beauty, and harmony.

Just as Teilhard de Chardin's "Mass on the World" was shaped into the mountains and hills which burst into song, and trees which clap their hands—so all creation will come to sit at table in the Kingdom of God. Theologian Catherine LaCugna writes:

> God is so thoroughly involved in every last detail of creation that if we could truly grasp this it would altogether change how we approach each moment of our lives. For everything that exists—insect, agate, galaxy—manifests the mystery of the living God.[11]

The Constitutions of the Society recognize that the activity of God in creation is "cooperating with Him and glorifying Him . . . that which he gives as Creator, nature."[12] Thus Ignatius offers a supernatural

---

9. See Teilhard de Chardin, *The Future of Man & The Hymn of the Universe*, trans. N. Denny (New York: Harper & Row, 1959), 76.
10. See Teilhard de Chardin, *The Phenomenon of Man*, trans. Bernard Wall (New York: Harper & Row, 1959), 287f.
11. Catherine Mowry LaCugna, *God for Us: The Trinity and Christian Life* (San Francisco, HarperCollins, 1991), 304.
12. *Constitutions* P.X, n. 3.

view of creation so that we might be led to render to God greater glory and service. This view leads us to be passionately concerned about healing humans and healing the earth, since humans and earth are seen as united in God's primary and communal act of love. This relational view provides the bridge between creation and redemption.

Ignatian Imagination and the Examen

The daily Examen and Ignatian imaginative prayer are two clear ways to cultivate an ecological sensitivity in our interior lives. We are well aware that God continually draws each one of us to himself in and through Christ. We experience God's activity in our feelings, moods, actions, and desires. We believe that God reveals himself in our feelings as much as in our clear and distinct ideas. Allowing God to draw us more intimately, we must first let him draw us at the core of our being, which means becoming more aware of our feelings. Here we recognize God's ceaseless invitation to come closer, to be more like God, to be one with God. Additionally, we become conscious of our resistance to God, which arises from sin in ourselves and in the world about us. Using the technique of the Examen with an ecological lens allows us to prayerfully reflect on the events of the day. We are able to witness our relationship with creation and to detect God's presence and discern God's direction for us. The goal of the Examen is a discerning heart. The purpose of the Ecological Examen is discerning how God is inviting us individually to see how we are responding with greater sensitivity.

The five movements in the Ecological Examen parallel the traditional Examen. We begin with thanksgiving and gratitude for the covenant God offers in the gift of God's self in all creation. Second, we make a specific request to have our eyes opened by the Spirit to the ways we might care for creation. Third, we undertake a review of the challenges and joy experienced in this care. We ask God how we were drawn into the divine presence today by creation, and how we were being invited to respond to God's action in that same creation. Is there some part of our relationship with creation that is in need of change? Fourth, we ask for a true and clear awareness of our sinfulness, whether found in our sense of superiority or in a failure to respond to the needs of other creatures. Finally, we ask for hope in the future, seeking greater sensitivity to trust in God's living presence in all creation.

Ecological Examen

All creation reflects the beauty and blessing of God's image. Where was I most aware of this today?

Can I identify specifically how I made a conscious effort to care for God's creation during this day?

What challenges or joys do I experience as I recall my care for creation?

How can I repair breaks in my relationship with creation, in my unspoken sense of superiority?

As I imagine tomorrow, I ask for the grace to see the Incarnate Christ in the dynamic interconnections of all creation.

Conclude with the prayer of Jesus: *The glory that you have given me I have given them, so that they may be one, as we are one, I in them and you in me, that they may become completely one, so that the world may know that you have sent me and have loved them even as you have loved me* (John 17:22–23).

Conclusion: Reconciliation, a Sacrament for the Society

The more I listen in the confessional, and in spiritual direction, the clearer it becomes that the oil that has ravaged the Gulf of Mexico abides in many of us deeply—forcing each of us to ask the question: "What is my part?" As we look on this "pierced side" of the earth, we feel a desire to act, to reconcile, to change habits, whether in our patterns of driving or in our use of plastics. Many I have encountered have spoken at length about how the crisis weighs heavily on their psyches, and how they are longing for a spiritual response.

As noted above in reflections on the ecological implications of the Spiritual Exercises, when the 35th General Congregation of the Society of Jesus sought to articulate the mission of the Society today, it spoke of our need to create right relationships, especially in three areas: first, reconciliation with God; second, reconciliation with one another; and third, reconciliation with creation. (I am reminded of Pope Paul III's charge to Ignatius to include the hearing of confessions when he sought approval of the founding documents of the Society.)[13] Reconciliation with God and neighbor has a long history in the Church. However, a reconciliation with creation has often been forgotten, emerging today in a time of grave ecological challenge and profound new insight into the richness of our incarnational heritage. The Congregation, realizing this new reality, challenged Jesuits and all those inspired by the spirituality of Ignatius to "move beyond doubts and indifference to take responsibility for our home, the Earth."[14] This investigation is my attempt to take the call of the Congregation seriously; but it is also a call to a eucharistic ecology

13. The text from the September 27 approval of the Society reads: ". . . that he is a part of a society founded for the especial purpose of providing for the advancement of souls in Christian life and doctrine and for the propagation of the faith through public preaching and the ministry of the Word of God, spiritual exercises and deeds of charity, and in particular through the training of the young and ignorant in Christianity and through the spiritual consolation of the faithful of Christ in hearing confessions."

14. Documents of the 35th General Congregation of the Society of Jesus, Decree 3: Challenges to our Mission Today, "Reconcilation with Creation," accessed March 1, 2009: Following the directive 30 of GC 34, Fr. Peter-Hans Kolvenbach commissioned a study and invited all "Jesuits and those who share our mission to show ever more effective ecological solidarity in our spiritual, communal, and apostolic lives." This invitation calls us to move beyond doubts and indifference to take responsibility for our home, the earth. Care for the environment affects the quality of our relationships with God, with other human beings, and with creation itself. It touches the core of our faith in, and love for, God, "from whom we come and towards whom we are journeying." It might be said that St. Ignatius teaches us this care of the environment in the Principle and Foundation when speaking of the goodness of creation, as well as in the Contemplatio ad Amorem when describing the active presence of God within creation. The drive to access and exploit sources of energy and other natural resources is very rapidly widening the damage to earth, air, water, and our whole environment, to the point that the future of our planet is threatened. Poisoned water, polluted air, massive deforestation, and deposits of atomic and toxic waste are causing death and untold suffering, particularly to the poor. Many poor communities have been displaced, and indigenous peoples have been the most affected. In heeding the call to restore right relationships with creation, we have been moved anew by the cry of those suffering the consequences of environmental destruction, by the many postulates received, and by the recent teaching of the Holy Father and many episcopal conferences on this issue.

that emerges from—and has often been overlooked within—the long sacramental tradition of the Church and the incarnational spirituality of Ignatius, especially as seen in the Spiritual Exercises.

When Teilhard de Chardin—inspired by his encounter with the Ignatian charism—looks at the breadth and depth of unfolding creation, he sees Christ, the Incarnate One, as not only the spiritual but also the physical center of the universe. Because the Word becomes flesh, no part of the physical universe is separable from the Spirit of God. All such dichotomies are overcome. Indeed, as Teilhard sings in the poetry of his Hymn of the Universe:

> All the things in the world to which this day will bring increase; all those that will diminish; all those too that will die: all of them, Lord, I try to gather into my arms, so as to hold them out to you in offering. This is the material of my sacrifice; the only material you desire. . . . Over every living thing which is to spring up, to grow, to flower, to ripen during this day say again the words: This is my Body. And over every death-force which waits in readiness to corrode, to wither, to cut down, speak again your commanding words which express the supreme mystery of faith: This is my Blood.[15]

For Teilhard, the Eucharist is an iconic prayer of the transformation of the universe in Christ, because it acknowledges and anticipates the divinization of the universe. The One we encounter sacramentally in the Eucharist is the One in whom all things are created and in whom all things are transfigured in an ongoing process. Our eucharistic communion is always a sharing in the transformation of the universe, as well as a sacramental expression of the already existent union with God in creation. Because the world is already "charged with the grandeur of God" through the covenant of creation and the indwelling of the Incarnation, the Eucharist reveals what is, even while moving the world toward what is coming to be.[16] Thus, the most intimate communion with God in Eucharist is at the same time an intense moment of intimacy with the evolving earth.

15. *Hymn of the Universe* was published in 1961 by Harper & Row, accessed March 1, 2013.
16. "God's Grandeur," accessed March 1, 2013.

This eucharistic covenant shapes our imaginations, minds, and hearts toward an ecological sensibility and spirituality, in which communion and love of creation is an essential dimension of communion and love of the resurrected Christ. An authentic eucharistic covenant leads to an ecological ethos, culture, and praxis; every eucharistic experience, therefore, calls us to ecological conversion and action to advance the salvation of all the world. As the source and summit of the whole life of the Church, the Eucharist relates us to Christ, connects us with one another, and re-members us with creation. It is the image of the covenant fully realized, where "God may be all in all" (1 Corinthians 15:28).

In his letter promulgating the decrees of General Congregation 35, the Superior General of the Society of Jesus, Adolfo Nicolás, wrote:

> The task now at hand lies with the whole Society. It is our responsibility to 'receive' the decrees and to give them life in our ministries, communities and personal lives. Our experience has taught us that the success or failure of a General Congregation does not lie in documents but in the quality of lives, which are inspired by them. Because of this, I earnestly exhort all Jesuits to read, study, meditate on and appropriate these decrees. Likewise, I encourage you to enrich them with the depth of your own faith and insight.[17]

In this investigation, I have attempted to respond to the call of Father General and to engage the mission offered by the most recent Congregation.[18] Today, since the world can no longer sustain the dichotomies of spirit versus matter or ecology versus spirituality, it is up to us—perhaps most especially those of us graced by the gift of Ignatian spirituality—to reconcile these historical "opposites" for the life of the world. Adhering to the encouragement expressed in the letter of promulgation for the General Congregation, I have attempted to set forth a variety of inspirations found in our tradition, and to "give them life" anew through my own "faith and insight."

---

17. "Letter of Promulgation," accessed March 1, 2013.
18. This mission is succinctly presented in the opening quotation and initial paragraphs of Part II.

Ignatian Spirituality and the Ecological Vision of *Laudato Si'*

Paul L. Younger

> The earth is the Lord's and all that is in it.
>
> —Psalm 24:1

Ignatius briefly sets out his understanding of the relationship between humans and the rest of creation right at the start of the First Week of the Spiritual Exercises, in the Principle and Foundation, where he states that "the other things on the face of the earth are created for the human beings, to help them in the pursuit of the end for which they are created" (SE 23). Taken at face value, these words might seem to be a simple extension of the injunction in the first of the creation myths in Genesis, where humankind is instructed to "fill the earth and subdue it; and have dominion . . . over every living thing . . ." (Genesis 1:28). More than any other line of scripture, this verse has been used to justify ever-greater human appropriation of the earth's primary biological production. Right-wing pressure groups that claim Christian affiliation—particularly in the USA—use this single sentence to justify unremitting and carefree subjugation of nature to any and all desires of humankind. Does the Principle and Foundation of the Spiritual Exercises also take such an instrumental view of creation? I should like to address this question here, particularly in the light of *Laudato Si'*—the second encyclical of the first Jesuit pope.

Laudato Si': A Brief Synopsis

The publication of *Laudato Si'* on May 24, 2015, had been much anticipated. Its focus was in many ways prefigured in 2013 in the final chapter of Pope Francis's first encyclical, *Lumen fidei*, where he wrote that:

> . . . by revealing the love of God the Creator, [faith] enables us to respect Nature all the more, and to discern in it a grammar written by the hand of God and a dwelling place entrusted to our protection and care. Faith also helps us to devise models of development which are based not simply on utility and profit but consider creation as a gift for which we are all indebted . . .[1]

Despite the wide-ranging nature of this antecedent, the press speculation that preceded publication of *Laudato Si'*, and the immediate reaction of most commentators (whether favorable or not) asserted that the encyclical letter was "on climate change." While climate change does indeed feature prominently in *Laudato Si'*, it is by no means the dominating topic: Quantitative analysis reveals that wider concerns, such as poverty, consumerism, waste, pollution, the environment more generally, ecology, and loss of biodiversity receive far more coverage.[2] Essentially, *Laudato Si'* is a call to a comprehensive "ecological conversion": to acknowledge that "the earth is the Lord's and all that is in it" (Psalm 24:1) and thus to "recognize that we are profoundly united with every creature" and hence act so as to "protect the world and not prey on it" (n. 246). Although the term *ecology* is widely misappropriated in contemporary culture, Pope Francis uses the term correctly, to designate the interactions between creatures, and between creatures and the environment.

1. *Lumen fidei*, n. 55.
2. Paul L. Younger, "Laudato? Sì! An Environmental Engineer Reads Pope Francis," *Open House*, 251 (August 2015), 3–4, accessed 10 September 2015.

It is important to note that, in contrast to all but one earlier encyclical by any Pope, *Laudato Si′* is explicitly directed to all of humankind rather than just to the Roman Catholic faithful.[3] Thus its mood and content contrast markedly with Pope Francis's earlier official documents, which were exhortations directed principally at the church community.[4] One manifestation of this contrast is that only two chapters of *Laudato Si′* (two and six) deal predominantly with theology and Christian pastoral practices, while the other four deal with issues of common interest to many individuals and groups in wider society.

Chapter 1 reviews the multifaceted challenges of anthropogenic environmental degradation, adopting the ecological concept of "common goods" as a means to understand the issues of injustice arising from pollution, greenhouse gas emissions, and biodiversity loss. The second chapter—"The Gospel of Creation"—proposes a theological framework for analyzing these issues, drawing predominantly on biblical, patristic, conciliar, and papal sources. In doing so, it localizes ecological issues firmly within the pre-existing framework of Catholic social teaching. Within this rich narrative, Pope Francis explicitly deals with the misuse of that troublesome verse from Genesis (1:28) mentioned above. While admitting that "we Christians have at times incorrectly interpreted the Scriptures," he goes on to argue that, approaching this text in its full context and with an appropriate hermeneutic, "we must forcefully reject the notion that our being created in God's image and given dominion over the earth justifies absolute domination over other creatures" (n. 67).[5] Rather, the full remit of humankind is:

3. I think of John XXIII's *Pacem in terris* (1963), which addressed all people of good will at a time when the Cold War risked tipping over into global nuclear holocaust.

4. *Lumen fidei* and the apostolic exhortation *Evangelii gaudium* (2013).

5. See Jeremy Cohen, Be Fertile and Increase, *Fill the Earth and Master It: The Ancient and Medieval Career of a Biblical Text* (Ithaca: Cornell UP, 1989), 314: "In the case of Gen 1:28, modern scholars have retrojected contemporary concern with dominion over nature onto scripture's call to 'fill the earth and master it,' assuming that here lies the source of western ecological attitudes . . . but . . . this study . . . has revealed otherwise."

> . . . to "till and keep" the garden of the world (cf. Genesis 2:15). "Tilling" refers to cultivating, ploughing or working, while "keeping" means caring, protecting, overseeing, and preserving. This implies a relationship of mutual responsibility between human beings and nature. Each community can take from the bounty of the earth whatever it needs for subsistence, but it also has the duty to protect the earth and to ensure its fruitfulness for coming generations. "The earth is the Lord's" (Psalm 24:1); to him belongs "the earth with all that is within it" (Deuteronomy 10:14). Thus God rejects every claim to absolute ownership: "The land shall not be sold in perpetuity, for the land is mine; for you are strangers and sojourners with me" (Leviticus 25:23). (n. 67)

The third chapter of *Laudato Si'* examines the disordered tendencies in individuals and society that give rise to ecological degradation, most notably blind faith in (unspecified) technological fixes and the tendency to anthropocentrism in our dealings with nature. Chapter 4 explores many facets of what an "integral" ecology might look like, with environmental, economic, social, and cultural dimensions. An "ecology of daily life" is advocated, in which the renewal of urban environments is undertaken in a manner that prioritizes the needs of the poor, minimizing the many environmental blights on their health and quality of life, such as those associated with overcrowding owing to inadequate housing, and with air pollution arising from unregulated transport. The principle of the common good is reiterated here, along with discussion of concepts of intra- and inter-generational justice. The final two chapters set out some parameters for action, both at the level of policymaking (chapter 5) and at the level of individual lifestyles, not least the ways in which these are influenced by education and spiritual development (chapter 6). The encyclical closes with two remarkable prayers: The first is written for use in interfaith contexts by any monotheistic believer, while the second is specifically Christian in language.

To summarize, *Laudato Si'* constitutes a radical call to what Pope Francis terms "ecological conversion," in which our personal and collective encounters with Jesus are realized in a "vocation to be protectors of God's handiwork" (n. 217). This "entails gratitude and gratuitousness, a recognition that the world is God's loving gift, and that we are called quietly to imitate his generosity in self-sacrifice and good works" (n. 220). However, personal conversion is insufficient: the "problems must be addressed by community networks and not simply by the sum of individual good deeds" (n. 219). Yet:

> . . . on many concrete questions, the Church has no reason to offer a definitive opinion; she knows that honest debate must be encouraged among experts, while respecting divergent views. But we need only take a frank look at the facts to see that our common home is falling into serious disrepair. Hope would have us recognize that . . . we can always do something to solve our problems. (n. 61)

Besides citing his own earlier papal statements, Pope Francis refers to only two other Jesuits in *Laudato Si′*: Juan Carlos Scannone, who has illuminated many of the ways in which the urban poor of Latin America are developing their own ecology of justice; and Pierre Teilhard de Chardin, the acknowledgment of whom feels like a healing touch for those geoscientists and spiritual writers who have long regarded him as a prophet unfairly rejected by the elders of his own people. Franciscan and Dominican sources are cited far more frequently than Jesuit ones. So, just how "Ignatian" is the spirituality advocated by *Laudato Si′*?

Ignatius and the "Gospel of Creation"

Ignatius himself clearly drew huge spiritual inspiration from the natural world. In the summary of his experiences dictated to Luis Gonçalves da Câmara, Ignatius relates how, during his convalescence in Loyola, he derived great consolation, and an impetus to serve the Lord, from his habit of gazing at the sky and the stars (*Autobiography*, n. 11). Subsequently, one of his most profound and memorable spiritual experiences occurred while he was staring into the Cardoner River near Manresa (*Autobiography*, n. 30). Thus it is unsurprising that natural imagery is frequently invoked in the Spiritual Exercises.

This tendency reaches its acme in the "Contemplation to Attain Love" in the Fourth Week, in which retreatants are encouraged to reflect repeatedly on the action of God in nature, thus:

- in the second point, to consider "how God dwells in creatures; in the elements, giving them existence; in the plants, giving them life; in the animals, giving them sensation; in human beings, giving them intelligence" (SE 235).
- in the third point to consider "how God labors and works for me in all the creatures on the face of the earth; that is, he acts in the manner of one who is laboring. For example, he is working in the heavens, elements, plants, fruits, cattle, and all the rest—giving them their existence, conserving them, concurring with their vegetative and sensitive activities, and so forth" (SE 236).
- in the fourth point, to consider how everything that is good emanates from God in an indivisible manner, "as the rays come down from the sun, or the rains from their source" (SE 237).

These lines echo the Principle and Foundation (SE 23) in that they identify God working for the good of humans through all other created things. This is an undeniably anthropocentric interpretation of nature. Intellectual assent to this point is not possible without accepting that the love of God is abundant to the point of profligacy: that all of the created universe has been called into existence simply to let a limited number of creatures on a tiny, insignificant planet experience that love.[6]

The psalmist marveled at this profligate love:

> When I look at your heavens, the work of your fingers, the moon and the stars that you have established; what are human beings that you are mindful of them, mortals that you care for them? (Psalm 8:3–4)

---

6. Even if life on other planets has reached the same level of consciousness as humankind, and is thus also fitted to experience God's love directly, those planets are certainly few and exceedingly far between. See, for instance, Simon Conway-Morris, *Life's Solution: Inevitable Humans in a Lonely Universe* (Cambridge: CUP, 2003).

Carlo Carretto, in the first chapter of his book *The God Who Comes*, memorably uses the modern understanding of the cosmos to express how the immensity of God's love is reconciled with the deeply personal manner in which that love is manifest to humans:

> God has always been coming; God is always coming. This evening, as I gazed at the sky, I saw the heavenly body farthest from the earth and still visible to the naked eye: the nebula of Andromeda. . . . The pale light of the nebula, which reached my eye this evening, left there a million years ago at the speed of 187,000 miles per second. From that time, and doubtless from before then, God has been coming to meet me."[7]

Summarily disregarding any such interpretation, the evangelical "new atheists" use the same observations of the vastness of the universe to ridicule Christian claims of human "specialness."[8] The dichotomy between the interpretations of Carretto and Dawkins is not amenable to scientific resolution. Rather, it highlights the key insight that the marvels of nature, in and of themselves, are profoundly ambiguous, and that their full interpretation is therefore dependent on the faith perspective of the beholder.[9]

There is, of course, no doubt over the stance of Ignatius of Loyola on the spiritual significance of nature: Our experience of nature is integral to God's exuberant outpouring of grace into our lives, and our task is to recognize this for what it is and respond to it. It is in precisely this sense that Ignatius states that "the other things on the face of the earth are created for man and that they may help him in prosecuting the end for which he is created." Acceptance of this basic premise is indispensable in Ignatian spirituality, for so much of what follows in the Spiritual Exercises is predicated on it.

---

7. Carlo Carretto, *The God Who Comes*, translated by Rose M. Hancock (London: Darton, Longman and Todd, 1974), 3–4.
8. See, for example, Richard Dawkins, *The God Delusion* (London: Bantam, 2006), 134–151.
9. See Alister E. McGrath, *The Open Secret: A New Vision for Natural Theology* (Oxford: Wiley-Blackwell, 2008).

Yet there is an undeniable tension between the notion of creatures being created for the benefit of humans and existing for their own sake. This tension is explicitly discussed by Pope Francis in *Laudato Si'*, where he notes:

> In our time, the Church does not simply state that other creatures are completely subordinated to the good of human beings, as if they have no worth in themselves and can be treated as we wish. The German bishops have taught that, where other creatures are concerned, "we can speak of the priority of being over that of being useful." The *Catechism* clearly and forcefully criticizes a distorted anthropocentrism: "Each creature possesses its own particular goodness and perfection. . . . each of the various creatures, willed in its own being, reflects in its own way a ray of God's infinite wisdom and goodness. Man must therefore respect the particular goodness of every creature, to avoid any disordered use of things. (n. 69)

The use of the characteristically Ignatian word *disordered* in the last sentence here offers the key to resolving any perceived tension between the perspectives of Ignatius and Pope Francis. This resolution is, to paraphrase Ignatius himself, to be found more in deeds than in words: in the time-honored practices of Ignatian spirituality as set forth in the Spiritual Exercises.

Ignatian Practices and Ecological Spirituality

Immediately following the statement that "the other things on the face of the earth are created for the human beings, to help them in the pursuit of the end for which they are created," Ignatius goes on to say that "it follows that we ought to use these things to the extent that they help us toward our end, and free ourselves from them to the extent that they hinder us from it." The end to which this limited use of the other things on the face of the earth is directed is spelt out by Ignatius as follows: "Human beings are created to praise, reverence and serve God our Lord, and by means of doing this to save their souls" (First Principle and Foundation). Only in so far as their use might advance us in that spiritual quest can we take advantage of other created things. And any such use must be as sparing as possible:

> To attain this it is necessary to make ourselves indifferent to all created things, in regard to everything which is left to our free will and is not forbidden. Consequently, on our own part we ought not to seek health rather than sickness, wealth rather than poverty, honor rather than dishonor, a long life rather than a short one, and so on in all other matters. (SE 23)

A range of structured reflections are provided by the Spiritual Exercises which nurture this indifference (perhaps better expressed as "detachment") in the retreatant. The aim is to remove disordered tendencies, especially disordered attachment to material possessions, to the prestige that goes with them, and to the power that such prestige often confers. It is with precisely this same understanding that Pope Francis warns against "any disordered use of things" (n. 69). It scarcely needs stating that if all inhabitants of our finite planet followed the Ignatian recommendation to use the good things of the earth only as sparingly as would be consistent with "praising, reverencing and serving God," then we would face no ecological crises.

Pope Francis makes much the same point at greater length in *Laudato Si′*:

> Christian spirituality proposes an alternative understanding of the quality of life, and encourages a prophetic and contemplative lifestyle, one capable of deep enjoyment free of the obsession with consumption. We need to take up an ancient lesson, found in different religious traditions and also in the Bible. It is the conviction that "less is more." A constant flood of new consumer goods can baffle the heart and prevent us from cherishing each thing and each moment. To be serenely present to each reality, however small it may be, opens us to much greater horizons of understanding and personal fulfilment. Christian spirituality proposes a growth marked by moderation and the capacity to be happy with little. It is a return to that simplicity which allows us to stop and appreciate the small things, to be grateful for the opportunities which

> life affords us, to be spiritually detached from what we possess, and not to succumb to sadness for what we lack. This implies avoiding the dynamic of dominion and the mere accumulation of pleasures. (n. 222)

This could equally serve as a succinct summary of the way of life that pursuit of the Spiritual Exercises seeks to promote. The strength of the Exercises is that they do not merely exhort the adoption of a "prophetic and contemplative lifestyle" but provide many techniques for opening ourselves up to the grace we need to achieve spiritual detachment. Of particular relevance to the issues covered by *Laudato Si'* are two of these techniques: the application of the senses and the Daily Examen.

Within the formal framework of the Exercises, the application of the senses is presented principally as a means of extracting as much meaning as possible from Lectio Divina on prescribed scripture passages. It involves the imaginative consideration of the sight, smell, taste, touch, and sound of specific scenes described in the scriptures. As it is fundamentally difficult to imagine realistically if you do not yourself pay attention to the experience of the senses in daily life, the development of this technique gradually leads to a more conscious appreciation of "the small things" in daily life, "cherishing each thing and each moment" so that we are "serenely present to each reality . . . open[ing] us to much greater horizons of understanding and personal fulfilment." Supporting this practice is the Daily Examen, in which we reflect on the many ways in which God got through to us during the day. The overall experience is that we gradually become accustomed to find God in all things or, perhaps more accurately, to allowing God to find us in all things.[10] In doing so, the application of the senses expands from an imaginative practice during periods of prayer to become an everyday habit that gradually transforms our consciousness.

Ignatian spirituality abounds with examples of such practices, very often in relation to the beauty of nature. Beauty is a recurrent theme in *Laudato Si'*; indeed the addition of beauty to justice and peace is

---

10. See Gerard W. Hughes, *God in All Things: Earthing Our Spirituality* (London: Hodder and Stoughton, 2003) and Paul Coutinho, *Ignatian Mysticism* (Rockville, MD: Now You Know Media, 2010), 5 CDs.

arguably the greatest contribution that *Laudato Si′* makes to the lexicon of Catholic social teaching.[11] *Laudato Si′* makes it clear that when we cultivate our appreciation of nature, we align our vision with the "gaze of Jesus," who "was in constant touch with nature, lending it an attention full of fondness and wonder" (n. 97).

Of all the figures in Christendom to have fully grasped this truth, no one did so more thoroughly or eloquently than the Jesuit poet Gerard Manley Hopkins. His poetry throbs with a profound delight at the myriad ways in which God makes himself manifest to us through the beauty of creatures, both animate and inanimate. Hopkins's sustained application of the senses reached such degrees of profundity and sophistication that it exhausted the descriptive ability of existing poetic techniques, prompting him not only to bend the meanings of nouns and verbs but to introduce entirely new terms, most notably *inscape* and *instress*. Frustratingly, Hopkins never formally defined these terms. But, as they have been understood by many scholars, and as they have entered the vocabulary of other writers, inscape is that internal and external essence of an entity that can objectively be seen, touched, heard and/or described, whereas instress refers to the mystical experience that a given inscape stirs within us; our emotional response to another creature, which will often defy description.[12]

The significance of this for spirituality is simple yet profound: From the faith perspective, the inscape of every creature is God-given. For non-human beings, fulfilment of their ordained inscape is intrinsic. Thus Thomas Merton wrote:

> A tree gives glory to God by being a tree. For in being what God means it to be it is obeying him. . . . The more a tree is like itself, the more it is like Him. . . . No two created things are exactly alike. And their individuality is no imperfection. On the contrary, the perfection of each created thing is not merely in its conformity to an abstract type,

11. See Paul L. Younger, "Groaning with Creation: Ecological Spirituality in *Laudato Si′*," Open House, 252 (October 2015), forthcoming.
12. See Evelyn Wilson, "Gerard Manley Hopkins and Transcendence," lecture given at the 2003 Hopkins Literary Festival, Newbridge College, Co. Kildare, available at https://gerardmanleyhopkins.org/lectures_2003/transcendence.html, accessed 24 September 2015; Dennis Sobolev, *The Split World of Gerard Manley Hopkins: An Essay in Semiotic Phenomenology* (Washington, DC: Catholic University of America, 2011), 27–42.

> but in its own individual identity with itself. The forms and individual characters of living and growing things [and] of inanimate beings . . . constitute their holiness in the sight of God. . . . Their inscape is their sanctity. It is the imprint of His wisdom and His reality in them. . . . The little yellow flowers that nobody notices on the edge of that road are saints looking up into the face of God.[13]

By contrast, human beings have the ability to resist the realization of their individual inscapes: to be other than God intends them to be. The essence of the spiritual quest, as Ignatius and so many of his followers have realized, is to abandon the false self and fully embrace the personhood that God desires for us.[14] In respecting our own inscape we cannot withhold respect from the inscapes of all other creatures. This is the firm foundation of an authentically Ignatian ecological spirituality. It does not lead to an empty sentimentalism of nature, but to a passionate advocacy of care for creation, as expressed so eloquently by Hopkins:

> What would the world be, once bereft
> of wet and of wildness? Let them be left.
> O let them be left, wildness and wet;
> Long live the weeds and the wilderness yet.[15]

That present-day son of Ignatius, Pope Francis, now calls us to renew our own spirituality so that such passionate advocacy becomes an integral part of our mission as Christians, moving from instress to action, making common cause with all people of good will who seek a better future for our common home.

---

13. Thomas Merton, *New Seeds of Contemplation* (London: Shambala, 1961), 31–32.
14. James Martin, *Becoming Who You Are: Insights on the True Self from Thomas Merton and Other Saints* (Mahwah: Paulist, 2006).
15. Gerard Manley Hopkins, "Inversnaid," *Poems and Prose*, selected by W. H. Garner (London: Penguin, 1953), 51.

Want to Be a Better Leader? Connect with Nature

Karin Botto

In April 2019, I was invited to attend a gathering in Rome, Italy, hosted by the Jesuits. The goal of the week-long retreat was to share best practices in developing Ignatian leaders. During our stay, Father General Arturo Sosa gave an inspiring talk about the newly announced Universal Apostolic Preferences (UAP), the guiding pillars of Jesuit work around the world for the next decade. The four UAPs are: showing the way to God, walking with the excluded, journeying with youth, and caring for our common home. Father Sosa encouraged us to return to our home country and engage others in conversation around the UAPs.

When I returned to the United States, I reflected on how best to integrate the UAPs with the Ignatian Leadership Model, a framework that I and two colleagues developed five years earlier and published in the *Journal of Jesuit Business Education.* The model is the backbone of several leadership programs, experiences, retreats, and talks given at schools and organizations across the Association of Jesuit Colleges and Universities (AJCU). As I contemplated the UAPs, I was particularly moved by the fourth preference, Care for our Common Home. I had a deep desire to better understand how to support and develop individuals to activate their leadership around environmental sustainability. It seemed that very few leaders in Jesuit organizations were actively engaging with this issue. At the time, I was a doctoral student

From *Conversations*, April 2023.

in the Interdisciplinary Leadership Program at Creighton University, and I was discerning the specific focus of my dissertation research. Given my emerging interest, I enrolled in a sustainability leadership course, read every article and book I could find about the integration of climate science and leadership theory, and expanded my network to those studying sustainability.

One of the most important documents in my learning was Pope Francis's encyclical, *Laudato Si'*. In this text, Pope Francis explains that human beings need ecological conversion to fully engage in the solutions required for the monumental crisis we face. I became profoundly curious as to how ecological conversion occurs in leaders particularly, as it seems as if many are too busy and overwhelmed with the crisis of the moment to pay attention to this much larger, looming catastrophe.

During this period, I also led the human resources function at Le Moyne College in Syracuse, New York, and like many other leaders who were working around the clock dealing with COVID-19 and other important and urgent matters, I experienced the exhausting and overwhelming pressure of making rapid decisions in an unknown environment. I found myself heading into nature as often as I could to walk alone or with a spiritual companion to find a centered space to reflect and discern. What became clear was that being with nature changed me and how I responded to the situations unfolding around me. Most importantly, connecting to nature in an intentional way solidified my deepest desire, or vocation, to become a better steward for God's creation.

My dissertation topic became crystal clear: utilize aspects of the Ignatian Leadership Model to create experiences of ecological conversation for leaders across the AJCU network to expedite commitment to the fourth Universal Apostolic Preference. During the summer of 2021, I offered a six-week Ignatian Leadership Program across the United States. Thirty-seven campus leaders participated, representing seventy percent of the Jesuit Colleges and Universities in the United States.

One of the core concepts of the Ignatian Leadership Model is becoming a *Contemplative in Action*, which describes the importance of developing a reflective stance while being active in the world. Many leaders today express that they are too busy to take time to reflect, so one of my goals in this experience was to encourage leaders to slow down and reflect more deeply and intentionally with nature. Every other week of this six-week program, I introduced a new contemplative practice ideally to be experienced in or near nature such as a tree, garden, or water. The three practices selected for this program were the Ignatian Ecological Examen, the Buddhist practice of loving kindness meditation, and *shinrin-yoku* (forest bathing) drawn from Japanese culture. Following each practice, participants e-journaled about their experience. They wrote about the effect the contemplative practice had on them personally, on their leadership, and on their connection to nature. Reading their reflections allowed me to see, in real time, the influence the practice was having on them in a variety of ways. In addition, at the end of the program, I interviewed thirty-five percent of the participants to delve deeper into the experience of ecological conversion. Here I share several key learnings discovered in this process that leaders can utilize to enhance their own well-being, improve their leadership, and more fully support the fourth UAP and *Laudato Si'*.

Learning to Be Present

It was clear that participants were living and working in a distracted and increasingly anxious world. While they recognized the importance of carving out intentional space to deeply reflect and discern, participants shared that they needed to learn to become present, which took practice and patience. They explained that being present in the moment is often countercultural to their organizational context. Individuals needed to leave technology behind and free themselves mentally from competing priorities to create space for solitude. This process of letting go felt awkward and brought up many challenging emotions. Despite the initial discomfort, many leaders discovered this to be a very healthy and important step in their transformation. At the end of the six-week program, eighty-six percent of the participants felt that the experience influenced them on a quite personal level.

Honoring Gratitude and Pain for the World

Participants shared how the contemplative practices in nature allowed them to experience a deep sense of gratitude for the earth. This helped them deal with challenging emotions related to climate change, also known as eco-anxiety. Many described how learning to be with the pain, despair, and grief of what humans are doing to the earth allowed those feelings to transform into a deeper love and connection. This is a significant learning because today climate change is often framed using intense and negative emotions that can paralyze thoughtful action. Contemplative practices in nature provide space for leaders to reflect, discern, and move through difficult emotions to a more positive place of aligned action.

Shifting One's Identity

Many individuals in the program described how coming into direct contact with nature in an intentional way shifted their identity to help them recognize or remember that they are part of something much larger. One person described this shift like the ability to use a new lens on a camera. This perspective helped them embrace a widening circle of care. Through this space of interconnectedness, leaders move from an ego-centered perspective to an eco-centered one.

Participants shared that the Ecological Examen provided a structured, earth-focused reflection that helped stir a desire to act. Loving-kindness meditation helped participants wrestle with issues of self-love and compassion while demonstrating the importance of working with others to solve complex issues in the world. Shinrin-yoku brought participants into direct contact with nature, providing a deep sense of curiosity, wonder, and awe. All three contemplative practices were effective in different ways in helping the leaders become present with themselves, those around them, and the earth. Finding the right practice or combination of practices for oneself is important for leaders to explore.

Going Forth in Meaningful Action

Finally, participants in this program shared how this experience stimulated the desire to act on behalf of the earth for a better future. Individuals started researching their local natural environments, picking up trash when walking, reducing food waste, analyzing their shopping behaviors, cutting back on meat consumption, reducing plastic usage, and spending more time in nature to maintain the connection. All these actions seemed to occur spontaneously because of ecological conversion. There was no formal conversation during the six-week program about actions one could take on behalf of the earth; rather, people seemed to feel called to commit themselves more wholly to the effort of addressing climate issues. In addition, individuals in this program spoke about developing future leaders in this area such as students in their classrooms, members of their families, or groups in their communities. It was clear that individuals wanted to share this experience and inspire others. Seventy-one percent of the participants in this program shared that the experience influenced their leadership.

Steps to Take for Ecological Conversion

Undertaking simple contemplative practices in nature such as the Ecological Examen, loving-kindness meditation, and shinrin-yoku can help individuals transform themselves into more effective leaders with and for others. Contemplative practices are one method leaders can utilize to transform themselves to be better stewards of the earth's precious gifts. This process can also ignite the collective commitment needed to better care for our common home and to tackle the immense challenges ahead on behalf of the earth.

If you are interested in deepening your connection to the earth so that you can enhance your well-being, improve your leadership, and more fully support the fourth UAP and *Laudato Si'*, here are a few steps you can take:

- Schedule time for quiet reflection with nature.
- Leave technology behind and attempt to let go of competing priorities. (Note: You can pick them up on the other side of the experience if they still seem important.)
- Explore integrating one or more contemplative practices into your nature time.
- Experiment with different practices to see which feels right to you.
- Savor the feelings of gratitude (consolation) for the gifts the earth has given us.
- Reframe your relationship with the earth as one of reciprocity whereby you recognize and embrace the wisdom of interconnectedness.
- Reflect on the strong emotions (desolation) climate issues elicit and allow them to transform into love, connection, and thoughtful action.
- Journal your experiences so that you can reflect on them over time.
- Allow yourself to see the world with new eyes.
- Engage others around you in this activity, especially if it seems countercultural. (Note: If this is countercultural to your team or organization, it likely means you need to do these activities more often.)

A Prayer for Our Earth

Pope Francis

At the conclusion of this lengthy reflection, which has been both joyful and troubling, I propose that we offer two prayers. The first we can share with all who believe in a God who is the all-powerful Creator, while in the other we Christians ask for inspiration to take up the commitment to creation set before us by the Gospel of Jesus.

A Prayer for Our Earth

All-powerful God, you are present in the whole universe
and in the smallest of your creatures.
You embrace with your tenderness all that exists.
Pour out upon us the power of your love,
that we may protect life and beauty.
Fill us with peace, that we may live
as brothers and sisters, harming no one.
O God of the poor,
help us to rescue the abandoned and forgotten of this earth,
so precious in your eyes.
Bring healing to our lives, that we may protect the world and not
prey on it,
that we may sow beauty, not pollution and destruction.
Touch the hearts

Encyclical Letter published by Pope Francis on May 24, 2015.

of those who look only for gain
at the expense of the poor and the earth.
Teach us to discover the worth of each thing,
to be filled with awe and contemplation,
to recognize that we are profoundly united
with every creature
as we journey towards your infinite light.
We thank you for being with us each day.
Encourage us, we pray, in our struggle
for justice, love, and peace.

A Christian Prayer in Union with Creation

Father, we praise you with all your creatures.
They came forth from your all-powerful hand;
they are yours, filled with your presence and your tender love.
Praise be to you!

Son of God, Jesus,
through you all things were made.
You were formed in the womb of Mary our Mother,
you became part of this earth,
and you gazed upon this world with human eyes.
Today you are alive in every creature
in your risen glory.
Praise be to you!

Holy Spirit, by your light
you guide this world towards the Father's love
and accompany creation as it groans in travail.
You also dwell in our hearts
and you inspire us to do what is good. Praise be to you!

Triune Lord, wondrous community of infinite love,
teach us to contemplate you
in the beauty of the universe, for all things speak of you.
Awaken our praise and thankfulness
for every being that you have made.
Give us the grace to feel profoundly joined
to everything that is.

God of love, show us our place in this world
as channels of your love
for all the creatures of this earth,
for not one of them is forgotten in your sight.
Enlighten those who possess power and money
that they may avoid the sin of indifference,
that they may love the common good, advance the weak,
and care for this world in which we live.
The poor and the earth are crying out.
O Lord, seize us with your power and light,
help us to protect all life,
to prepare for a better future,
for the coming of your Kingdom
of justice, peace, love, and beauty.
Praise be to you!
Amen.

Contributors

Matthew Ashley, PhD, is professor of systematic theology at Notre Dame University, in South Bend, Indiana. He earned a Master of Theological Studies degree at the Weston Jesuit School of Theology, and his doctoral degree at the University of Chicago Divinity School. Dr. Ashley's published articles and books cover a range of topics including political theology, liberation theology, and Ignatian spirituality, with particular attention to memory that is transformative, and the theology of mercy and care for the environment.

Maka Akan Najin Black Elk (Oglala Lakȟóta) is a teacher at the American School in Japan and the former executive director for truth and healing at Maȟpiya Lúta (formerly Red Cloud Indian School) in Pine Ridge, South Dakota. After graduating from the University of San Francisco he earned Master's degrees in Peace and Human Rights Education at Columbia University's Teachers College, and Educational Leadership at the University of Notre Dame. He served as chair of the American Indian Catholic Schools Network for four years and has advocated for truth and healing in Catholic ministries and schools serving Indigenous peoples.

Karin Botto, EdD, serves as a senior human resource business partner at Syracuse University. She facilitates leadership development programs and organizational development initiatives in the Jesuit network and beyond, and has published an Ignatian Leadership model in the *Journal of Jesuit Business Education*. She serves as a principal of One Earth Leadership, which focuses on environmental sustainability, contemplative practices, and personal, community, and planetary wellbeing.

Sarah Broscombe is a learning and development consultant for social justice and educational organizations. A graduate of the Jesus College at Oxford University, she teaches, writes, and leads retreats in the areas of Ignatian spirituality, leadership development, and transformational change. She is a frequent contributor to *Thinking Faith*, the online journal of the British Jesuits.

Kevin F. Burke, SJ, is the vice president for university mission and professor of theology at Regis University. He has held faculty and administrative positions at the Weston Jesuit School of Theology (Cambridge, Massachusetts) and the Jesuit School of Theology (Berkeley, California). He is the author of several books including *The Theology of Ignacio Ellacuría* (Georgetown University Press, 2000) and *Pedro Arrupe: Essential Writings* (Orbis Books, 2004).

Joseph Carver is the system director of ethics and spiritual health for the Bozeman Health System in Missoula, Montana. Born and raised on a farm in rural New York, his interest in our relationship with creation has deep roots. Carver was a Jesuit for twenty-three years and has worked in ministry in numerous settings for nearly thirty years. He sees the Incarnate Christ as not only the spiritual but also the physical center of the universe, and regards embodied spirituality as a path into the breadth and depth of instruction unfolding in creation.

Marcia Chatelain, PhD, is the Presidential Penn Compact Professor of Africa Studies at the University of Pennsylvania. The author of *South Side Girls: Growing Up in the Great Migration* (Duke University Press Books, 2015), Chatelain is a scholar of African American life and culture. Her most recent book, *Franchise: The Golden Arches in Black America* (Liveright, 2020), was awarded the Pulitzer Prize in 2021. She previously taught at Georgetown University where she won several teaching awards and served on its Working Group on Slavery, Memory, and Reconciliation.

Eric Clayton is the award-winning author of *Cannonball Moments: Telling Your Story, Deepening Your Faith* (Loyola Press, 2022) and *My Life with the Jedi: The Spirituality of Star Wars* (Loyola Press, 2024). Clayton is the deputy director of communications for the Jesuit Conference of Canada and the United States. His essays on spirituality, parenting, and pop culture have appeared in *National Catholic Reporter*, *America*, *US Catholic* and more. He lives near Baltimore, Maryland, with his wife and two daughters. Learn more at ericclaytonwrites.com.

Erin Cline, PhD, is the Tagliabue Professor at Georgetown University. She specializes in Chinese philosophy, Chinese religions, and comparative philosophy and theology. The author of five books, she focuses her work on how the virtues, values, and rituals of classical Chinese philosophers can help people live better today. In *A World on Fire: Sharing the Ignatian Spiritual Exercises with Other Religions* (The Catholic University of America Press, 2018), she places the Ignatian tradition into conversation with selected Asian spiritual traditions, showing how and why the Spiritual Exercises might be adapted for non-Christian retreatants.

William Critchley-Menor, SJ, is a Jesuit of the Midwest Province of the Society of Jesus. He teaches American literature and liberation theology at Makȟpiya Luta-Red Cloud School in Pine Ridge, South Dakota, where he has also served as the project assistant for truth and healing. Before his current position, he completed a master's degree in American studies at Saint Louis University.

Bert Daelemans, SJ, graduated as engineer-architect and theologian (KU Leuven, PhD, 2013) and currently teaches on the faculty of theology at KU Leuven and Universidad Pontificia Comillas, Madrid. He has published ten books in which he bridges art and theology, with particular attention to Ignatian spirituality.

Thanh-Thao (Sue) Do is an alumna and current graduate student at Santa Clara University, currently serving as a young-adult ministry volunteer at Most Holy Trinity Parish in San Jose, California, and hospice administrative assistant at Gentiva Healthcare. She is a self-published author of three books including, most recently, *At Full Brightness* (2021).

Becky Eldredge is an Ignatian-trained spiritual director who accompanies people through spiritual direction, writing, retreats, and as founder of Ignatian Ministries. She is part of the Archdiocese of New Orleans Spirituality Center teaching staff, where she trains spiritual directors in the Ignatian tradition. Becky is the author of *The Inner Chapel* (Loyola Press, 2020) and of *Busy Lives and Restless Souls* (Loyola Press, 2017).

Philip Endean, SJ, was a British Jesuit who worked at the Centre Sèvres, home of the Jesuit faculties of philosophy and theology in Paris. He served for many years as the editor-in-chief of *The Way*, a spirituality magazine published by the British Jesuits. A long list of academic accomplishments and pastoral commitments inform his work on the Spiritual Exercises. Philip Endean passed away in September of 2023.

Jean Luc Enyegue, SJ, is a Jesuit from Cameroon. He obtained his doctorate from Boston University and is the director of the Jesuit Historical Institute in Africa, based in Nairobi, Kenya. He is the author of *The Jesuit Ethos: A Social and Spiritual History* (Paulist Press, 2023) and *Competing Catholicisms: The Jesuits, the Vatican and the Making of Postcolonial French Africa* (James Currey, 2024).

Alex Hale, SJ, met the Jesuits at the University of Detroit Jesuit High School, where he was moved to a deeper relationship with God through a silent retreat and leadership on a Kairos retreat. He went on to attend Xavier University, where he would work in local politics in Cincinnati, Ohio, as a legislative aide, campaign manager, and project manager for a political development consulting firm. He is currently a Jesuit regent teaching at St. Xavier High School in Cincinnati, Ohio.

Margo J. Heydt, EdD, is associate professor of social work at Xavier University in Cincinnati. She holds a Master of Social Work degree from West Virginia University and an EdD in counseling from the University of Cincinnati. Along with members of Xavier's theology department, she developed and team-teaches the interdisciplinary Religion, Ethics and Professional Practice course. She incorporates spirituality into her work, often in the context of Jesuit and Ignatian spirituality.

Ken Homan, SJ, is a Jesuit brother from the Midwest Province. He is currently working on a doctorate in history at Georgetown University, where he is a graduate assistant for the Kalmanovitz Initiative for Labor and the Working Poor.

Joshua Hren is founder of Wiseblood Books and co-founder of the Master of Fine Arts program at the University of St. Thomas. His books include the novel *Infinite Regress* (Angelico Press, 2022); the short story collections *This Our Exile* (Angelico Press, 2018) and *In the Wine Press* (Angelico Press, 2020); *How to Read (and Write) Like a Catholic* (TAN Books, 2021); and *Contemplative Realism: A Theological-Aesthetical Manifesto* (Benedict XVI Institute, 2022).

Eric Immel, SJ, currently works as a vocation promoter for the Midwest Province of the Society of Jesus. For a decade, he has practiced Ignatian spiritual direction and has studied the *Spiritual Exercises of St. Ignatius* and the discernment of spirits in the Christian tradition. He has a particular interest in exploring the overlap and confluence of Ignatian and Black spiritualities.

Christopher Kerr joined the Ignatian Solidarity Network (ISN) as executive director in 2011 and has more than twenty years of experience in Catholic education and social justice ministry. In December 2020, he was appointed by Superior General Rev. Arturo Sosa, SJ, to serve as a lay delegate on a six-member Advisory Committee for the Social Justice and Ecology Secretariat of the Jesuit Curia in Rome.

Barbara Lee is a spiritual director and a retired lawyer and federal judge. While serving as a member of the Ignatian Volunteer Corps, during her mid-seventies, she enrolled in the Creighton University Graduate School of Theology to qualify as a spiritual director. Her first book is *God Isn't Finished with Me Yet: A Guide to Discovering the Spiritual Graces of Later Life* (Loyola Press, 2018).

Elizabeth Liebert, SNJM, is professor emeritus of the San Francisco Theological Seminary (SFTS) and the Graduate Theological Union, and affiliate faculty at Jesuit School of Theology (Berkeley, California) and Lancaster Theological Seminary (Lancaster, Pennsylvania). She has authored and co-authored six highly affirmed books on spirituality including *The Spiritual Exercises Reclaimed: Uncovering Possibilities for Women* (Paulist Press, 2022) and *Soul of Discernment: A Spiritual Practice for Communities and Institutions* (Westminster John Knox Press, 2015).

Mary J. Lomax-Ghirarduzzi, EdD, is vice president for diversity, equity, and inclusion, chief diversity officer, and professor of communications at the University of the Pacific. She previously served as vice provost of diversity and community engagement at the University of San Francisco. She is a nationally recognized speaker and author on race, leadership, and faith-informed social justice.

Thomas Lucas, SJ, is an artist and scholar with a varied portfolio of liturgical design and stained-glass works internationally, including the restoration of the original apartment of St. Ignatius at the Gesù in Rome. He is the author of *Landmarking: City, Church, and Jesuit Urban Strategy* (Loyola Press, 1997). He has held faculty and administrative positions at the University of San Francisco and Seattle University, and is currently pastor of St. Ignatius Loyola Parish in Sacramento, California.

Ryan Mak, SJ, is a Jesuit brother from San Francisco, California, currently living in Chicago. He is a family medicine resident at McGaw Medical Center at Northwestern University, working in everything from delivering babies to taking care of the elderly in the last days of life. His background in Ignatian spirituality began when he was a high school student at St. Ignatius College Preparatory in San Francisco and has continued throughout the past ten years as a Jesuit engaging in spiritual conversations with many great Jesuit mentors and friends.

Bryan N. Massingale, STD, is a Catholic priest, professor of theological and social ethics, and holds the James and Nancy Buckman Chair in Applied Christian Ethics at Fordham University. He is the author of two books and more than 170 articles, book chapters, and book reviews. An award-winning scholar, teacher, and activist, Fr. Massingale frequently addresses issues of racial and sexual justice in venues such as NPR, ABC News, PBS NewsHour, HuffPost, Canadian Public Radio, *The South African Times*, and the Associated Press.

Tim McEvoy has a doctorate in early modern history from the University of Warwick and is assistant director at St. Beuno's Jesuit Spirituality Centre in North Wales, UK. He writes for *The Way* and *Thinking Faith*, both periodicals of the British Jesuits.

Sarah J. Melcher, PhD, is professor emerita of Hebrew Scriptures at Xavier University in Cincinnati. She earned a PhD in Hebrew Bible from Emory University. She has published widely on the theology of disability and is a retired minister of the United Church of Christ. She served as a mentor to David Frost in his study of "The Ignatian Body and Its Role in Jesuit Education."

Debra K. Mooney, PhD, was vice president for mission and ministry and chief mission officer at Xavier University until her retirement in 2025. She is a licensed clinical psychologist and the founding director of the Ruth J. and Robert A. Conway Institute for Jesuit Education.

Maddie Murphy was a volunteer with Jesuit Volunteer Corps Northwest in 2017–2018, serving as the community support coordinator at Wintonia Community Housing. She graduated from Fordham University and is from Wayzata, Minnesota.

Michele C. Murray, PhD, is senior vice president for student development and mission at the College of the Holy Cross. She is co-author of *Helping College Students Find Purpose* (Jossey-Bass, 2010) and *Teaching College Students Communication Strategies for Effective Social Justice Advocacy* (Peter Lang Inc., International Academic Publishers, 2012), and has written numerous articles on Ignatian spirituality and meaning-making.

Hung T. Pham, SJ, currently serves as provincial assistant for formation and director of the Office of Ignatian Spirituality for the Central and Southern Province for the Society of Jesus. He completed his doctorate degree in Ignatian spirituality from Universidad Comillas de Madrid and has held teaching positions at the Jesuit School of Theology (Berkeley, California) and Regis University. He was a delegate to the 36th General Congregation of the Society of Jesus.

Pope Francis, born Jorge Mario Bergoglio, was the first pope from the Americas, hailing from Argentina, and the first Jesuit pope. He was elected to the papacy in March of 2013 and died in office in April 2025. His apostolic exhortations on care for the earth, *Laudato Si'* and *Laudato Deum*, continue to challenge and inspire Catholics and non-Catholics alike.

Patrick Saint-Jean, SJ, PsyD, originally from Haiti, is a member of the USA Midwest Jesuit Province and the author of *The Crucible of Racism: Ignatian Spirituality and the Power of Hope*. He currently teaches in the Department of Psychology at Creighton University in Omaha, Nebraska.

Holly Schapker is an American artist whose work is displayed internationally and throughout the Midwest region of the United States. A graduate of Xavier University, she continued her painting education by studying under Michael Scott for ten years, whose fine art teaching process has a strong focus on painting outdoors. For the past fifteen years she has focused her time and talents on Catholic art. Her work has been the subject of many publications, including print, television, and radio. She also travels to give lectures as a creative Catholic and hosts spiritual retreats.

Gemma Simmonds, CJ, is a sister of the Congregation of Jesus, director of the Religious Life Institute, and senior research fellow in pastoral theology at the Margaret Beaufort Institute of Theology (Cambridge, UK). She has been a spiritual director, retreat giver, and lecturer for more than twenty-five years, as well as having worked as a prison and university chaplain. She is the author of numerous books and articles including *The Way of Ignatius: A Prayer Journey through Lent* (SPCK Publishing, 2018) and *Dancing at the Still Point: Retreat Practices for a Busy Life* (Form, 2021).

Arturo Sosa, SJ, a Venezuelan, serves as the 31st and present Superior General of the Society of Jesus, discerned and elected by the delegates of the 36th General Congregation on October 14, 2016, succeeding Adolfo Nicolás, SJ. Father Sosa received his degrees from the Universidad Central de Venezuela and Andrés Bello

Catholic University. In addition to a number of letters, homilies, and addresses, Fr. Sosa has published *Walking with Ignatius: In Conversation with Dario Menor* (Loyola Press, 2021).

Thomas D. Stegman, SJ, was a member of the USA Midwest Province of the Society of Jesus from Nebraska. Fr. Stegman held degrees in scripture from Weston School of Theology and his PhD in New Testament studies from Emory University. A teacher and scholar, he wrote more than eleven books, numerous articles, and addresses. He served as dean of the Pontifical School of Theology and Ministry at Boston College and participated in the 36th General Congregation in Rome (2016). Fr. Stegman died in April of 2023.

Mark Thibodeaux, SJ, entered the Jesuits in 1988. He holds degrees in philosophy, psychology, and theology from Loyola University of New Orleans and Weston School of Theology in Cambridge, Massachusetts. He worked in Jesuit secondary schools for nine years and was novice director for the Jesuits for ten years. He is currently the pastor of Holy Name of Jesus Church and School in New Orleans, Louisiana. He is the author of six books on prayer and spirituality, including *Reimagining the Ignatian Examen: Fresh Ways to Pray from Your Day* (Loyola Press, 2015), *Armchair Mystic* (Franciscan Media, 2019), *God's Voice Within* (Loyola Press, 2010), *Ignatian Discernment of Spirits for Spiritual Direction and Pastoral Care: Going Deeper* (Loyola Press, 2020), *Ascending with Ignatius: A 30-Day At-Home Retreat* (Word Among Us Press, 2020), and *Discern: Listening for God's Whispers* (Loyola Press, 2024).

Jennifer Tilghman-Havens is a writer, facilitator, teacher, and spiritual director who serves as the executive director of the Center for Jesuit Education at Seattle University. She has published research on the intersections of servant-leadership, diversity and equity, transformative pedagogy, women's leadership, Ignatian spirituality, and environmental sustainability.

Michelle Wheatley, DMin, is the co-founder of the Wheatley Leadership Group and former vice president for Mission Integration at Gonzaga University. She earned a Doctor of Ministry degree from San Francisco Theological Seminary in the area of spirituality and leadership.

Paul L. Younger, PhD, held the Rankine Chair of Engineering at the University of Glasgow, where he served as professor of energy engineering. He was formerly pro-vice-chancellor for engagement and founder-director of the Institute for Sustainability at Newcastle University. During his time at Newcastle, he was honored as a Fellow of the Royal Academy of Engineering in 2007, and as a Fellow of the Royal Society of Edinburgh in 2016. He worked extensively with community groups on water supply and pollution remediation projects worldwide. Dr. Younger completed the Spiritual Exercises under Annotation 19, in 2014. He died in April 2018.

Co-Editors

Eileen Burke-Sullivan, STD, served as vice president for mission and ministry and held the Barbara Reardon Heaney Chair in Pastoral and Liturgical Theology at Creighton University, where she directed graduate programs in ministry and Christian spirituality until her retirement in 2022. She is the co-author of *The Ignatian Tradition: Spirituality in History* (Liturgical Press, 2009) and *The Church in the Modern World: Gaudiem et Spes Then and Now* (Liturgical Press, 2014). In addition to her scholarly work, Eileen served as spiritual director, retreat leader, and was a member of Christian Life Community USA for fifty years. Eileen passed away in November 2024.

Julia A. Dowd, DMin, is director of mission integration for the U.S. East-West Province of the Sisters of Notre Dame de Namur. She has served for twenty-five years in Ignatian pastoral, social, and educational ministries, most recently as director of university ministry at the University of San Francisco. She earned a Doctor of Ministry degree from the Pacific School of Religion in women's spirituality, the Spiritual Exercises, and Jesuit education.

Mark Mossa, SJ, is a professor of religious studies at Loyola University of New Orleans, where he also serves as program director of the Canizaro Center for Catholic Studies. He has served as director of campus ministry at Spring Hill College and St. Mary Student Parish in Ann Arbor, Michigan, and also has taught at Fordham University and University of Detroit-Mercy. He is the author of *Already There: Letting God Find You* (Audible Audiobook, 2011) and *Saint Ignatius Loyola: The Spiritual Writings* (SkyLight Paths, 2012).

Stephanie Russell, EdD, serves as vice president for mission integration at the Association of Jesuit Colleges and Universities, where she develops formation programs and resources for faculty, staff, and university leaders. She is a co-creator of the Ignatian Colleagues Program and AJCU Trustee Forum, maintaining in her work a strong focus on Catholic social teaching and intellectual tradition, the Ignatian spiritual and educational heritage, and interreligious dialogue as means for deepening the mission of Jesuit schools.

Lori Stanley is the executive director, and the first layperson to hold the role, of the Loyola Institute for Spirituality in Orange, CA, where the Spiritual Exercises in Daily Life retreat, Ignatian spirituality formation, and Ignatian pilgrimages are offered. In 2020 she was appointed to the United States Conference of Catholic Bishops (USCCB) anti-racism taskforce for the state of California, and is a collaborator with the Jesuit Antiracism Sodality (JARS) and the Jesuits West Collaborative for Racial Equity (CORE). She earned a master's degree in pastoral theology from Loyola Marymount University, specializing in spiritual direction, and writes for the Ignatian Solidarity Network series.

Index

B

C

J

K

S

T

Acknowledgments

I. Foundations, History, and Current Context

Eileen Burke-Sullivan, "The Biographical Roots of the Ignatian Tradition." *The Ignatian Tradition: Spirituality in History*, edited by Kevin F. Burke and Eileen Burke-Sullivan (Liturgical Press, 2009), xxii–xxxi. Copyright © 2009 by Liturgical Press. Used with permission.

Mark Mossa, SJ, "Letters to the Twenty-First Century: The Incomparable Value of Ignatius's Letters for Understanding the Practicality of Ignatian Spirituality Then and Now." Adapted from *Saint Ignatius Loyola: The Spiritual Writings, Selections Annotated and Explained* (SkyLight Paths Publishing, 2012). Copyright © 2012 by Turner Publishing. Adapted with permission.

Margo J. Heydt and Sarah J. Melcher, "Mary, the Hidden Catalyst: Reflections from an Ignatian Pilgrimage to Spain and Rome." *Jesuit and Feminist Education: Intersections in Teaching and Learning for the Twenty-first Century*, edited by Jocelyn M. Borczyka and Elizabeth A. Petrino (Fordham University Press, 2012), 37–55. Copyright © 2012 by Fordham University Press. Used with permission.

Jean Luc Enyegue, SJ, "What the Conversation of St. Ignatius Can Teach Us 500 Years Later." *America*, Vol. 224, No. 6 (May 2021), 50–51. Copyright © 2021 by America Media. Used with permission.

Arturo Sosa, SJ, "Universal Apostolic Preferences of the Society of Jesus, 2019–2029." Copyright © 2019 by the Jesuit Curia. Used with permission.

Arturo Sosa, SJ, "Showing the Way to God." *Walking with Ignatius: Arturo Sosa, SJ, Superior General of the Society of Jesus in Conversation with Darío Menor* (Messenger Publications, 2021), 124–135. Copyright © 2021 by Loyola Press. Used with permission.

II. Contemporary Interpretations

Pope Francis, *Address of His Holiness Pope Francis to the 36th General Congregation of the Society of Jesus* (Vatican Publishing House: 2016). Copyright © 2016 by Vatican Publishing House. Used with permission.

Matthew Ashley, "Pope Francis as Interpreter of Ignatius's Spiritual Exercises." *Spiritus: A Journal of Christian Spirituality*, Vol. 17, No. 2 (Fall 2017), 165–180. Copyright © 2017 by Johns Hopkins Press. Used with permission.

Julia A. Dowd, "In Our Bones: The Spiritual Exercises and Call to Justice in Jesuit Education." *Conversations on Jesuit Higher Education*, No. 58 (Fall 2020), 6–9. Copyright © 2020 by Julia A. Dowd. Used with permission.

Ryan Mak, SJ, "Something I Never Thought About: Jesuits as Plastic Surgeons?" *The Jesuit Post* (March 23, 2021). Available at: https://thejesuitpost.org/2021/03/something-i-never-thought-about-jesuits-as-plastic-surgeons/. Copyright © 2021 by America Media. Used with permission.

Alex Hale, SJ, "Catholics Need to Learn How to Deal with Disagreements. St. Peter Faber Can Help." *The Jesuit Post* (March 15, 2021). Available at: https://thejesuitpost.org/2021/03/catholics-need-to-learn-how-to-deal-with-disagreements-st-peter-faber-can-help/. Copyright © 2021 by America Media. Used with permission.

Thanh-Thao (Sue) Do, "How Ignatian Spirituality Enhanced My Cognitive Behavioral Therapy." *America* (July 30, 2021). Available at: https://www.americamagazine.org/faith/2021/07/30/mental-health-ignatian-spirituality-college-241140/. Copyright © 2021 by America Media. Used with permission.

Eric Clayton, *Cannonball Moment: Telling Your Story, Deepening Your Faith* (Loyola Press, 2022). Copyright © 2022 by Eric A. Clayton. Used with permission.

III. Freedom and Discernment

Mark Thibodeaux, SJ, *Ignatian Discernment of Spirits for Spiritual Direction and Pastoral Care: Going Deeper* (Loyola Press, 2020). Copyright © 2020 at Loyola Press. Used with permission.

Gemma Simmonds, CJ, "Discernment: Becoming Who We Are." *The Tablet* (May 25, 2021), 6–9. Copyright © 2021 by the DeSales Media Group. Used with permission.

Hung T. Pham, SJ, "To Allow the Creator to Deal Immediately with the Creature." *Studies in the Spirituality of Jesuits*, Vol. 49, No. 3 (September 1, 2017). Copyright © 2017 by the Institute for Advanced Jesuit Studies. Used with permission of the Institute for Advanced Jesuit Studies.

Eileen Burke-Sullivan, "Maintaining the Tension: Freedom, Commitment, and Discernment." *The Way*, Vol. 43, No. 4 (October 2004), 7–18. Copyright © 2004 by The Way http://www.theway.org.uk/. Used with permission.

Barbara Lee, *God Isn't Finished with Me Yet* (Loyola Press, 2018), 101–113. Copyright © 2018 by Loyola Press. Used with permission.

Arturo Sosa, SJ, "On Discernment in Common" letter to the Whole Society, September 17, 2017, on the Anniversary of the Bull *Regimini militantis* of Pope Paul III (1540). Copyright © 2017 by the Jesuit Curia. Used with permission.

IV. Reconciliation

General Congregation 36, Decree 1: *Companions in a Mission of Reconciliation*. Copyright © 2016 by the Jesuit Curia. Used with permission.

Thomas D. Stegman, SJ, "The Moment of GC 36 for Its Members." *Studies in the Spirituality of Jesuits*, Vol. 49, No. 3 (September 1, 2017). Copyright © 2017 by the Institute for Advanced Jesuit Studies. Used with permission of the Institute for Advanced Jesuit Studies.

David Collins, SJ, et al., Georgetown University Working Group on Slavery, Memory, and Reconciliation, "Report of the Working Group on Slavery, Memory, and Reconciliation to The President of Georgetown University" (Summer 2016), 28–31. Used with permission.

Pope Francis, *Address of His Holiness to a Meeting with Young People and Elders, Primary School in Iqualuit, Friday, July 29, 2022* (Vatican Publishing House: 2022). Copyright © 2022 by Vatican Publishing House. Used with permission.

Maka Black Elk and William Critchley-Menor, SJ, "Atoning for Sins Against Indigenous People Begins with Confronting the Past. Red Cloud Indian School is Showing the Way." *America* (October 8, 2021). Available at: https://www.americamagazine.org/politics-society/2021/10/08/indigenous-peoples-day-orange-shirt-culture-jesuits-boarding-school/. Copyright © 2021 by America Media. Used with permission.

V. Leadership and Mission

Sarah Broscombe, "What is Ignatian Leadership? *Thinking Faith* (September 1, 2017). Copyright © 2017 by Sarah Broscombe. Used with permission.

Michelle Wheatley, "What Does the Ignatian Leader Do?" *Jesuit Higher Education: A Journal,* Vol. 12, No. 1 (2023). Available at: https://digitalcommons.lmu.edu/jhe/vol12/iss1/2. Copyright © 2023 by Michelle Wheatley. Used with permission.

Jennifer Tilghman-Havens, "Ignatian Leadership for Love and Liberation." *Jesuit Higher Education: A Journal,* Vol. 12, No. 1 (2023). Published under the title "Ignatian Leadership as a Mechanism for Human Liberation: 'What's Love Got to Do with It?'" Available at: https://digitalcommons.lmu.edu/jhe/vol12/iss1/8. Copyright © 2023 by Jennifer Tilghman-Havens. Used with permission.

Debra K. Mooney, "A New Ignatian Virtue Necessary for Promoting Justice: Cura Propria." *Conversations on Jesuit Higher Education* (September 6, 2021). Available at: https://conversationsmagazine.org/cura-propria-a-new-ignatian-virtue-necessary-for-promoting-justice-57e36f2286da. Copyright © 2021 by Debra K. Mooney. Used with permission.

Michele C. Murray, "Suppose Leaders Presupposed?" *Conversations on Jesuit Higher Education* (March 16, 2023). Published under the title "Suppose we all presupposed? Applying the Ignatian plus-sign in everyday life." Available at : https://conversations-magazine.org/suppose-we-all-presupposed-applying-the-ignatian-plus-sign-in-everyday-life-d6319130e601. Copyright © 2023 by Michele C. Murray. Used with permission.

Kevin F. Burke, SJ, "Introduction: A Mysticism of Open Eyes." *Pedro Arrupe, Essential Writings*, edited with an introduction by Kevin F. Burke (Orbis Books, 2004), 26–34. Copyright © 2004 by Orbis Books. Used with permission.

VI. Adaptations

Philip Endean, SJ, "How Far Can You Go? Ignatius's Exercises, Fidelity, and Adaptation." *Review of Ignatian Spirituality*, Vol. 29, No. 1 (Spring 1998), 35–49. Copyright © 1998 by Philip Endean, SJ. Used with permission.

Elizabeth Liebert, SNJM, "The Spiritual Exercises and Gender." Lecture, Symposium on Mystagogy in the Spiritual Exercises, Manresa, Spain, June 13, 2022. Copyright © 2022 by Elizabeth Liebert, SNJM. Used with permission.

Erin M. Cline, "Jesuit Norms for Choice of Mission and the Exercises." *A World on Fire: Sharing the Ignatian Spiritual Exercises with Other Religions* (Catholic University Press, 2018), 52–64. Copyright © 2018 by Catholic University Press. Used with permission.

VII. Imagination and Creativity

Thomas Lucas, SJ, "The Spiritual Exercises and Art." *Conversations on Jesuit Higher Education*, Vol. 47, Issue 1 (2015), 8–10. Copyright © 2015 by Thomas Lucas, SJ. Used with permission.

Bert Daelemans, SJ, "The Wound of Ignatius in Art." *Jesuitas: Revista de la Provencia de España de la Compañía de Jesús*, No. 148 (Summer 2021). Copyright © 2021 by Bert Daelemans, SJ. Used with permission.

Holly Schapker, "Available and Willing." *Conversations on Jesuit Higher Education*, Vol. 47, Issue 1 (2015), 8–10. Copyright © 2015 by Holly Schapker. Used with permission.

Joshua Hren, "David Foster Wallace's Denomination of Joy." *America*, Vol. 227, No. 3 (October 2022), 56–58. Copyright © 2022 by America Media. Used with permission.

Tim McEvoy, "Ignatius and the Stars." *The Way*, Vol. 60, No. 2 (April 2021), 8–17. Copyright © 2021 by The Way. Available at: http://www.theway.org.uk/. Used with permission.

Eric Immel, SJ, "Touching Jesus' Cloak: Imaginative Prayer in Action." *The Jesuit Post* (November 4, 2021). Available at: https://thejesuitpost.org/2021/11/touching-jesuss-cloak-imaginative-prayer-in-action/. Copyright © 2021 by America Media. Used with permission.

VIII. Ignatian Spirituality and Anti-Racism

Marcia Chatelain, "The Jesuit Spirituality of Martin Luther King, Jr." *America* (January 18, 2021). Published under the title "Martin Luther King Jr. shows us how Jesuit spirituality can be lived—in and outside the church." Available at: https://www.americamagazine.org/faith/2021/01/18/martin-luther-king-saint-ignatius-jesuit-spirituality-239742/. Copyright © 2021 by America Media. Used with permission.

Becky Eldredge, "Racism and the Gift of Sorrow." *Jesuits Magazine Central and Southern Province*, Vol. VIII, No. 3 (Fall 2021), 10–12. Used with permission.

Mary J. Lomax-Ghirarduzzi, "How to Use Ignatian Spirituality for Anti-Racism and Racial Justice." *Alpha Sigma Nu Magazine* (October 2021), 6–7. Copyright © 2021 by Alpha Sigma Nu. Used with permission.

Ken Homan, SJ, "What Dr. King and St. Ignatius Taught Me about Discernment and Anti-Racism." *The Jesuit Post* (January 18, 2021). Available at: https://thejesuitpost.org/2021/01/what-dr-king-and-st-ignatius-taught-me-about-discernment-and-anti-racism/. Copyright © 2021 by America Media. Used with permission.

Christopher Kerr, "Remembering George Floyd with a Steadfast Commitment to Racial Justice." *Ignatian Solidarity Network Blog* (May 25, 2021). Available at: https://ignatiansolidarity.net/blog/2021/05/25/george-floyd-racial-justice/. Used with permission.

Bryan N. Massingale, "The Ignatian Witness to Truth in a Climate of Injustice." *Conversations on Jesuit Higher Education*, Vol. 52, Article 3 (2017). Copyright © 2017 by Bryan N. Massingale. Used with permission.

Maddie Murphy, "An Examen for White Allies." *Ignatian Spirituality Network Blog* (December 12, 2018). Available at: https://ignatiansolidarity.net/blog/2018/12/12/an-examen-for-white-allies/. Copyright © 2018 by Maddie Murphy. Used with permission.

Patrick Saint-Jean, SJ, "A Doorway to Racial Healing." *The Crucible of Racism: Ignatian Spirituality and the Power of Hope* (Orbis Books, 2022). Copyright © 2022 by Orbis Books. Used with permission.

IX. Care for Our Common Home

Joseph Carver, "Ignatian Spirituality and Ecology: Entering into Conversation with the Earth." *Jesuit Higher Education: A Journal,* Vol. 4, No. 2 (January 2015). Available at: https://digitalcommons.lmu.edu/jhe/vol4/iss2/10. Copyright © 2015 by Joseph Carver. Used with permission.

Paul L. Younger, "Ignatian Spirituality and the Ecological Vision of Laudato Si'." *The Way*, Vol. 54, No. 4 (October 2015), 57–67. Copyright © 2015 by The Way. Available at: http://www.theway.org.uk/. Used with permission.

Karin Botto, "Want to Be a Better Leader? Connect with Nature." *Conversations on Jesuit Higher Education* (April 16, 2023). Available at: https://conversationsmagazine.org/want-to-be-a-better-leader-connect-with-nature-6713a72f6231. Copyright © 2023 by Karin Botto. Used with permission.

Pope Francis, "A Prayer for Our Earth." *Laudato Si': On Care for Our Common Home: Encyclical Letter*, section 246. (Vatican Publishing House, 2015). Copyright © 2015 by Vatican Publishing House. Used with permission.